Dengeki Daisy

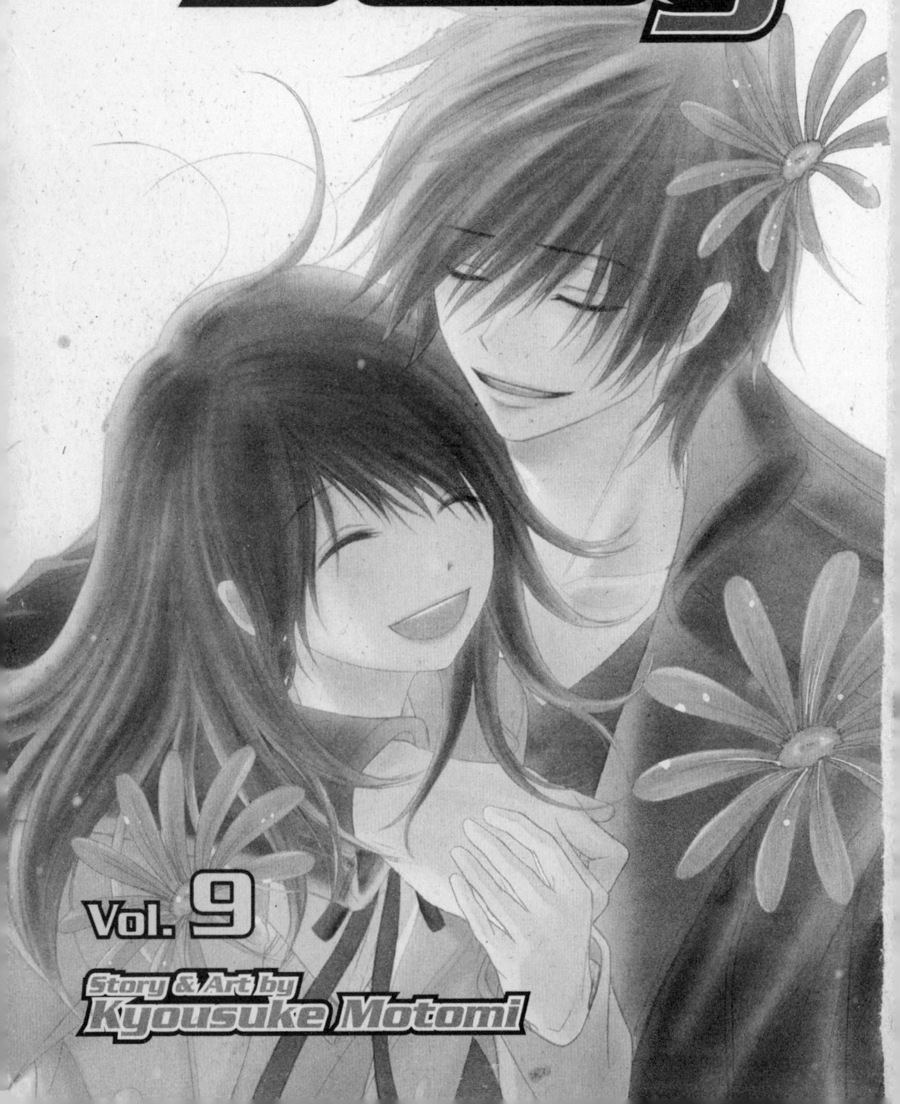

Vol. 9

Story & Art by
Kyousuke Motomi

Dengeki Daisy

Volume 9 CONTENTS

DAISY

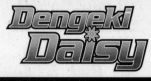

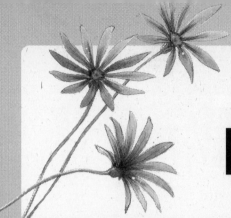

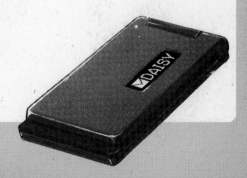

Dengeki Daisy Vol. 9

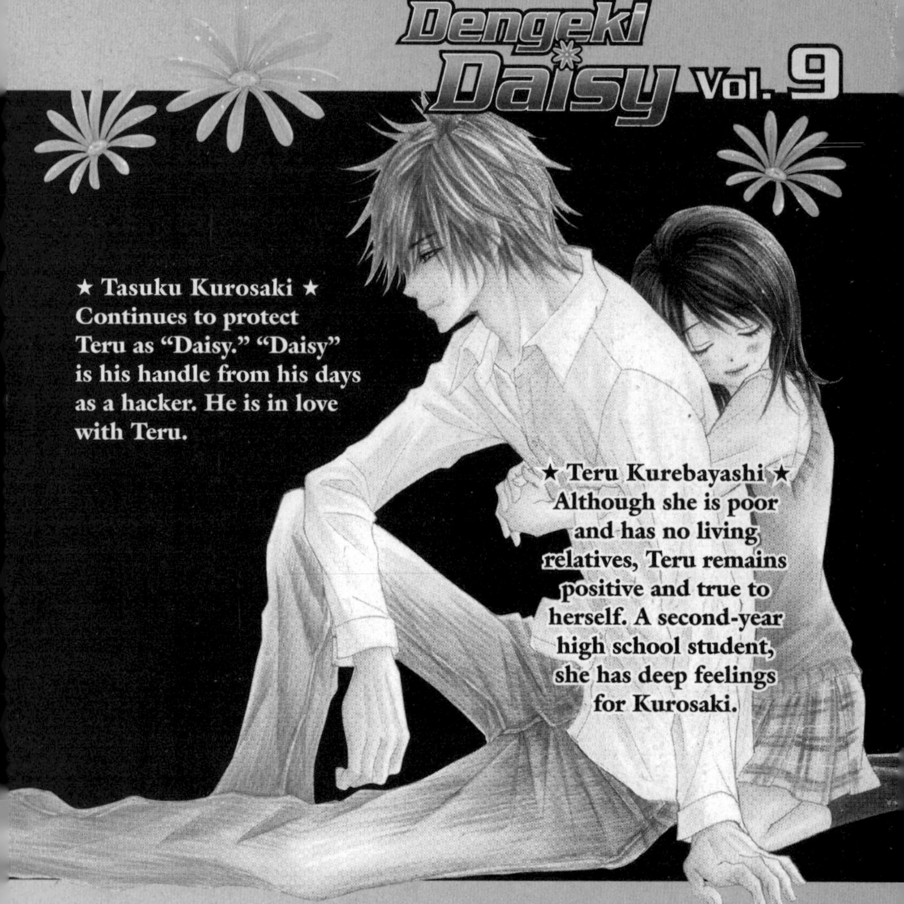
★ Tasuku Kurosaki ★
Continues to protect Teru as "Daisy." "Daisy" is his handle from his days as a hacker. He is in love with Teru.
★ Teru Kurebayashi ★
Although she is poor and has no living relatives, Teru remains positive and true to herself. A second-year high school student, she has deep feelings for Kurosaki.

★ After losing her brother, Soichiro, Teru's sole consolation was the cell phone he left her because she received messages from a mysterious person known only as "Daisy" on it. Whatever hardships she faced, Teru was able to endure them because of the encouragement these messages gave her.

★ Teru discovers that Kurosaki, the delinquent school custodian, is Daisy. Thinking that there must be a reason why Kurosaki has chosen to hide his identity, Teru decides to keep this knowledge to herself.

★ During this time, a fake Daisy appears, Teru's life is threatened, and strange incidents involving Teru and Kurosaki occur. Teru vows to stay close to Kurosaki, who has protected her at every turn. Meanwhile, Kurosaki begins to realize that in order to be with Teru, he will have to disclose the truth. The fake Daisy incident nears its climax, and it is learned that the real culprit behind it is Chiharu Mori.

CHARACTERS...

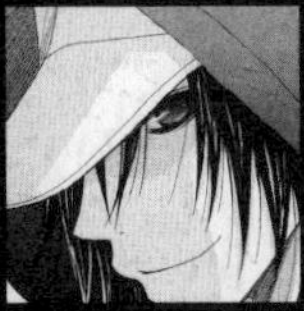

★ Akira ★
The culprit behind the Fake Daisy incident. Chiharu Mori's partner-in-crime.

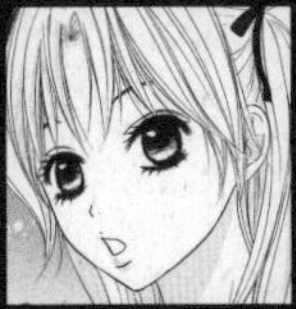

★ Rena ★
Teru's friend. She once was romantically involved with Arai.

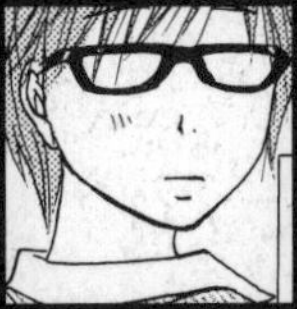

★ Kiyoshi Hasegawa ★
Teru's friend since grade school and Kurosaki's number two servant.

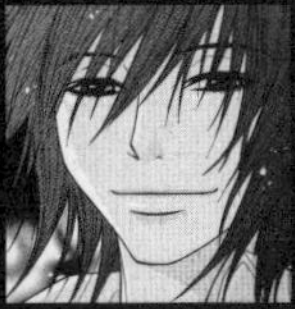

★ Soichiro Kurebayashi ★
Teru's older brother and a genius systems engineer. He died after leaving Teru in Kurosaki's care.

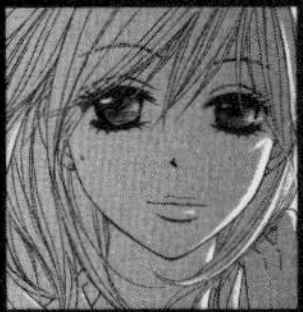

★ Chiharu Mori ★
She used to work at Teru's school and was the perpetrator behind the fake Daisy incident.

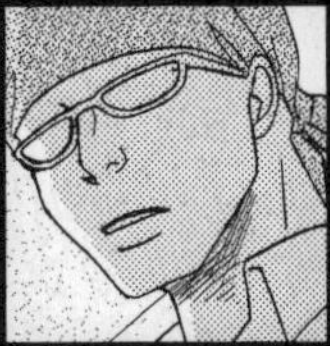

★ Boss (Masuda) ★
Currently runs the snack shop "Flower Garden" but has ties to the Ministry of Internal Affairs and Communications.

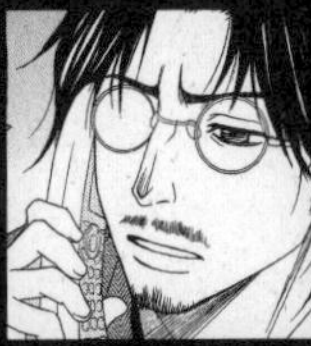

★ Director (Kazumasa Ando) ★
He used to work with Soichiro and is currently the director of Teru's school.

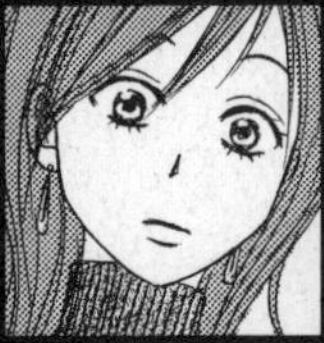

★ Riko Onizuka ★
She was Soichiro's girlfriend and is now a counselor at Teru's school.

STORY...

Teru falls for Mori's trap and ends up sending Kurosaki this message: "I can't forgive you for killing my brother. Please just disappear from my life." Kurosaki replies with, "It's true that I killed your beloved brother" and disappears. Despondent, Teru asks the Director and Riko to tell her the truth about Kurosaki's past and his "sin."

★ Teru learns that Kurosaki's father was involved with the development of a top-secret government code, and his death was shrouded in mystery. Kurosaki became a hacker to clear his father's name and created the code virus known as "Jack Frost." In order to save Kurosaki from being charged with a "Jack Frost"-related murder, Soichiro worked nonstop to decipher the code and died in the process. Teru now accepts everything she has learned about Kurosaki. She still loves him and decides to search for him...

HAPPY NEW YEAR 2011

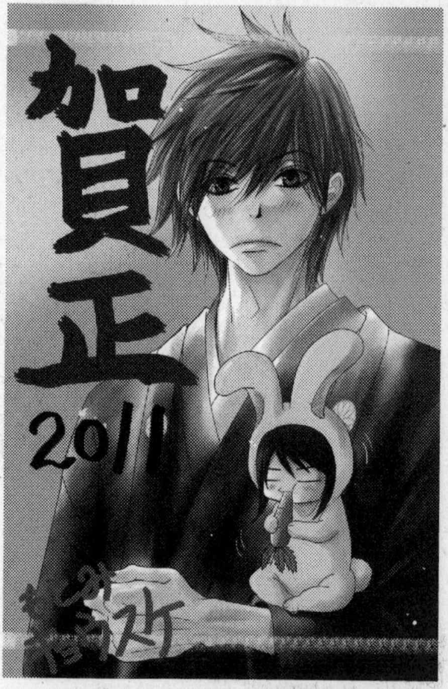
賀正
2011

KYOUSUKE MOTOMI

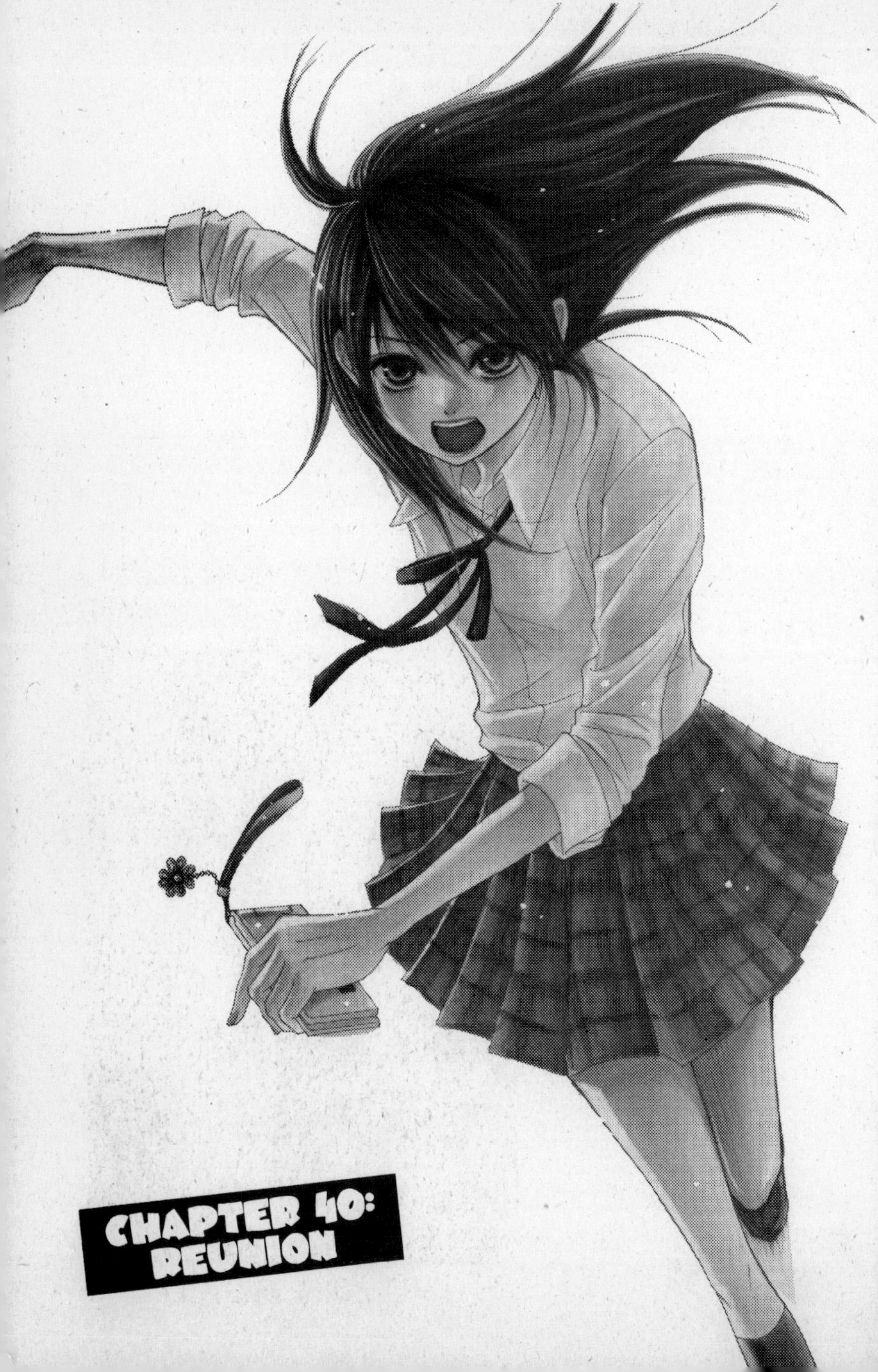

CHAPTER 40: REUNION

I FINALLY FOUND YOU, KUROSAKI.

I'VE COME FOR YOU. LET'S GO BACK TOGETHER.

IT'S NO USE RUNNING AWAY. I'LL CATCH YOU WHEREVER YOU GO.

HELLO, EVERYONE!! IT'S KYOUSUKE MOTOMI. DENGEKI DAISY... WE'VE REACHED VOLUME 9 AT LAST!!!

THANK YOU FOR PICKING IT TO READ. AND IF YOU LIKE IT, I'D BE EVEN MORE GRATEFUL. PLEASE ENJOY IT!!

THE BLUE DAISIES IN MY GARDEN BLOOMED HERE AND THERE, EVEN DURING THE WINTER. THEY'RE ACTUALLY SPRING-TO-AUTUMN FLOWERS THOUGH.

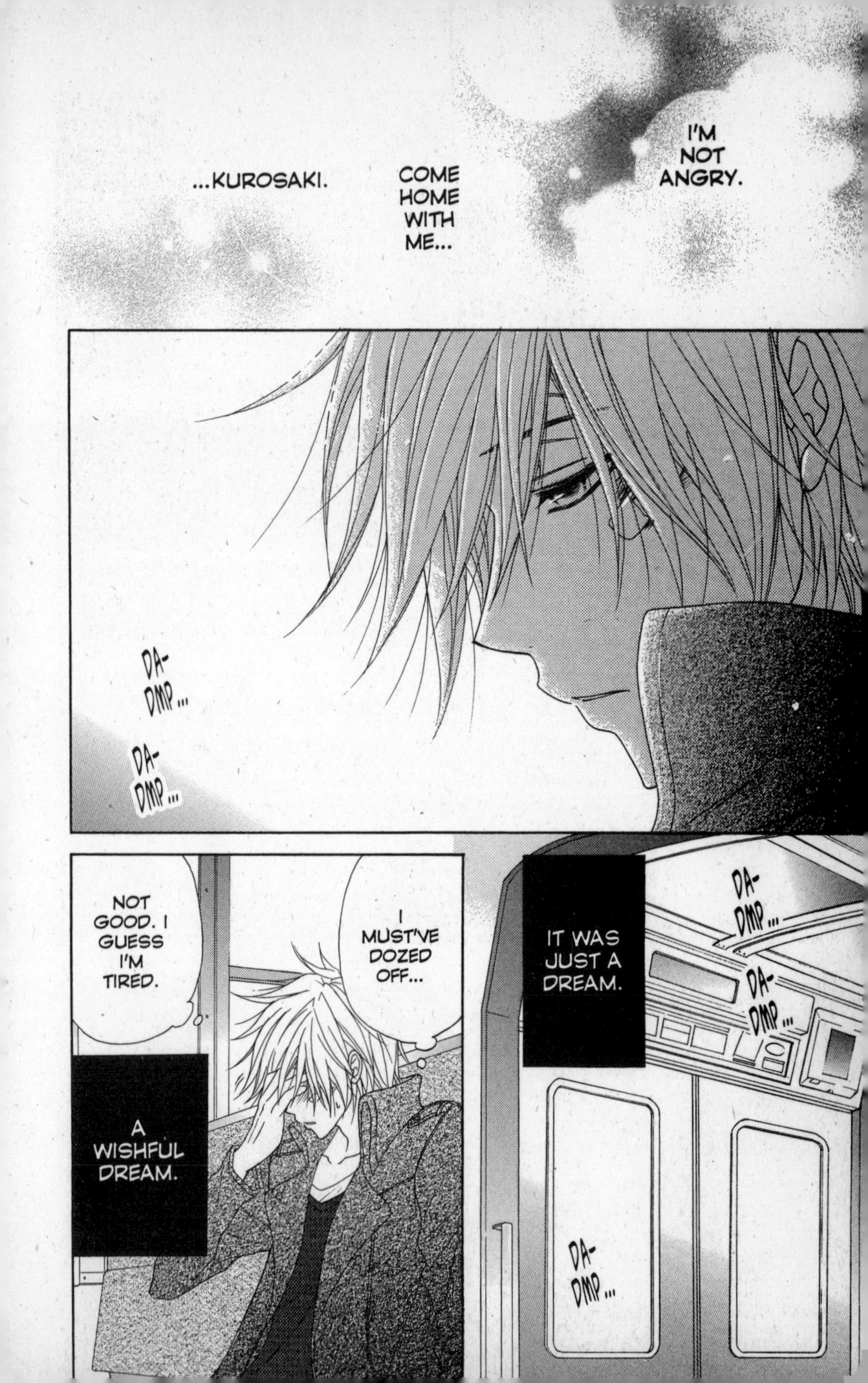
I'M NOT ANGRY.
COME HOME WITH ME...
...KUROSAKI.
DA-DMP...
DA-DMP...
DA-DMP...
DA-DMP...
IT WAS JUST A DREAM.
DA-DMP...
I MUST'VE DOZED OFF...
NOT GOOD. I GUESS I'M TIRED.
A WISHFUL DREAM.

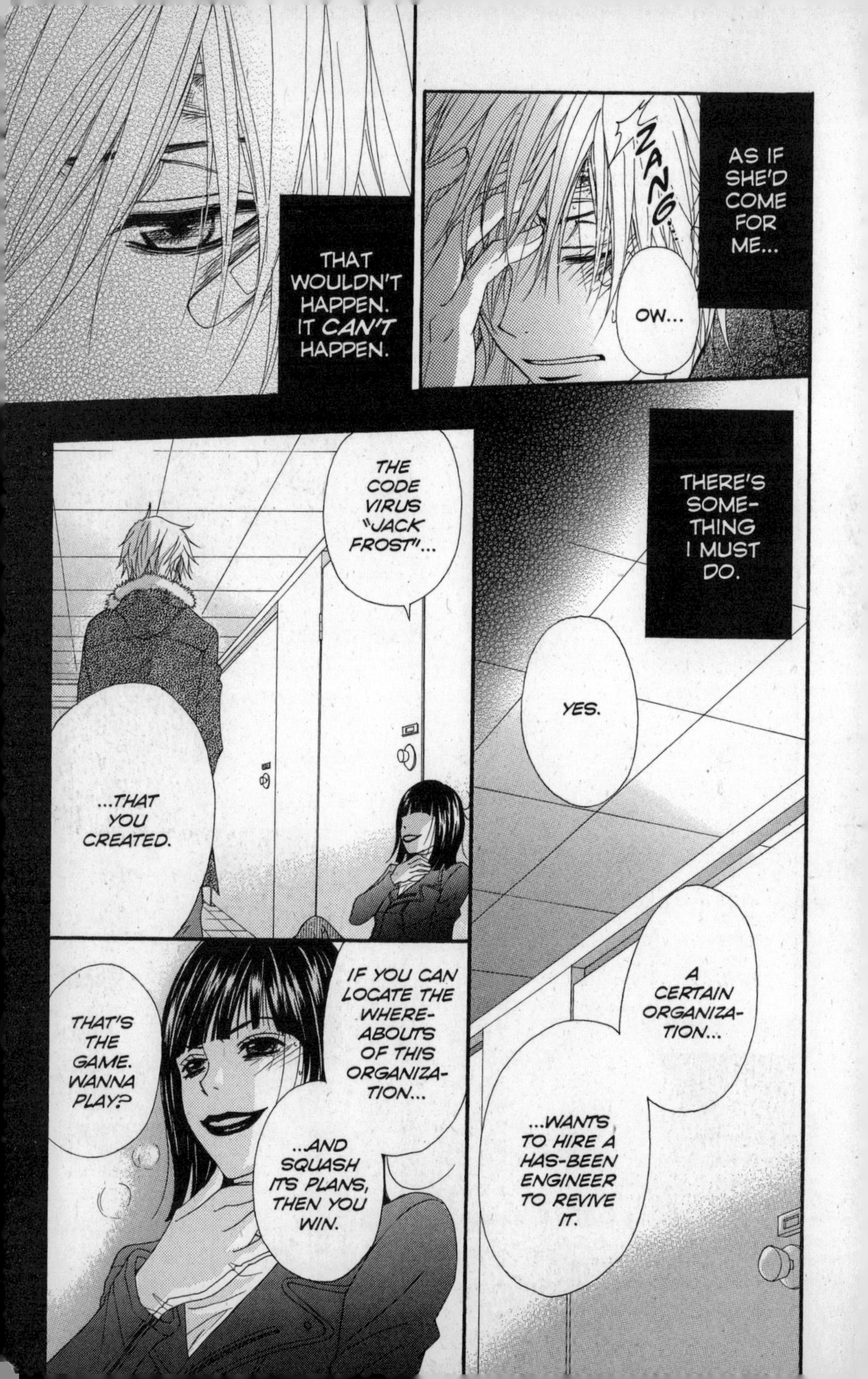
AS IF SHE'D COME FOR ME...
ZANG...
OW...
THAT WOULDN'T HAPPEN. IT *CAN'T* HAPPEN.
THERE'S SOME-THING I MUST DO.
YES.
A CERTAIN ORGANIZA-TION...
...WANTS TO HIRE A HAS-BEEN ENGINEER TO REVIVE IT.
THE CODE VIRUS "JACK FROST"...
...THAT YOU CREATED.
IF YOU CAN LOCATE THE WHERE-ABOUTS OF THIS ORGANIZA-TION...
...AND SQUASH ITS PLANS, THEN YOU WIN.
THAT'S THE GAME. WANNA PLAY?

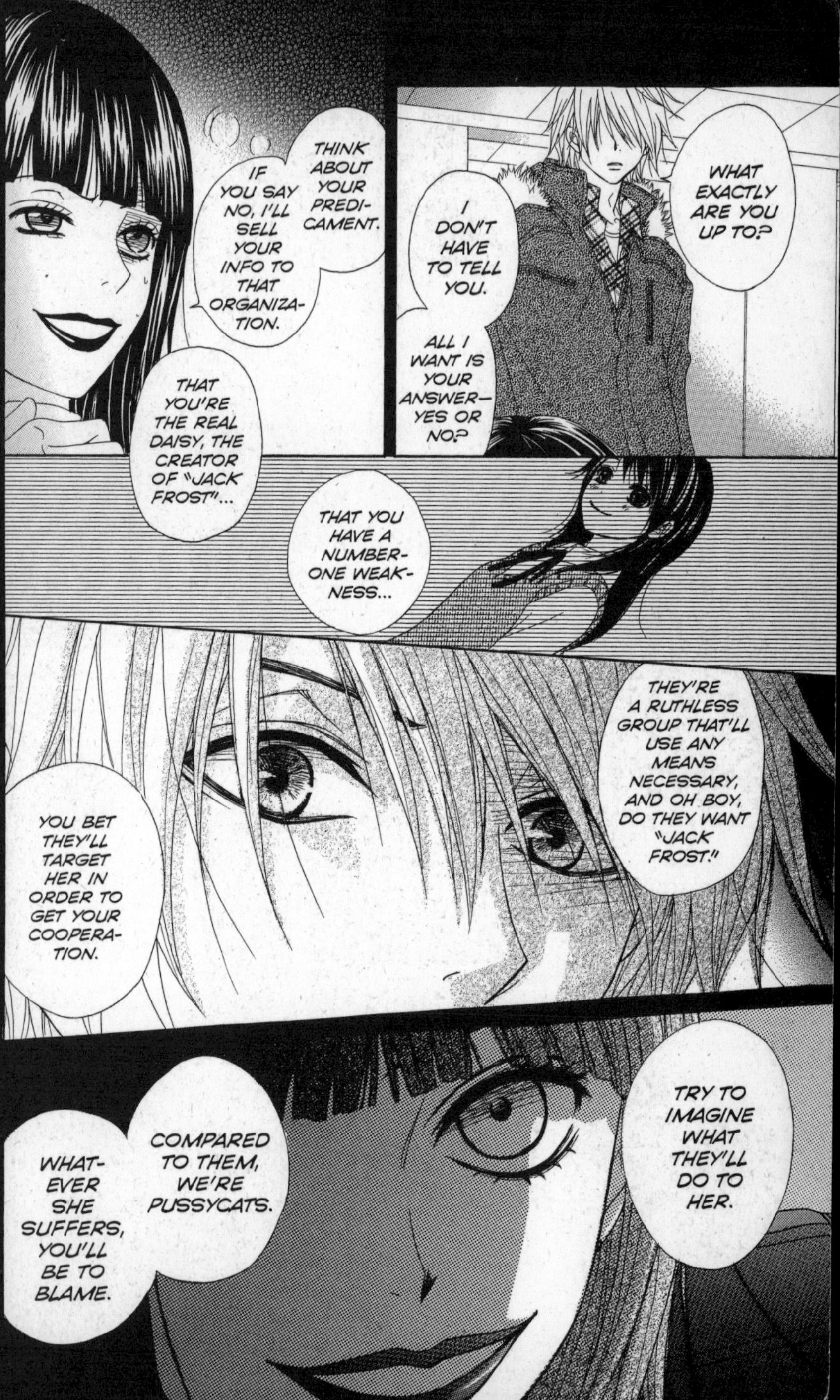
WHAT EXACTLY ARE YOU UP TO?
I DON'T HAVE TO TELL YOU.
ALL I WANT IS YOUR ANSWER—YES OR NO?
THINK ABOUT YOUR PREDICAMENT.
IF YOU SAY NO, I'LL SELL YOUR INFO TO THAT ORGANIZATION.
THAT YOU'RE THE REAL DAISY, THE CREATOR OF "JACK FROST"...
THAT YOU HAVE A NUMBER-ONE WEAKNESS...
THEY'RE A RUTHLESS GROUP THAT'LL USE ANY MEANS NECESSARY, AND OH BOY, DO THEY WANT "JACK FROST."
YOU BET THEY'LL TARGET HER IN ORDER TO GET YOUR COOPERATION.
TRY TO IMAGINE WHAT THEY'LL DO TO HER.
COMPARED TO THEM, WE'RE PUSSYCATS.
WHATEVER SHE SUFFERS, YOU'LL BE TO BLAME.

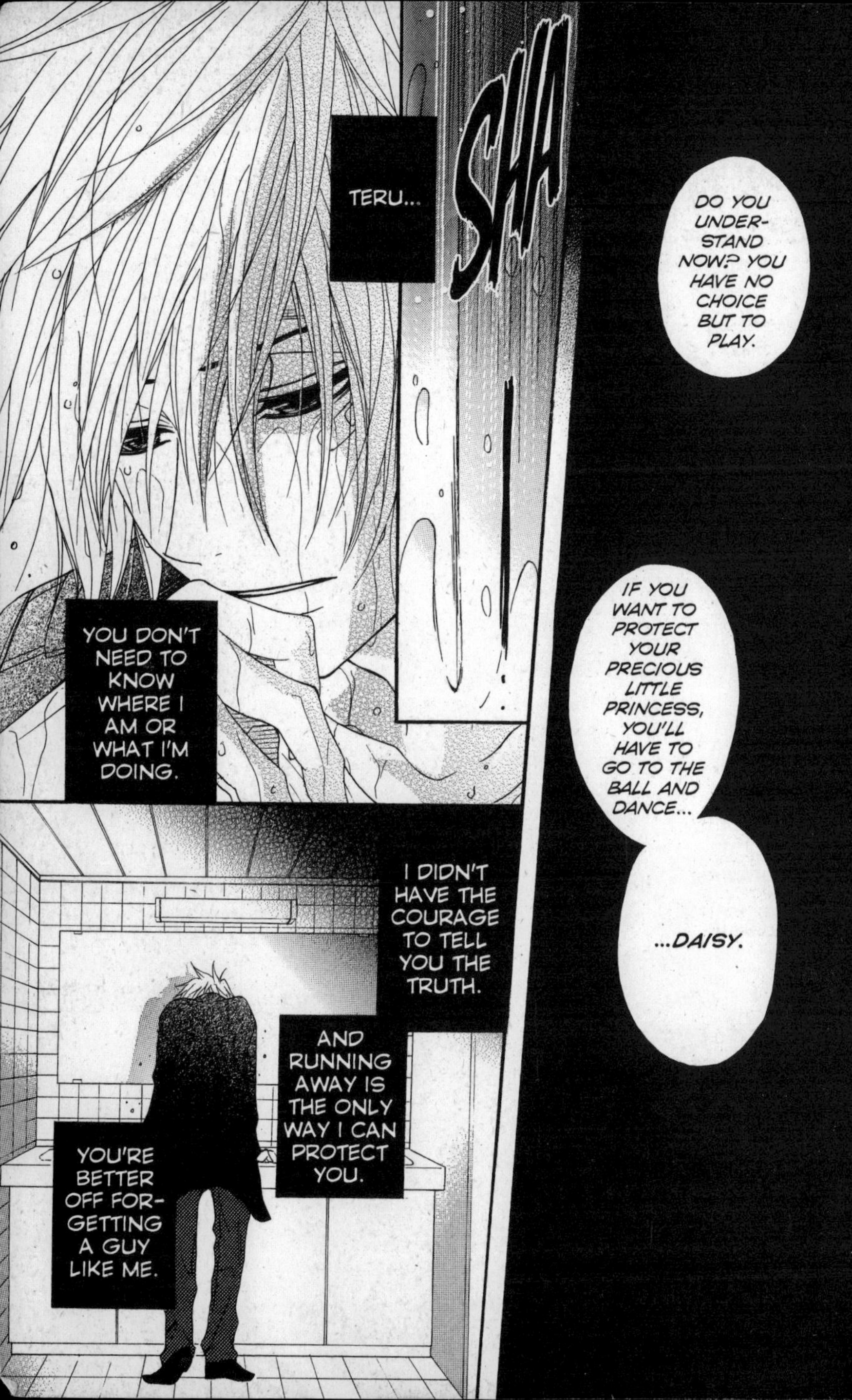
DO YOU UNDER-STAND NOW? YOU HAVE NO CHOICE BUT TO PLAY.
IF YOU WANT TO PROTECT YOUR PRECIOUS LITTLE PRINCESS, YOU'LL HAVE TO GO TO THE BALL AND DANCE...
...DAISY.
SHA
TERU...
YOU DON'T NEED TO KNOW WHERE I AM OR WHAT I'M DOING.
I DIDN'T HAVE THE COURAGE TO TELL YOU THE TRUTH.
AND RUNNING AWAY IS THE ONLY WAY I CAN PROTECT YOU.
YOU'RE BETTER OFF FOR-GETTING A GUY LIKE ME.

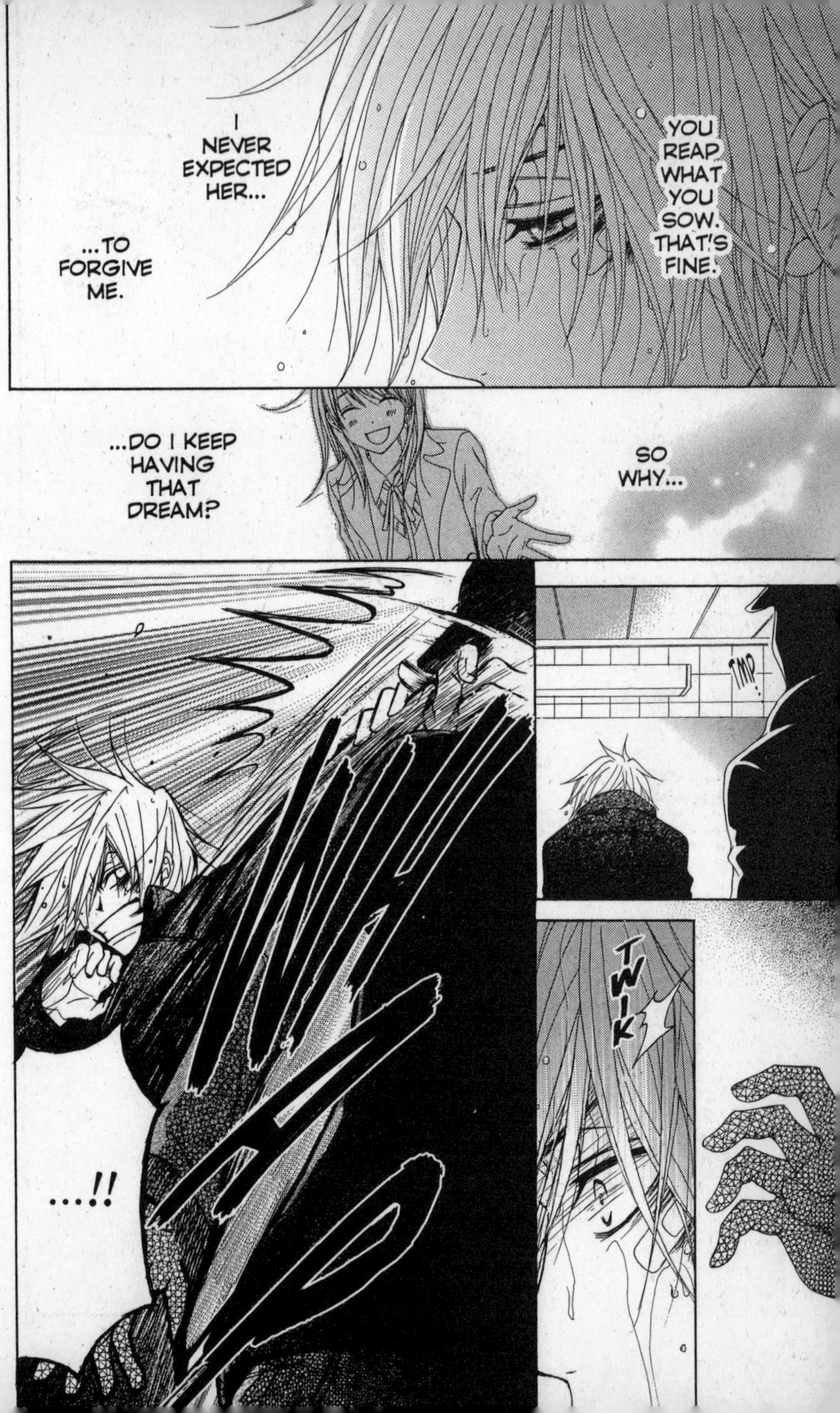
YOU REAP WHAT YOU SOW. THAT'S FINE.
I NEVER EXPECTED HER...
...TO FORGIVE ME.
SO WHY...
...DO I KEEP HAVING THAT DREAM?
TMP
TWIK
...!!

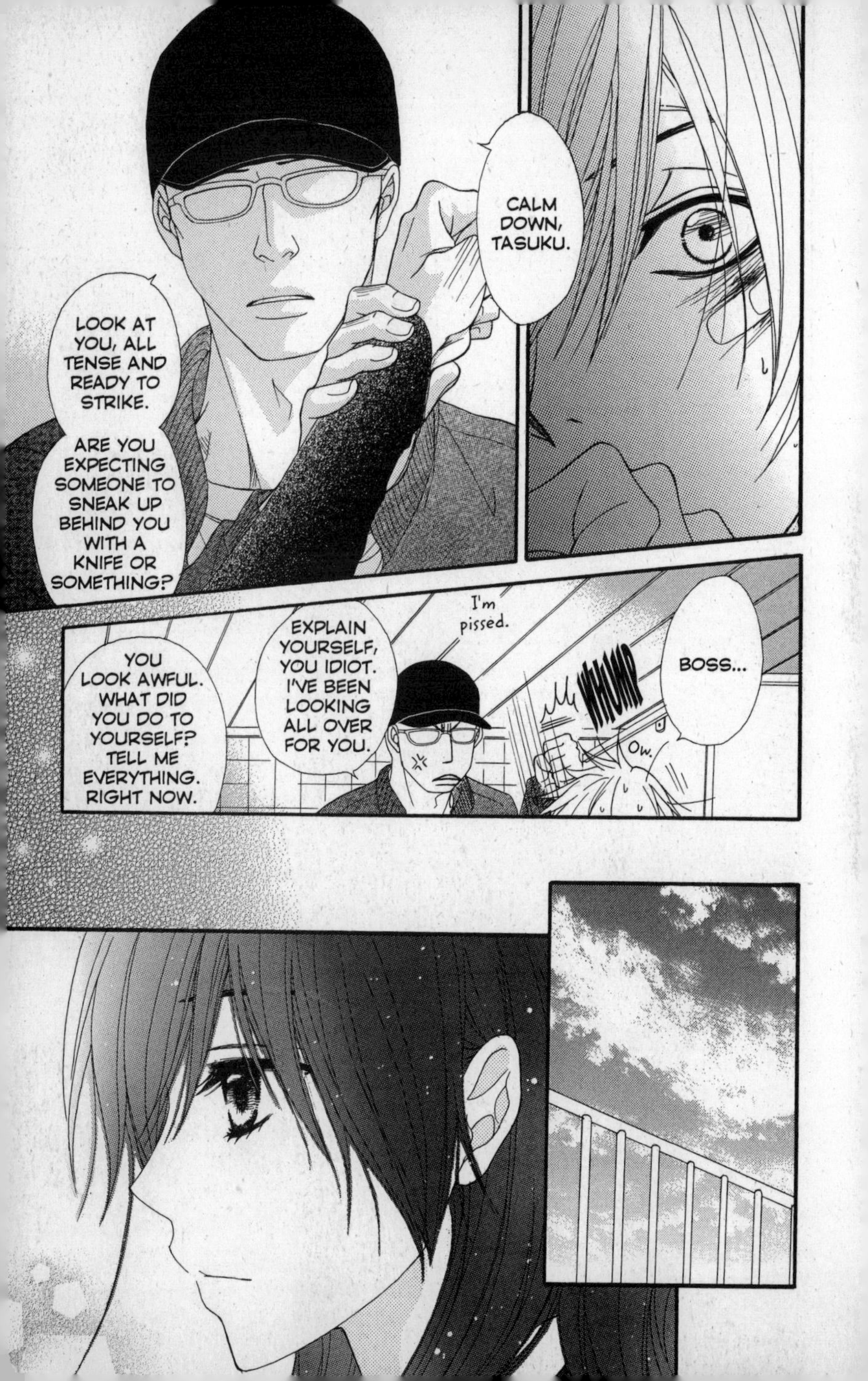
CALM DOWN, TASUKU.
LOOK AT YOU, ALL TENSE AND READY TO STRIKE.
ARE YOU EXPECTING SOMEONE TO SNEAK UP BEHIND YOU WITH A KNIFE OR SOMETHING?
BOSS...
I'm pissed.
WHUMP
Ow.
EXPLAIN YOURSELF, YOU IDIOT. I'VE BEEN LOOKING ALL OVER FOR YOU.
YOU LOOK AWFUL. WHAT DID YOU DO TO YOURSELF? TELL ME EVERYTHING. RIGHT NOW.

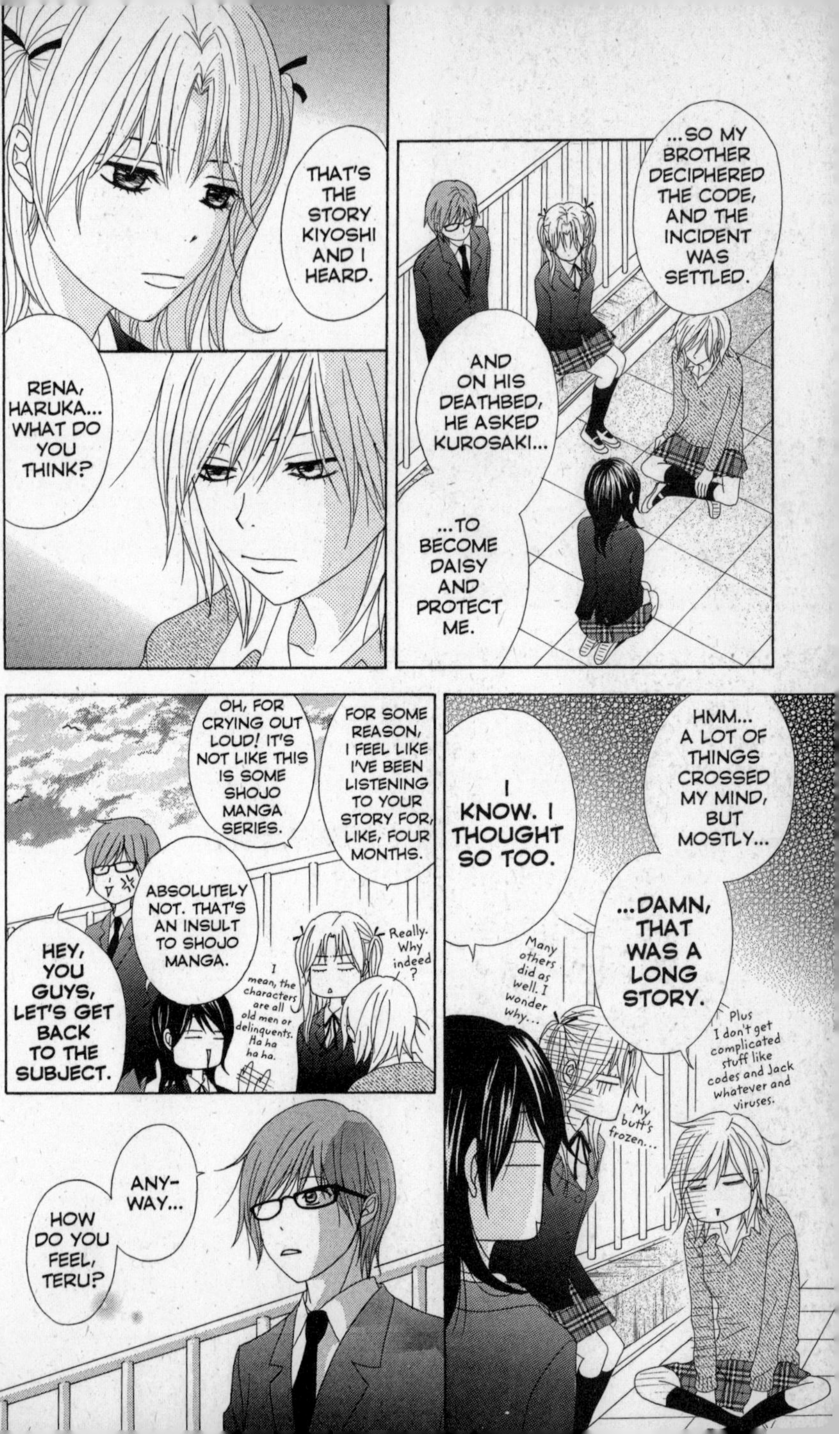
...SO MY BROTHER DECIPHERED THE CODE, AND THE INCIDENT WAS SETTLED.
AND ON HIS DEATHBED, HE ASKED KUROSAKI...
...TO BECOME DAISY AND PROTECT ME.
THAT'S THE STORY KIYOSHI AND I HEARD.
RENA, HARUKA... WHAT DO YOU THINK?
HMM... A LOT OF THINGS CROSSED MY MIND, BUT MOSTLY...
I KNOW. I THOUGHT SO TOO.
...DAMN, THAT WAS A LONG STORY.
Many others did as well. I wonder why...
Plus I don't get complicated stuff like codes and Jack whatever and viruses.
My butt's frozen...
FOR SOME REASON, I FEEL LIKE I'VE BEEN LISTENING TO YOUR STORY FOR, LIKE, FOUR MONTHS.
OH, FOR CRYING OUT LOUD! IT'S NOT LIKE THIS IS SOME SHOJO MANGA SERIES.
Really. Why indeed?
ABSOLUTELY NOT. THAT'S AN INSULT TO SHOJO MANGA.
I mean, the characters are all old men or delinquents. Ha ha ha ha.
HEY, YOU GUYS, LET'S GET BACK TO THE SUBJECT.
ANY-WAY...
HOW DO YOU FEEL, TERU?

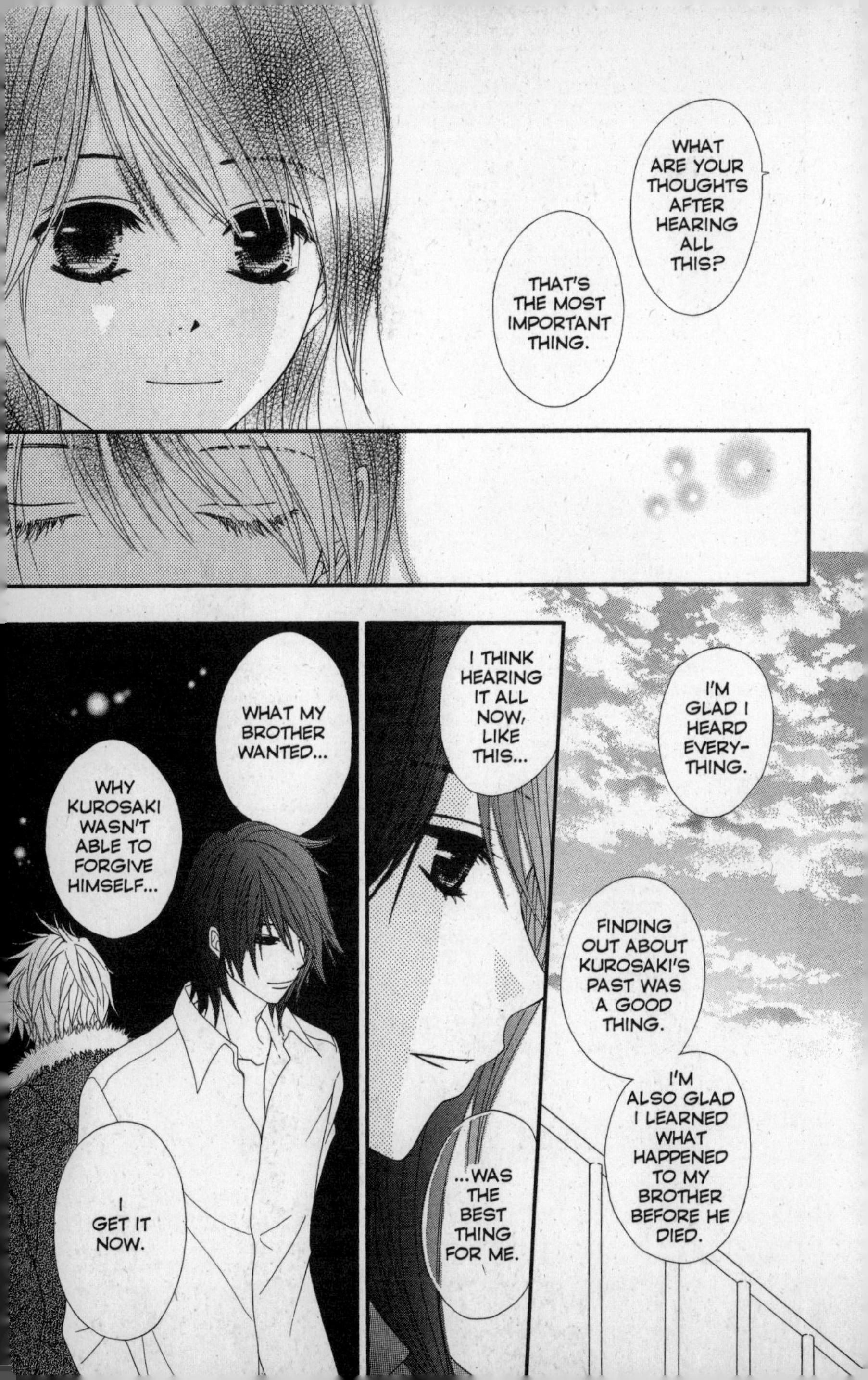
WHAT ARE YOUR THOUGHTS AFTER HEARING ALL THIS?
THAT'S THE MOST IMPORTANT THING.
I'M GLAD I HEARD EVERY-THING.
FINDING OUT ABOUT KUROSAKI'S PAST WAS A GOOD THING.
I'M ALSO GLAD I LEARNED WHAT HAPPENED TO MY BROTHER BEFORE HE DIED.
I THINK HEARING IT ALL NOW, LIKE THIS...
...WAS THE BEST THING FOR ME.
WHAT MY BROTHER WANTED...
WHY KUROSAKI WASN'T ABLE TO FORGIVE HIMSELF...
I GET IT NOW.

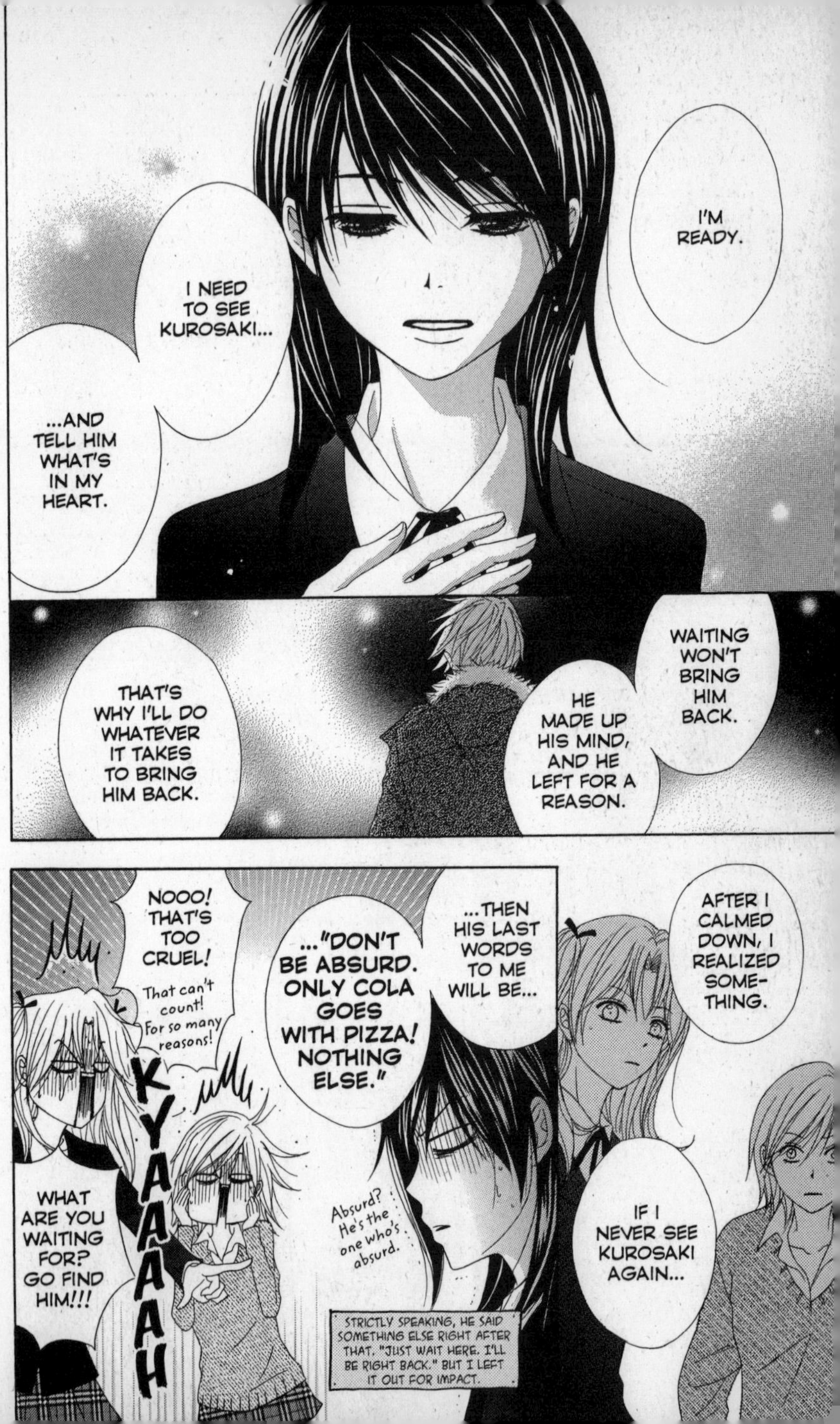
I'M READY.
I NEED TO SEE KUROSAKI...
...AND TELL HIM WHAT'S IN MY HEART.
WAITING WON'T BRING HIM BACK.
HE MADE UP HIS MIND, AND HE LEFT FOR A REASON.
THAT'S WHY I'LL DO WHATEVER IT TAKES TO BRING HIM BACK.
AFTER I CALMED DOWN, I REALIZED SOME-THING.
IF I NEVER SEE KUROSAKI AGAIN...
...THEN HIS LAST WORDS TO ME WILL BE...
..."DON'T BE ABSURD. ONLY COLA GOES WITH PIZZA! NOTHING ELSE."
Absurd? He's the one who's absurd.
STRICTLY SPEAKING, HE SAID SOMETHING ELSE RIGHT AFTER THAT. "JUST WAIT HERE. I'LL BE RIGHT BACK." BUT I LEFT IT OUT FOR IMPACT.
NOOO! THAT'S TOO CRUEL!
That can't count! For so many reasons!
KYAAAAH
WHAT ARE YOU WAITING FOR? GO FIND HIM!!!

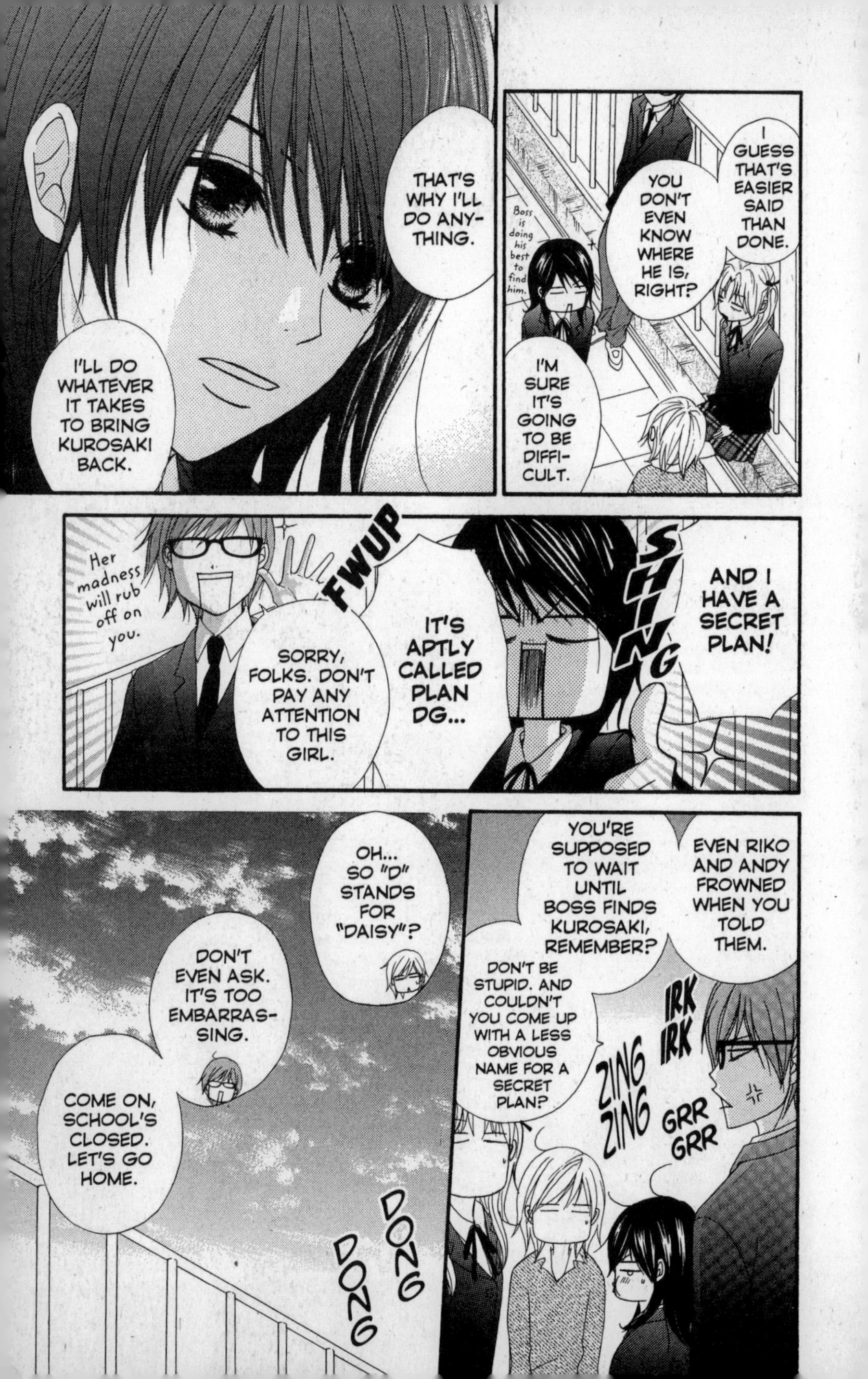
I GUESS THAT'S EASIER SAID THAN DONE.
YOU DON'T EVEN KNOW WHERE HE IS, RIGHT?
Boss is doing his best to find him.
I'M SURE IT'S GOING TO BE DIFFICULT.
THAT'S WHY I'LL DO ANYTHING.
I'LL DO WHATEVER IT TAKES TO BRING KUROSAKI BACK.
AND I HAVE A SECRET PLAN!
SHING
IT'S APTLY CALLED PLAN DG...
FWUP
SORRY, FOLKS. DON'T PAY ANY ATTENTION TO THIS GIRL.
Her madness will rub off on you.
EVEN RIKO AND ANDY FROWNED WHEN YOU TOLD THEM.
YOU'RE SUPPOSED TO WAIT UNTIL BOSS FINDS KUROSAKI, REMEMBER?
IRK IRK
DON'T BE STUPID. AND COULDN'T YOU COME UP WITH A LESS OBVIOUS NAME FOR A SECRET PLAN?
GRR GRR
ZING ZING
OH... SO "D" STANDS FOR "DAISY"?
DON'T EVEN ASK. IT'S TOO EMBARRAS-SING.
COME ON, SCHOOL'S CLOSED. LET'S GO HOME.
DONG
DONG
DONG

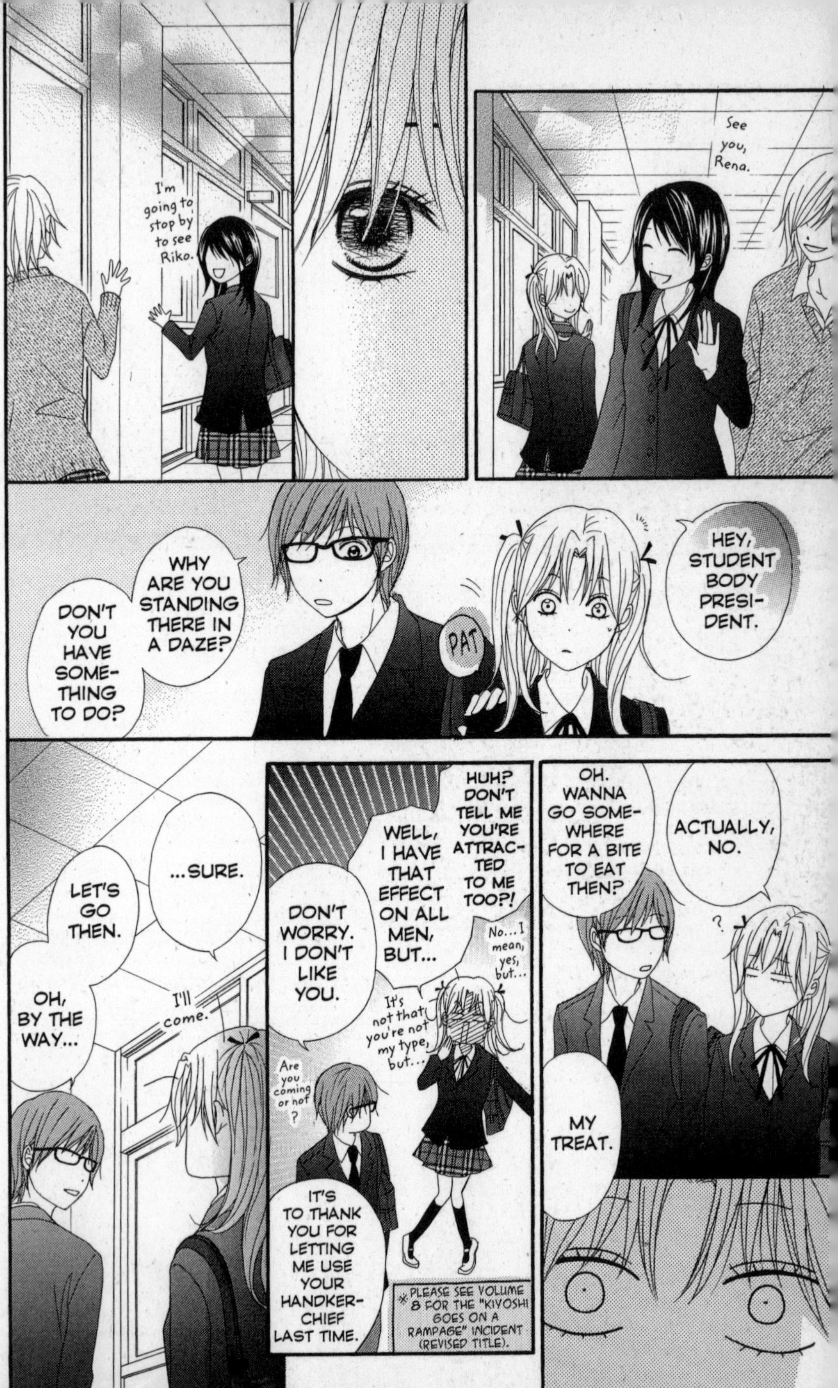
See you, Rena.
I'm going to stop by to see Riko.
HEY, STUDENT BODY PRESIDENT.
PAT
WHY ARE YOU STANDING THERE IN A DAZE?
DON'T YOU HAVE SOMETHING TO DO?
ACTUALLY, NO.
OH. WANNA GO SOMEWHERE FOR A BITE TO EAT THEN?
?
MY TREAT.
HUH? DON'T TELL ME YOU'RE ATTRACTED TO ME TOO?!
WELL, I HAVE THAT EFFECT ON ALL MEN, BUT...
DON'T WORRY. I DON'T LIKE YOU.
No... I mean, yes, but...
It's not that you're not my type, but...
Are you coming or not?
IT'S TO THANK YOU FOR LETTING ME USE YOUR HANDKERCHIEF LAST TIME.
※ PLEASE SEE VOLUME 8 FOR THE "KIYOSHI GOES ON A RAMPAGE" INCIDENT (REVISED TITLE).
...SURE.
LET'S GO THEN.
I'll come.
OH, BY THE WAY...

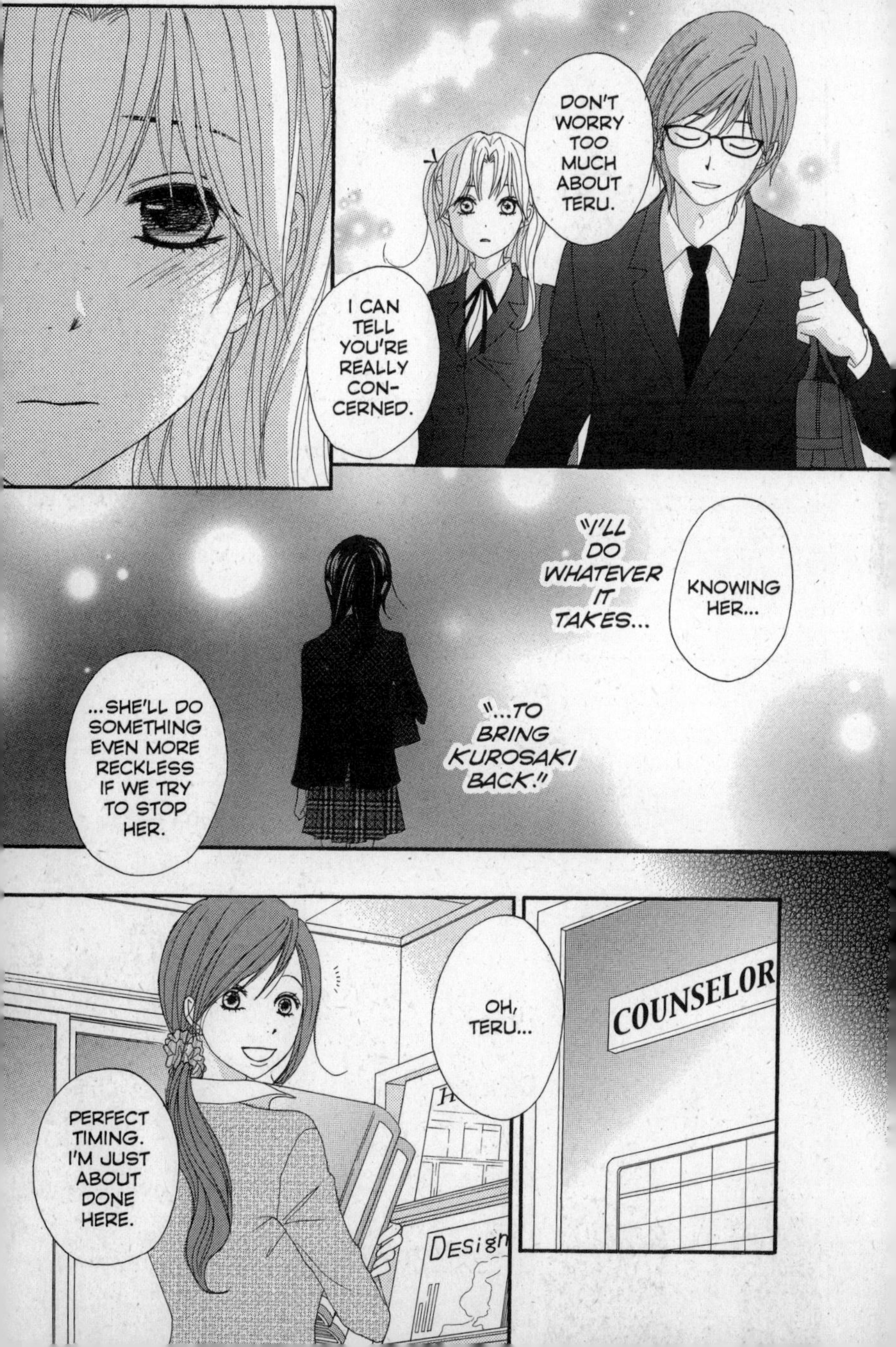
DON'T WORRY TOO MUCH ABOUT TERU.
I CAN TELL YOU'RE REALLY CON-CERNED.
KNOWING HER...
"I'LL DO WHATEVER IT TAKES...
"...TO BRING KUROSAKI BACK!"
...SHE'LL DO SOMETHING EVEN MORE RECKLESS IF WE TRY TO STOP HER.
COUNSELOR
OH, TERU...
PERFECT TIMING. I'M JUST ABOUT DONE HERE.
Design

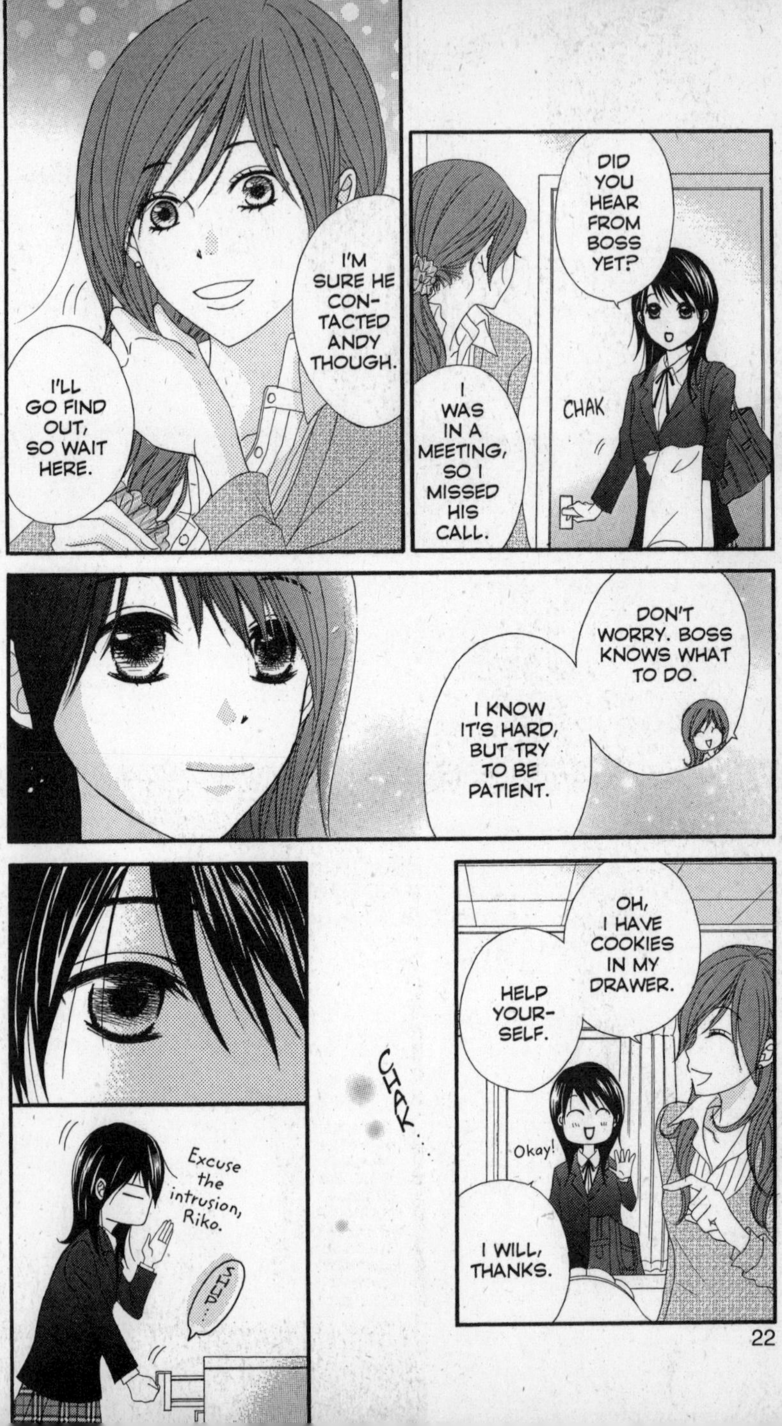
DID YOU HEAR FROM BOSS YET?
I WAS IN A MEETING, SO I MISSED HIS CALL.
CHAK
I'M SURE HE CONTACTED ANDY THOUGH.
I'LL GO FIND OUT, SO WAIT HERE.
DON'T WORRY. BOSS KNOWS WHAT TO DO.
I KNOW IT'S HARD, BUT TRY TO BE PATIENT.
OH, I HAVE COOKIES IN MY DRAWER.
HELP YOURSELF.
Okay!
I WILL, THANKS.
CHAK...
Excuse the intrusion, Riko.
SLIP...

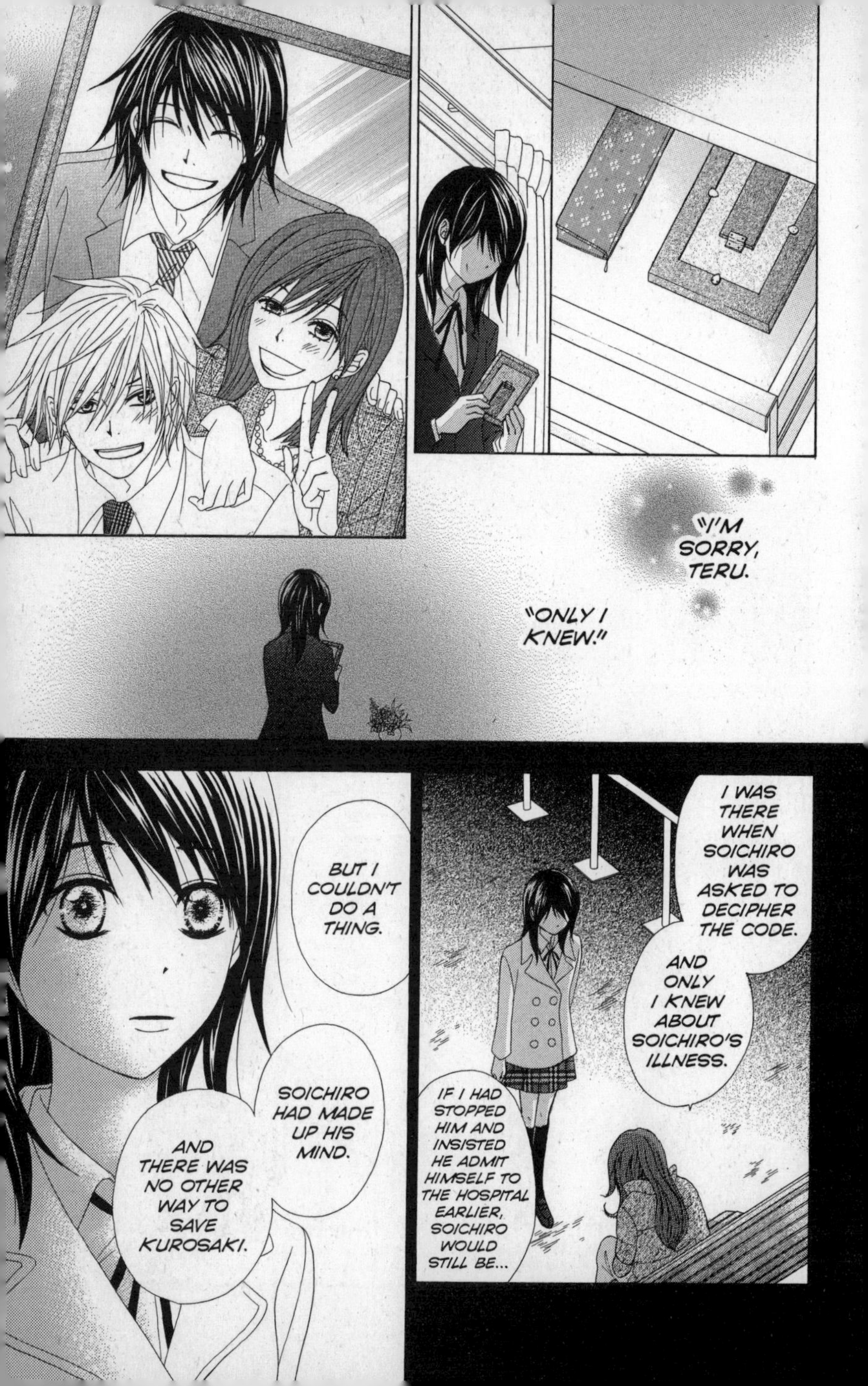
"I'M SORRY, TERU.
"ONLY I KNEW."
I WAS THERE WHEN SOICHIRO WAS ASKED TO DECIPHER THE CODE.
AND ONLY I KNEW ABOUT SOICHIRO'S ILLNESS.
IF I HAD STOPPED HIM AND INSISTED HE ADMIT HIMSELF TO THE HOSPITAL EARLIER, SOICHIRO WOULD STILL BE...
BUT I COULDN'T DO A THING.
SOICHIRO HAD MADE UP HIS MIND.
AND THERE WAS NO OTHER WAY TO SAVE KUROSAKI.

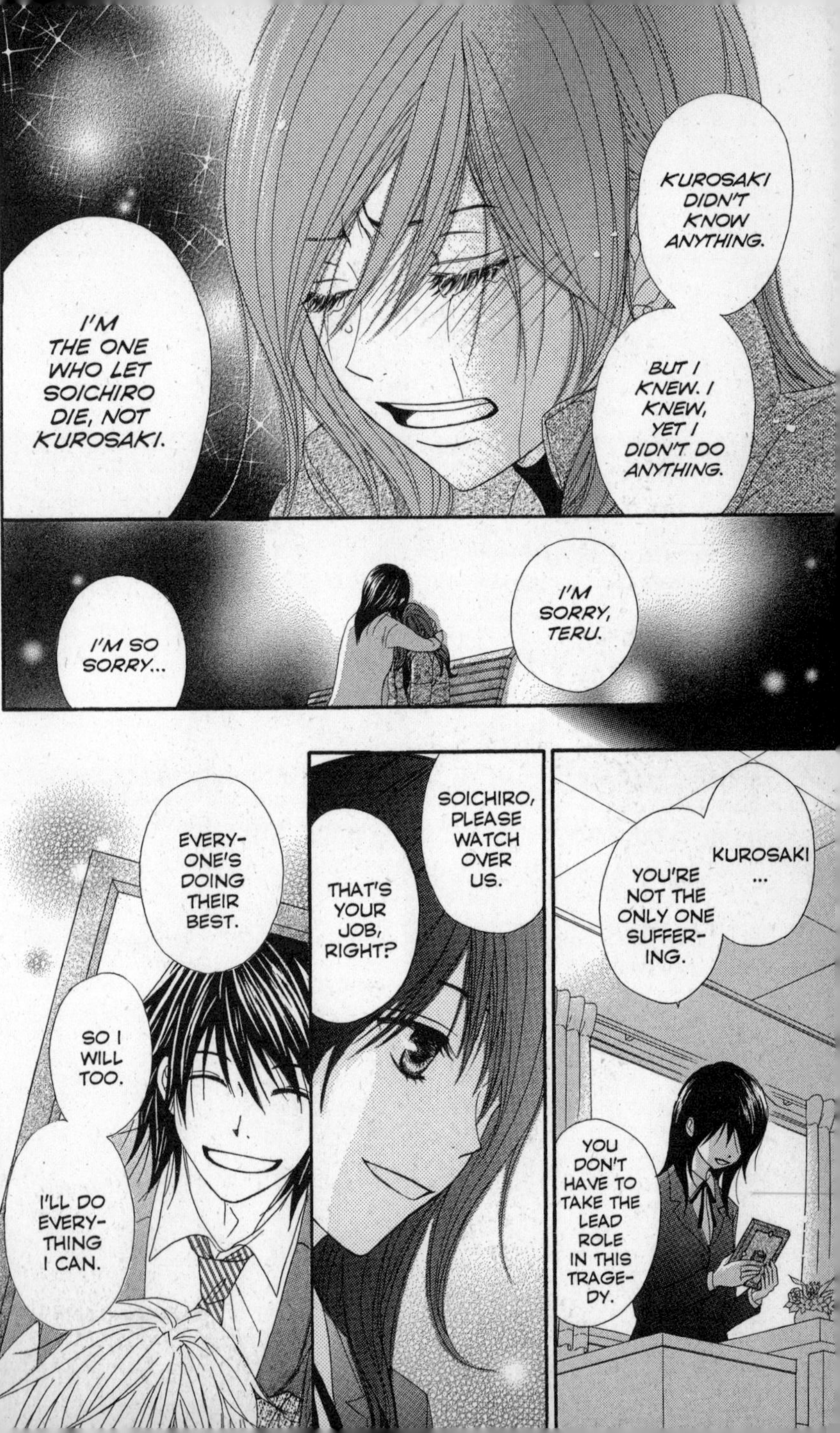
KUROSAKI DIDN'T KNOW ANYTHING.
BUT I KNEW. I KNEW, YET I DIDN'T DO ANYTHING.
I'M THE ONE WHO LET SOICHIRO DIE, NOT KUROSAKI.
I'M SORRY, TERU.
I'M SO SORRY...
KUROSAKI ...
YOU'RE NOT THE ONLY ONE SUFFERING.
YOU DON'T HAVE TO TAKE THE LEAD ROLE IN THIS TRAGEDY.
SOICHIRO, PLEASE WATCH OVER US.
THAT'S YOUR JOB, RIGHT?
EVERYONE'S DOING THEIR BEST.
SO I WILL TOO.
I'LL DO EVERYTHING I CAN.

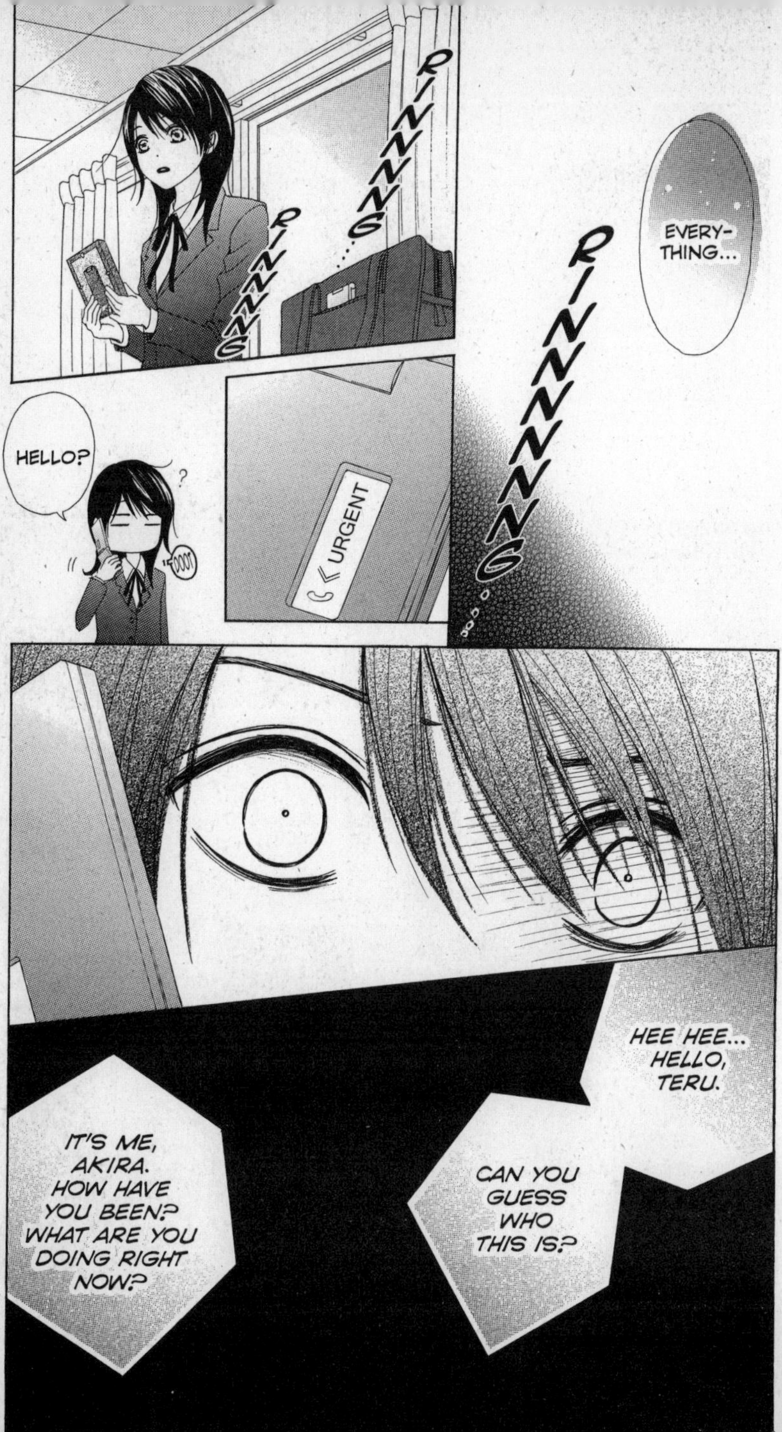
EVERYTHING...
RINNNNNNNG...
RINNNNG...
RINNNNG
URGENT
HELLO?
?
HEE HEE... HELLO, TERU.
CAN YOU GUESS WHO THIS IS?
IT'S ME, AKIRA. HOW HAVE YOU BEEN? WHAT ARE YOU DOING RIGHT NOW?

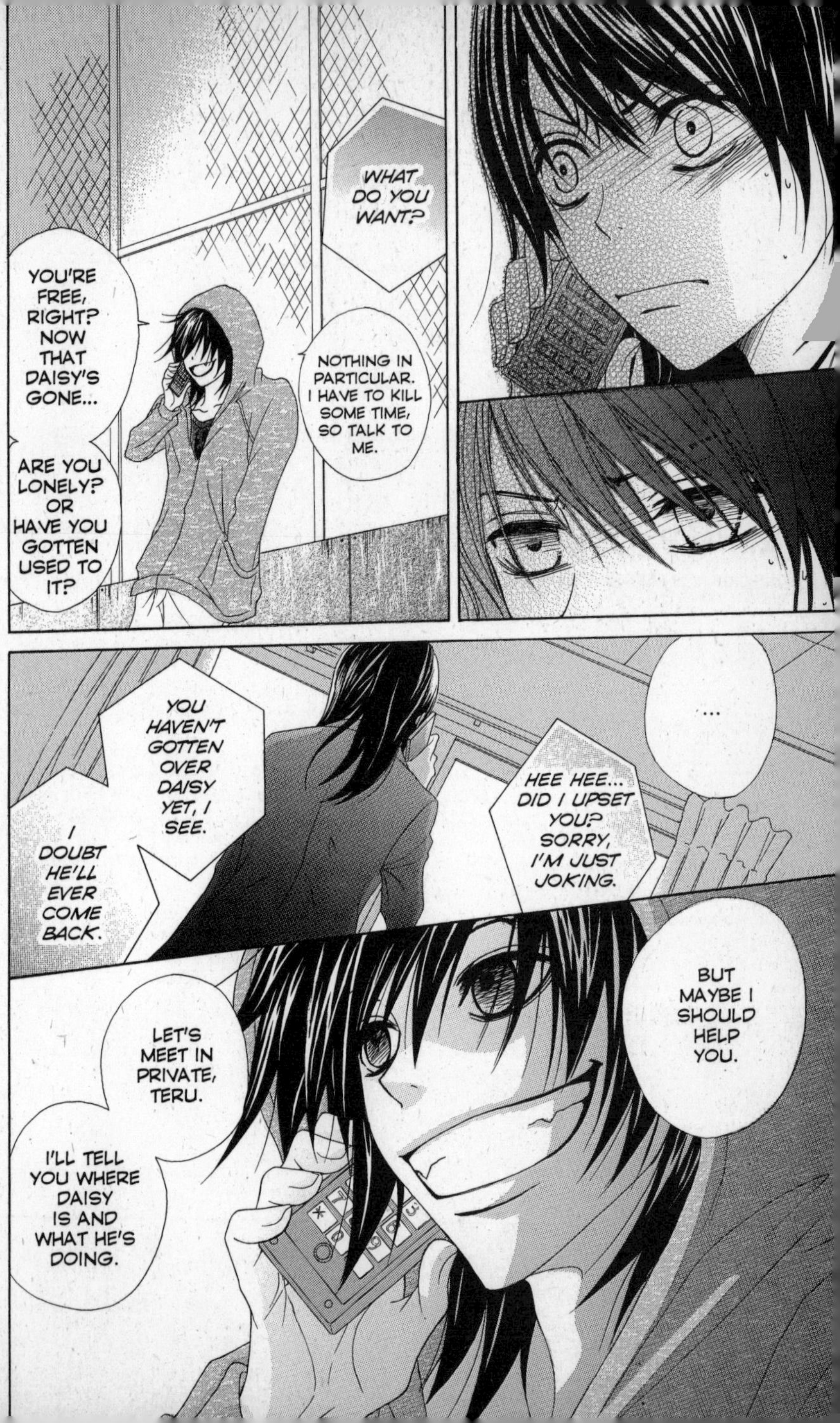
WHAT DO YOU WANT?
NOTHING IN PARTICULAR. I HAVE TO KILL SOME TIME, SO TALK TO ME.
YOU'RE FREE, RIGHT? NOW THAT DAISY'S GONE...
ARE YOU LONELY? OR HAVE YOU GOTTEN USED TO IT?
...
HEE HEE... DID I UPSET YOU? SORRY, I'M JUST JOKING.
YOU HAVEN'T GOTTEN OVER DAISY YET, I SEE.
I DOUBT HE'LL EVER COME BACK.
BUT MAYBE I SHOULD HELP YOU.
LET'S MEET IN PRIVATE, TERU.
I'LL TELL YOU WHERE DAISY IS AND WHAT HE'S DOING.

ARE YOU JUST GOING TO SIT THERE AND DO NOTHING?

YOU SHOULD TRY TO HELP DAISY.

RIGHT, TERU?

EXPRESS TRAIN TO ☐☐

SO...

I GUESS YOU REALLY HAVE BEEN LOOKING FOR "JACK FROST."

ONLY A FEW RESEARCHERS AT KENBASHI ELECTRONICS USE IT.

GOING ON JUST THAT, YOU MANAGED TO DIG UP QUITE A BIT OF INFO.

NOW, THE PROBLEM IS...

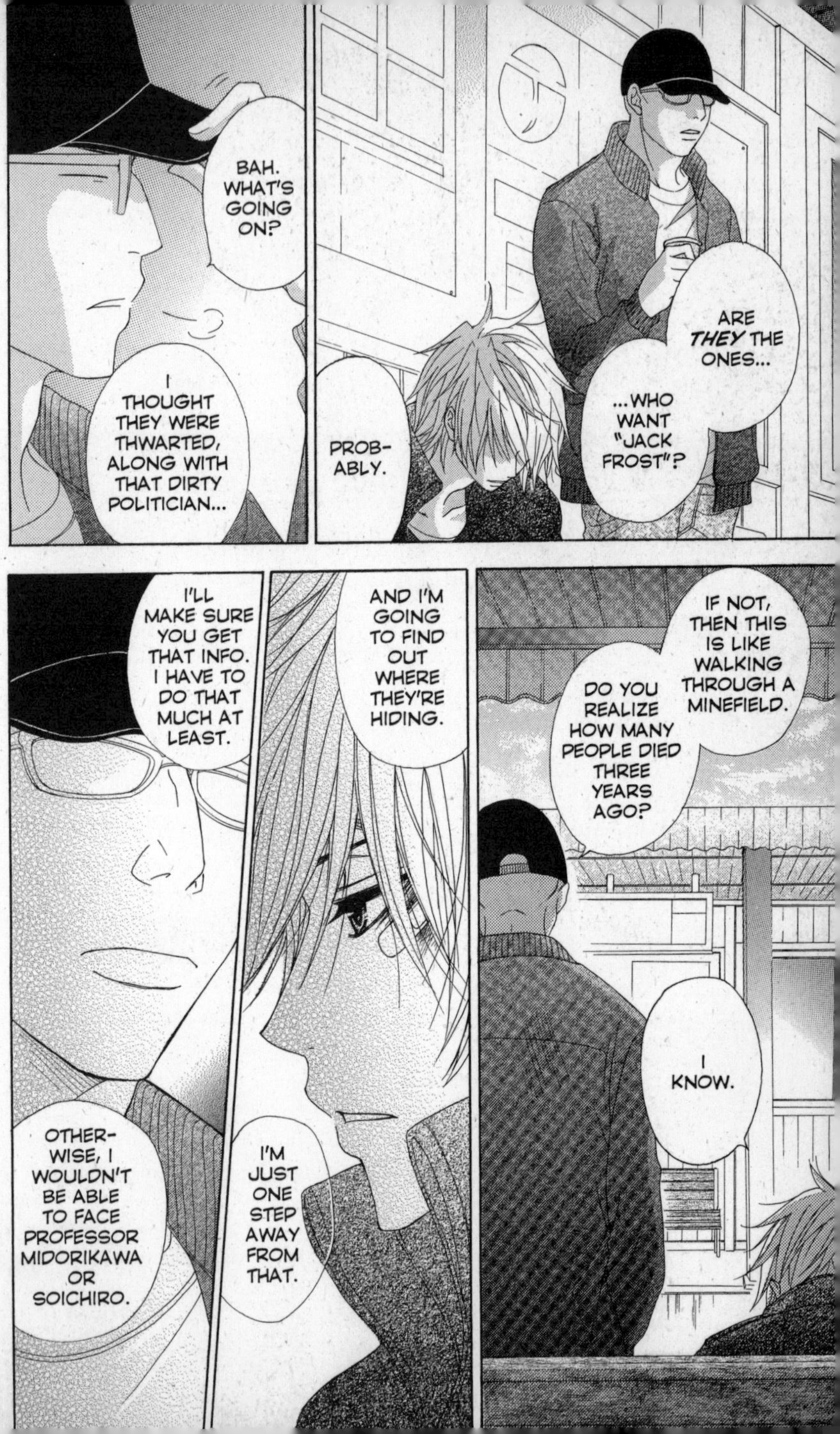
ARE *THEY* THE ONES...
...WHO WANT "JACK FROST"?
PROB-ABLY.
BAH. WHAT'S GOING ON?
I THOUGHT THEY WERE THWARTED, ALONG WITH THAT DIRTY POLITICIAN...
IF NOT, THEN THIS IS LIKE WALKING THROUGH A MINEFIELD.
DO YOU REALIZE HOW MANY PEOPLE DIED THREE YEARS AGO?
I KNOW.
AND I'M GOING TO FIND OUT WHERE THEY'RE HIDING.
I'M JUST ONE STEP AWAY FROM THAT.
I'LL MAKE SURE YOU GET THAT INFO. I HAVE TO DO THAT MUCH AT LEAST.
OTHER-WISE, I WOULDN'T BE ABLE TO FACE PROFESSOR MIDORIKAWA OR SOICHIRO.

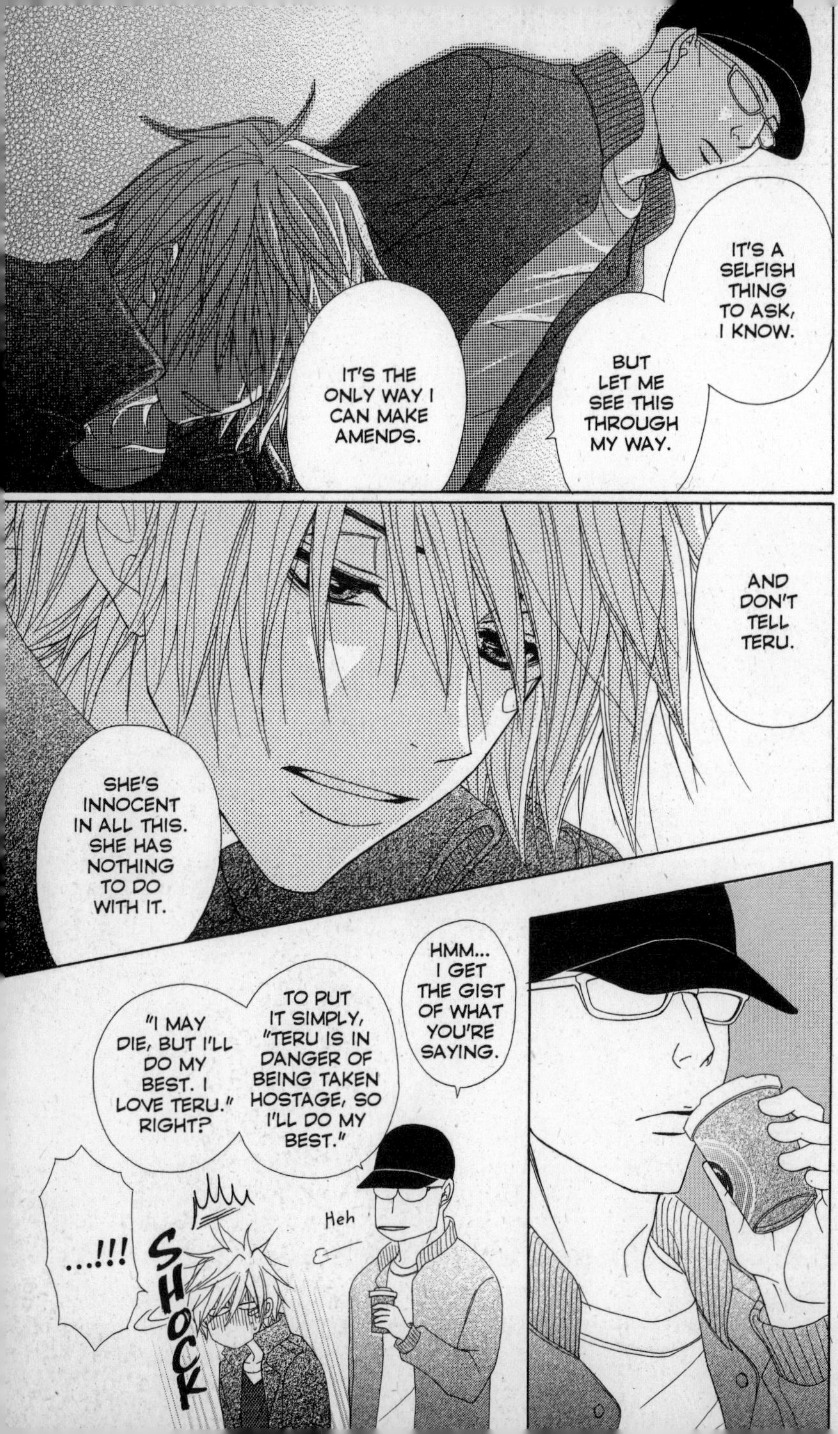
IT'S A SELFISH THING TO ASK, I KNOW.
BUT LET ME SEE THIS THROUGH MY WAY.
IT'S THE ONLY WAY I CAN MAKE AMENDS.
AND DON'T TELL TERU.
SHE'S INNOCENT IN ALL THIS. SHE HAS NOTHING TO DO WITH IT.
HMM... I GET THE GIST OF WHAT YOU'RE SAYING.
TO PUT IT SIMPLY, "TERU IS IN DANGER OF BEING TAKEN HOSTAGE, SO I'LL DO MY BEST."
"I MAY DIE, BUT I'LL DO MY BEST. I LOVE TERU." RIGHT?
Heh
SHOCK
...!!!

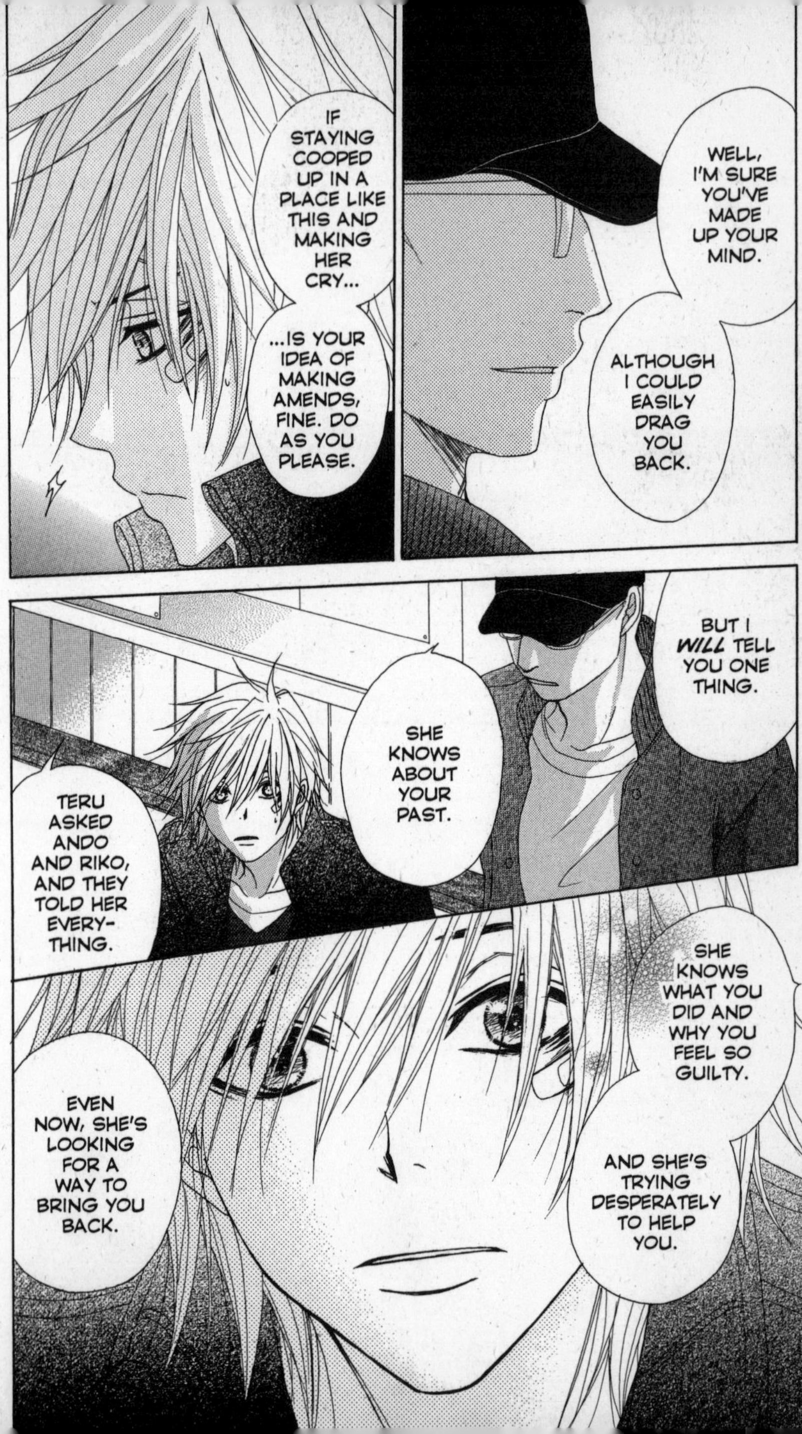
WELL, I'M SURE YOU'VE MADE UP YOUR MIND.
ALTHOUGH I COULD EASILY DRAG YOU BACK.
IF STAYING COOPED UP IN A PLACE LIKE THIS AND MAKING HER CRY...
...IS YOUR IDEA OF MAKING AMENDS, FINE. DO AS YOU PLEASE.
BUT I *WILL* TELL YOU ONE THING.
SHE KNOWS ABOUT YOUR PAST.
TERU ASKED ANDO AND RIKO, AND THEY TOLD HER EVERY-THING.
SHE KNOWS WHAT YOU DID AND WHY YOU FEEL SO GUILTY.
AND SHE'S TRYING DESPERATELY TO HELP YOU.
EVEN NOW, SHE'S LOOKING FOR A WAY TO BRING YOU BACK.

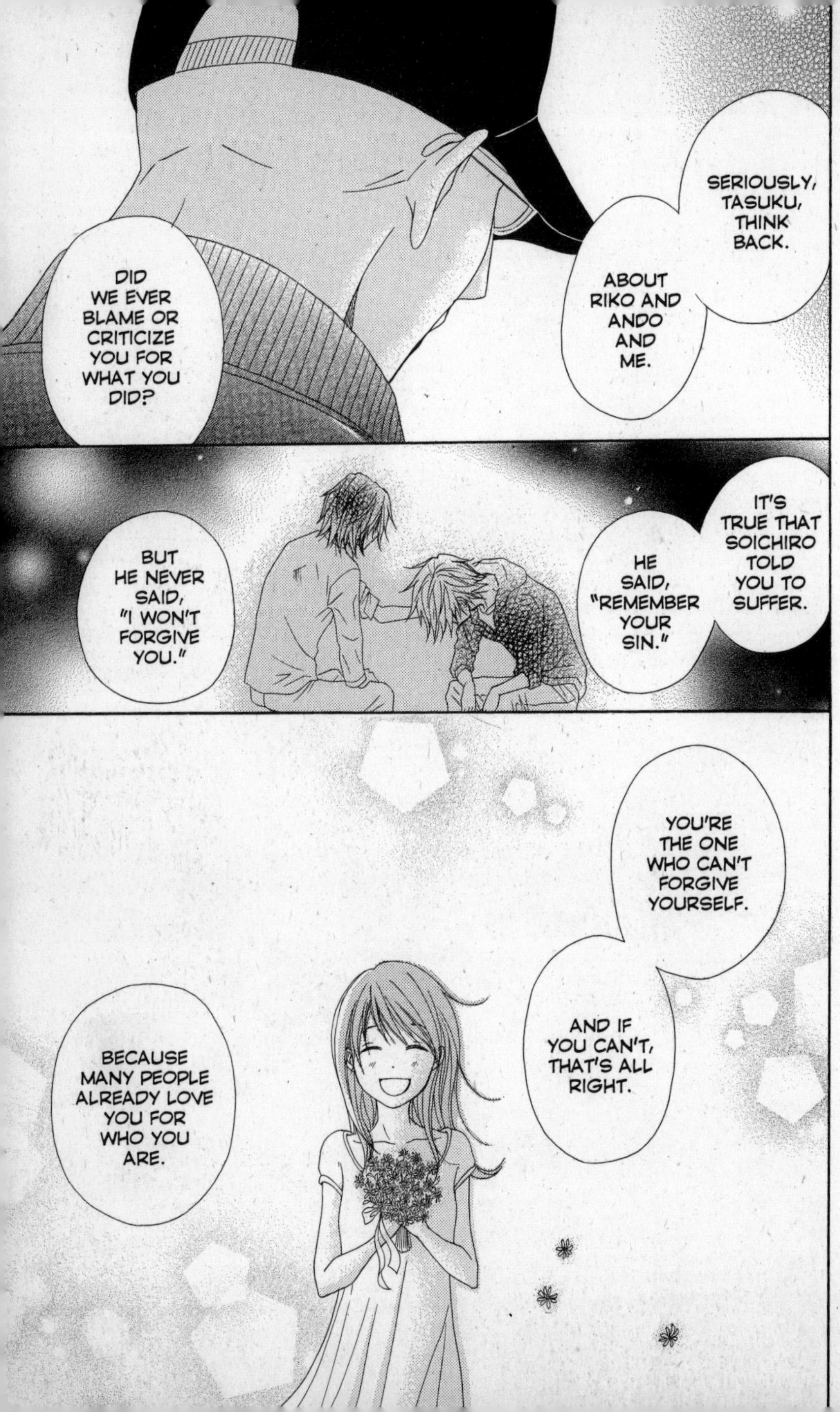
SERIOUSLY, TASUKU, THINK BACK.
ABOUT RIKO AND ANDO AND ME.
DID WE EVER BLAME OR CRITICIZE YOU FOR WHAT YOU DID?
IT'S TRUE THAT SOICHIRO TOLD YOU TO SUFFER.
HE SAID, "REMEMBER YOUR SIN."
BUT HE NEVER SAID, "I WON'T FORGIVE YOU."
YOU'RE THE ONE WHO CAN'T FORGIVE YOURSELF.
AND IF YOU CAN'T, THAT'S ALL RIGHT.
BECAUSE MANY PEOPLE ALREADY LOVE YOU FOR WHO YOU ARE.

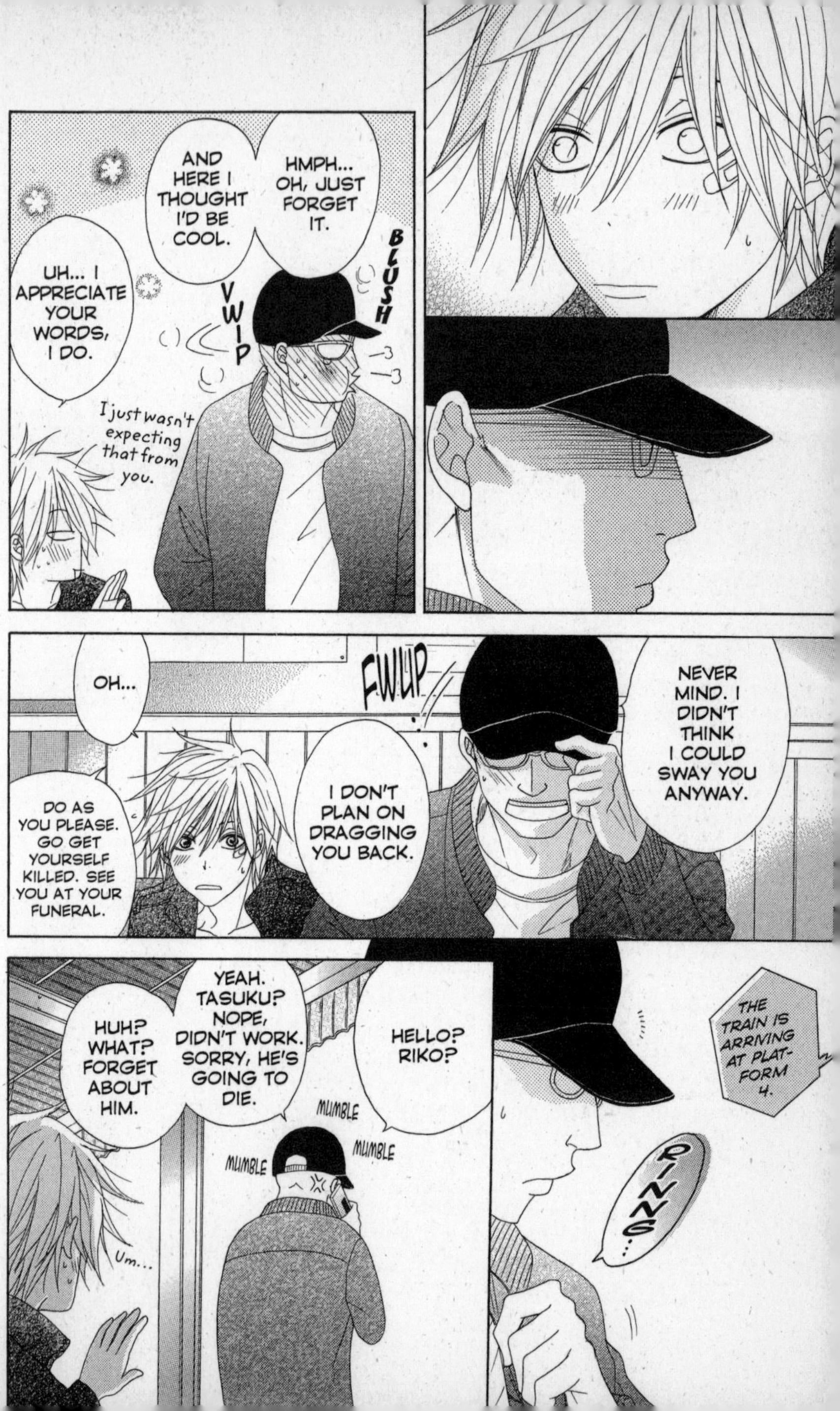
HMPH... OH, JUST FORGET IT.
AND HERE I THOUGHT I'D BE COOL.
BLUSH
VWIP
UH... I APPRECIATE YOUR WORDS, I DO.
I just wasn't expecting that from you.
NEVER MIND. I DIDN'T THINK I COULD SWAY YOU ANYWAY.
FWUP
I DON'T PLAN ON DRAGGING YOU BACK.
OH...
DO AS YOU PLEASE. GO GET YOURSELF KILLED. SEE YOU AT YOUR FUNERAL.
THE TRAIN IS ARRIVING AT PLAT-FORM 4.
RINNG...
HELLO? RIKO?
YEAH. TASUKU? NOPE, DIDN'T WORK. SORRY, HE'S GOING TO DIE.
HUH? WHAT? FORGET ABOUT HIM.
MUMBLE
MUMBLE
MUMBLE
Um...

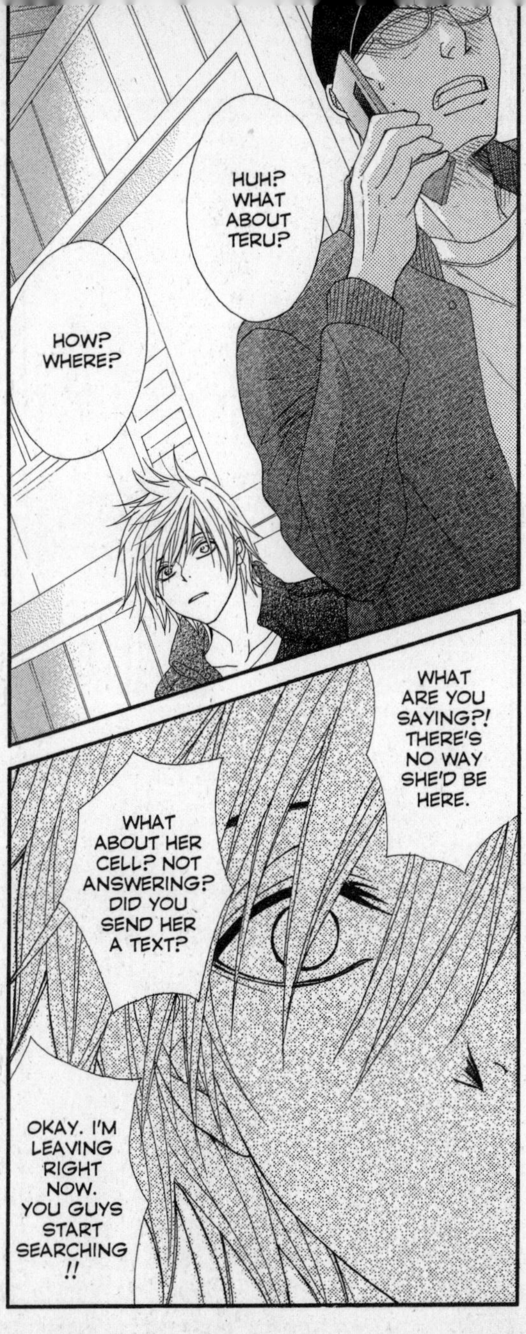
HUH? WHAT ABOUT TERU?
HOW? WHERE?
WHAT ARE YOU SAYING?! THERE'S NO WAY SHE'D BE HERE.
WHAT ABOUT HER CELL? NOT ANSWERING? DID YOU SEND HER A TEXT?
OKAY. I'M LEAVING RIGHT NOW. YOU GUYS START SEARCHING!!

DENGEKI DAISY QUESTION CORNER

BALDLY ASK!!

①

...HI!! I'VE BROUGHT YOU THIS CORNER WHERE I ASK FOR YOUR KINDNESS AND UNDERSTANDING. DUE TO CIRCUMSTANCES, THERE ARE ONLY FOUR QUESTION CORNERS IN THIS VOLUME. I DON'T THINK THAT WILL DISAPPOINT TOO MANY OF YOU, BUT ANYWAY, HERE WE GO!!!

Q.
HOW DID YOU COME TO NAME THE CHARACTERS IN *DENGEKI DAISY*, LIKE TASUKU, TERU AND SOICHIRO?

(MICRO MAPLE AND OTHERS, AICHI PREFECTURE)

A.
I'VE GOTTEN QUITE A FEW INQUIRIES ABOUT THIS. THIS MAY NOT SOUND TOO EXCITING, BUT FOR TASUKU AND TERU, I WANTED A ONE-KANJI NAME.

MY MANGA TENDS TO HAVE LOTS OF DIALOGUE... SO IT WAS A WAY TO SHORTEN THE LINES... THAT WAS THE MAIN REASON...
ALSO FOR TERU, I HAD IN MIND SOMEONE WHO SEEMS COMMONPLACE BUT ISN'T, LEAVES A LASTING IMPRESSION, AND TENDS TO BE SIMPLE RATHER THAN SOPHISTICATED.
I BORROWED THE NAME TASUKU FROM A FAVORITE RADIO SHOW HOST THAT I OFTEN LISTEN TO.
I COULDN'T DECIDE BETWEEN SOICHIRO AND SHIGERU. SO I ENDED UP SURVEYING THE PEOPLE AROUND ME. (IT'S TRUE.)

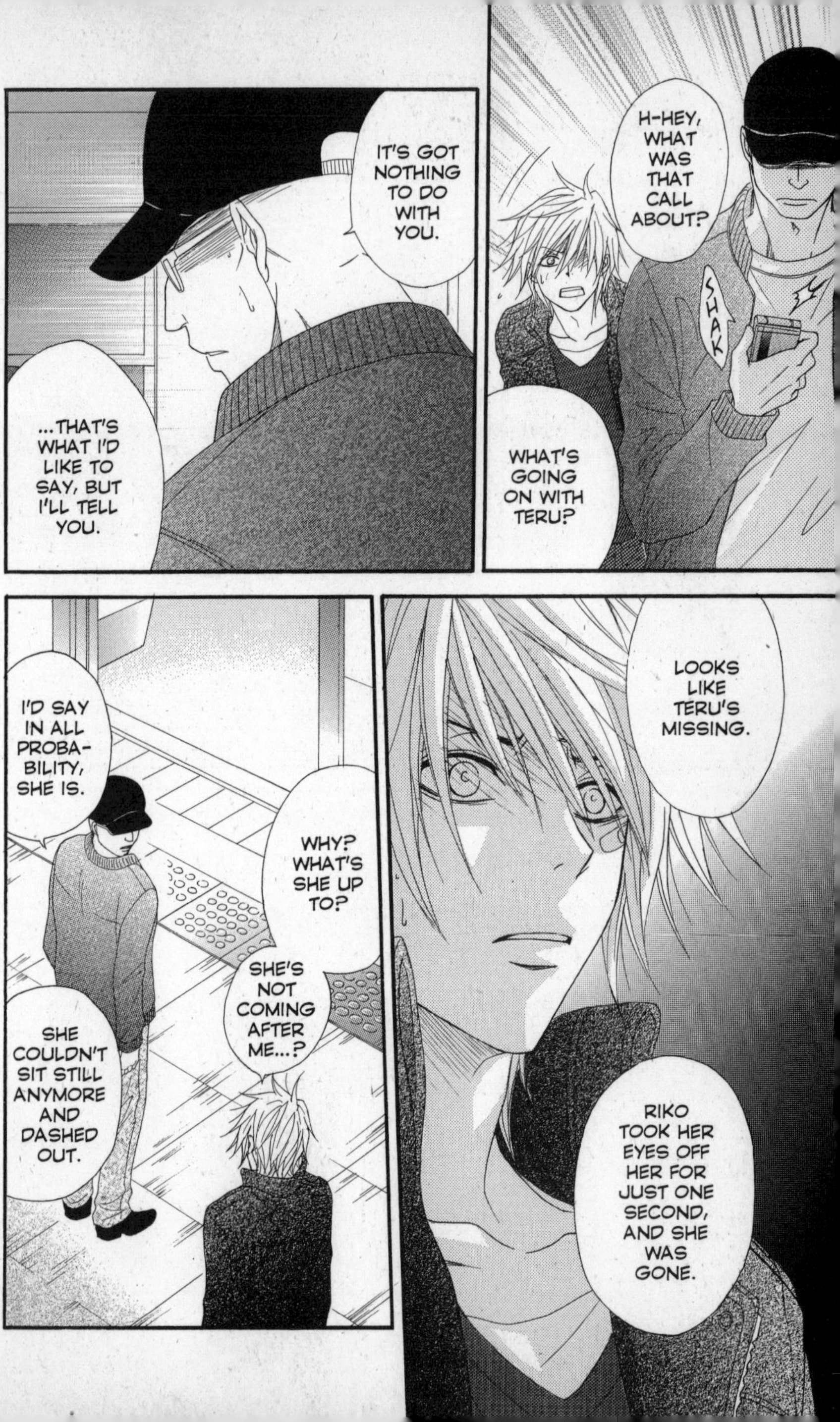
H-HEY, WHAT WAS THAT CALL ABOUT?
SHAK
WHAT'S GOING ON WITH TERU?
IT'S GOT NOTHING TO DO WITH YOU.
...THAT'S WHAT I'D LIKE TO SAY, BUT I'LL TELL YOU.
LOOKS LIKE TERU'S MISSING.
RIKO TOOK HER EYES OFF HER FOR JUST ONE SECOND, AND SHE WAS GONE.
WHY? WHAT'S SHE UP TO?
I'D SAY IN ALL PROBA-BILITY, SHE IS.
SHE'S NOT COMING AFTER ME...?
SHE COULDN'T SIT STILL ANYMORE AND DASHED OUT.

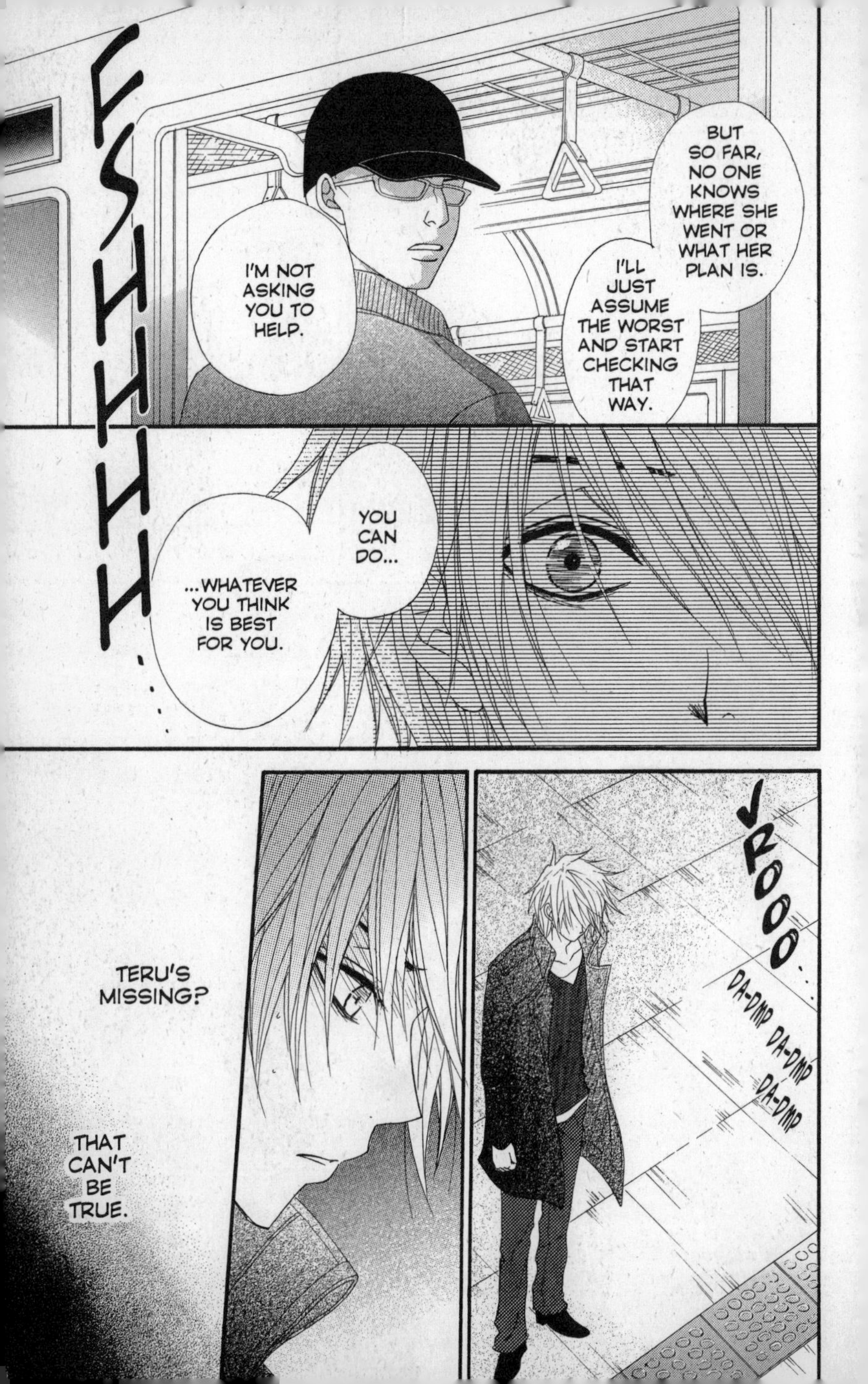
BUT SO FAR, NO ONE KNOWS WHERE SHE WENT OR WHAT HER PLAN IS.
I'LL JUST ASSUME THE WORST AND START CHECKING THAT WAY.
I'M NOT ASKING YOU TO HELP.
FSHHHHH...
YOU CAN DO...
...WHATEVER YOU THINK IS BEST FOR YOU.
VROOO...
DA-DMP DA-DMP DA-DMP
TERU'S MISSING?
THAT CAN'T BE TRUE.

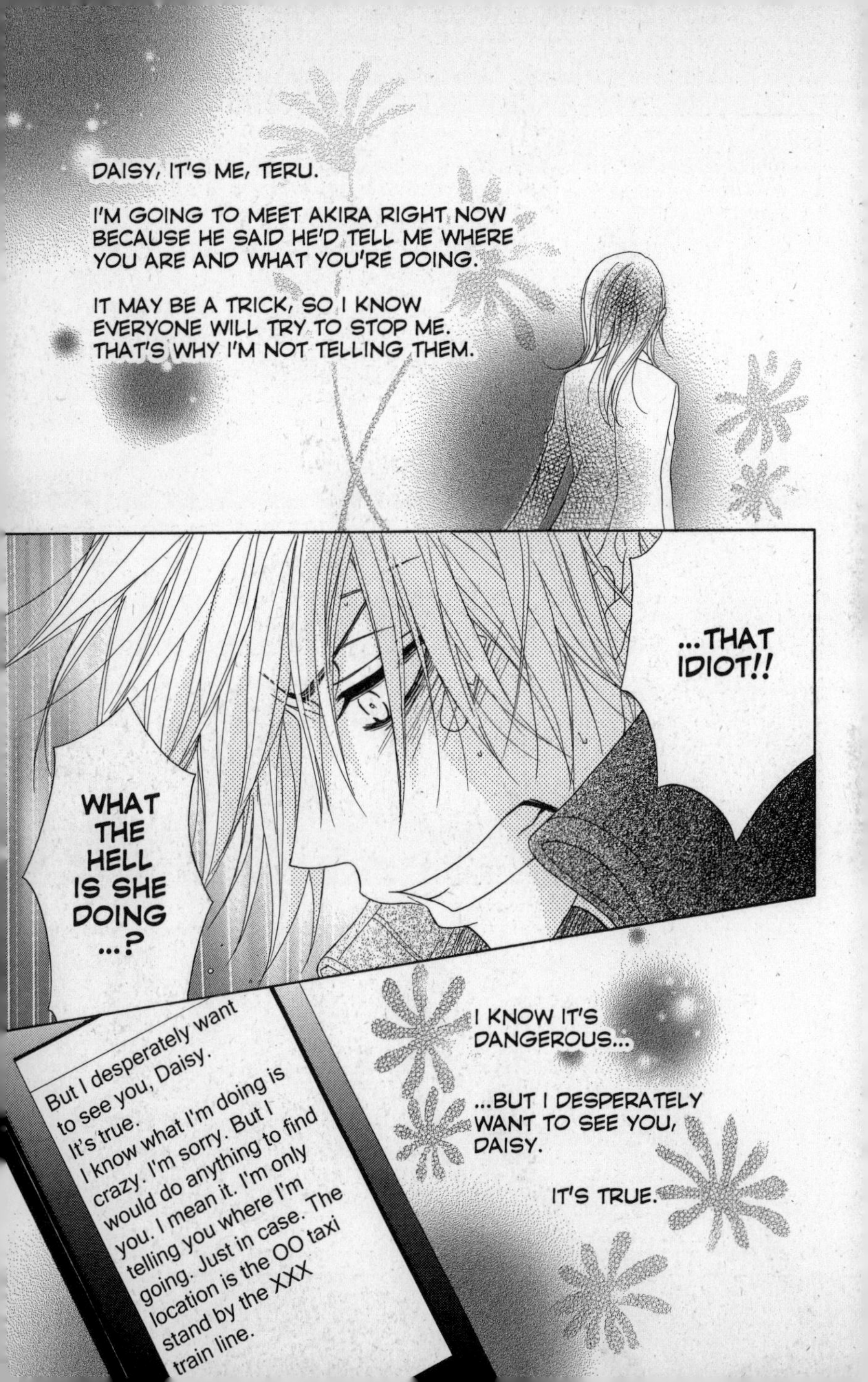
DAISY, IT'S ME, TERU.
I'M GOING TO MEET AKIRA RIGHT NOW BECAUSE HE SAID HE'D TELL ME WHERE YOU ARE AND WHAT YOU'RE DOING.
IT MAY BE A TRICK, SO I KNOW EVERYONE WILL TRY TO STOP ME. THAT'S WHY I'M NOT TELLING THEM.
...THAT IDIOT!!
WHAT THE HELL IS SHE DOING ...?
I KNOW IT'S DANGEROUS...
...BUT I DESPERATELY WANT TO SEE YOU, DAISY.
IT'S TRUE.
But I desperately want to see you, Daisy. It's true. I know what I'm doing is crazy. I'm sorry. But I would do anything to find you. I mean it. I'm only telling you where I'm going. Just in case. The location is the OO taxi stand by the XXX train line.

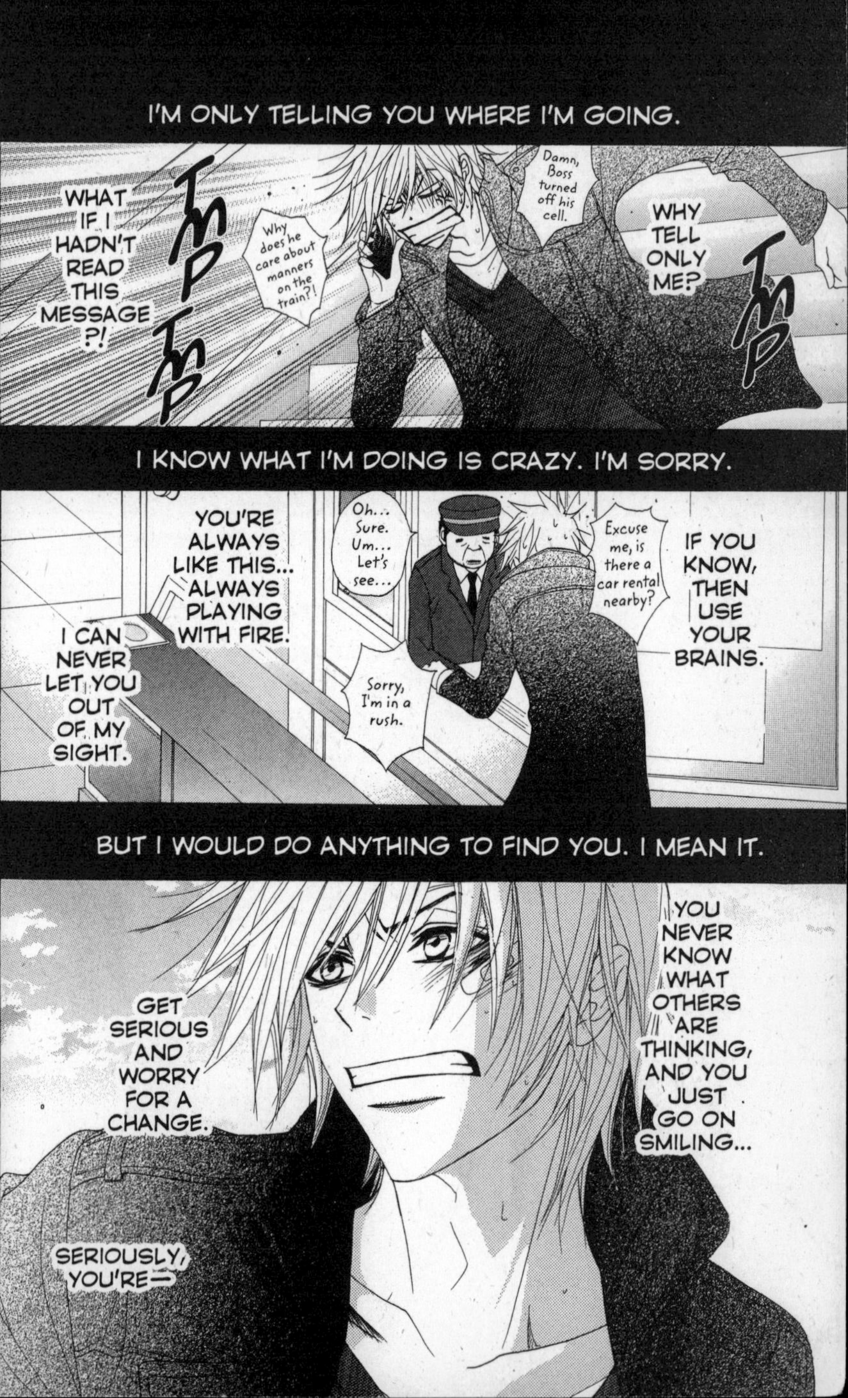
I'M ONLY TELLING YOU WHERE I'M GOING.
WHY TELL ONLY ME?
Damn, Boss turned off his cell.
TMP
Why does he care about manners on the train?!
WHAT IF I HADN'T READ THIS MESSAGE?!
TMP TMP
I KNOW WHAT I'M DOING IS CRAZY. I'M SORRY.
IF YOU KNOW, THEN USE YOUR BRAINS.
Excuse me, is there a car rental nearby?
Oh... Sure. Um... Let's see...
YOU'RE ALWAYS LIKE THIS... ALWAYS PLAYING WITH FIRE.
Sorry, I'm in a rush.
I CAN NEVER LET YOU OUT OF MY SIGHT.
BUT I WOULD DO ANYTHING TO FIND YOU. I MEAN IT.
YOU NEVER KNOW WHAT OTHERS ARE THINKING, AND YOU JUST GO ON SMILING...
GET SERIOUS AND WORRY FOR A CHANGE.
SERIOUSLY, YOU'RE—

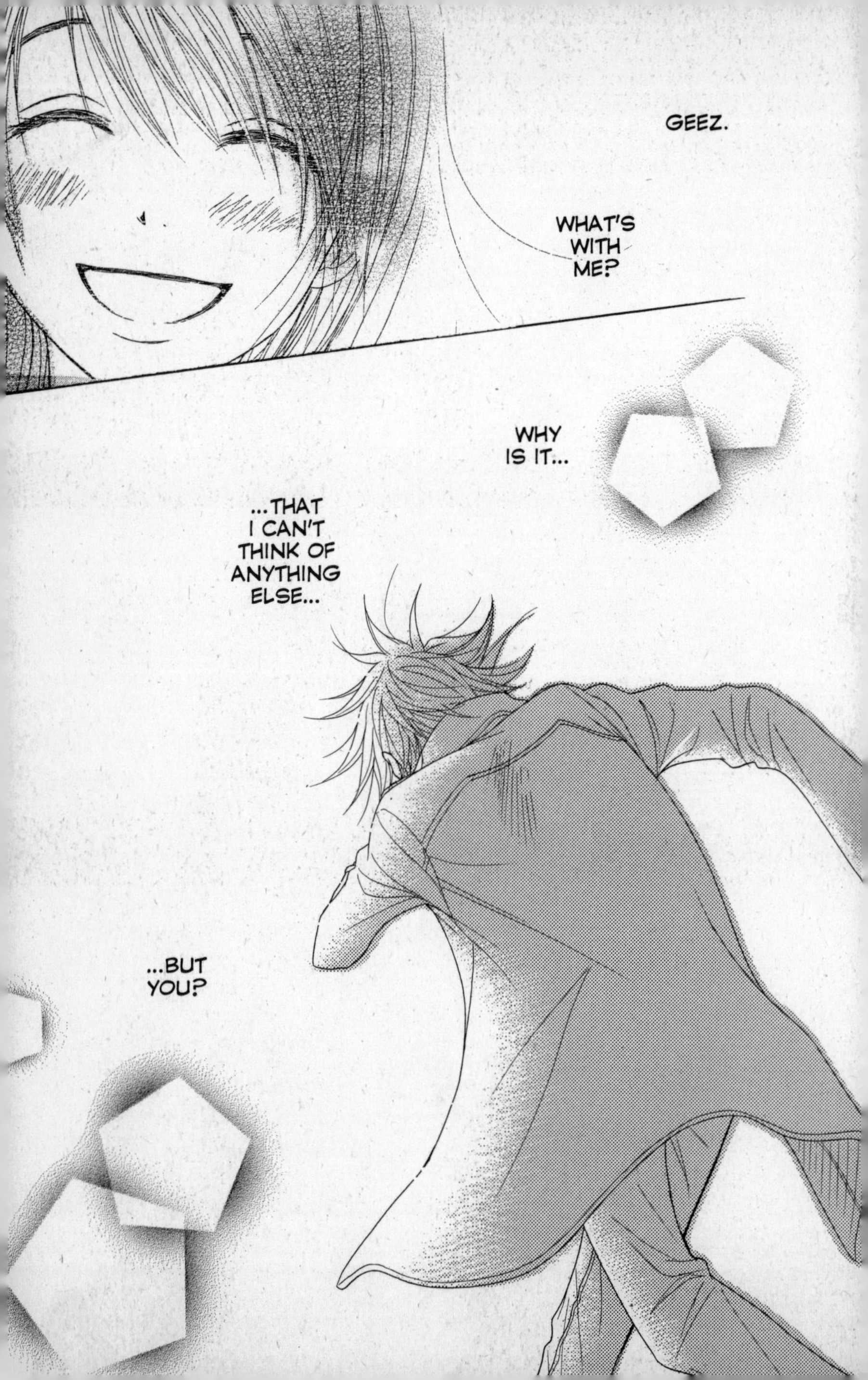
GEEZ.
WHAT'S WITH ME?
WHY IS IT...
...THAT I CAN'T THINK OF ANYTHING ELSE...
...BUT YOU?

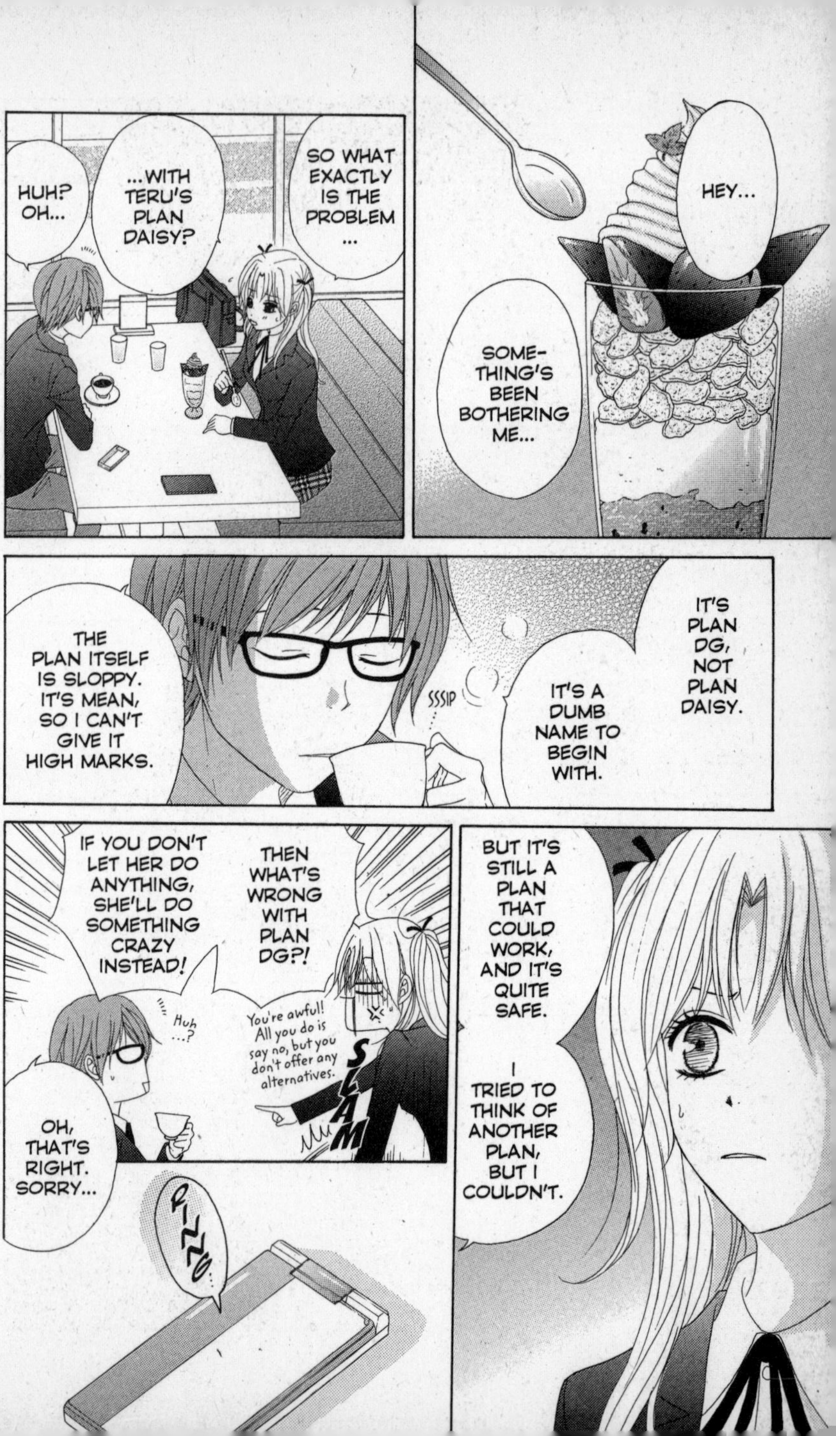
HEY...
SOMETHING'S BEEN BOTHERING ME...
SO WHAT EXACTLY IS THE PROBLEM...
...WITH TERU'S PLAN DAISY?
HUH? OH...
IT'S PLAN DG, NOT PLAN DAISY.
IT'S A DUMB NAME TO BEGIN WITH.
SSSIP
THE PLAN ITSELF IS SLOPPY. IT'S MEAN, SO I CAN'T GIVE IT HIGH MARKS.
BUT IT'S STILL A PLAN THAT COULD WORK, AND IT'S QUITE SAFE.
I TRIED TO THINK OF ANOTHER PLAN, BUT I COULDN'T.
THEN WHAT'S WRONG WITH PLAN DG?!
IF YOU DON'T LET HER DO ANYTHING, SHE'LL DO SOMETHING CRAZY INSTEAD!
SLAM
You're awful! All you do is say no, but you don't offer any alternatives.
Huh ...?
OH, THAT'S RIGHT. SORRY...
RINNG...

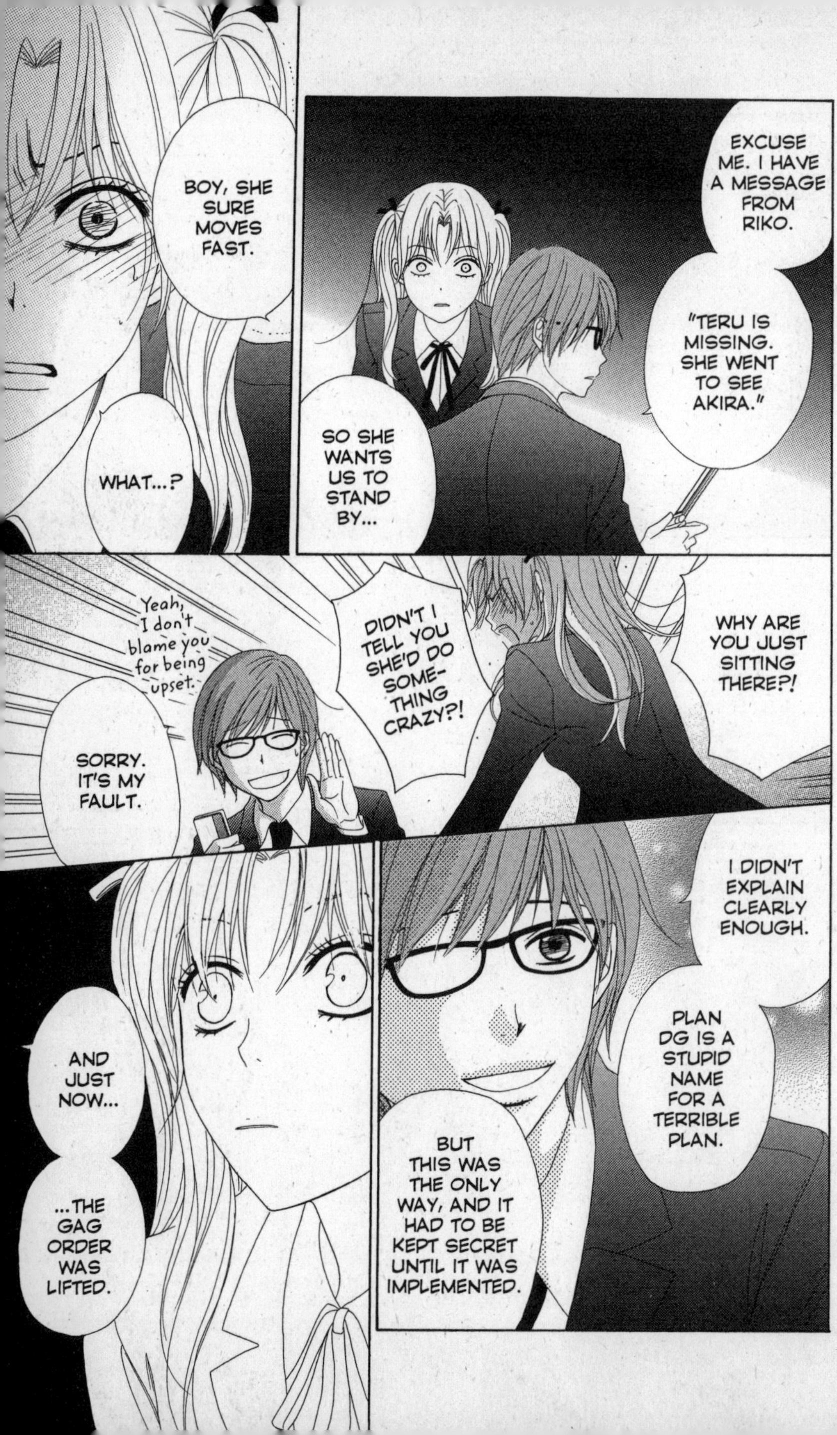
EXCUSE ME. I HAVE A MESSAGE FROM RIKO.
"TERU IS MISSING. SHE WENT TO SEE AKIRA."
SO SHE WANTS US TO STAND BY...
BOY, SHE SURE MOVES FAST.
WHAT...?
WHY ARE YOU JUST SITTING THERE?!
DIDN'T I TELL YOU SHE'D DO SOME-THING CRAZY?!
Yeah, I don't blame you for being upset.
SORRY. IT'S MY FAULT.
I DIDN'T EXPLAIN CLEARLY ENOUGH.
PLAN DG IS A STUPID NAME FOR A TERRIBLE PLAN.
BUT THIS WAS THE ONLY WAY, AND IT HAD TO BE KEPT SECRET UNTIL IT WAS IMPLEMENTED.
AND JUST NOW...
...THE GAG ORDER WAS LIFTED.

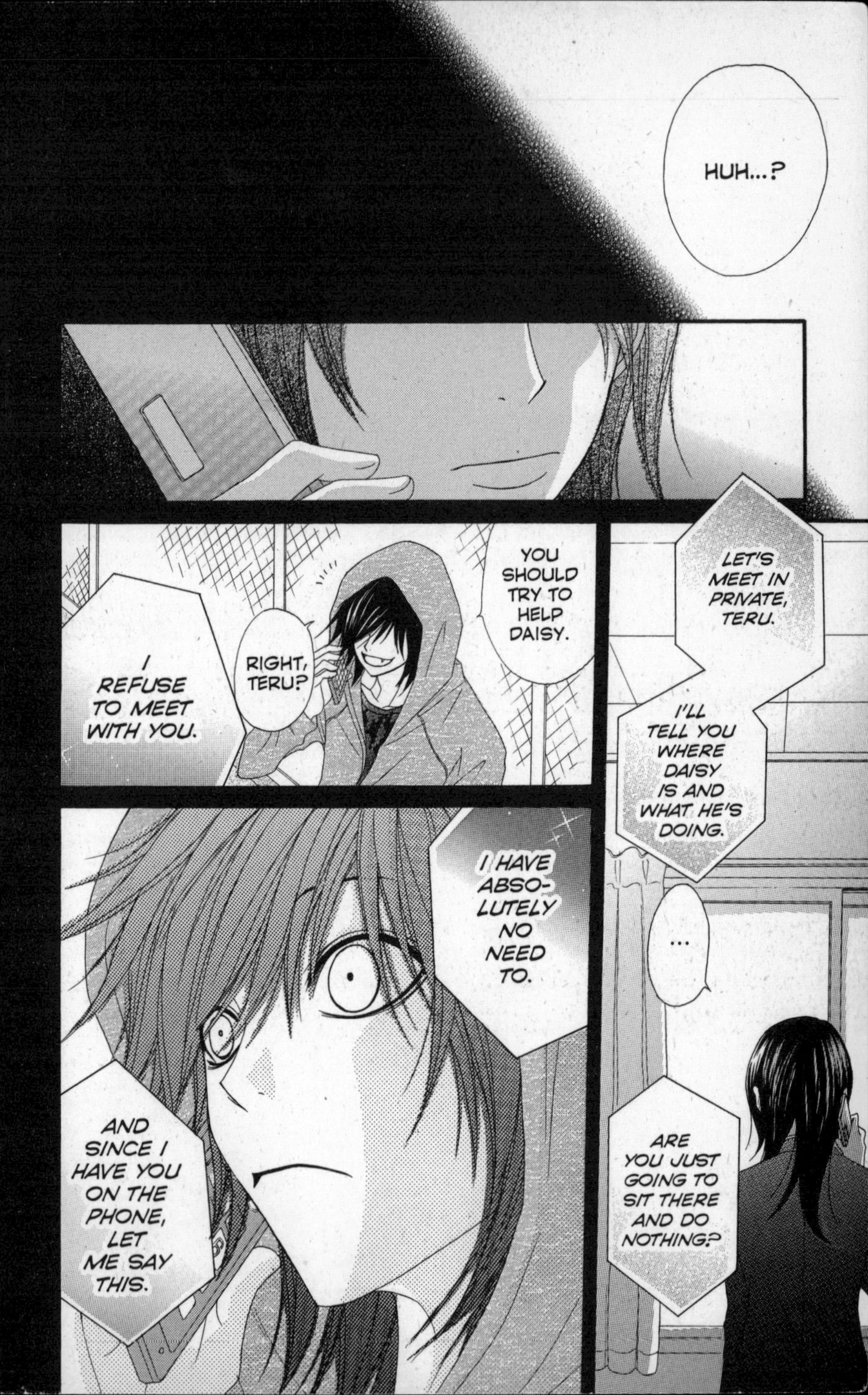
HUH...?
LET'S MEET IN PRIVATE, TERU.
I'LL TELL YOU WHERE DAISY IS AND WHAT HE'S DOING.
...
ARE YOU JUST GOING TO SIT THERE AND DO NOTHING?
YOU SHOULD TRY TO HELP DAISY.
RIGHT, TERU?
I REFUSE TO MEET WITH YOU.
I HAVE ABSOLUTELY NO NEED TO.
AND SINCE I HAVE YOU ON THE PHONE, LET ME SAY THIS.

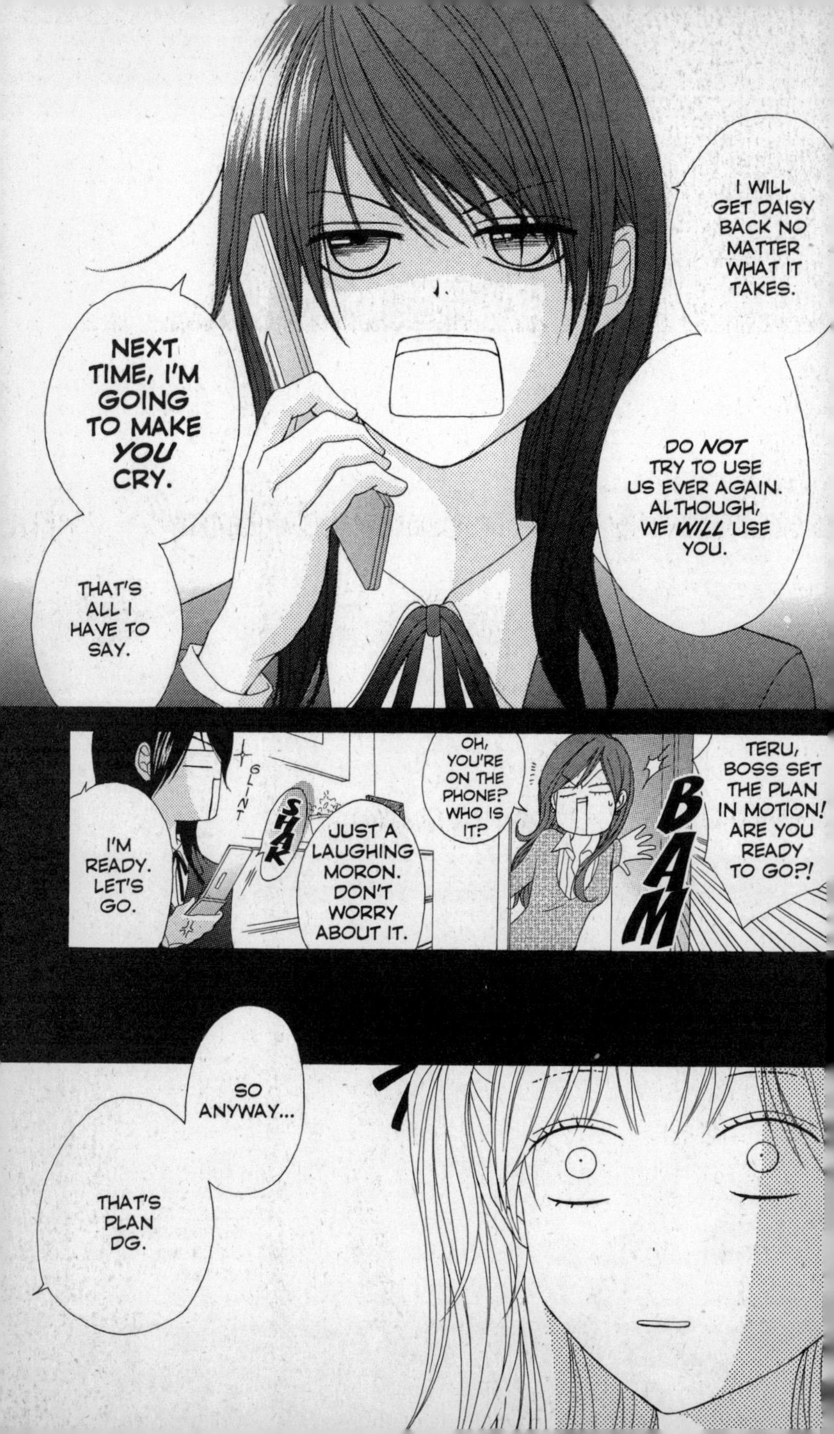
I WILL GET DAISY BACK NO MATTER WHAT IT TAKES.
DO NOT TRY TO USE US EVER AGAIN. ALTHOUGH, WE WILL USE YOU.
NEXT TIME, I'M GOING TO MAKE YOU CRY.
THAT'S ALL I HAVE TO SAY.
TERU, BOSS SET THE PLAN IN MOTION! ARE YOU READY TO GO?!
BAM
OH, YOU'RE ON THE PHONE? WHO IS IT?
SHAK
JUST A LAUGHING MORON. DON'T WORRY ABOUT IT.
GLINT
I'M READY. LET'S GO.
SO ANYWAY...
THAT'S PLAN DG.

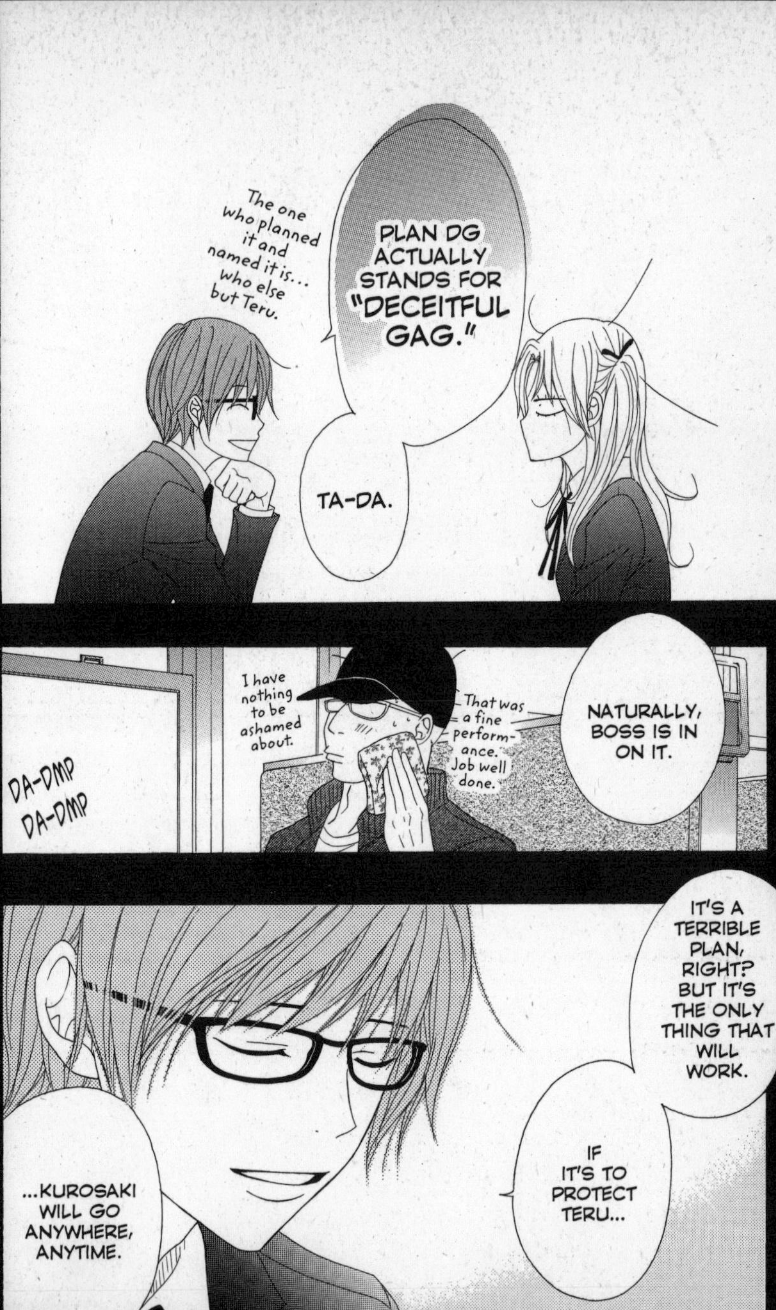
PLAN DG ACTUALLY STANDS FOR "DECEITFUL GAG."
TA-DA.
The one who planned it and named it is... who else but Teru.
NATURALLY, BOSS IS IN ON IT.
That was a fine performance. Job well done.
I have nothing to be ashamed about.
DA-DMP DA-DMP
IT'S A TERRIBLE PLAN, RIGHT? BUT IT'S THE ONLY THING THAT WILL WORK.
IF IT'S TO PROTECT TERU...
...KUROSAKI WILL GO ANYWHERE, ANYTIME.

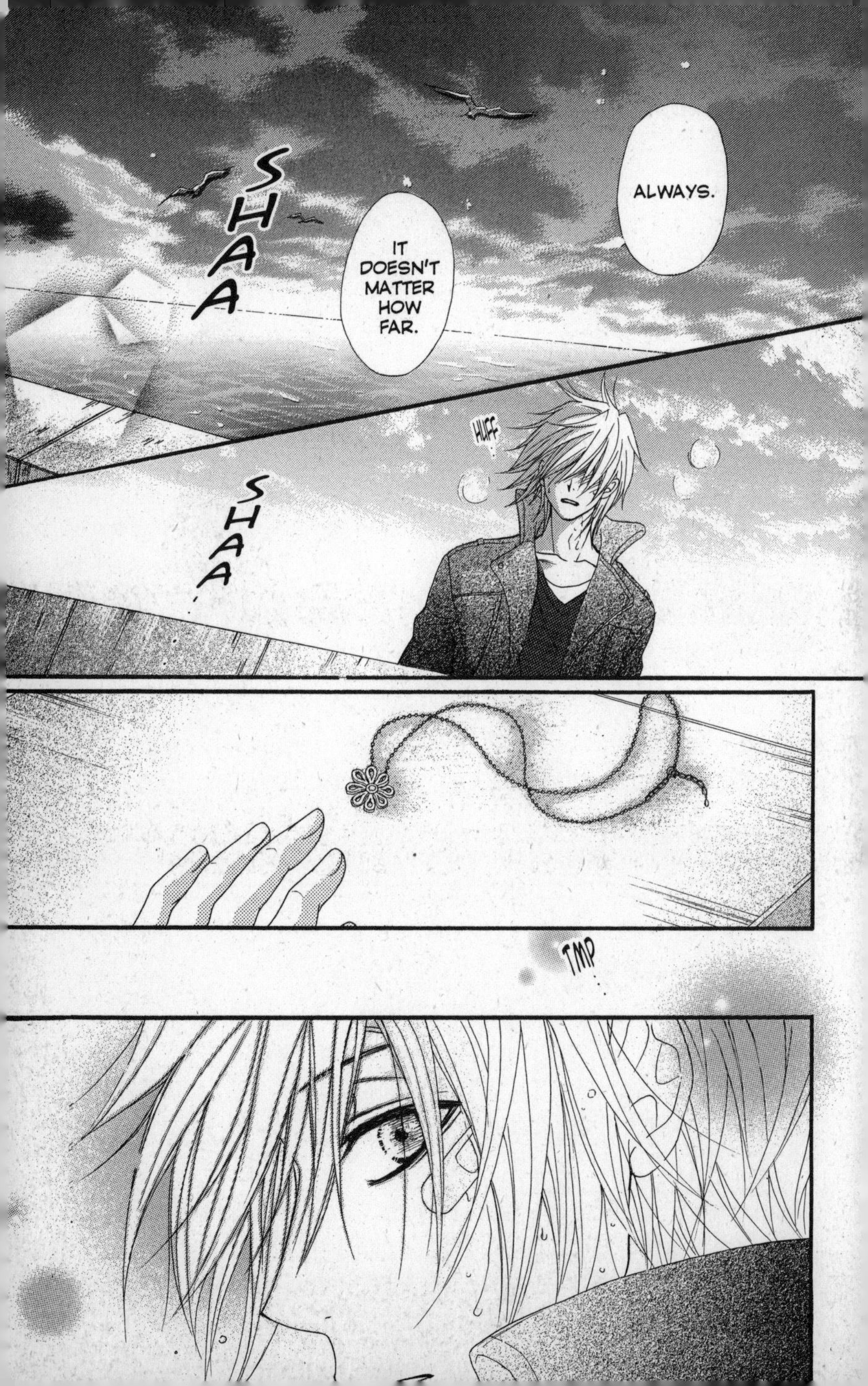
ALWAYS.
IT DOESN'T MATTER HOW FAR.
SHAAA
HUFF
SHAA...
TMP...

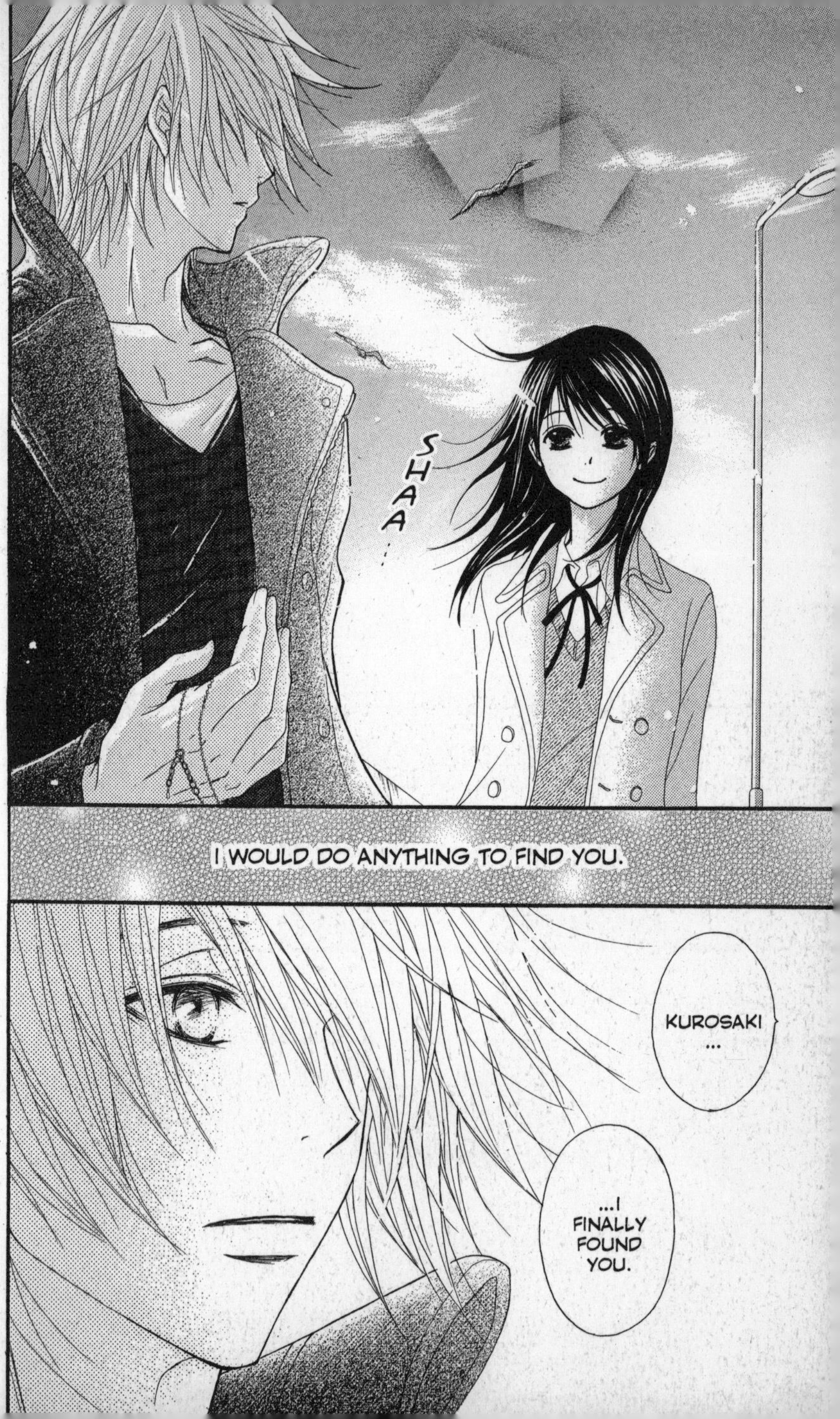
SHAA...
I WOULD DO ANYTHING TO FIND YOU.
KUROSAKI...
...I FINALLY FOUND YOU.

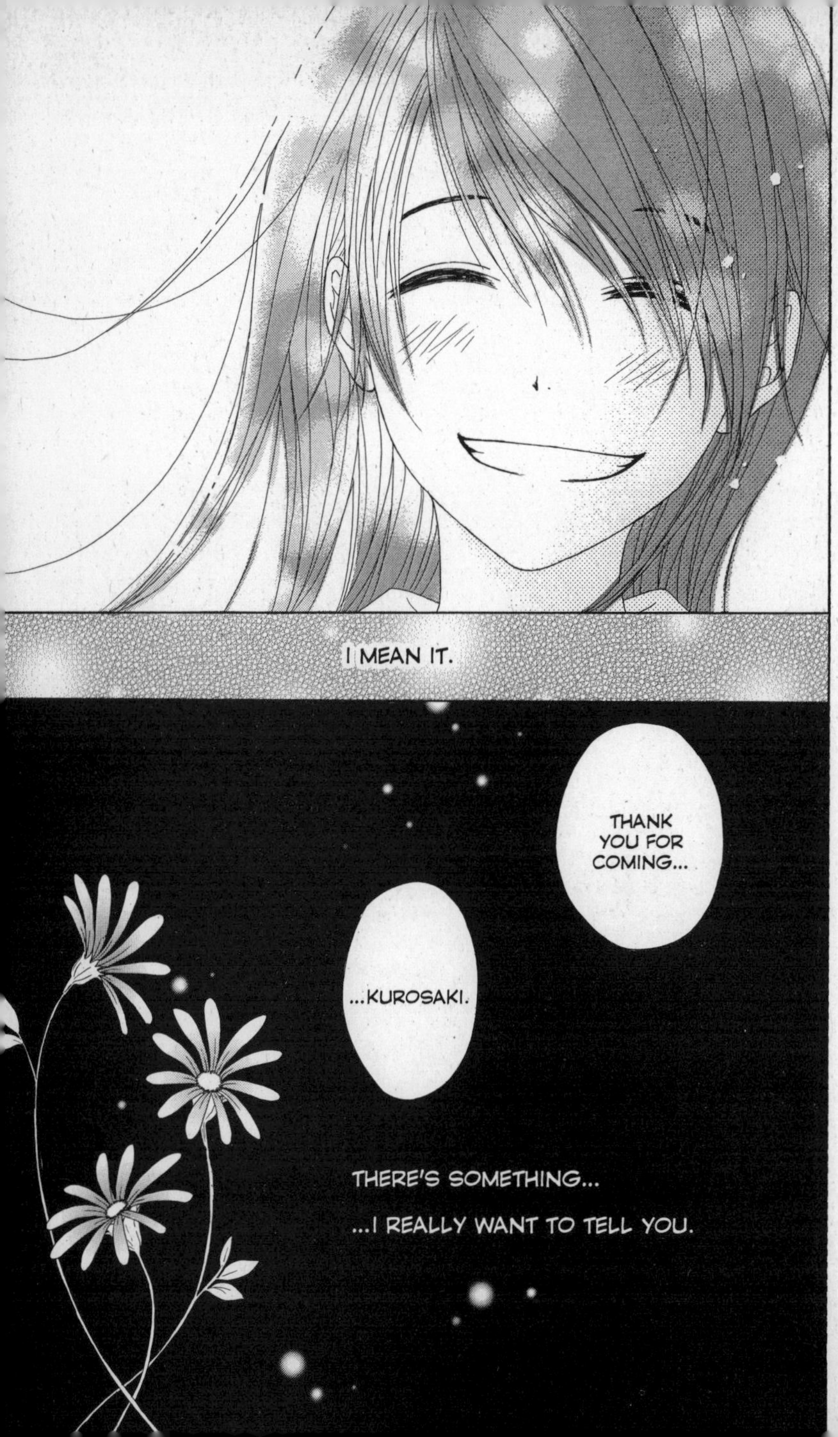
I MEAN IT.
THANK YOU FOR COMING...
...KUROSAKI.
THERE'S SOMETHING...
...I REALLY WANT TO TELL YOU.

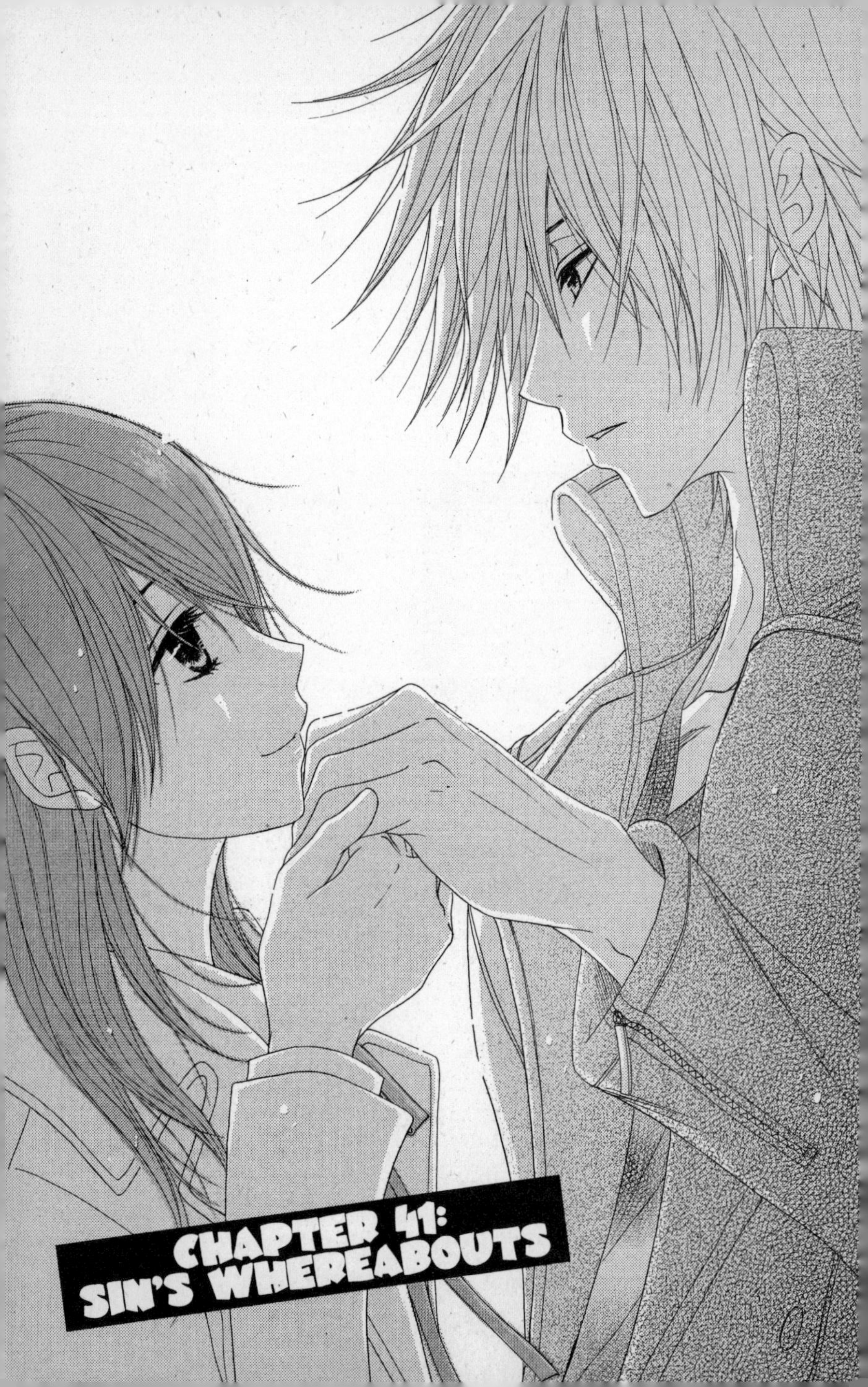
CHAPTER 41:
SIN'S WHEREABOUTS

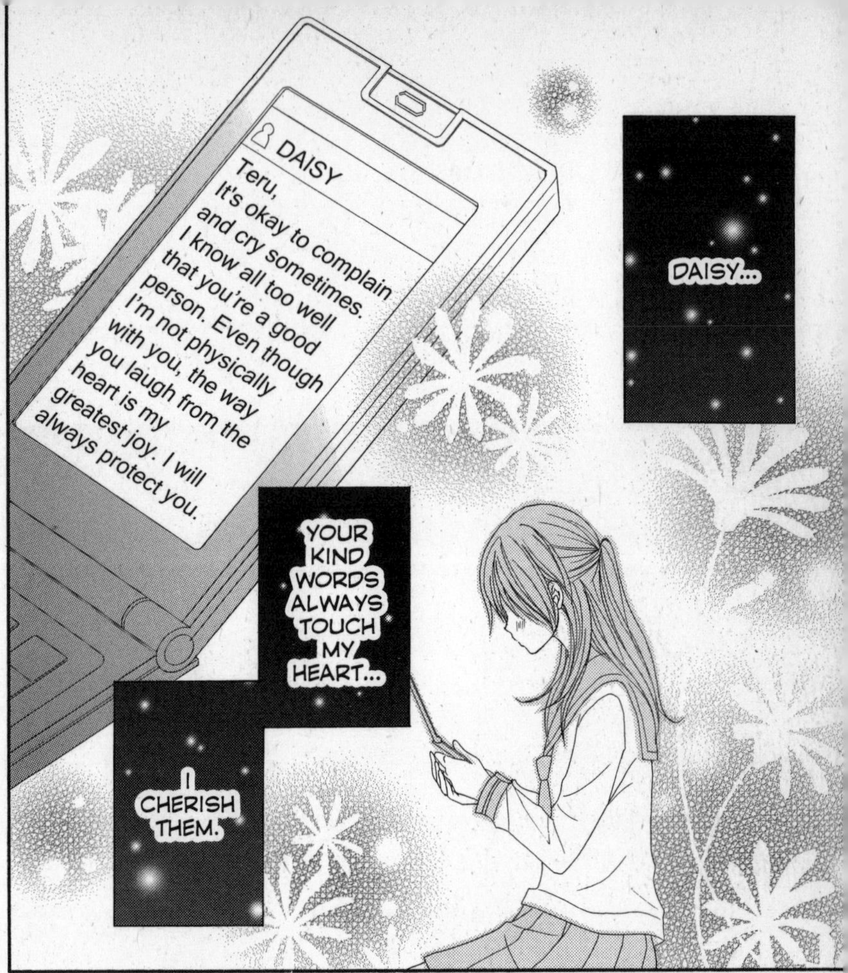
DAISY
Teru,
It's okay to complain and cry sometimes. I know all too well that you're a good person. Even though I'm not physically with you, the way you laugh from the heart is my greatest joy. I will always protect you.
DAISY...
YOUR KIND WORDS ALWAYS TOUCH MY HEART...
I CHERISH THEM.

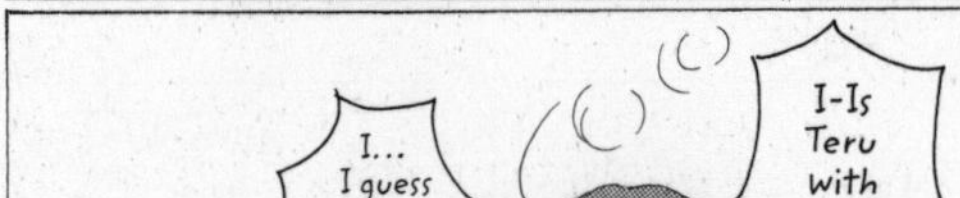
I-Is Teru with you?
I... I guess she's not... Where could she have gone?
FLUSTERED
Put more emotion into it! Get upset!
OT HERE
BOSS WHY? WHERE?
RIKO IS TERU WITH YOU?

IN CHAPTER 40, BOSS IS THE ONE WHO DECEIVES KUROSAKI WITH A FINE PERFORMANCE. (LAUGH) HOWEVER, HE WAS NOT THE ONLY ONE WHO PUT ON A SHOW. RIKO ALSO ASSISTED VIA CELL PHONE. ANDY PROBABLY WROTE THE SCREENPLAY. SO BESIDES TERU, EVEN THE OLDER ONES ARE DOING THEIR BEST FOR KUROSAKI.

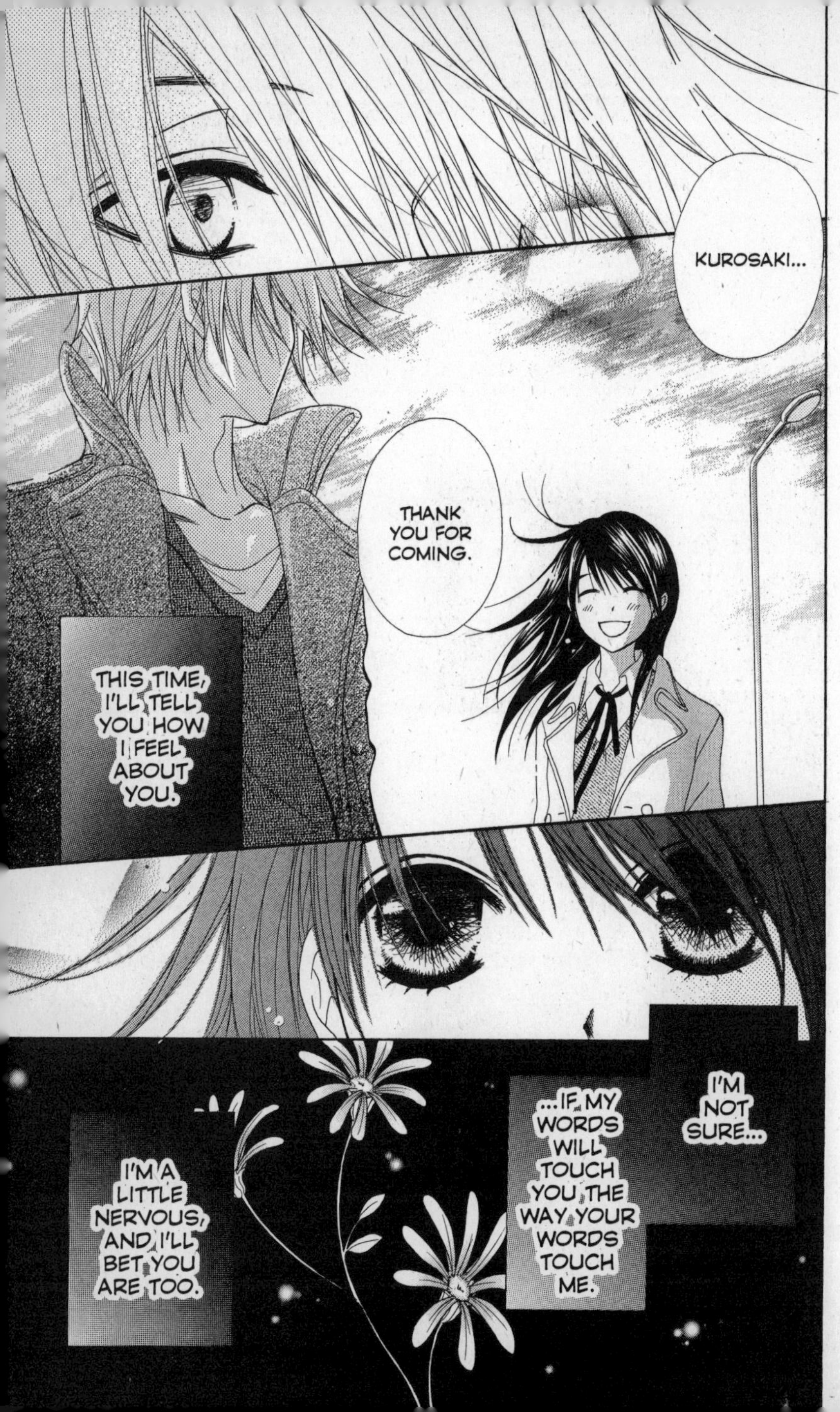
KUROSAKI...
THANK YOU FOR COMING.
THIS TIME, I'LL TELL YOU HOW I FEEL ABOUT YOU.
I'M NOT SURE...
...IF MY WORDS WILL TOUCH YOU THE WAY YOUR WORDS TOUCH ME.
I'M A LITTLE NERVOUS, AND I'LL BET YOU ARE TOO.

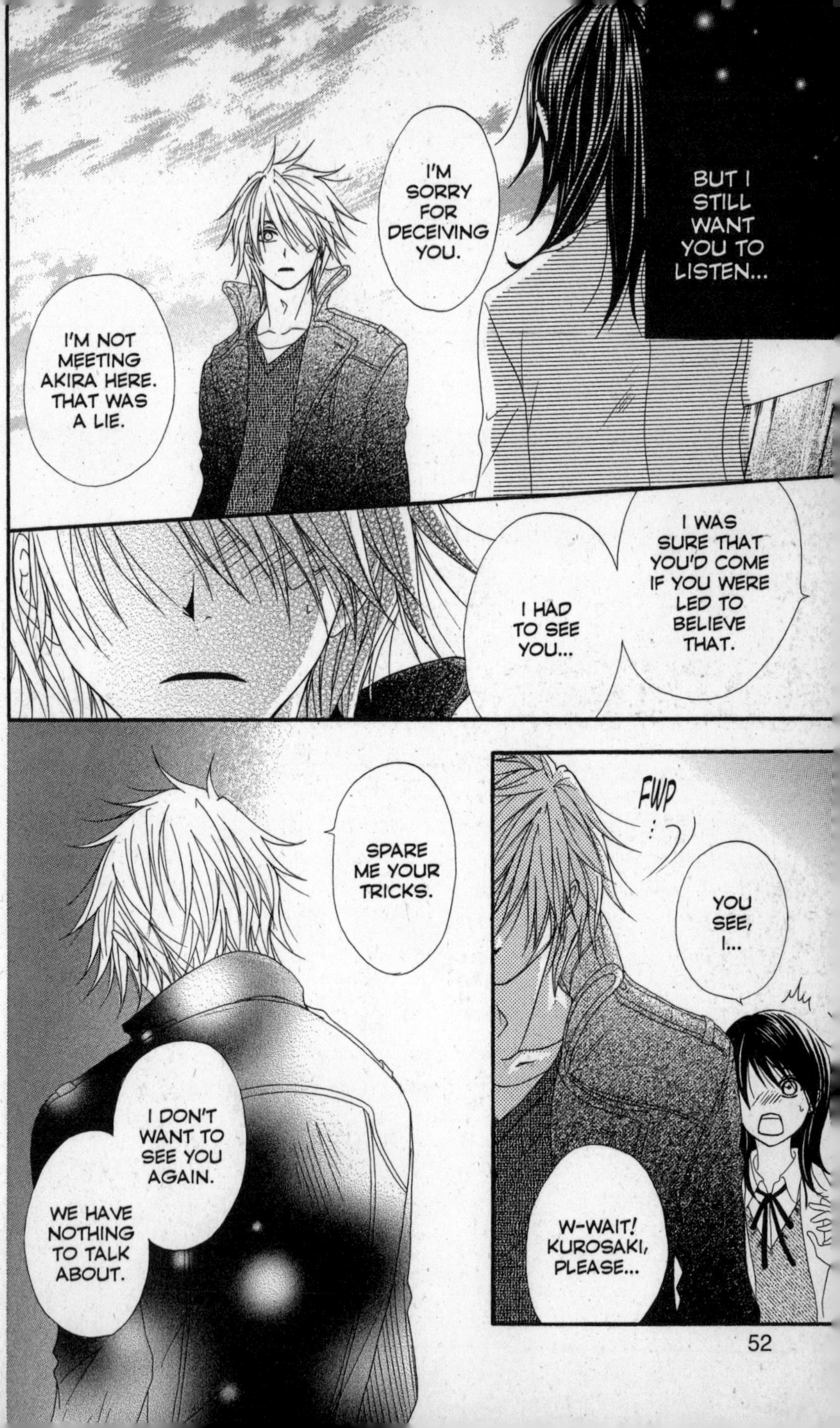
BUT I STILL WANT YOU TO LISTEN...
I'M SORRY FOR DECEIVING YOU.
I'M NOT MEETING AKIRA HERE. THAT WAS A LIE.
I WAS SURE THAT YOU'D COME IF YOU WERE LED TO BELIEVE THAT.
I HAD TO SEE YOU...
FWP
YOU SEE, I...
W-WAIT! KUROSAKI, PLEASE...
SPARE ME YOUR TRICKS.
I DON'T WANT TO SEE YOU AGAIN.
WE HAVE NOTHING TO TALK ABOUT.

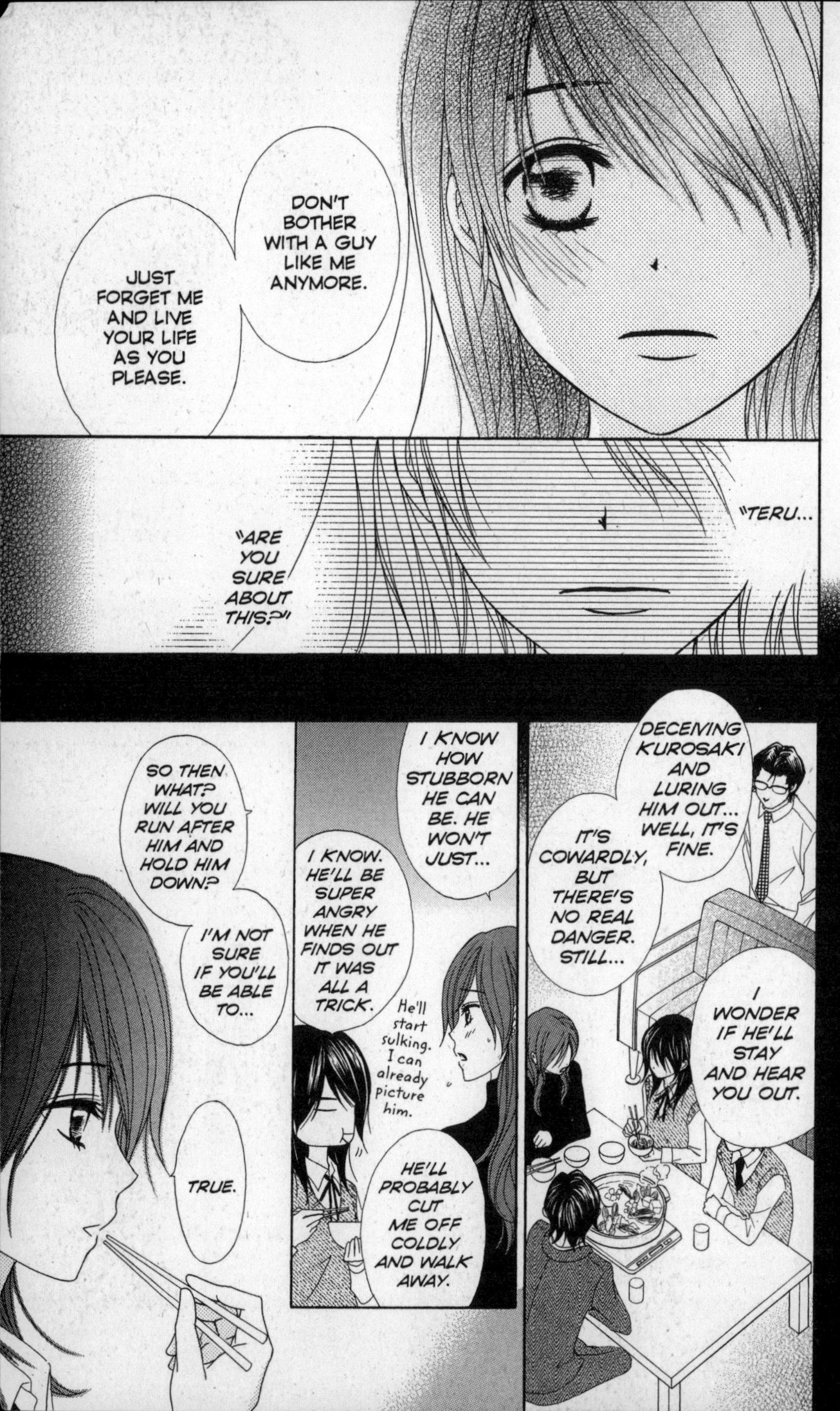
DON'T BOTHER WITH A GUY LIKE ME ANYMORE.
JUST FORGET ME AND LIVE YOUR LIFE AS YOU PLEASE.
"TERU...
"ARE YOU SURE ABOUT THIS?"
DECEIVING KUROSAKI AND LURING HIM OUT... WELL, IT'S FINE.
IT'S COWARDLY, BUT THERE'S NO REAL DANGER. STILL...
I WONDER IF HE'LL STAY AND HEAR YOU OUT.
I KNOW HOW STUBBORN HE CAN BE. HE WON'T JUST...
I KNOW. HE'LL BE SUPER ANGRY WHEN HE FINDS OUT IT WAS ALL A TRICK.
He'll start sulking. I can already picture him.
HE'LL PROBABLY CUT ME OFF COLDLY AND WALK AWAY.
SO THEN WHAT? WILL YOU RUN AFTER HIM AND HOLD HIM DOWN?
I'M NOT SURE IF YOU'LL BE ABLE TO...
TRUE.

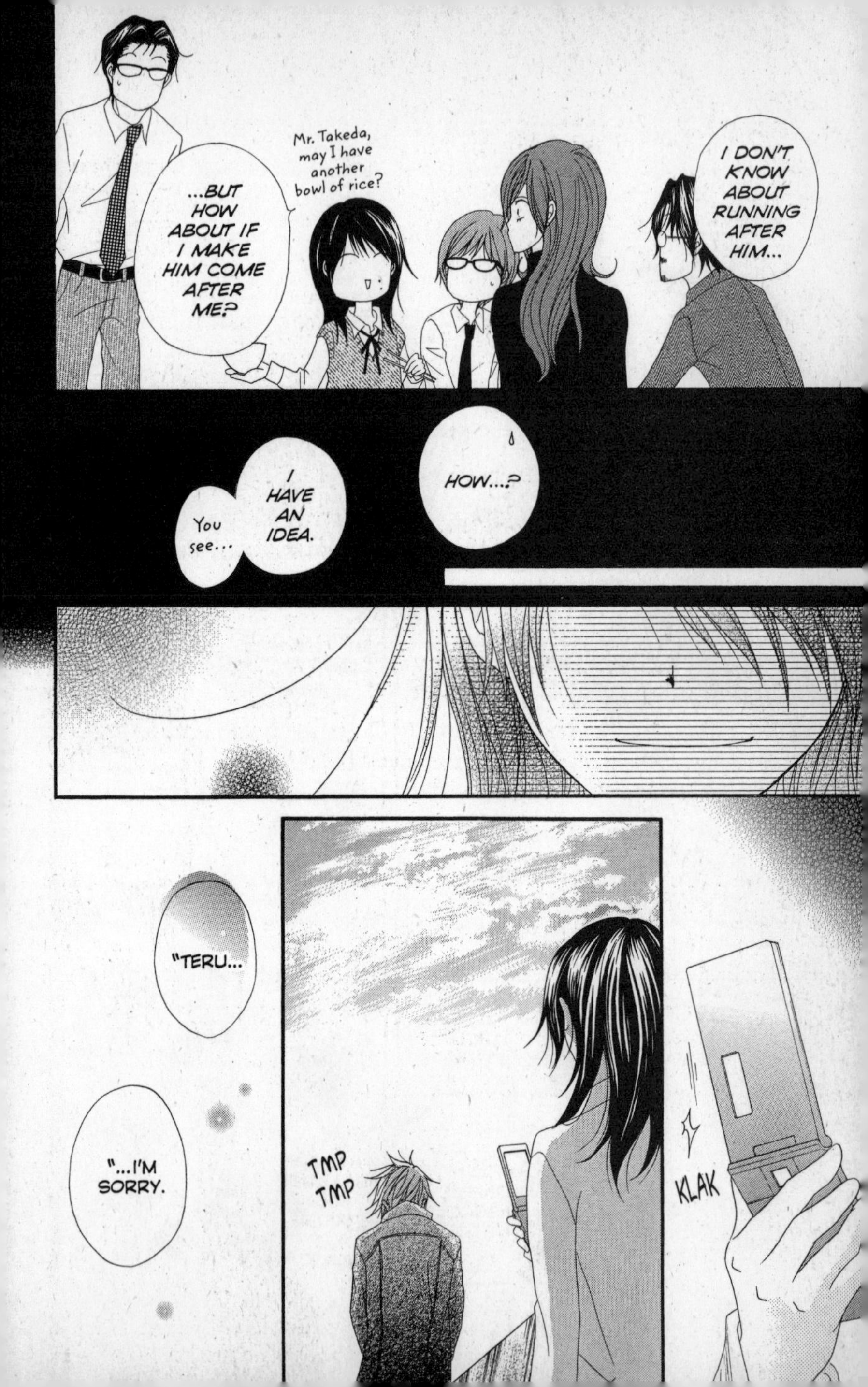
I DON'T KNOW ABOUT RUNNING AFTER HIM...
Mr. Takeda, may I have another bowl of rice?
...BUT HOW ABOUT IF I MAKE HIM COME AFTER ME?
HOW...?
I HAVE AN IDEA.
You see...
KLAK
TMP TMP
"TERU...
"...I'M SORRY.

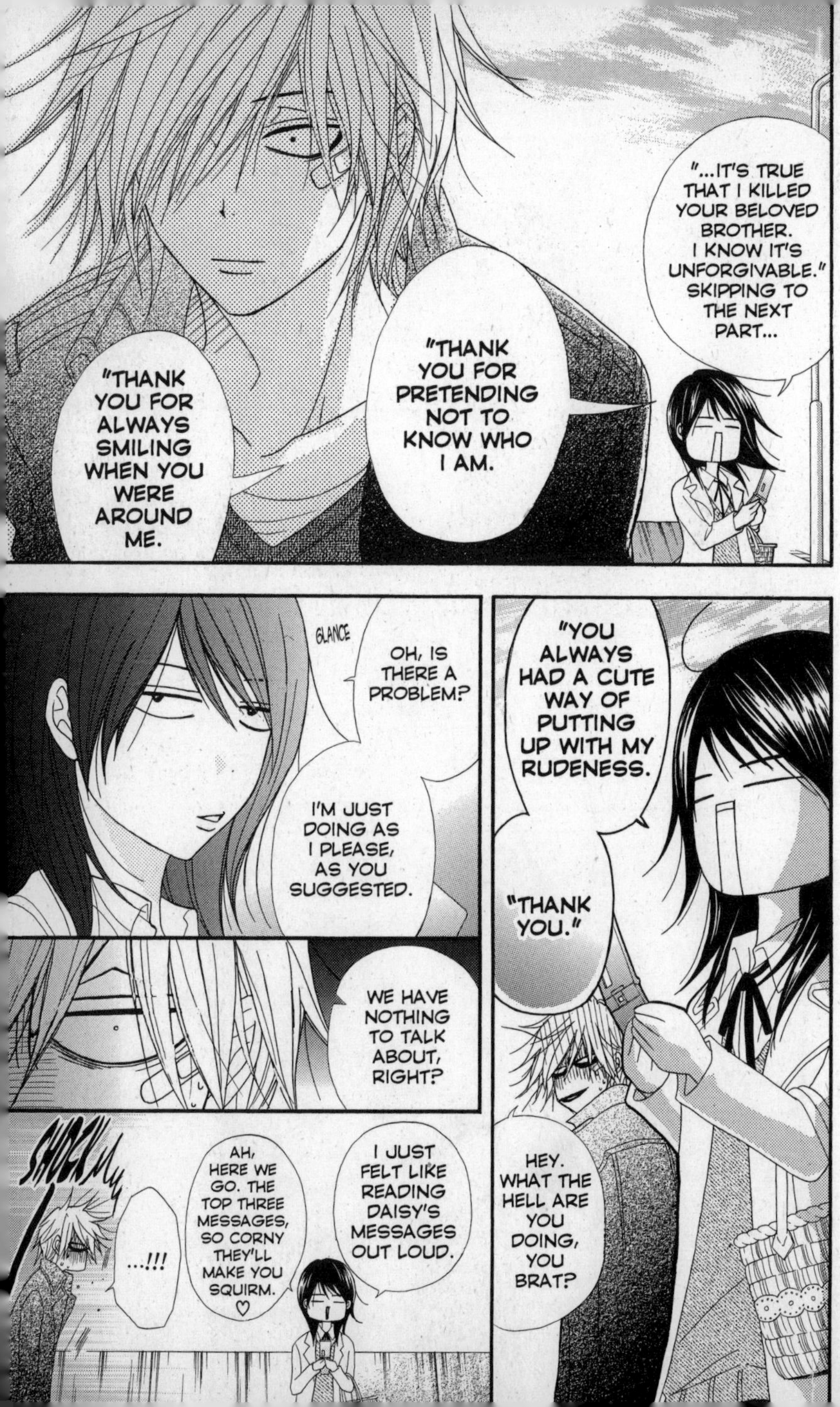
"...IT'S TRUE THAT I KILLED YOUR BELOVED BROTHER. I KNOW IT'S UNFORGIVABLE." SKIPPING TO THE NEXT PART...
"THANK YOU FOR PRETENDING NOT TO KNOW WHO I AM.
"THANK YOU FOR ALWAYS SMILING WHEN YOU WERE AROUND ME.
"YOU ALWAYS HAD A CUTE WAY OF PUTTING UP WITH MY RUDENESS.
"THANK YOU."
HEY. WHAT THE HELL ARE YOU DOING, YOU BRAT?
GLANCE
OH, IS THERE A PROBLEM?
I'M JUST DOING AS I PLEASE, AS YOU SUGGESTED.
WE HAVE NOTHING TO TALK ABOUT, RIGHT?
I JUST FELT LIKE READING DAISY'S MESSAGES OUT LOUD.
AH, HERE WE GO. THE TOP THREE MESSAGES, SO CORNY THEY'LL MAKE YOU SQUIRM. ♡
...!!!
SHOCK

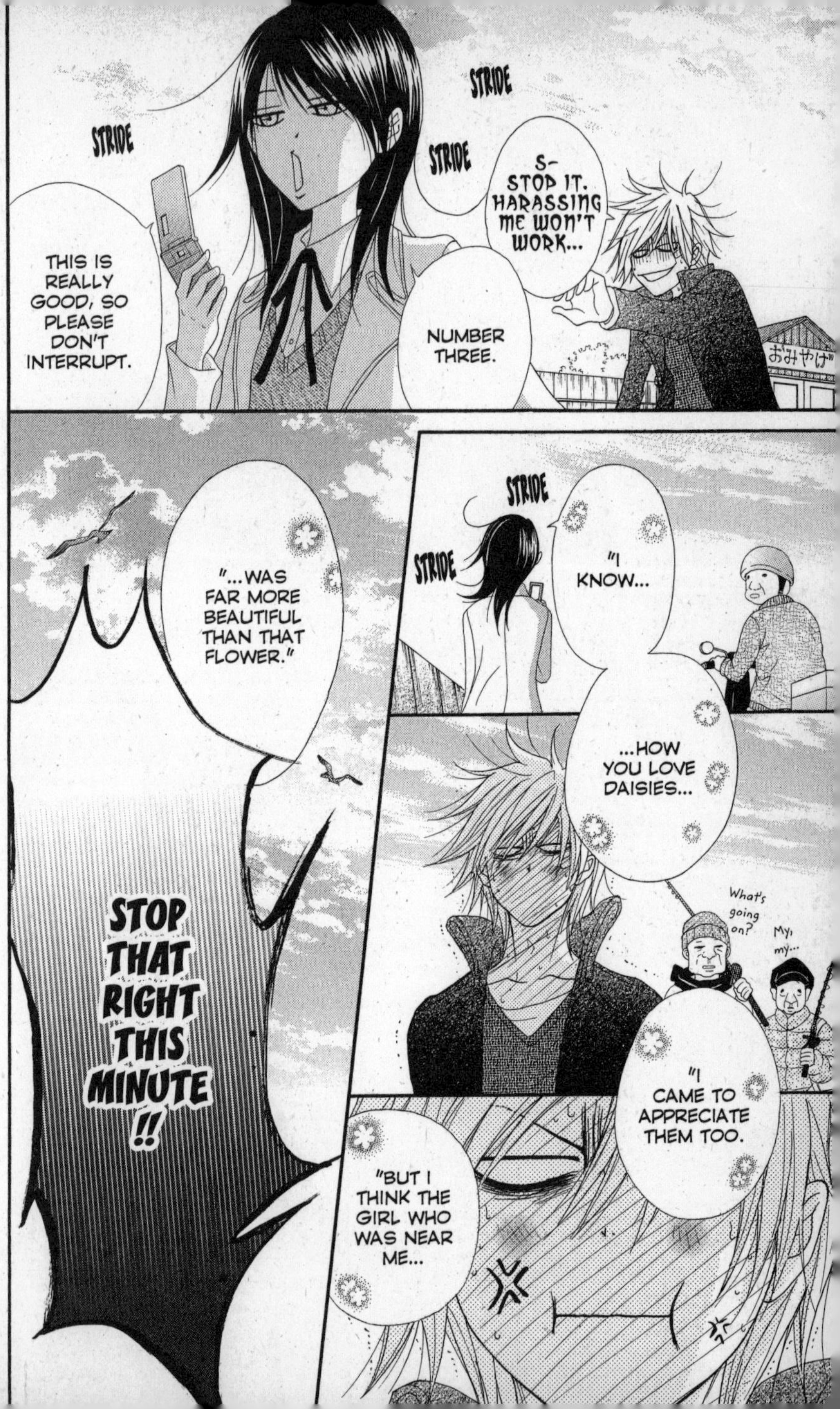
STRIDE
S-STOP IT. HARASSING ME WON'T WORK...
STRIDE
NUMBER THREE.
おみやげ
STRIDE
THIS IS REALLY GOOD, SO PLEASE DON'T INTERRUPT.
STRIDE
STRIDE
"I KNOW...
...HOW YOU LOVE DAISIES...
What's going on?
My, my...
"I CAME TO APPRECIATE THEM TOO.
"BUT I THINK THE GIRL WHO WAS NEAR ME...
"...WAS FAR MORE BEAUTIFUL THAN THAT FLOWER."
STOP THAT RIGHT THIS MINUTE!!

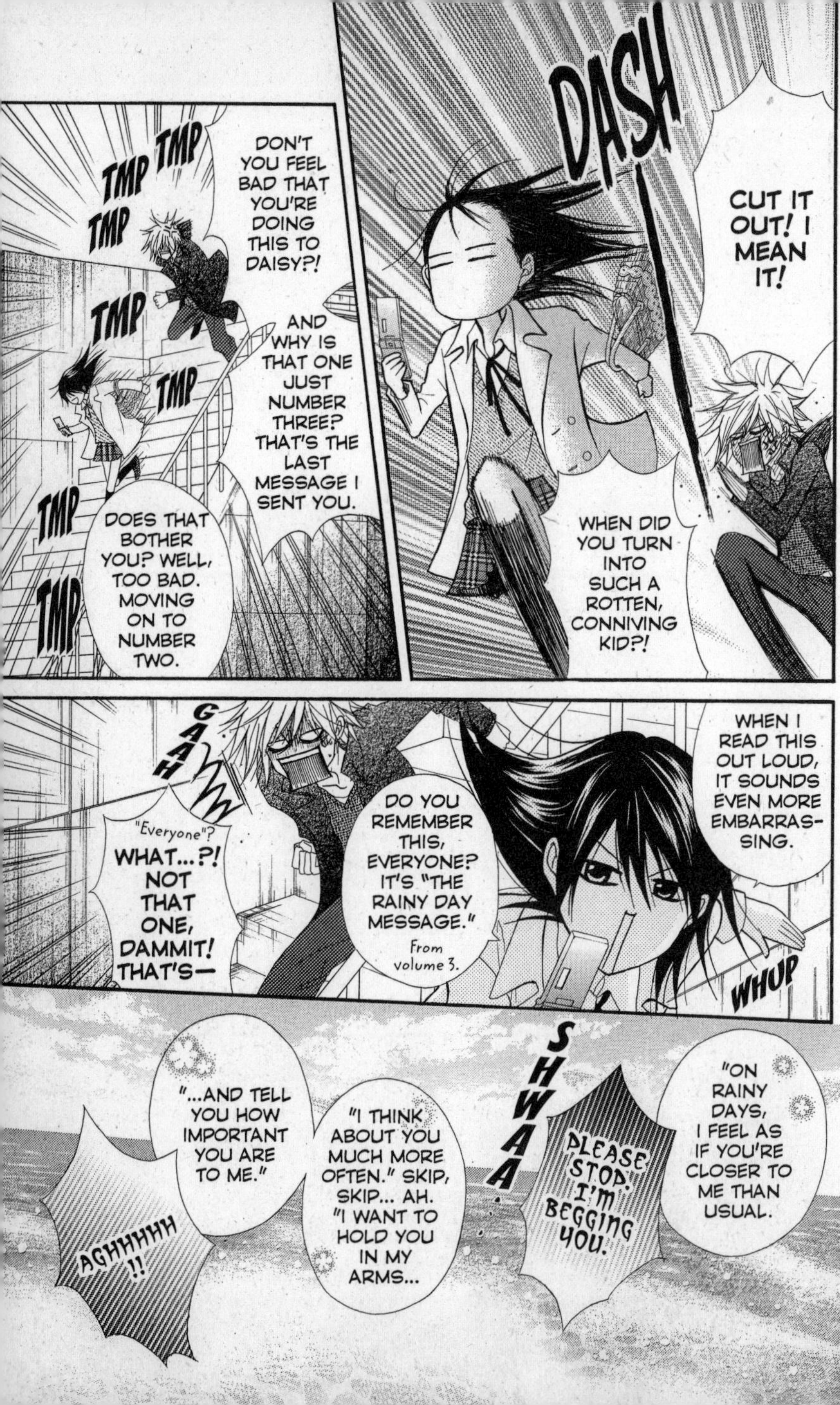
CUT IT OUT! I MEAN IT!
DASH
WHEN DID YOU TURN INTO SUCH A ROTTEN, CONNIVING KID?!
TMP TMP
TMP
DON'T YOU FEEL BAD THAT YOU'RE DOING THIS TO DAISY?!
TMP
AND WHY IS THAT ONE JUST NUMBER THREE? THAT'S THE LAST MESSAGE I SENT YOU.
TMP
TMP
DOES THAT BOTHER YOU? WELL, TOO BAD. MOVING ON TO NUMBER TWO.
TMP
WHEN I READ THIS OUT LOUD, IT SOUNDS EVEN MORE EMBARRAS-SING.
WHUP
DO YOU REMEMBER THIS, EVERYONE? IT'S "THE RAINY DAY MESSAGE."
From volume 3.
GAAH
"Everyone"? WHAT...?! NOT THAT ONE, DAMMIT! THAT'S—
"ON RAINY DAYS, I FEEL AS IF YOU'RE CLOSER TO ME THAN USUAL.
SHWAA
PLEASE STOP. I'M BEGGING YOU.
"I THINK ABOUT YOU MUCH MORE OFTEN." SKIP, SKIP... AH. "I WANT TO HOLD YOU IN MY ARMS...
"...AND TELL YOU HOW IMPORTANT YOU ARE TO ME."
AGHHHHH!!

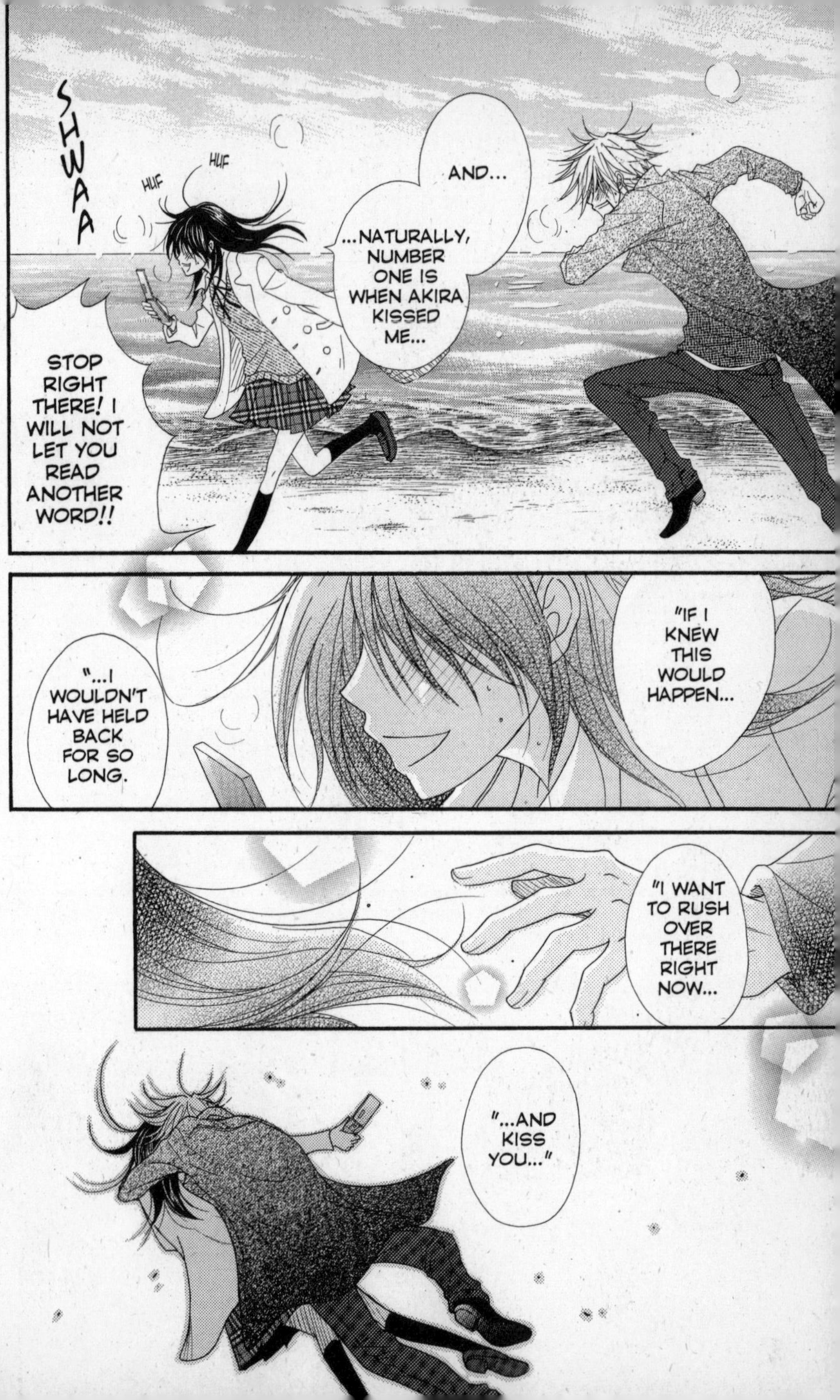
AND...
...NATURALLY, NUMBER ONE IS WHEN AKIRA KISSED ME...
HUF
HUF
SHWAA
STOP RIGHT THERE! I WILL NOT LET YOU READ ANOTHER WORD!!
"IF I KNEW THIS WOULD HAPPEN...
"...I WOULDN'T HAVE HELD BACK FOR SO LONG.
"I WANT TO RUSH OVER THERE RIGHT NOW...
"...AND KISS YOU..."

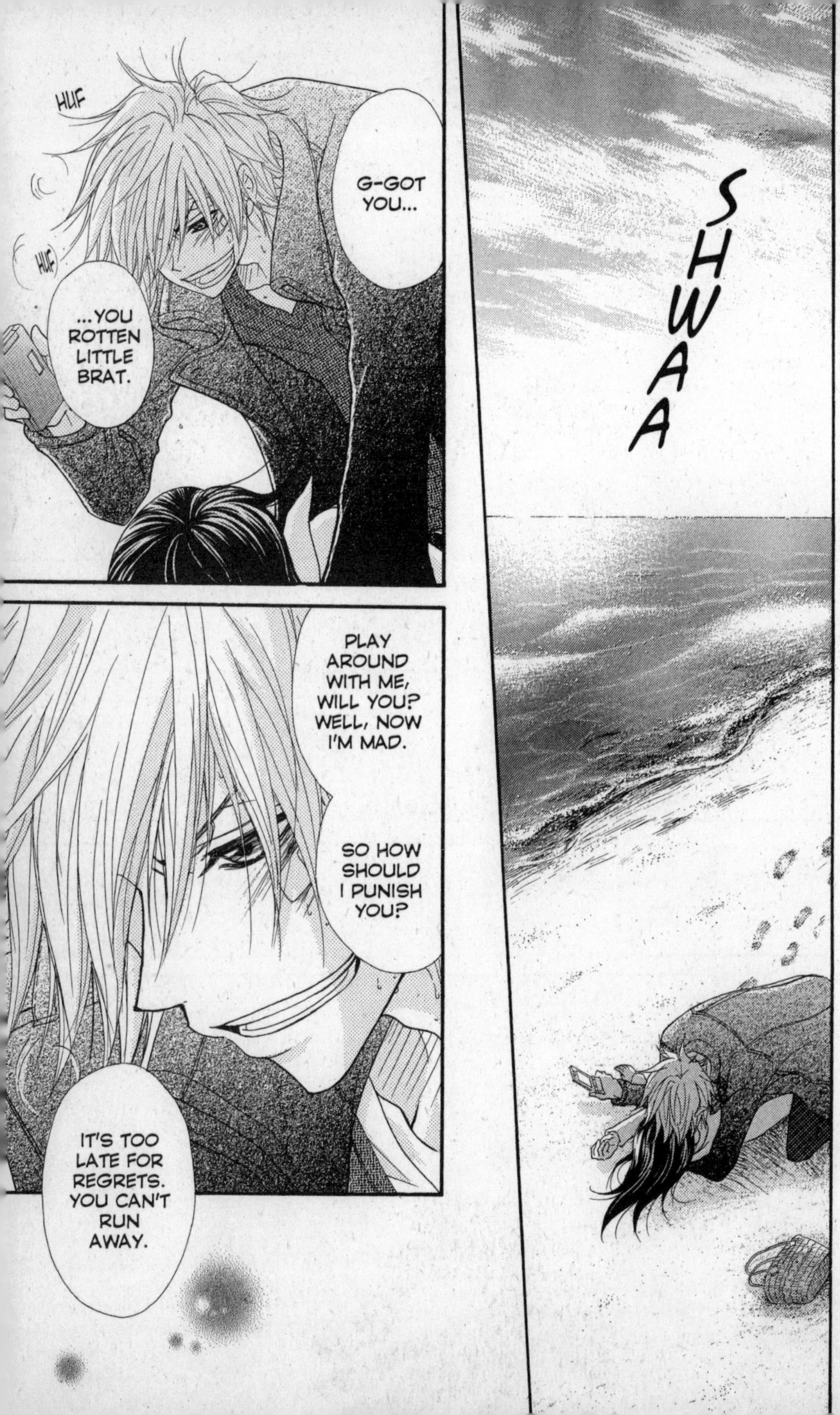
SHWAA
HUF
G-GOT YOU...
HUF
...YOU ROTTEN LITTLE BRAT.
PLAY AROUND WITH ME, WILL YOU? WELL, NOW I'M MAD.
SO HOW SHOULD I PUNISH YOU?
IT'S TOO LATE FOR REGRETS. YOU CAN'T RUN AWAY.

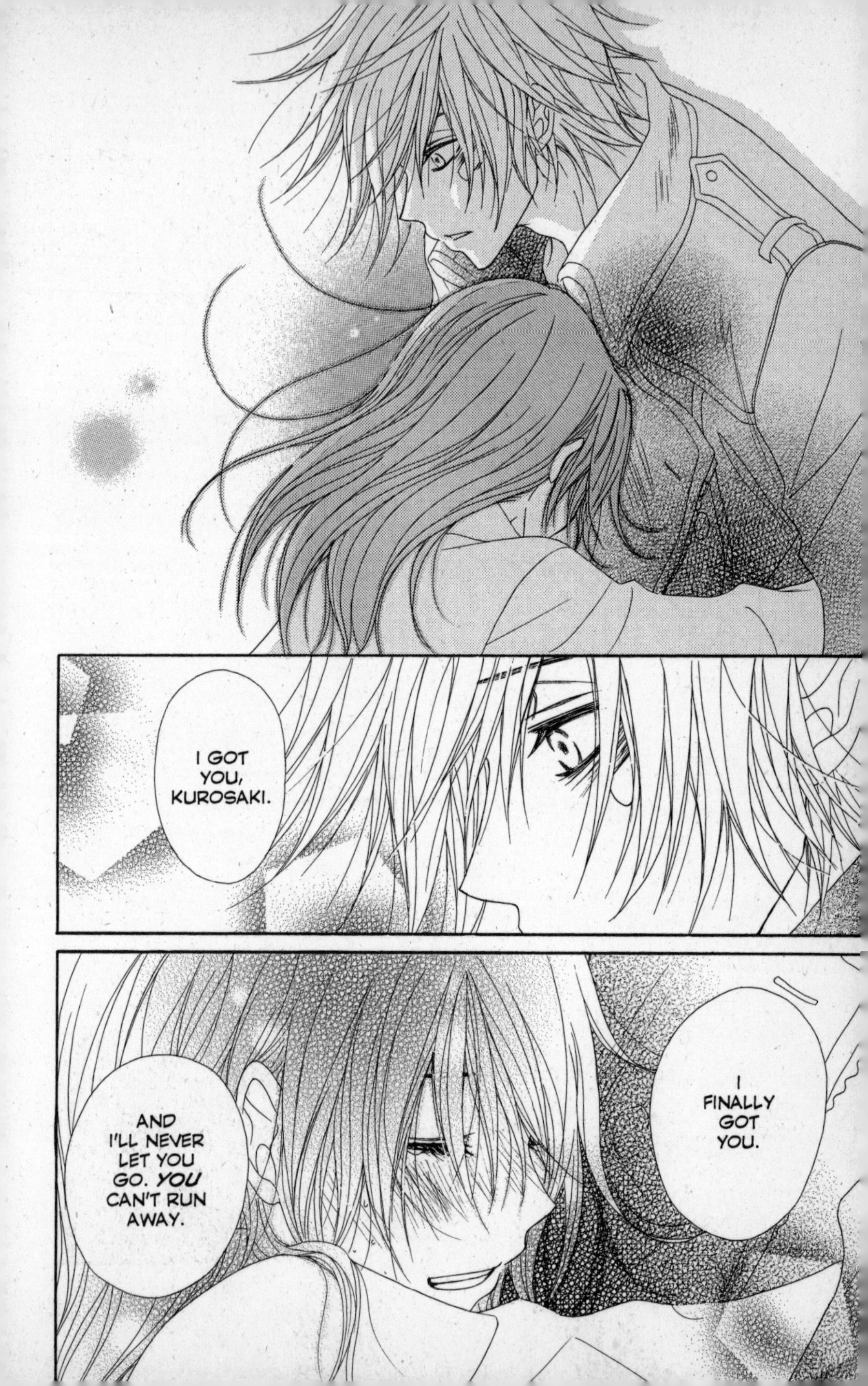
I GOT YOU, KUROSAKI.
I FINALLY GOT YOU.
AND I'LL NEVER LET YOU GO. *YOU* CAN'T RUN AWAY.

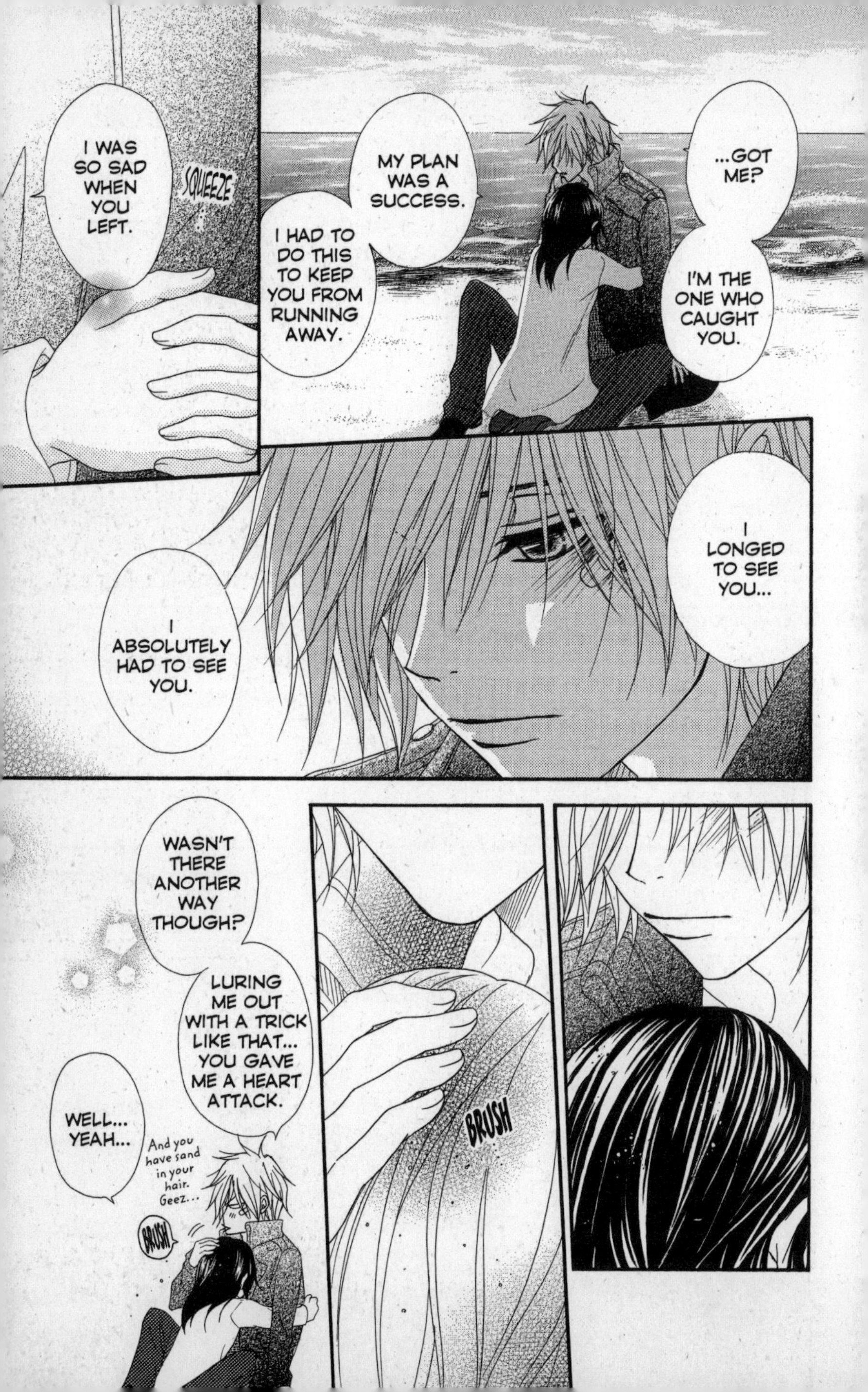
...GOT ME?
I'M THE ONE WHO CAUGHT YOU.
MY PLAN WAS A SUCCESS.
I HAD TO DO THIS TO KEEP YOU FROM RUNNING AWAY.
I WAS SO SAD WHEN YOU LEFT.
SQUEEZE
I LONGED TO SEE YOU...
I ABSOLUTELY HAD TO SEE YOU.
BRUSH
WASN'T THERE ANOTHER WAY THOUGH?
LURING ME OUT WITH A TRICK LIKE THAT... YOU GAVE ME A HEART ATTACK.
WELL... YEAH...
And you have sand in your hair. Geez...
BRUSH

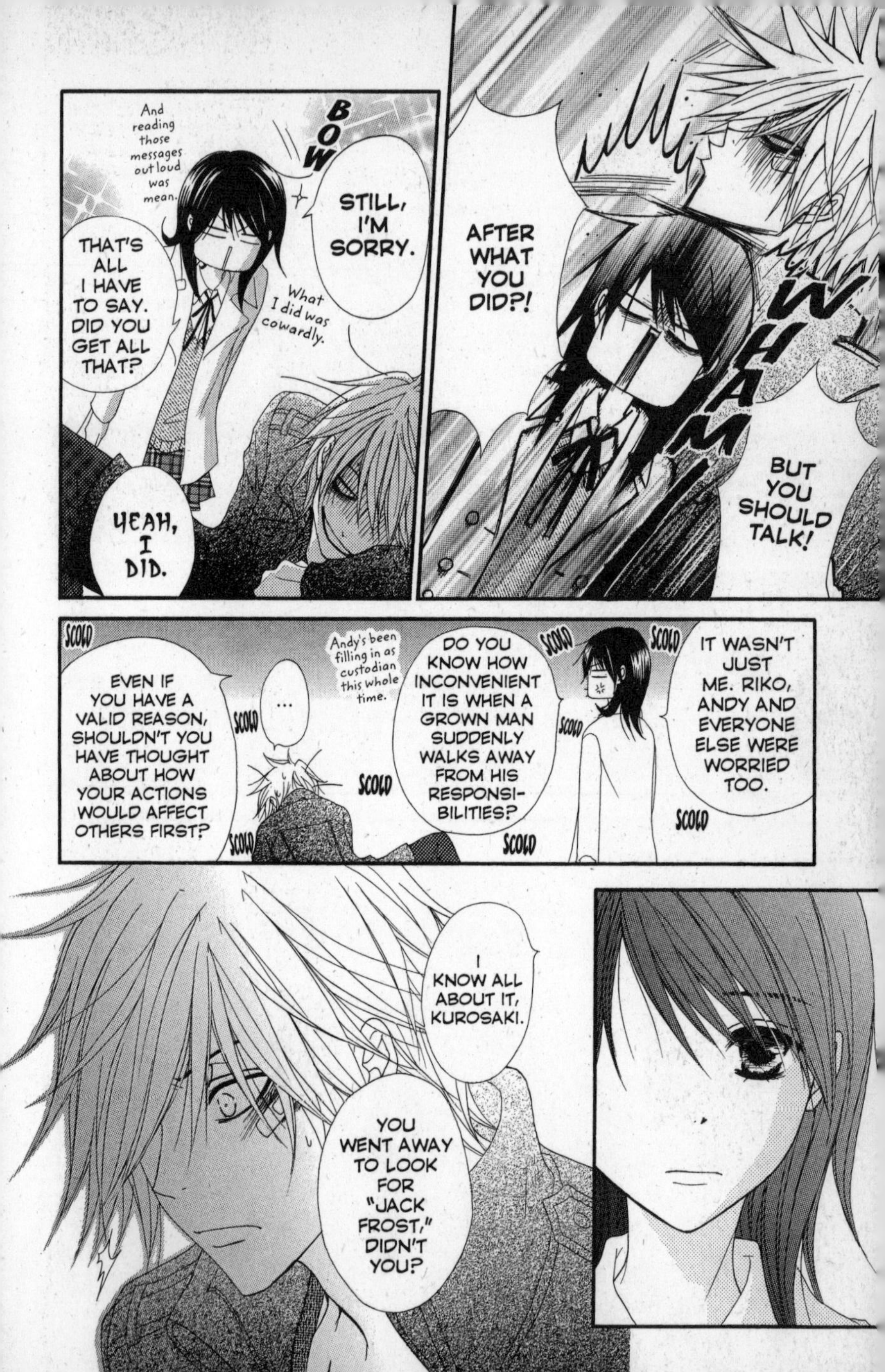
WHAM
AFTER WHAT YOU DID?!
BUT YOU SHOULD TALK!
BOW
STILL, I'M SORRY.
And reading those messages out loud was mean.
What I did was cowardly.
THAT'S ALL I HAVE TO SAY. DID YOU GET ALL THAT?
YEAH, I DID.
IT WASN'T JUST ME. RIKO, ANDY AND EVERYONE ELSE WERE WORRIED TOO.
SCOLD SCOLD SCOLD SCOLD
DO YOU KNOW HOW INCONVENIENT IT IS WHEN A GROWN MAN SUDDENLY WALKS AWAY FROM HIS RESPONSIBILITIES?
Andy's been filling in as custodian this whole time.
SCOLD SCOLD
...
SCOLD SCOLD SCOLD
EVEN IF YOU HAVE A VALID REASON, SHOULDN'T YOU HAVE THOUGHT ABOUT HOW YOUR ACTIONS WOULD AFFECT OTHERS FIRST?
I KNOW ALL ABOUT IT, KUROSAKI.
YOU WENT AWAY TO LOOK FOR "JACK FROST," DIDN'T YOU?

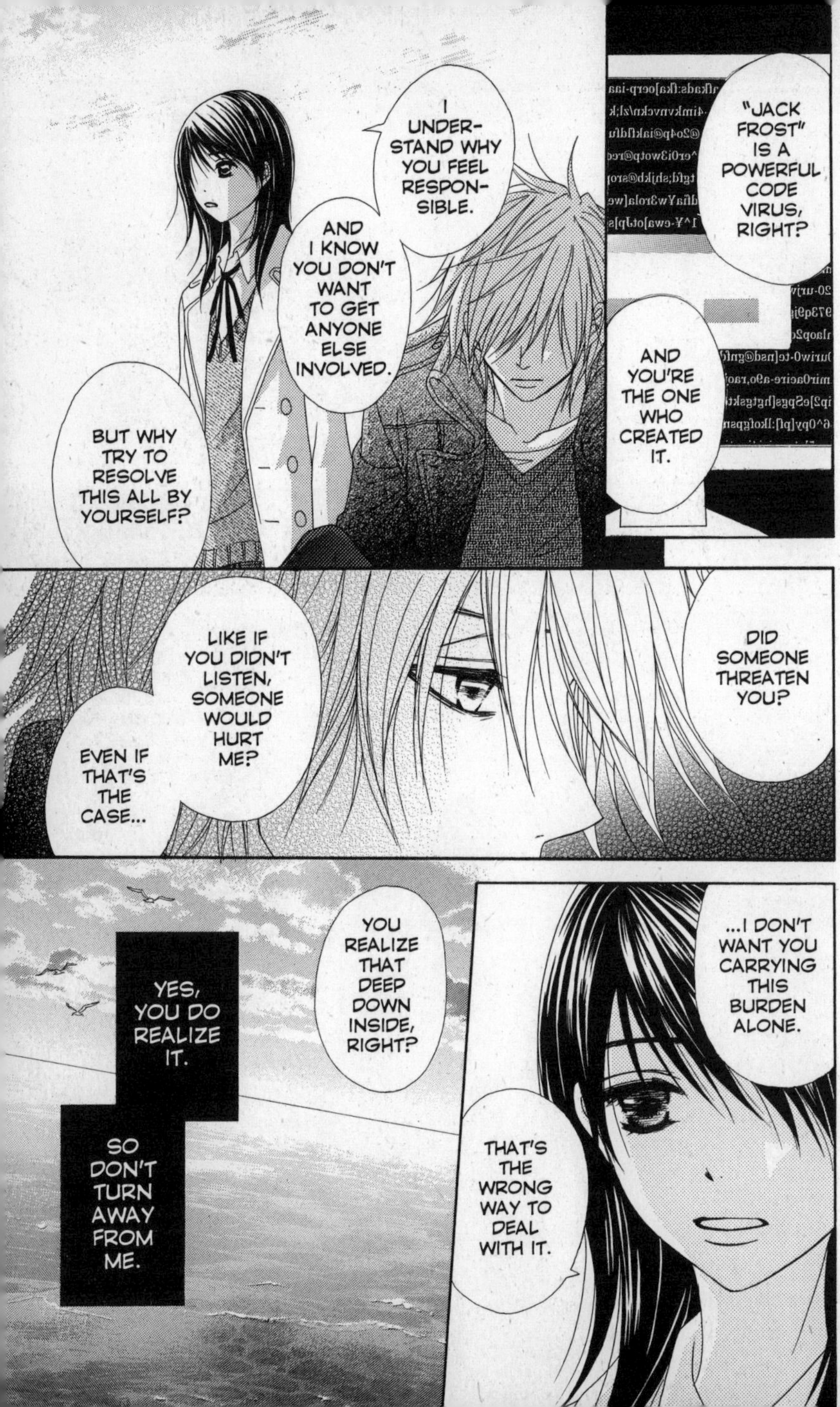
"JACK FROST" IS A POWERFUL CODE VIRUS, RIGHT?
AND YOU'RE THE ONE WHO CREATED IT.
I UNDER-STAND WHY YOU FEEL RESPON-SIBLE.
AND I KNOW YOU DON'T WANT TO GET ANYONE ELSE INVOLVED.
BUT WHY TRY TO RESOLVE THIS ALL BY YOURSELF?
DID SOMEONE THREATEN YOU?
LIKE IF YOU DIDN'T LISTEN, SOMEONE WOULD HURT ME?
EVEN IF THAT'S THE CASE...
...I DON'T WANT YOU CARRYING THIS BURDEN ALONE.
THAT'S THE WRONG WAY TO DEAL WITH IT.
YOU REALIZE THAT DEEP DOWN INSIDE, RIGHT?
YES, YOU DO REALIZE IT.
SO DON'T TURN AWAY FROM ME.

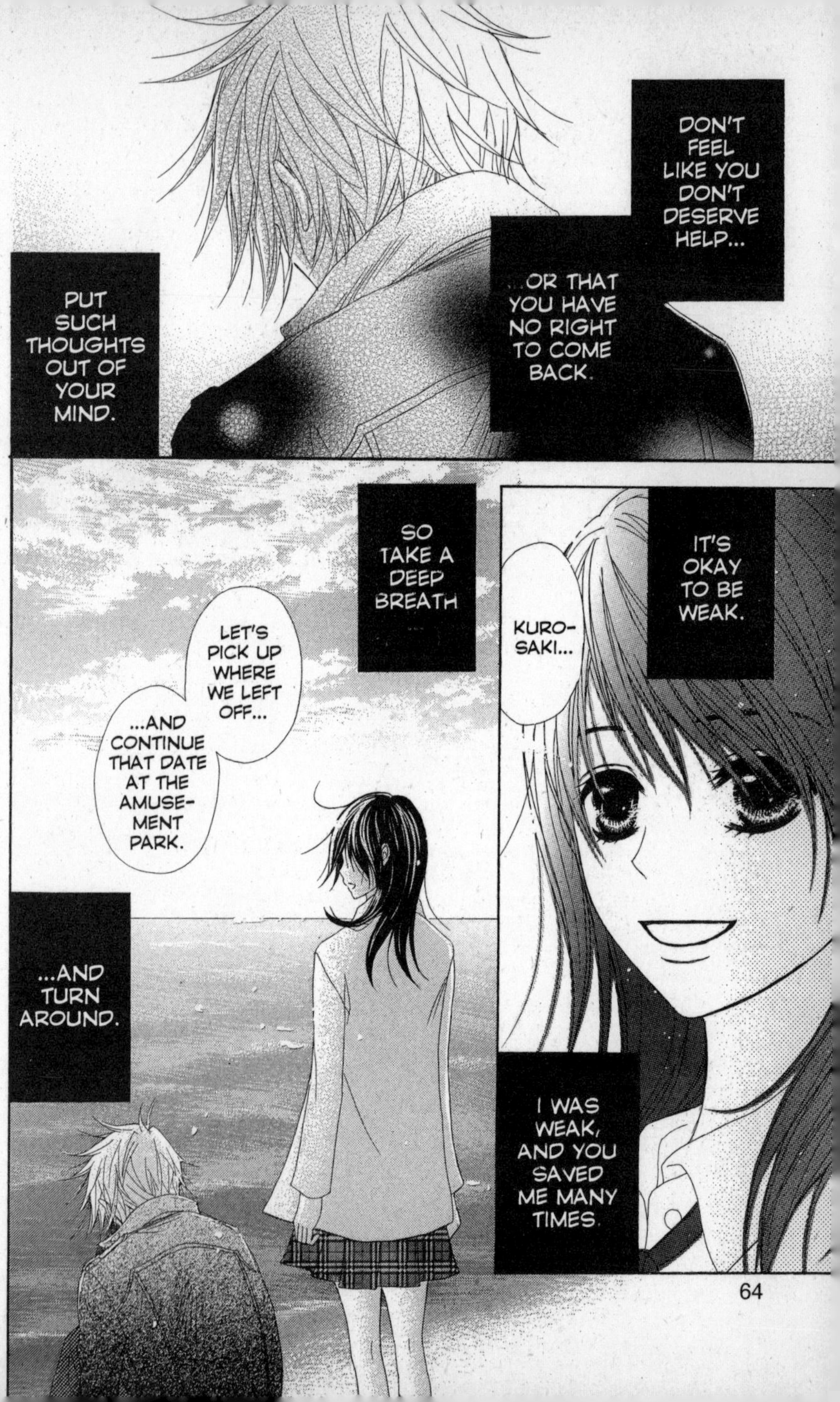
DON'T FEEL LIKE YOU DON'T DESERVE HELP...
...OR THAT YOU HAVE NO RIGHT TO COME BACK.
PUT SUCH THOUGHTS OUT OF YOUR MIND.
IT'S OKAY TO BE WEAK.
KURO-SAKI...
I WAS WEAK, AND YOU SAVED ME MANY TIMES.
SO TAKE A DEEP BREATH ...
LET'S PICK UP WHERE WE LEFT OFF...
...AND CONTINUE THAT DATE AT THE AMUSE-MENT PARK.
...AND TURN AROUND.

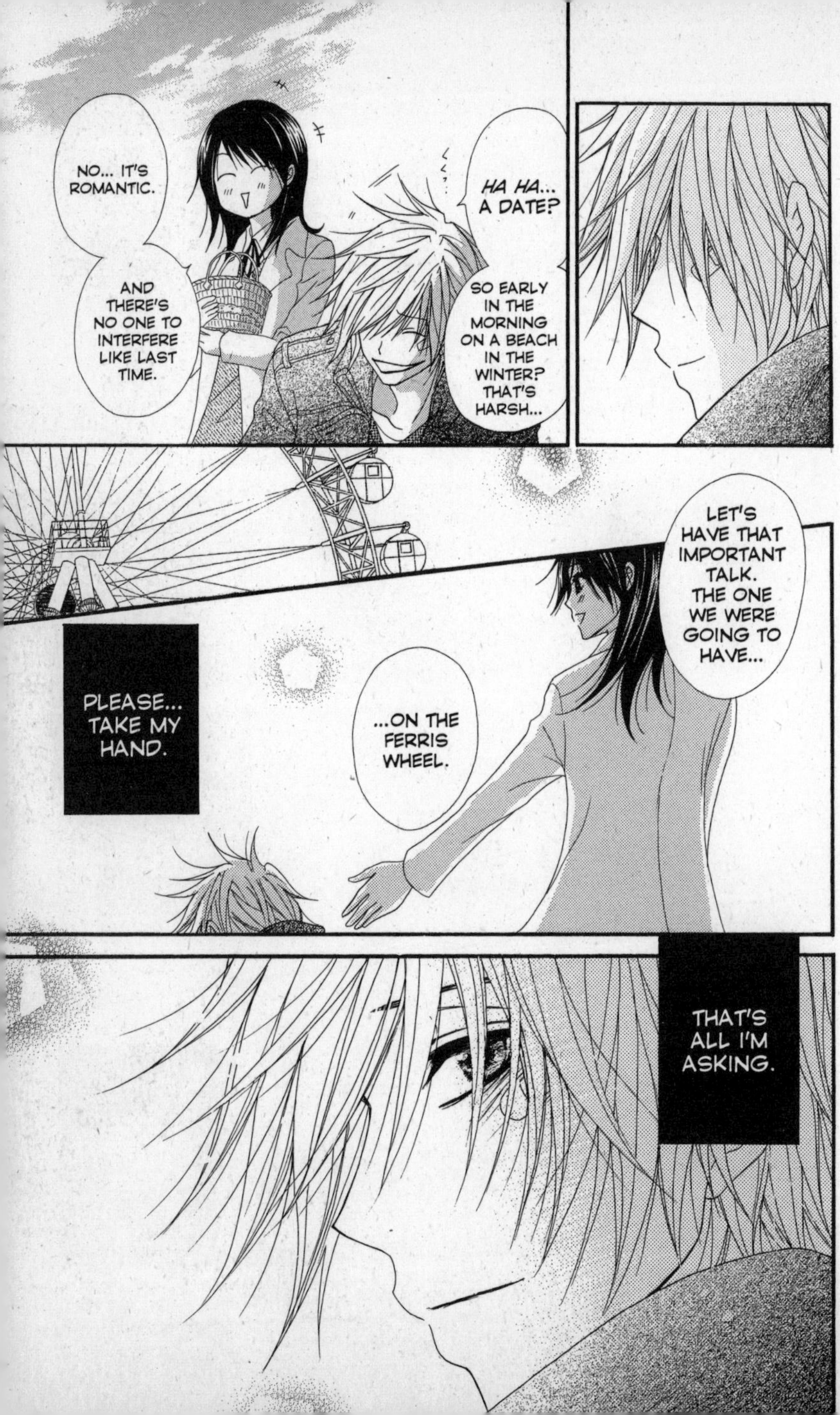
HA HA... A DATE?
SO EARLY IN THE MORNING ON A BEACH IN THE WINTER? THAT'S HARSH...
NO... IT'S ROMANTIC.
AND THERE'S NO ONE TO INTERFERE LIKE LAST TIME.
LET'S HAVE THAT IMPORTANT TALK. THE ONE WE WERE GOING TO HAVE...
...ON THE FERRIS WHEEL.
PLEASE... TAKE MY HAND.
THAT'S ALL I'M ASKING.

LET'S HAVE THAT TALK...
...ABOUT YOUR PAST SIN.
WE NEED TO...
...IN ORDER FOR US TO WALK TOGETHER TOWARDS THE FUTURE.

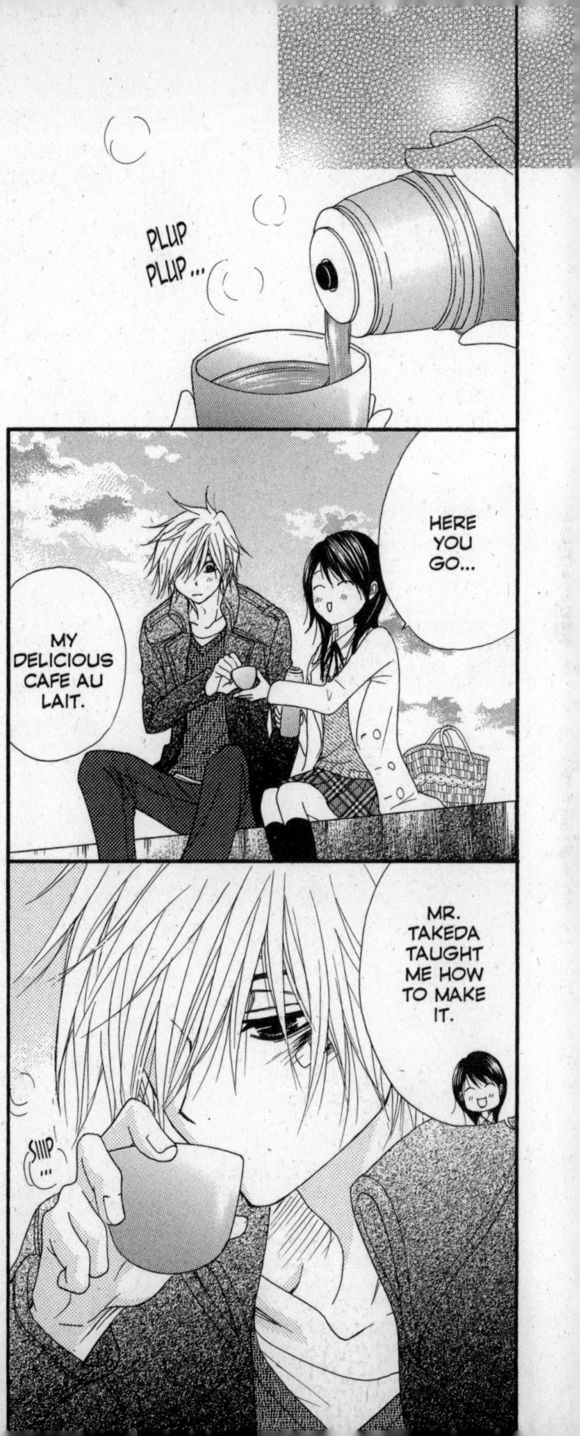
PLUP PLUP...
HERE YOU GO...
MY DELICIOUS CAFE AU LAIT.
MR. TAKEDA TAUGHT ME HOW TO MAKE IT.
SIIIP...

DENGEKI DAISY QUESTION CORNER

BALDLY ASK!! ②

Q.
I CAN'T FIND ANY GOOD-LOOKING HUNKS LIKE KUROSAKI. WHERE ARE THEY? ALSO, THAT "DO ONE GOOD DEED EACH DAY" MASK THAT HE TOOK IN CHAPTER 32 (VOLUME 7)—DOES KUROSAKI STILL HAVE IT?
(K.I., KANAGAWA PREFECTURE)

A.
I THINK WHETHER KUROSAKI IS GOOD-LOOKING OR NOT IS A MATTER OF PERSONAL TASTE. ALTHOUGH ONCE IN A WHILE, HE SHOWS SOME FIGHTING SPIRIT TO MAKE HIMSELF LOOK COOL.
...AS FOR THE MASK, YOU'RE VERY OBSERVANT, AREN'T YOU? SINCE THEN, KUROSAKI HAS TAKEN EVEN THE PLAIN MASKS. I'LL BET HE'S OFTEN THOUGHT ABOUT PUTTING THEM ON HIMSELF IN PRIVATE. AND THIS IS THE GUY YOU'RE CALLING A HUNK? I THINK YOU SHOULD THINK IT OVER.

Q.
HARUKA IS SUCH A CHEERFUL, FUN GIRL. HOW COME SHE DOESN'T HAVE A BOYFRIEND?
(KURO MICKY, AICHI PREFECTURE)

A
THAT'S WHAT I WANT TO KNOW!!!!
...OH, WHY AM I GETTING UPSET?
...I'M NOT CHEERFUL AND I'M CERTAINLY NOT MUCH FUN... OH WELL...
(AUTHOR)

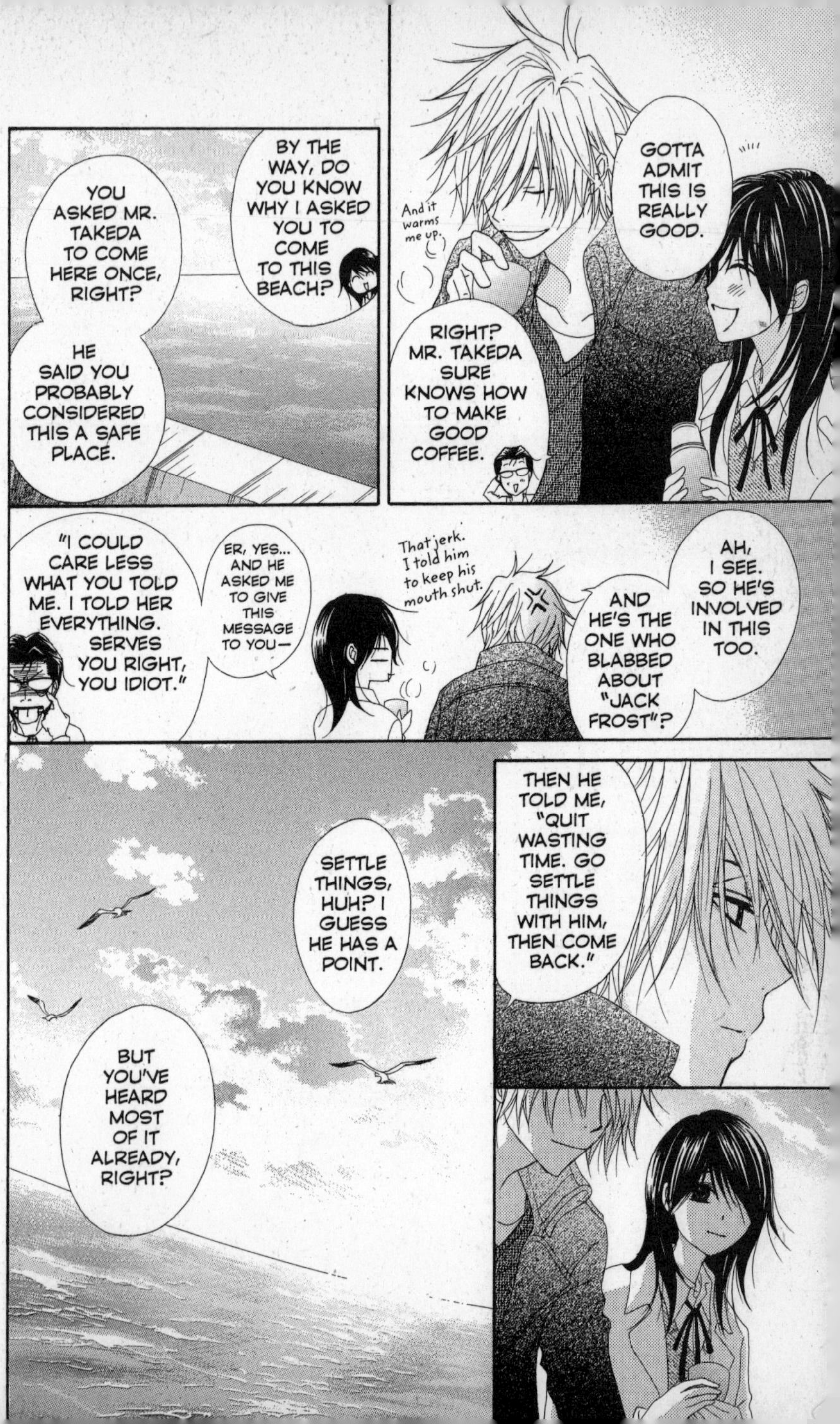
GOTTA ADMIT THIS IS REALLY GOOD.
And it warms me up.
RIGHT? MR. TAKEDA SURE KNOWS HOW TO MAKE GOOD COFFEE.
BY THE WAY, DO YOU KNOW WHY I ASKED YOU TO COME TO THIS BEACH?
YOU ASKED MR. TAKEDA TO COME HERE ONCE, RIGHT?
HE SAID YOU PROBABLY CONSIDERED THIS A SAFE PLACE.
AH, I SEE. SO HE'S INVOLVED IN THIS TOO.
AND HE'S THE ONE WHO BLABBED ABOUT "JACK FROST"?
That jerk. I told him to keep his mouth shut.
ER, YES... AND HE ASKED ME TO GIVE THIS MESSAGE TO YOU—
"I COULD CARE LESS WHAT YOU TOLD ME. I TOLD HER EVERYTHING. SERVES YOU RIGHT, YOU IDIOT."
THEN HE TOLD ME, "QUIT WASTING TIME. GO SETTLE THINGS WITH HIM, THEN COME BACK."
SETTLE THINGS, HUH? I GUESS HE HAS A POINT.
BUT YOU'VE HEARD MOST OF IT ALREADY, RIGHT?

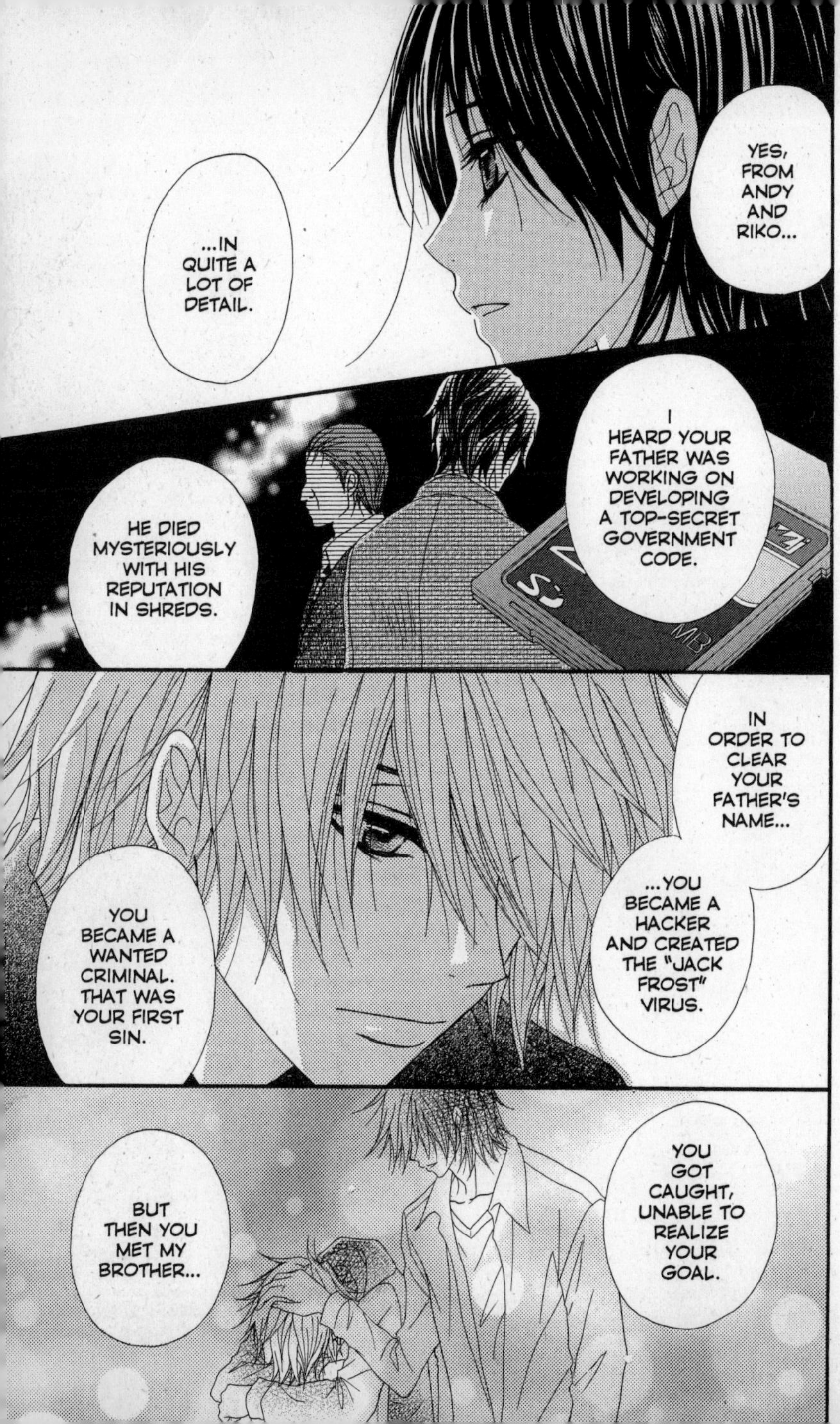
YES, FROM ANDY AND RIKO...
...IN QUITE A LOT OF DETAIL.
I HEARD YOUR FATHER WAS WORKING ON DEVELOPING A TOP-SECRET GOVERNMENT CODE.
HE DIED MYSTERIOUSLY WITH HIS REPUTATION IN SHREDS.
IN ORDER TO CLEAR YOUR FATHER'S NAME...
...YOU BECAME A HACKER AND CREATED THE "JACK FROST" VIRUS.
YOU BECAME A WANTED CRIMINAL. THAT WAS YOUR FIRST SIN.
YOU GOT CAUGHT, UNABLE TO REALIZE YOUR GOAL.
BUT THEN YOU MET MY BROTHER...

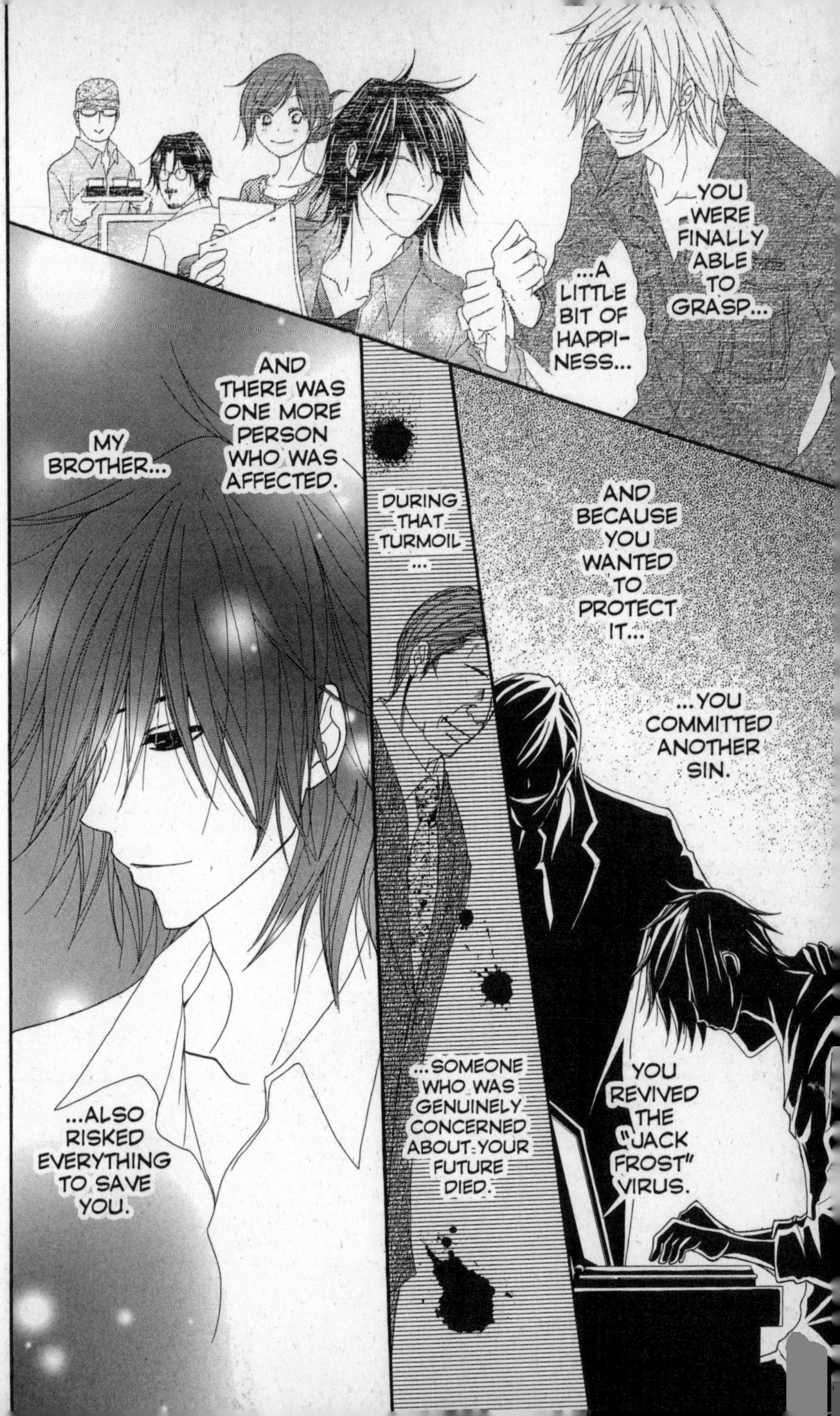
YOU WERE FINALLY ABLE TO GRASP...
...A LITTLE BIT OF HAPPINESS...
AND BECAUSE YOU WANTED TO PROTECT IT...
...YOU COMMITTED ANOTHER SIN.
YOU REVIVED THE "JACK FROST" VIRUS.
DURING THAT TURMOIL...
...SOMEONE WHO WAS GENUINELY CONCERNED ABOUT YOUR FUTURE DIED.
AND THERE WAS ONE MORE PERSON WHO WAS AFFECTED.
MY BROTHER...
...ALSO RISKED EVERYTHING TO SAVE YOU.

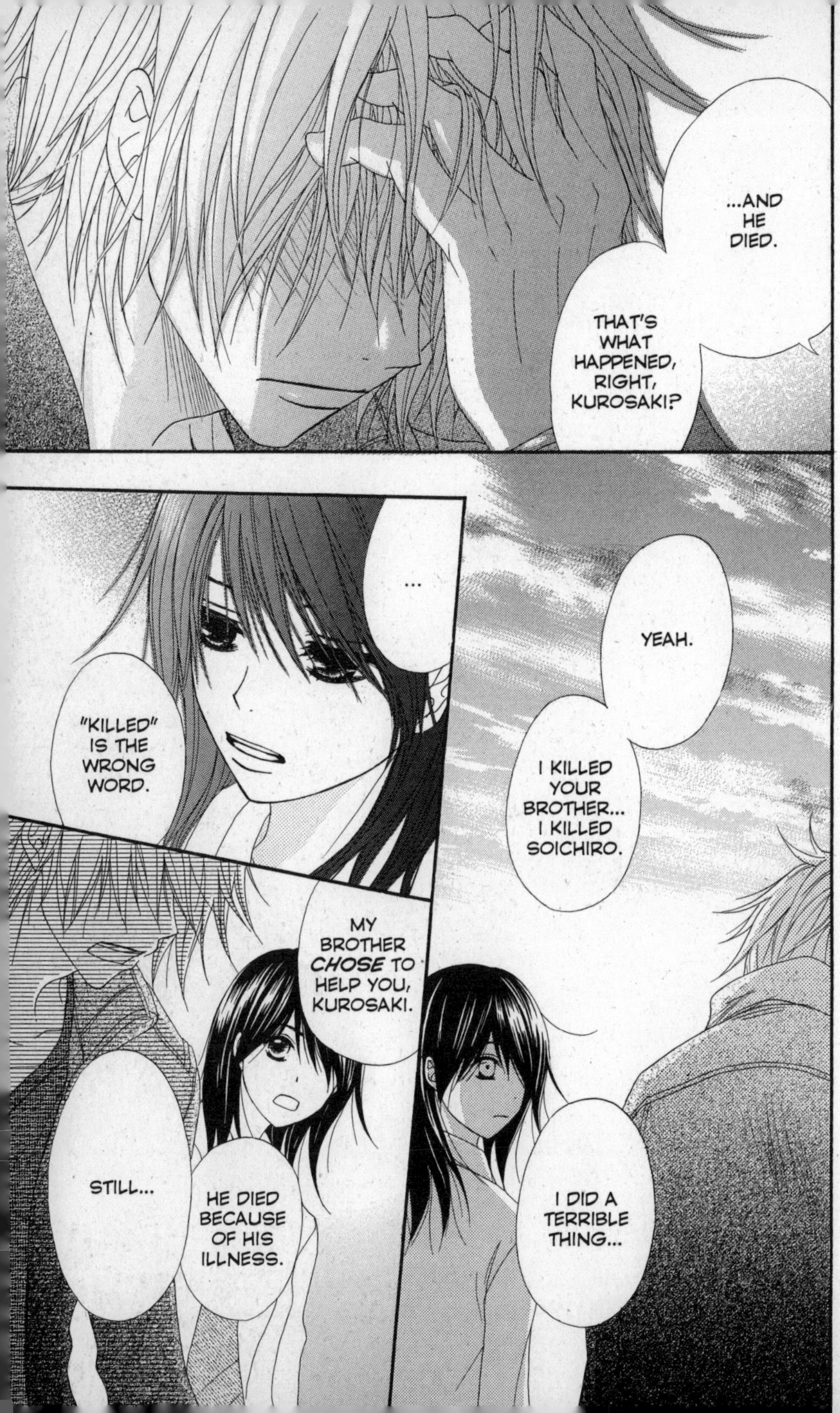
...AND HE DIED.
THAT'S WHAT HAPPENED, RIGHT, KUROSAKI?
YEAH.
I KILLED YOUR BROTHER... I KILLED SOICHIRO.
I DID A TERRIBLE THING...
...
"KILLED" IS THE WRONG WORD.
MY BROTHER *CHOSE* TO HELP YOU, KUROSAKI.
HE DIED BECAUSE OF HIS ILLNESS.
STILL...

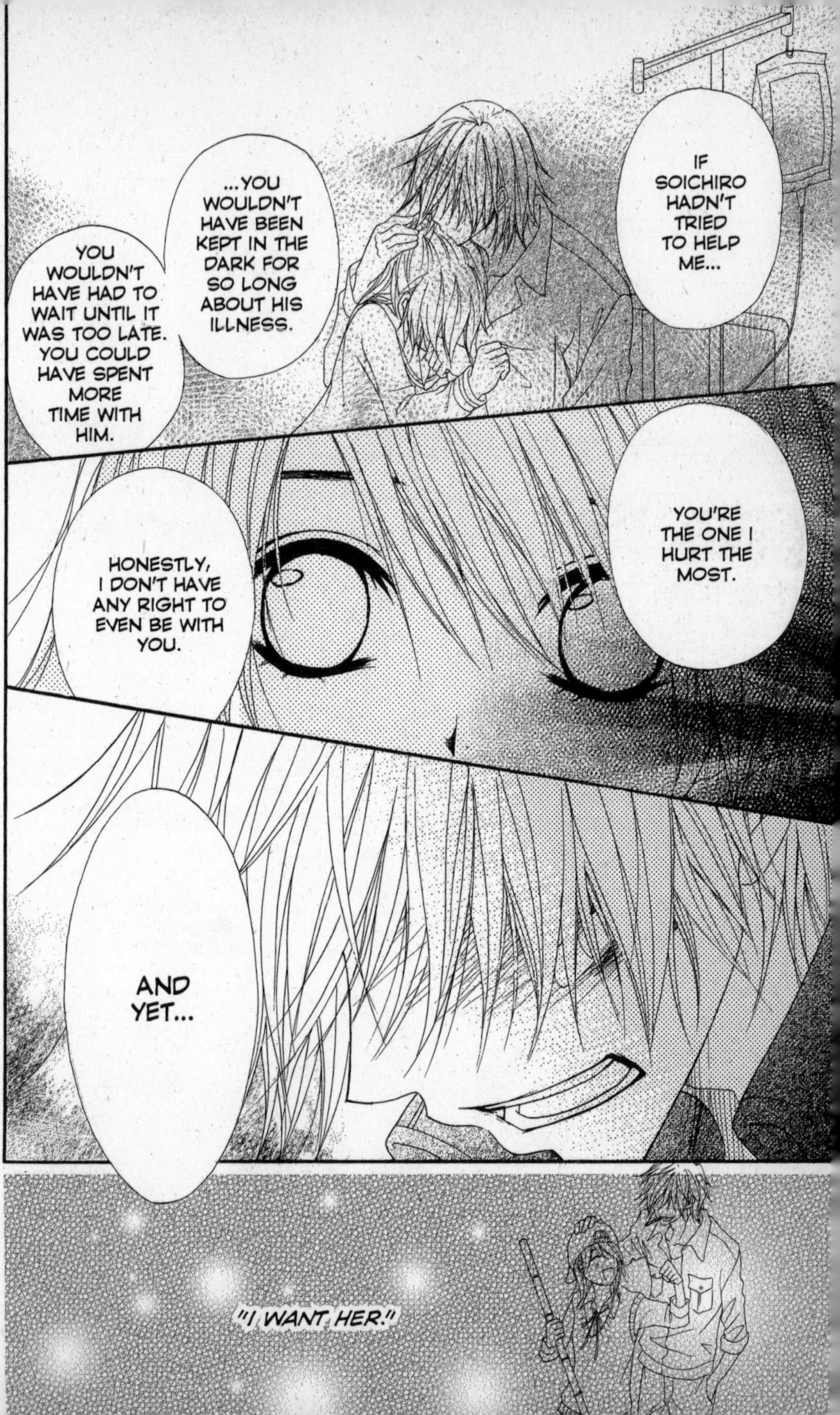
IF SOICHIRO HADN'T TRIED TO HELP ME...
...YOU WOULDN'T HAVE BEEN KEPT IN THE DARK FOR SO LONG ABOUT HIS ILLNESS.
YOU WOULDN'T HAVE HAD TO WAIT UNTIL IT WAS TOO LATE. YOU COULD HAVE SPENT MORE TIME WITH HIM.
YOU'RE THE ONE I HURT THE MOST.
HONESTLY, I DON'T HAVE ANY RIGHT TO EVEN BE WITH YOU.
AND YET...
"I WANT HER."

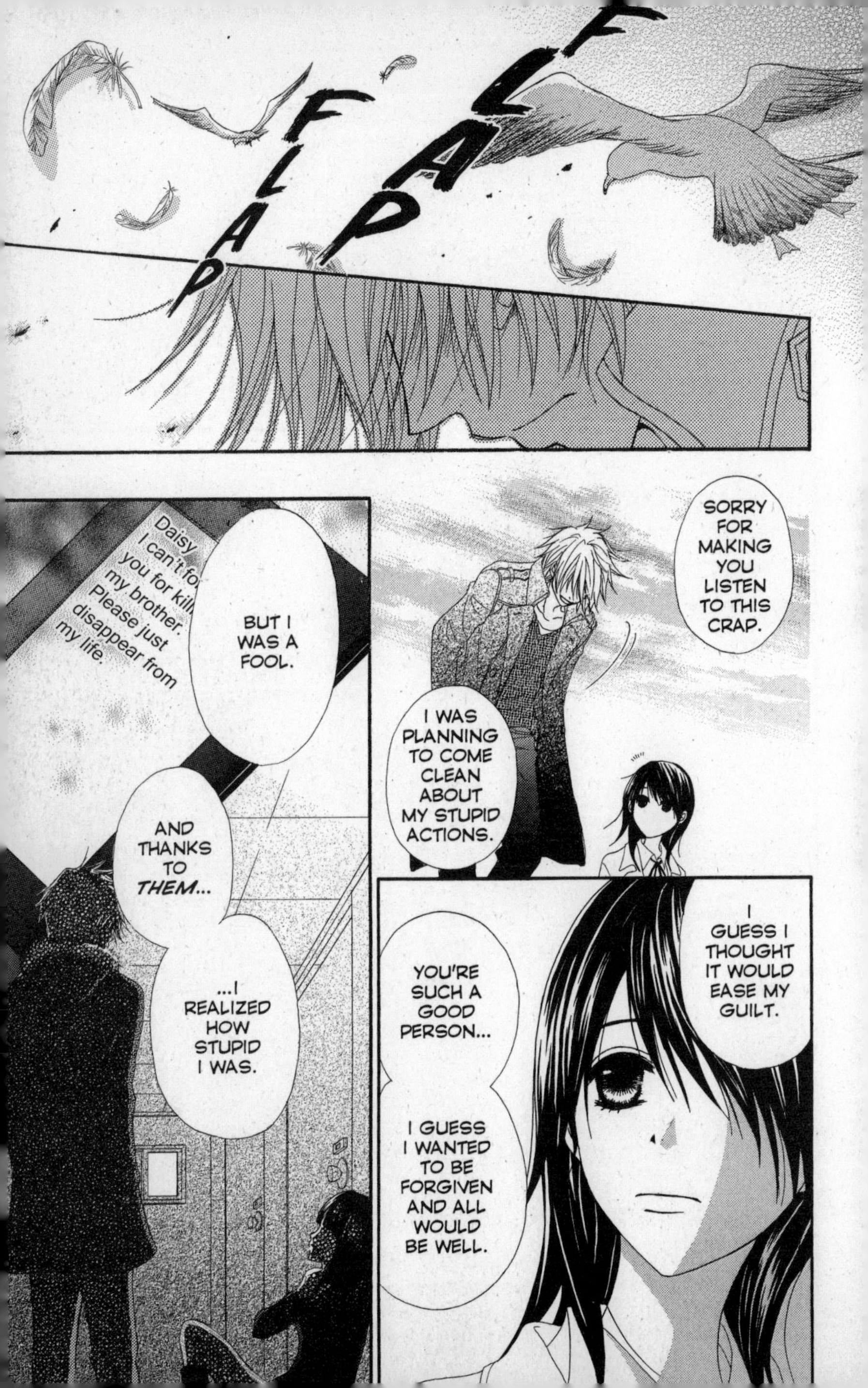
FLAP
FLAP
SORRY FOR MAKING YOU LISTEN TO THIS CRAP.
I WAS PLANNING TO COME CLEAN ABOUT MY STUPID ACTIONS.
I GUESS I THOUGHT IT WOULD EASE MY GUILT.
YOU'RE SUCH A GOOD PERSON...
I GUESS I WANTED TO BE FORGIVEN AND ALL WOULD BE WELL.
Daisy
my brother.
Please just disappear from my life.
BUT I WAS A FOOL.
AND THANKS TO *THEM*...
...I REALIZED HOW STUPID I WAS.

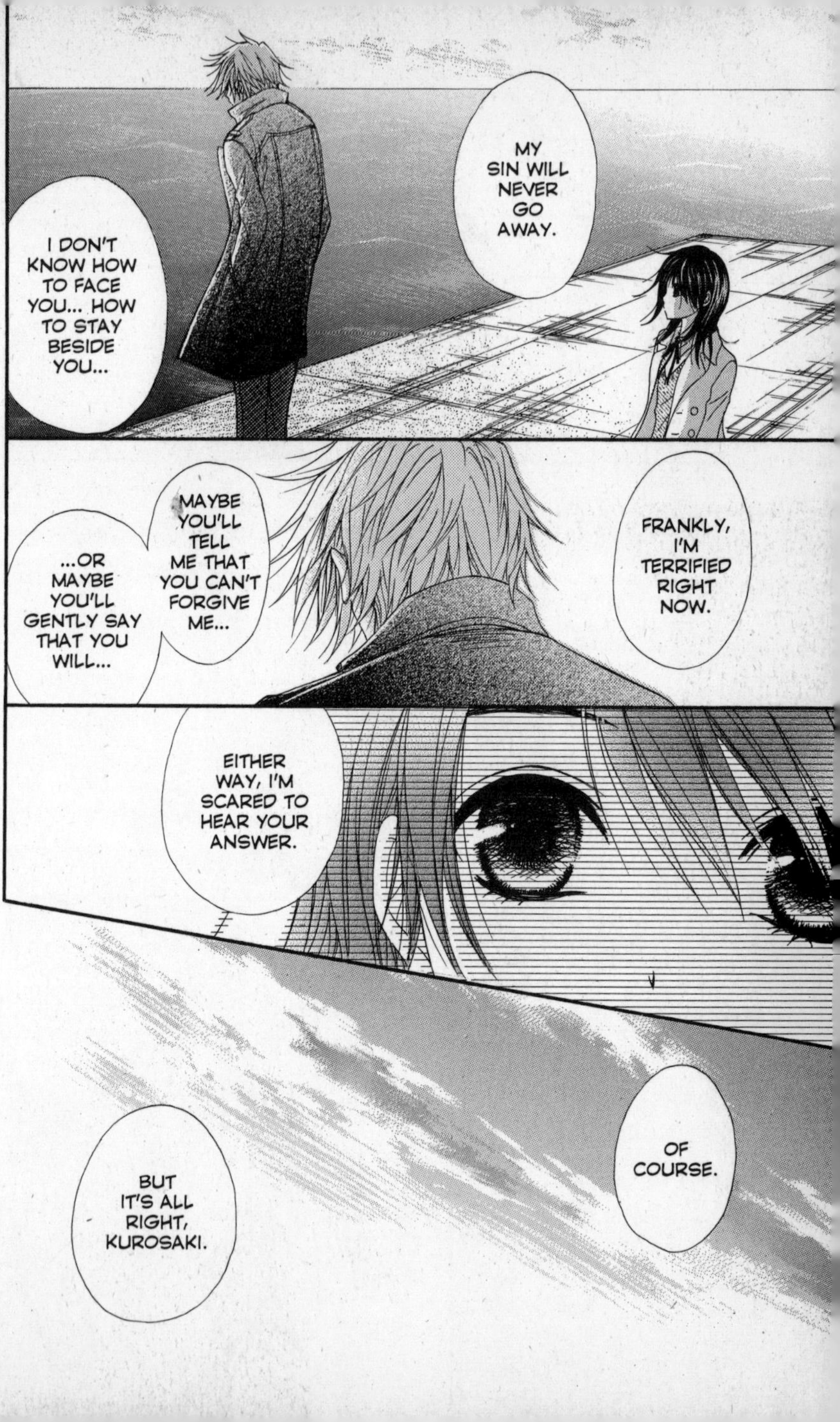
MY SIN WILL NEVER GO AWAY.
I DON'T KNOW HOW TO FACE YOU... HOW TO STAY BESIDE YOU...
FRANKLY, I'M TERRIFIED RIGHT NOW.
MAYBE YOU'LL TELL ME THAT YOU CAN'T FORGIVE ME...
...OR MAYBE YOU'LL GENTLY SAY THAT YOU WILL...
EITHER WAY, I'M SCARED TO HEAR YOUR ANSWER.
OF COURSE.
BUT IT'S ALL RIGHT, KUROSAKI.

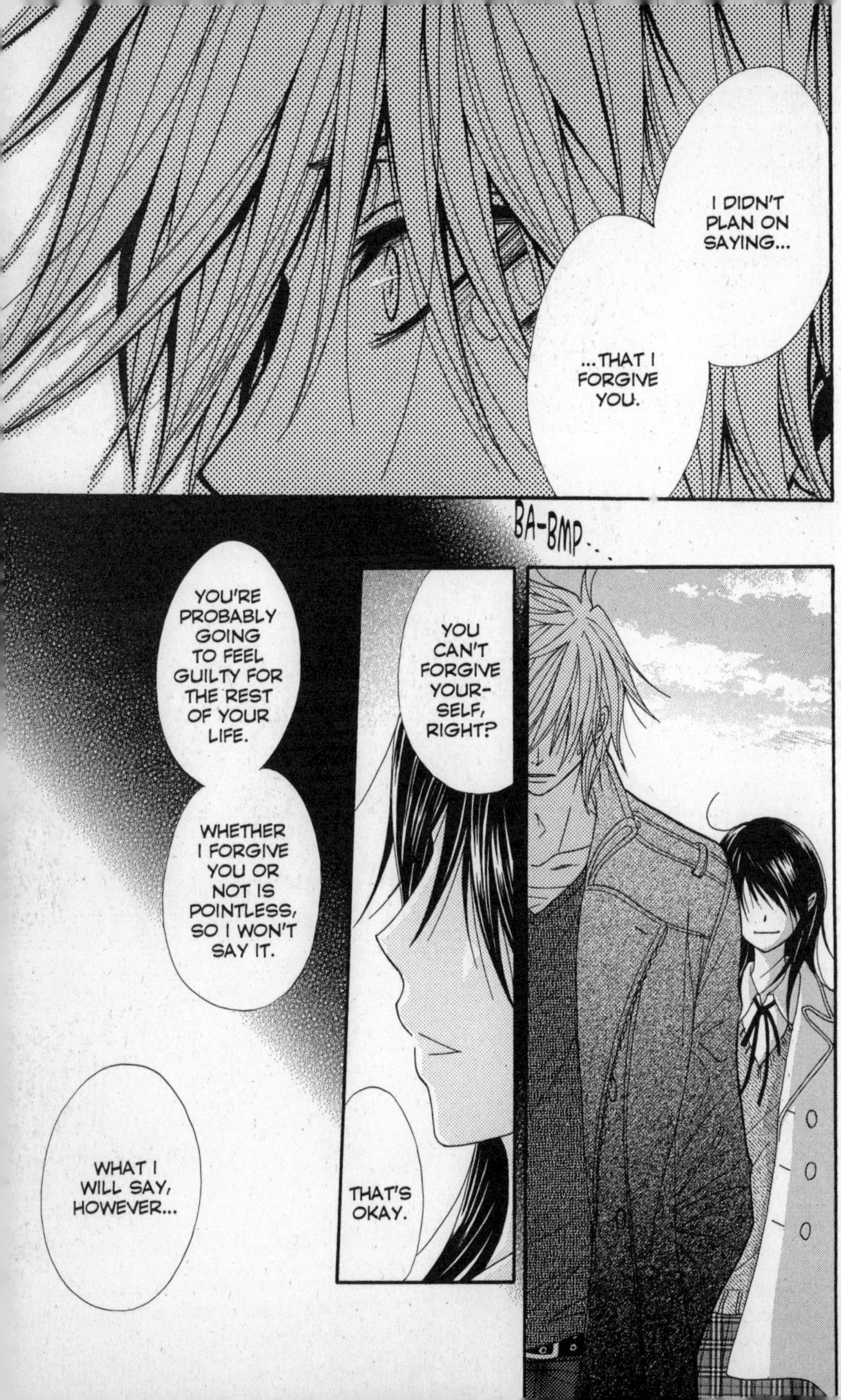

I DIDN'T PLAN ON SAYING...
...THAT I FORGIVE YOU.
BA-BMP...
YOU CAN'T FORGIVE YOURSELF, RIGHT?
THAT'S OKAY.
YOU'RE PROBABLY GOING TO FEEL GUILTY FOR THE REST OF YOUR LIFE.
WHETHER I FORGIVE YOU OR NOT IS POINTLESS, SO I WON'T SAY IT.
WHAT I WILL SAY, HOWEVER...

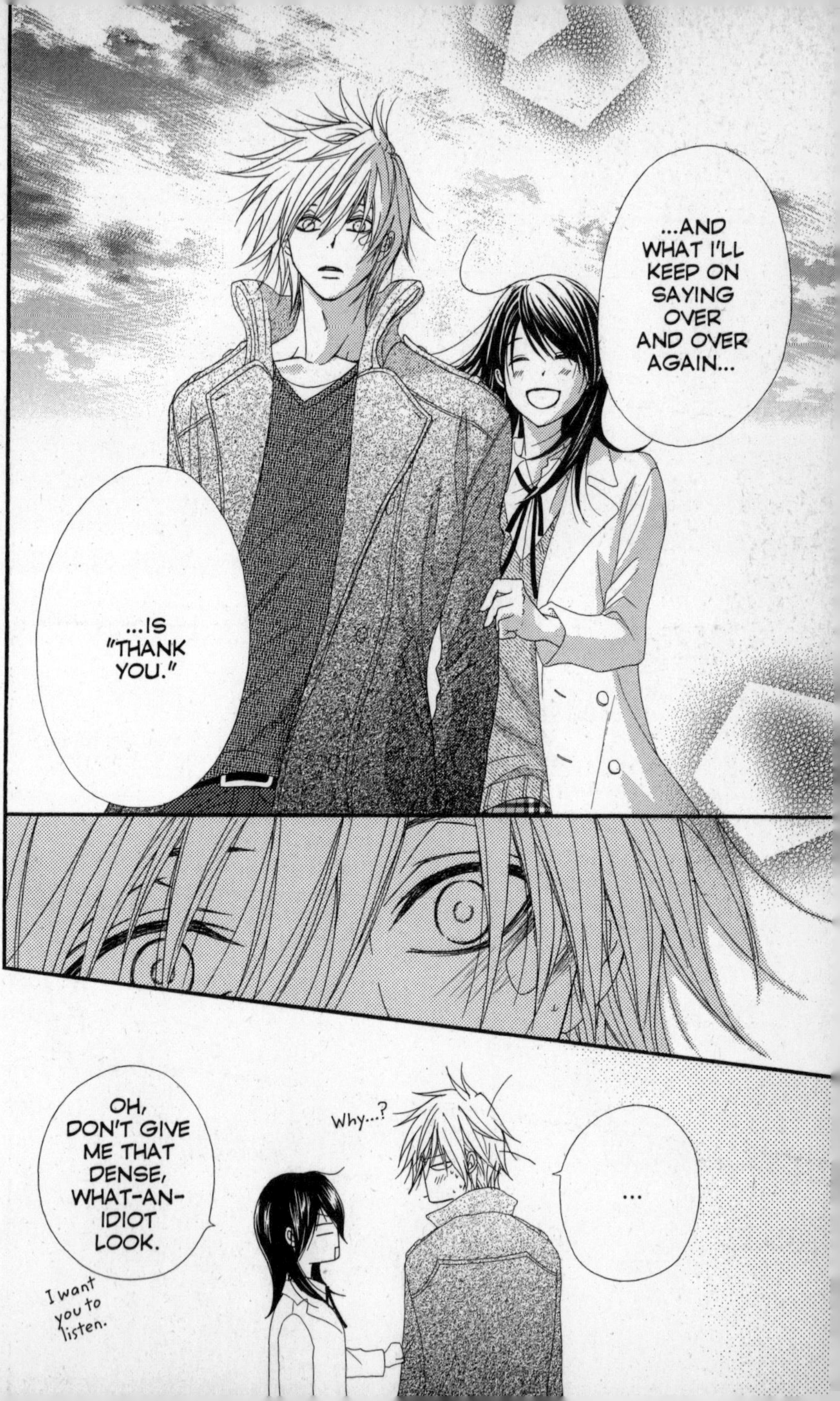
...AND WHAT I'LL KEEP ON SAYING OVER AND OVER AGAIN...
...IS "THANK YOU."
...
Why...?
OH, DON'T GIVE ME THAT DENSE, WHAT-AN-IDIOT LOOK.
I want you to listen.

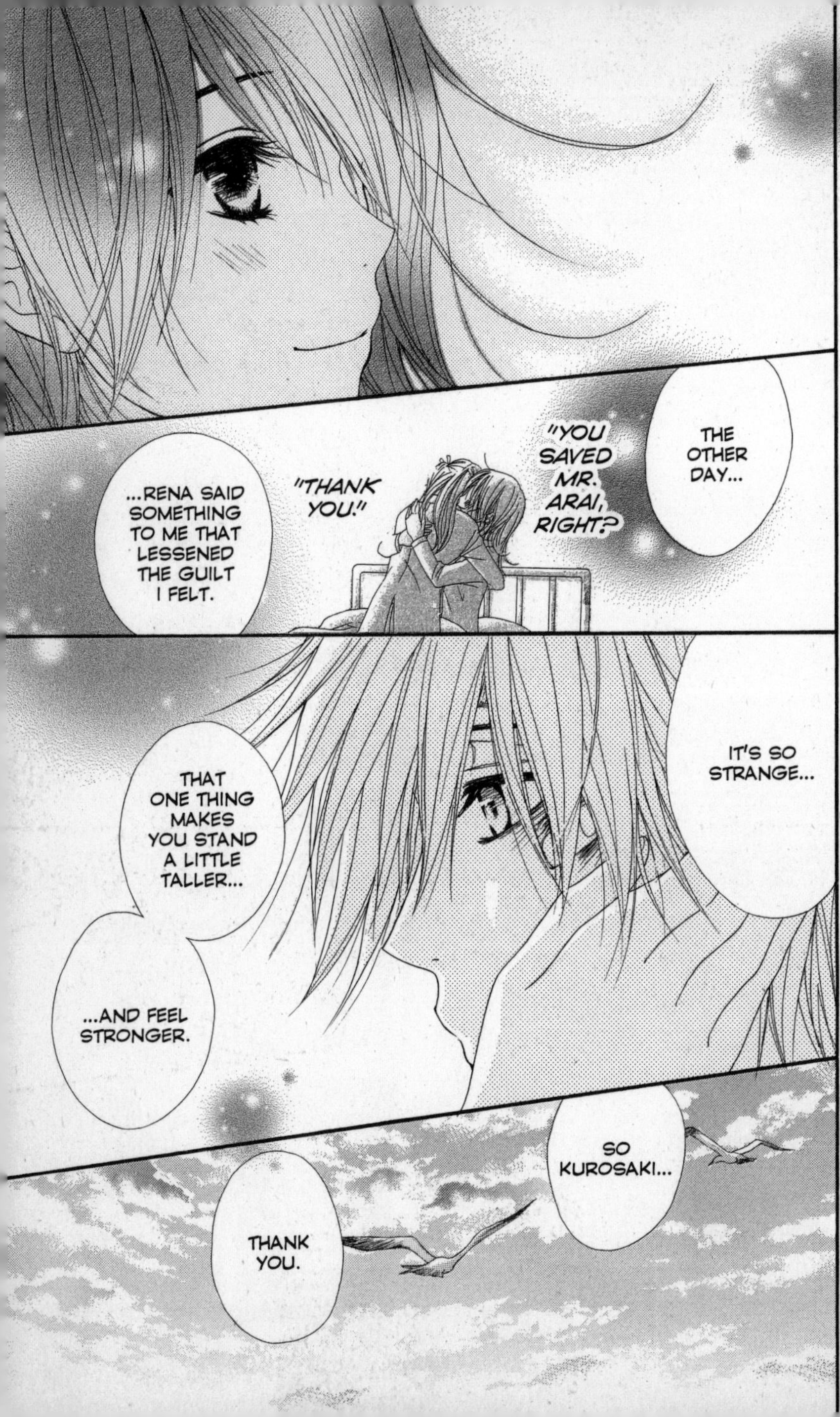
THE OTHER DAY...
"YOU SAVED MR. ARAI, RIGHT?
"THANK YOU."
...RENA SAID SOMETHING TO ME THAT LESSENED THE GUILT I FELT.
IT'S SO STRANGE...
THAT ONE THING MAKES YOU STAND A LITTLE TALLER...
...AND FEEL STRONGER.
SO KUROSAKI...
THANK YOU.

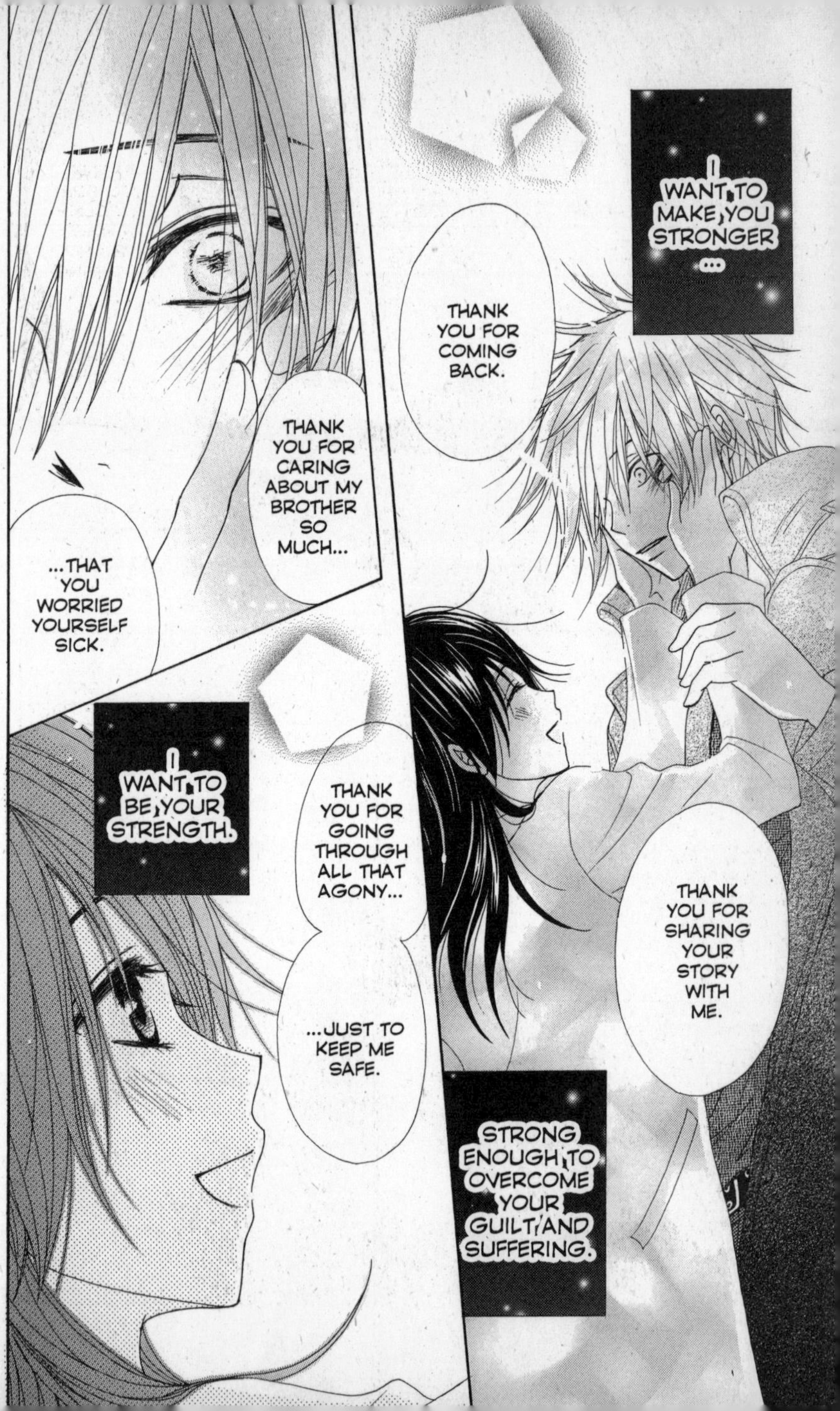
I WANT TO MAKE YOU STRONGER...
THANK YOU FOR COMING BACK.
THANK YOU FOR SHARING YOUR STORY WITH ME.
STRONG ENOUGH TO OVERCOME YOUR GUILT AND SUFFERING.
THANK YOU FOR CARING ABOUT MY BROTHER SO MUCH...
...THAT YOU WORRIED YOURSELF SICK.
I WANT TO BE YOUR STRENGTH.
THANK YOU FOR GOING THROUGH ALL THAT AGONY...
...JUST TO KEEP ME SAFE.

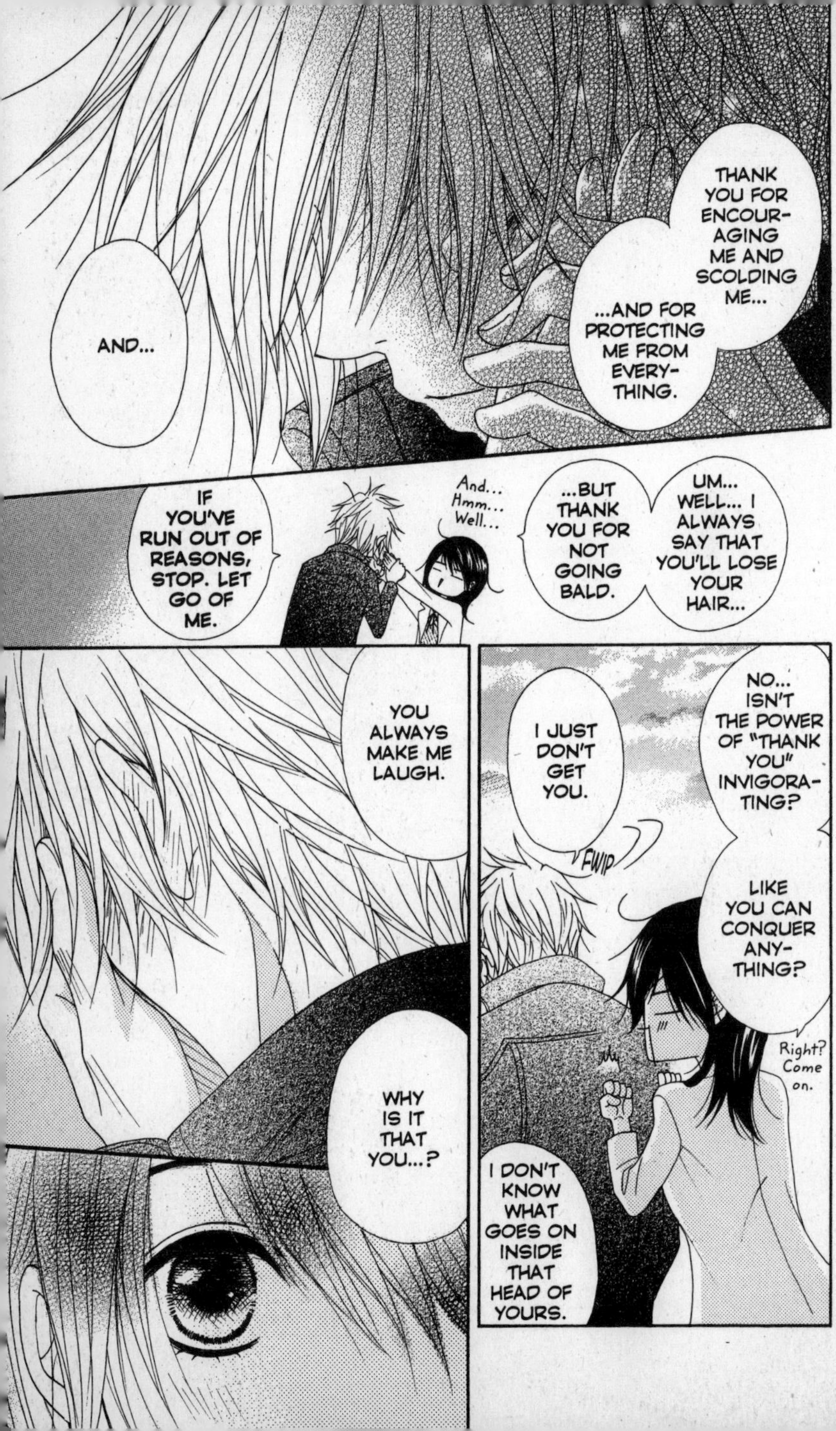
THANK YOU FOR ENCOURAGING ME AND SCOLDING ME...
...AND FOR PROTECTING ME FROM EVERYTHING.
AND...
UM... WELL... I ALWAYS SAY THAT YOU'LL LOSE YOUR HAIR...
...BUT THANK YOU FOR NOT GOING BALD.
And... Hmm... Well...
IF YOU'VE RUN OUT OF REASONS, STOP. LET GO OF ME.
NO... ISN'T THE POWER OF "THANK YOU" INVIGORATING?
LIKE YOU CAN CONQUER ANYTHING?
Right? Come on.
I JUST DON'T GET YOU.
FWIP
I DON'T KNOW WHAT GOES ON INSIDE THAT HEAD OF YOURS.
YOU ALWAYS MAKE ME LAUGH.
WHY IS IT THAT YOU...?

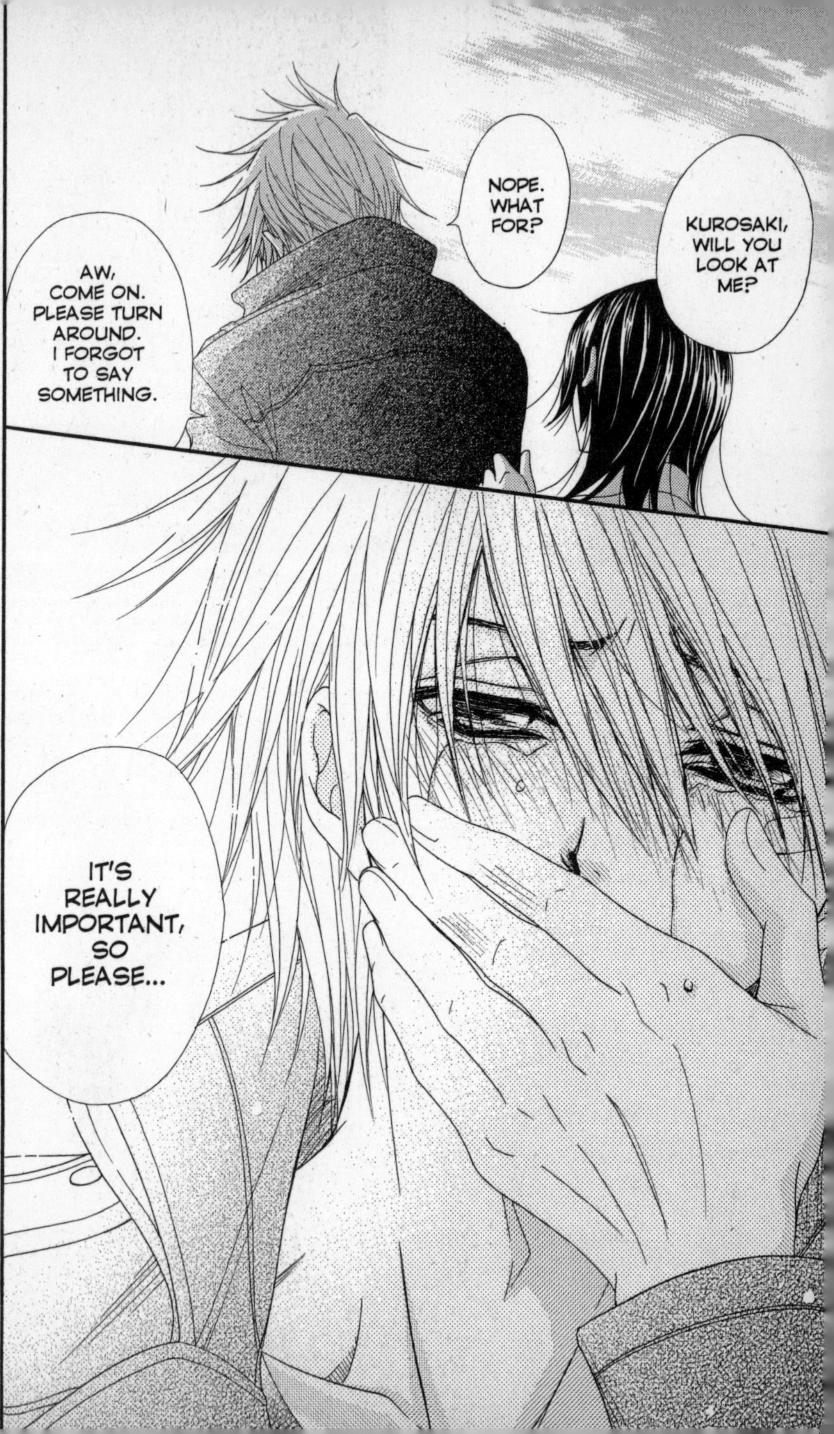
KUROSAKI, WILL YOU LOOK AT ME?
NOPE. WHAT FOR?
AW, COME ON. PLEASE TURN AROUND. I FORGOT TO SAY SOMETHING.
IT'S REALLY IMPORTANT, SO PLEASE...

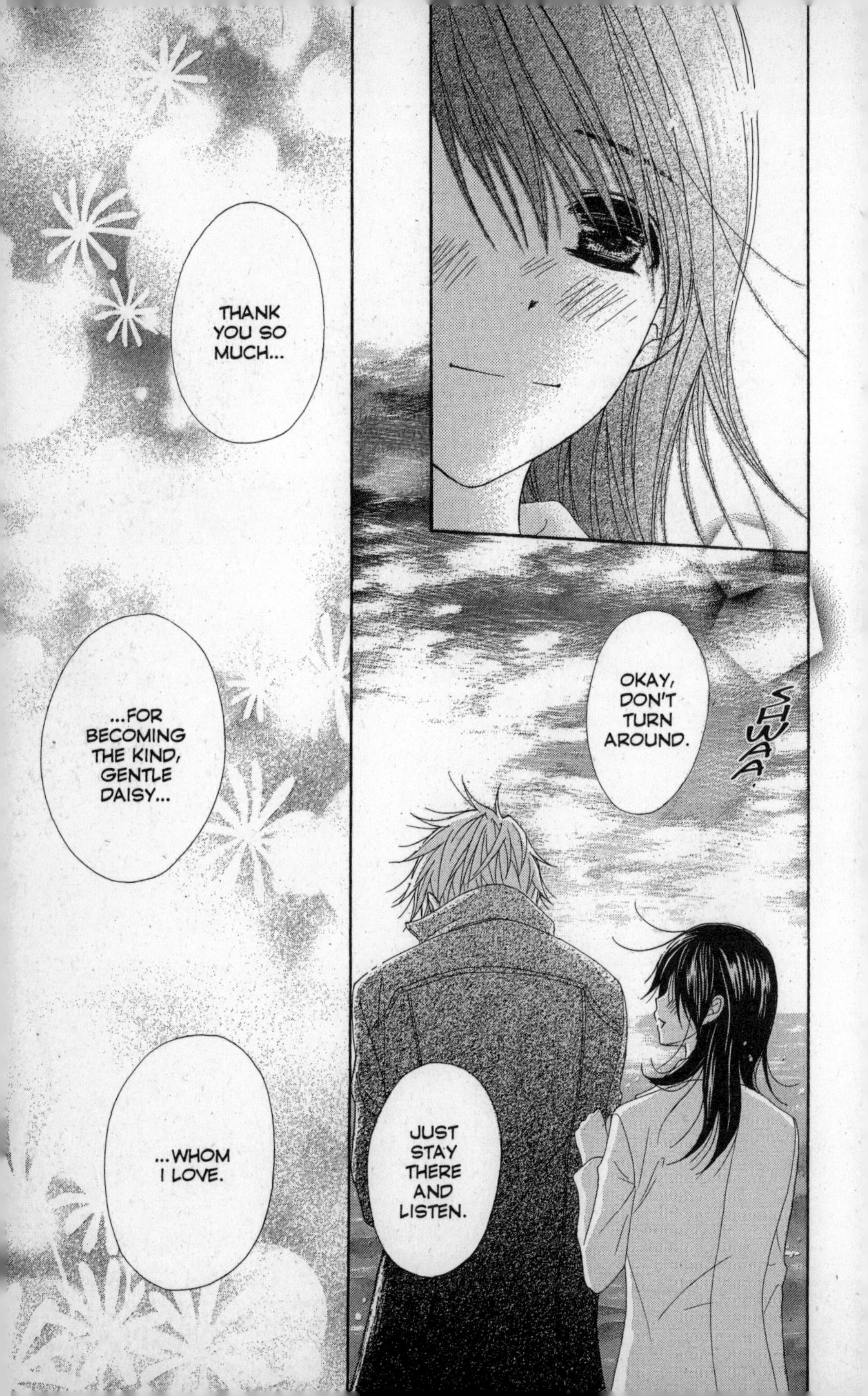
OKAY, DON'T TURN AROUND.
SHWAA
JUST STAY THERE AND LISTEN.
THANK YOU SO MUCH...
...FOR BECOMING THE KIND, GENTLE DAISY...
...WHOM I LOVE.

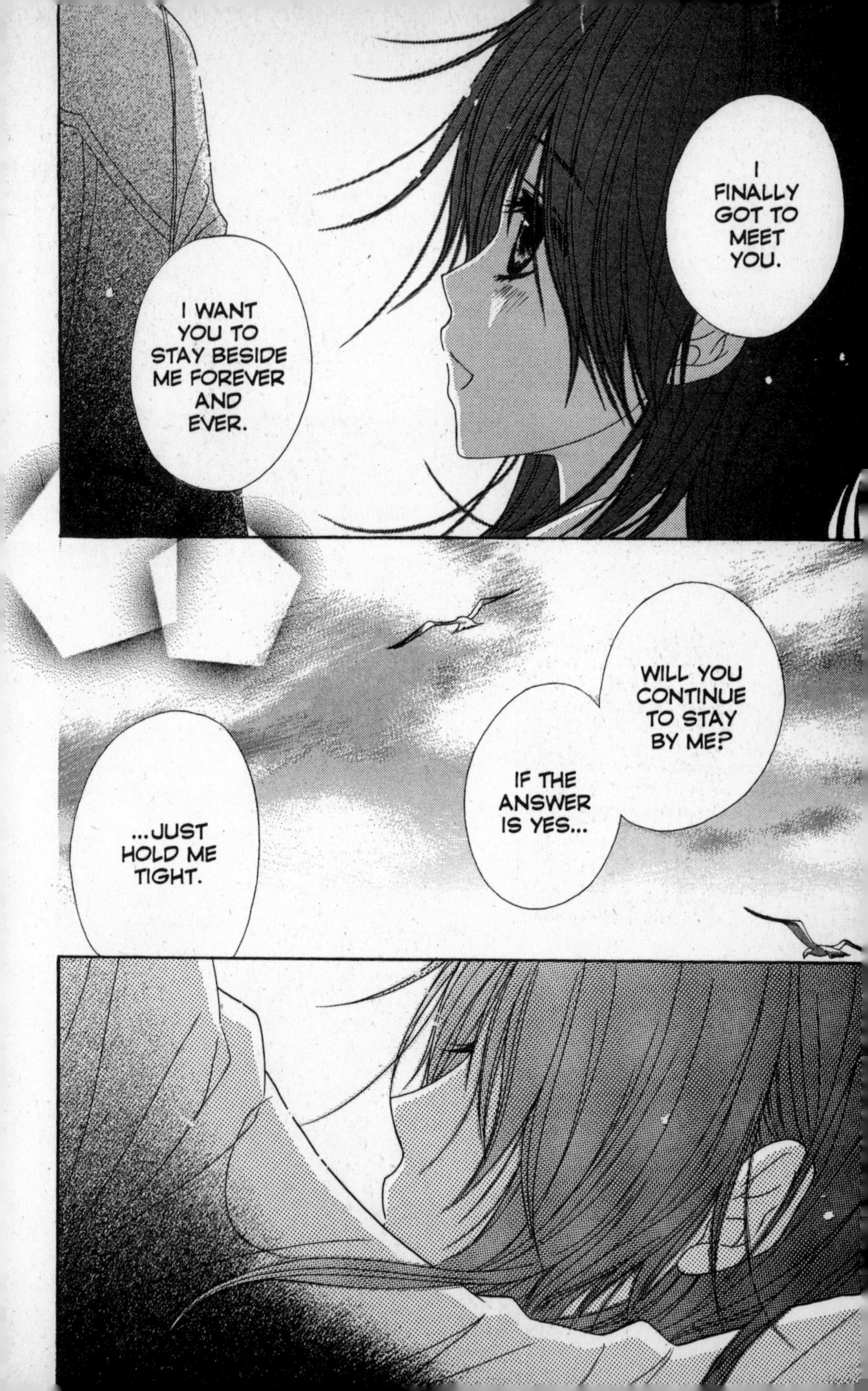
I FINALLY GOT TO MEET YOU.
I WANT YOU TO STAY BESIDE ME FOREVER AND EVER.
WILL YOU CONTINUE TO STAY BY ME?
IF THE ANSWER IS YES...
...JUST HOLD ME TIGHT.

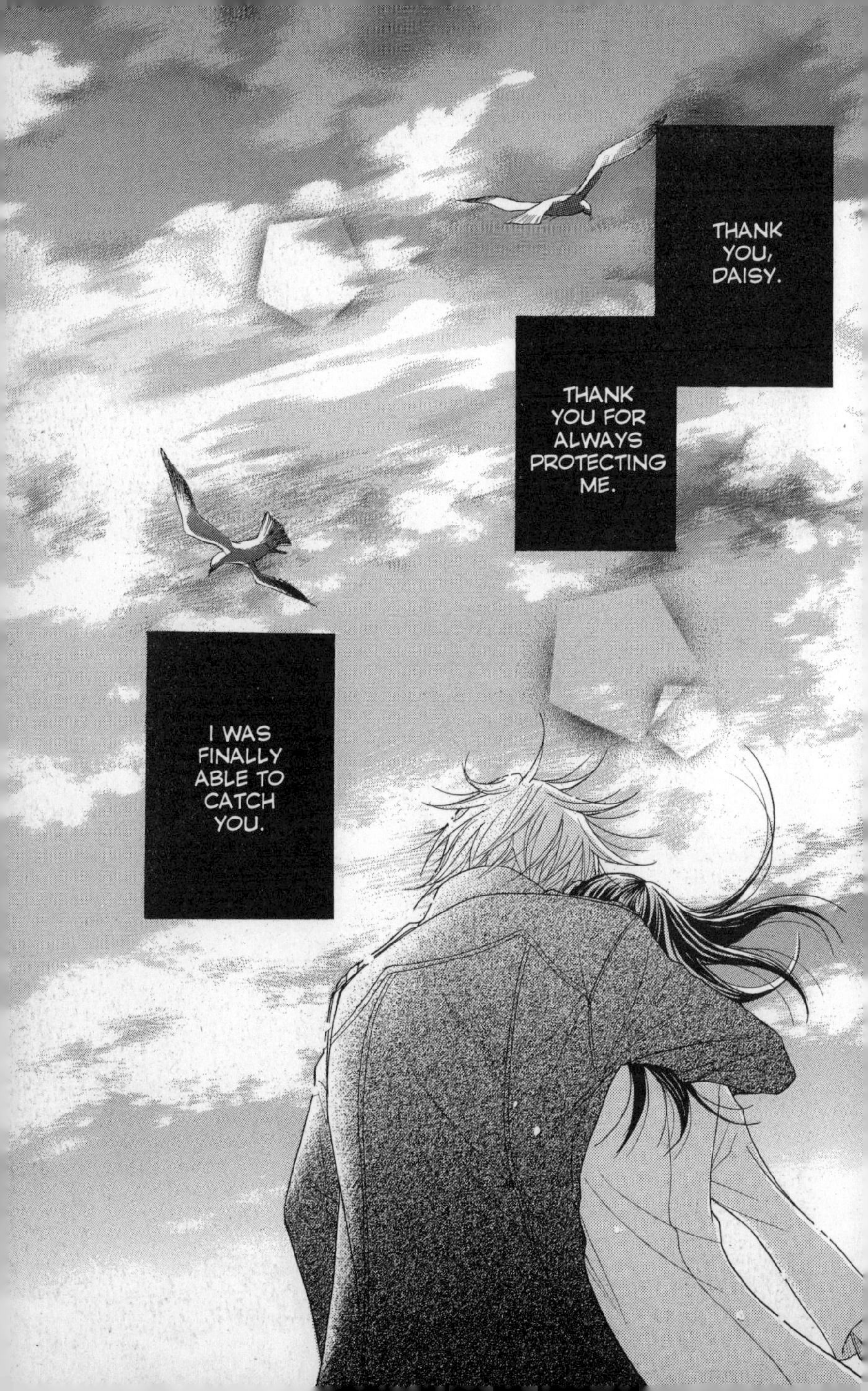
THANK YOU, DAISY.
THANK YOU FOR ALWAYS PROTECTING ME.
I WAS FINALLY ABLE TO CATCH YOU.

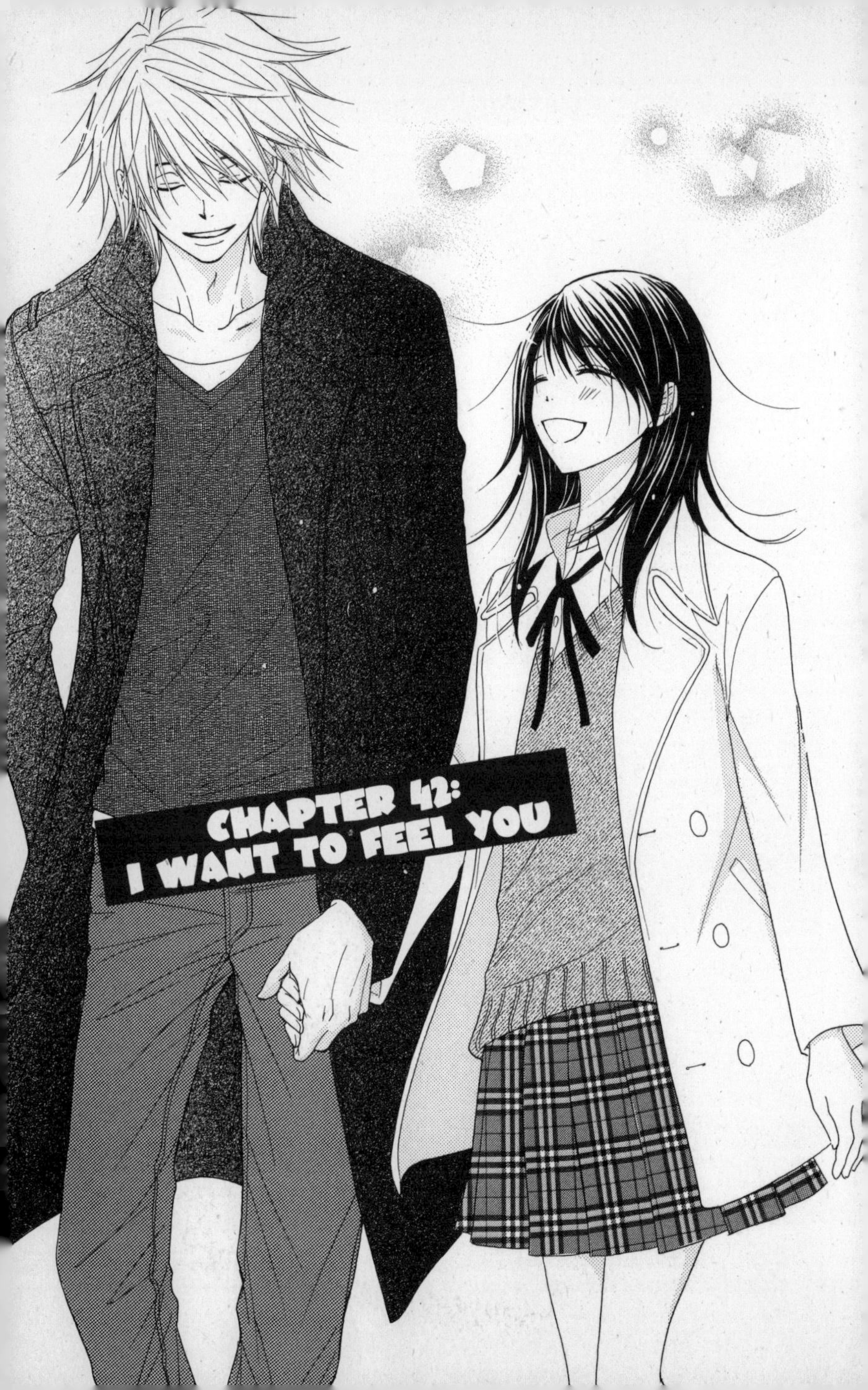
CHAPTER 42:
I WANT TO FEEL YOU

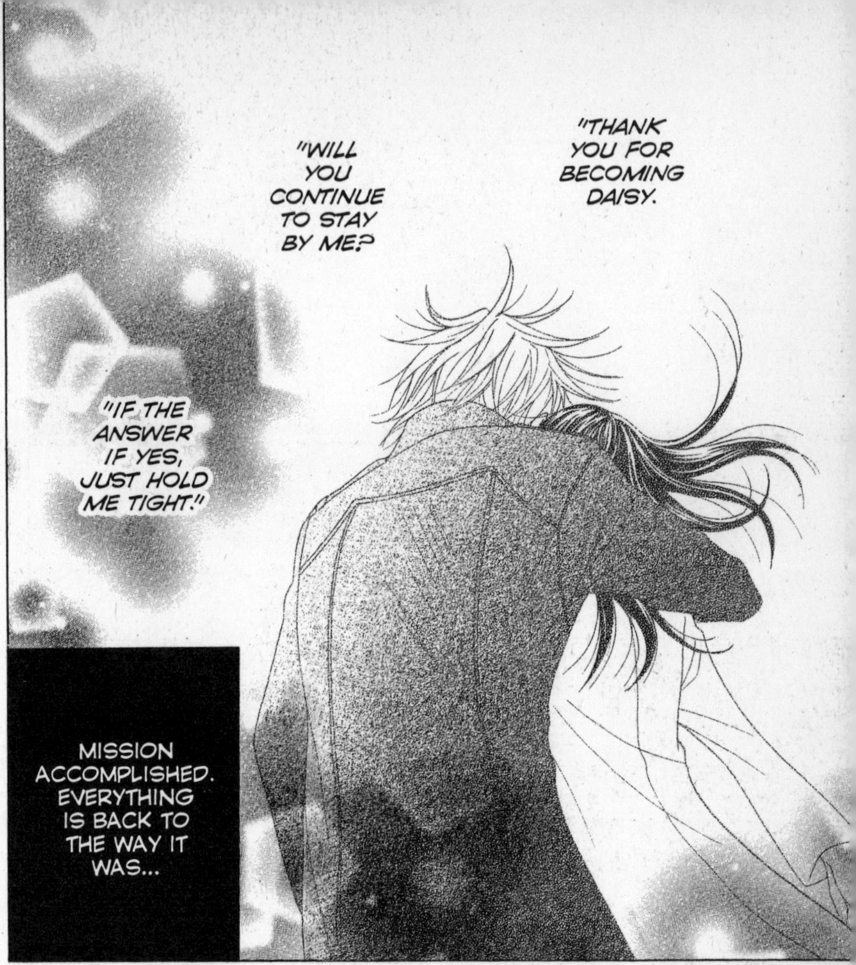
"THANK YOU FOR BECOMING DAISY.
"WILL YOU CONTINUE TO STAY BY ME?
"IF THE ANSWER IF YES, JUST HOLD ME TIGHT."
MISSION ACCOMPLISHED. EVERYTHING IS BACK TO THE WAY IT WAS...

ABOUT THE PART DURING THEIR REUNION WHERE KUROSAKI IS PUNISHED BY HAVING DAISY'S MESSAGE READ ALOUD... THIS WAS SOMETHING I HAD DEFINITELY DECIDED TO DO FROM AROUND THE TIME KUROSAKI DISAPPEARS. HENCE, THE REASON FOR DAISY'S MESSAGE AT THE END OF VOLUME 7, AS KUROSAKI LEAVES AND TERU IS IN TEARS. I GAVE SERIOUS CONSIDERATION TO "WHAT WOULD EMBARRASS KUROSAKI THE MOST" AND COULDN'T HELP BUT SMILE OCCASIONALLY THINKING ABOUT IT.
IF ANYTHING, I TEND TO BE PRETTY MASOCHISTIC, BUT WHEN IT COMES TO KUROSAKI, I TEND TO TURN BRUTAL. IT'S VERY STRANGE.

BUT READING MESSAGES YOU RECEIVE ALOUD IN FRONT OF OTHERS ISN'T NORMALLY A COOL THING. READERS, PLEASE DON'T EVER DO THIS!! HUMAN RELATIONSHIPS ARE PRECIOUS!!!

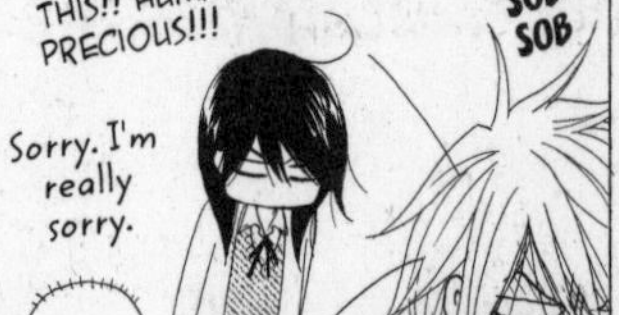
SOB SOB
Sorry. I'm really sorry.

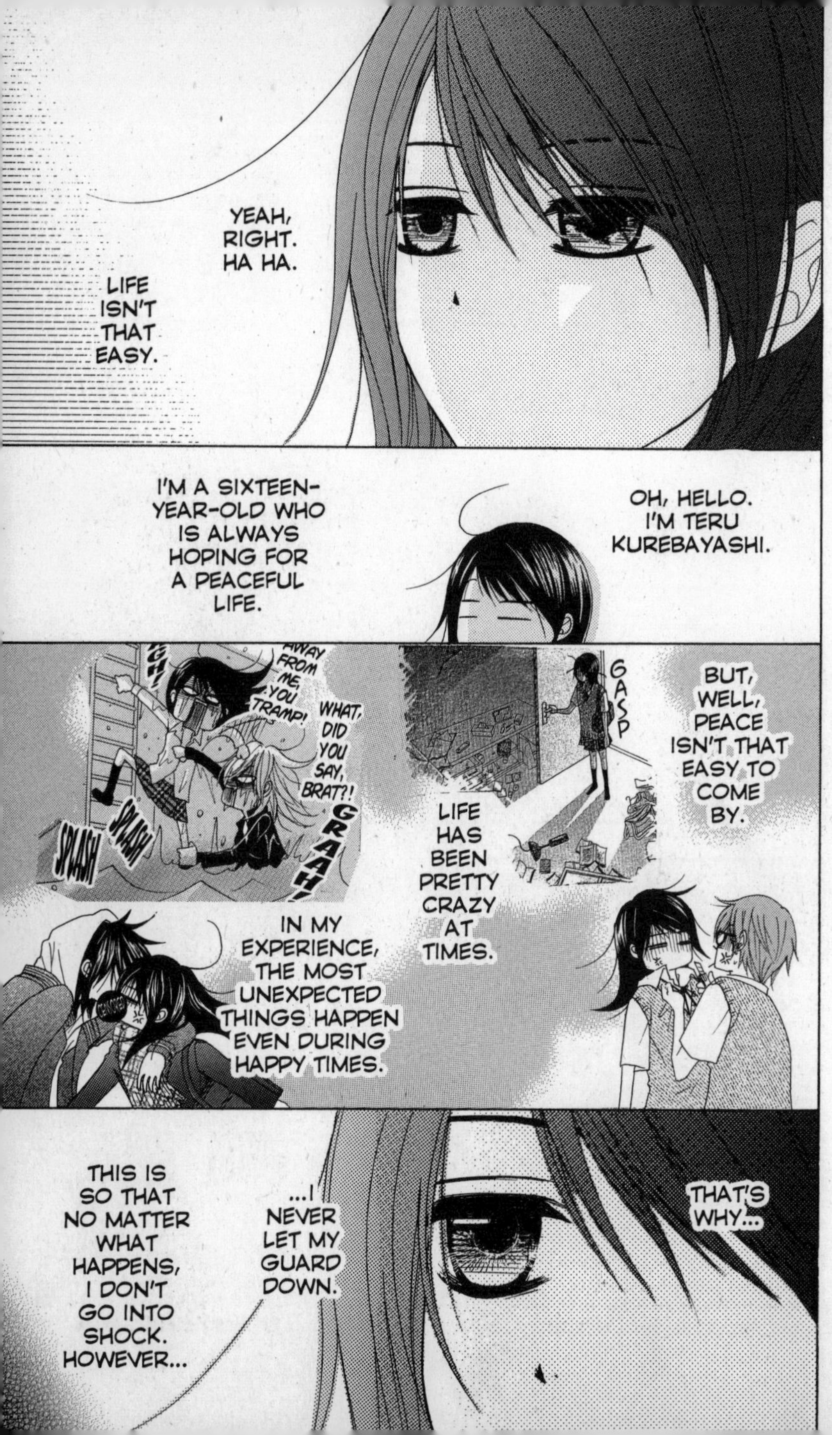
YEAH, RIGHT. HA HA.
LIFE ISN'T THAT EASY.
OH, HELLO. I'M TERU KUREBAYASHI.
I'M A SIXTEEN-YEAR-OLD WHO IS ALWAYS HOPING FOR A PEACEFUL LIFE.
BUT, WELL, PEACE ISN'T THAT EASY TO COME BY.
GASP
LIFE HAS BEEN PRETTY CRAZY AT TIMES.
AWAY FROM ME, YOU TRAMP!
WHAT, DID YOU SAY, BRAT?!
GRAAAH!
SPLASH
SPLASH
IN MY EXPERIENCE, THE MOST UNEXPECTED THINGS HAPPEN EVEN DURING HAPPY TIMES.
THAT'S WHY...
...I NEVER LET MY GUARD DOWN.
THIS IS SO THAT NO MATTER WHAT HAPPENS, I DON'T GO INTO SHOCK. HOWEVER...

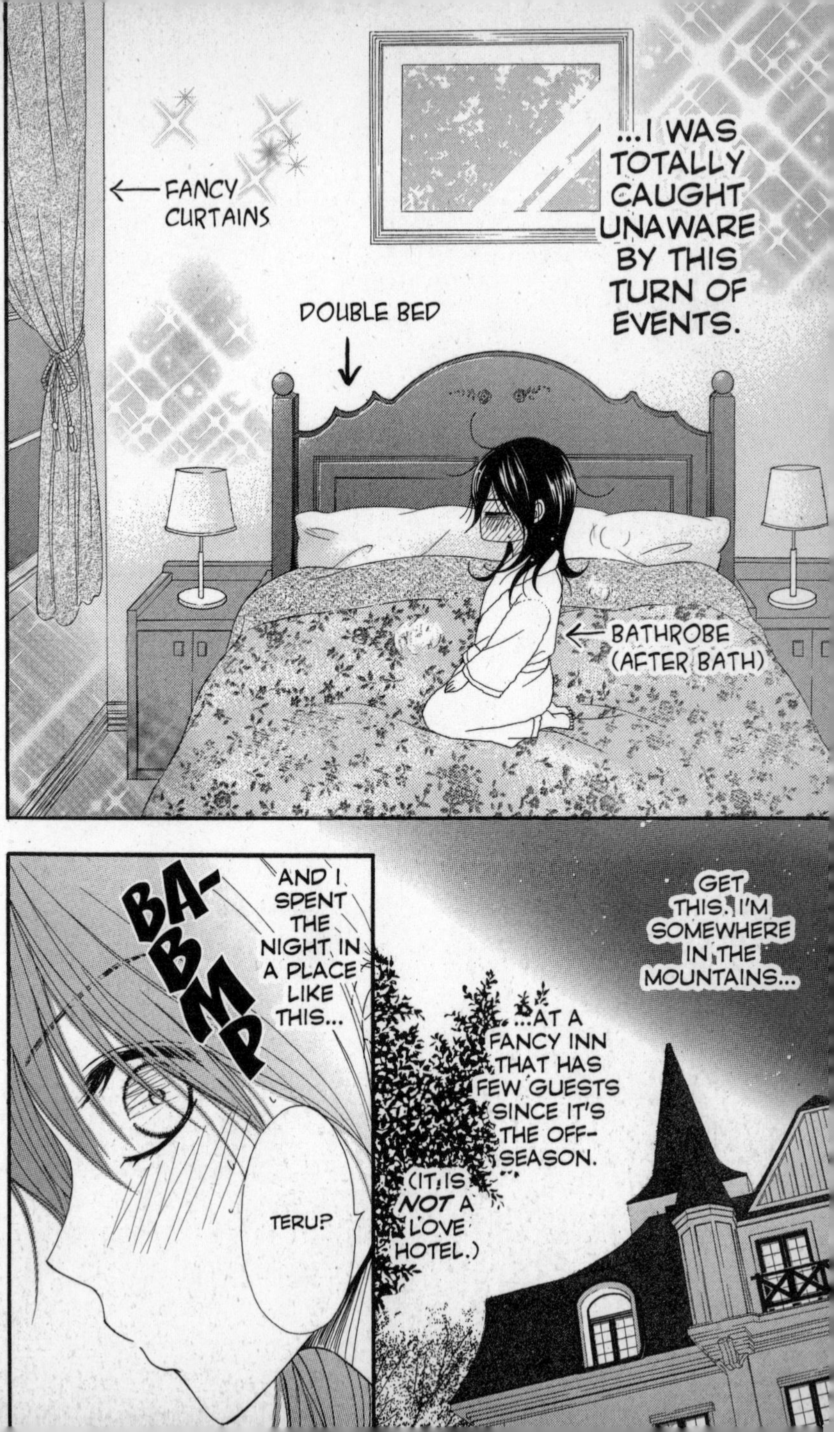
...I WAS TOTALLY CAUGHT UNAWARE BY THIS TURN OF EVENTS.
DOUBLE BED
FANCY CURTAINS
BATHROBE (AFTER BATH)
GET THIS. I'M SOMEWHERE IN THE MOUNTAINS...
...AT A FANCY INN THAT HAS FEW GUESTS SINCE IT'S THE OFF-SEASON.
(IT IS *NOT* A LOVE HOTEL.)
AND I SPENT THE NIGHT IN A PLACE LIKE THIS...
BA-BMP
TERU?

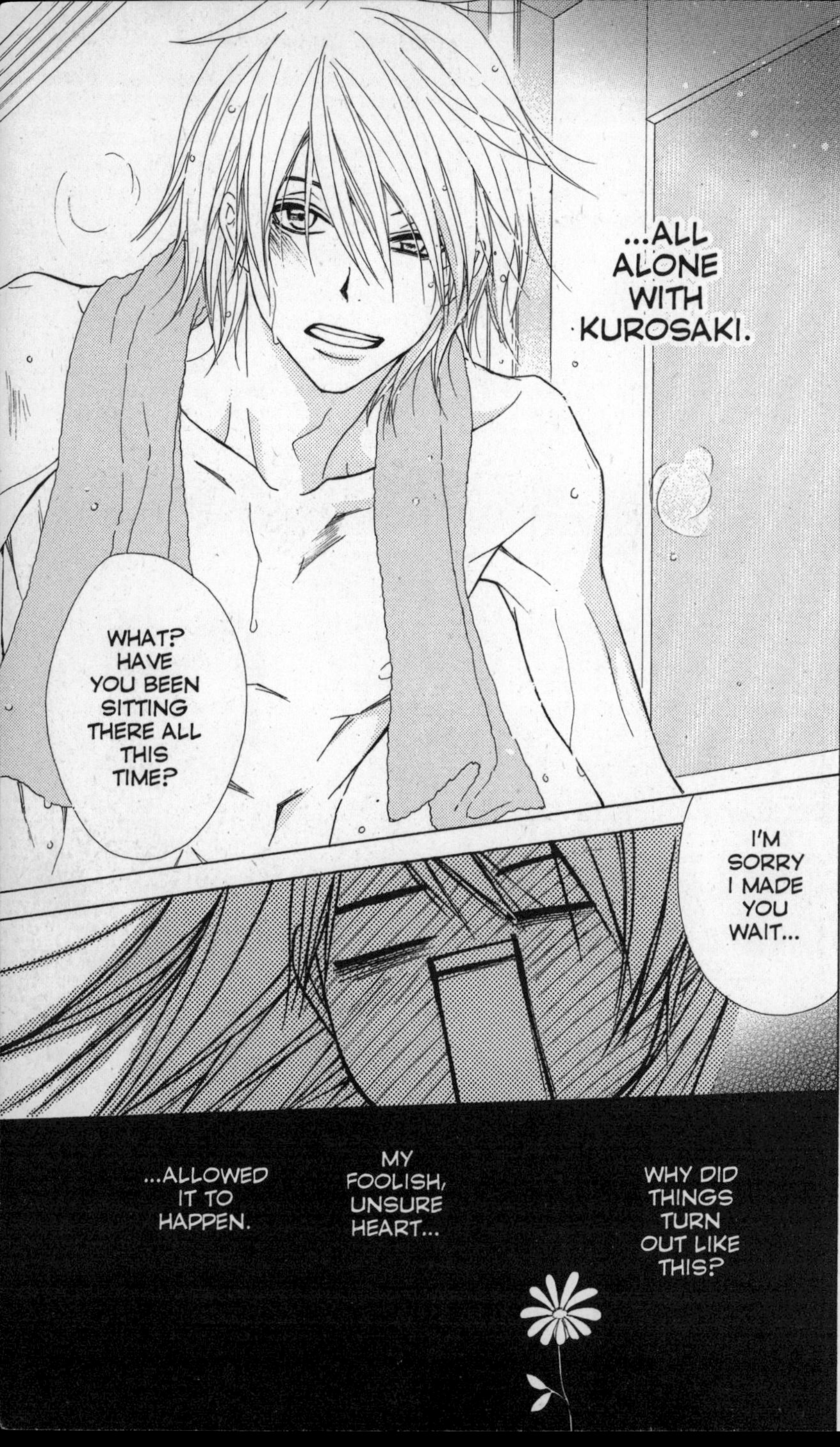
...ALL ALONE WITH KUROSAKI.
WHAT? HAVE YOU BEEN SITTING THERE ALL THIS TIME?
I'M SORRY I MADE YOU WAIT...
WHY DID THINGS TURN OUT LIKE THIS?
MY FOOLISH, UNSURE HEART...
...ALLOWED IT TO HAPPEN.

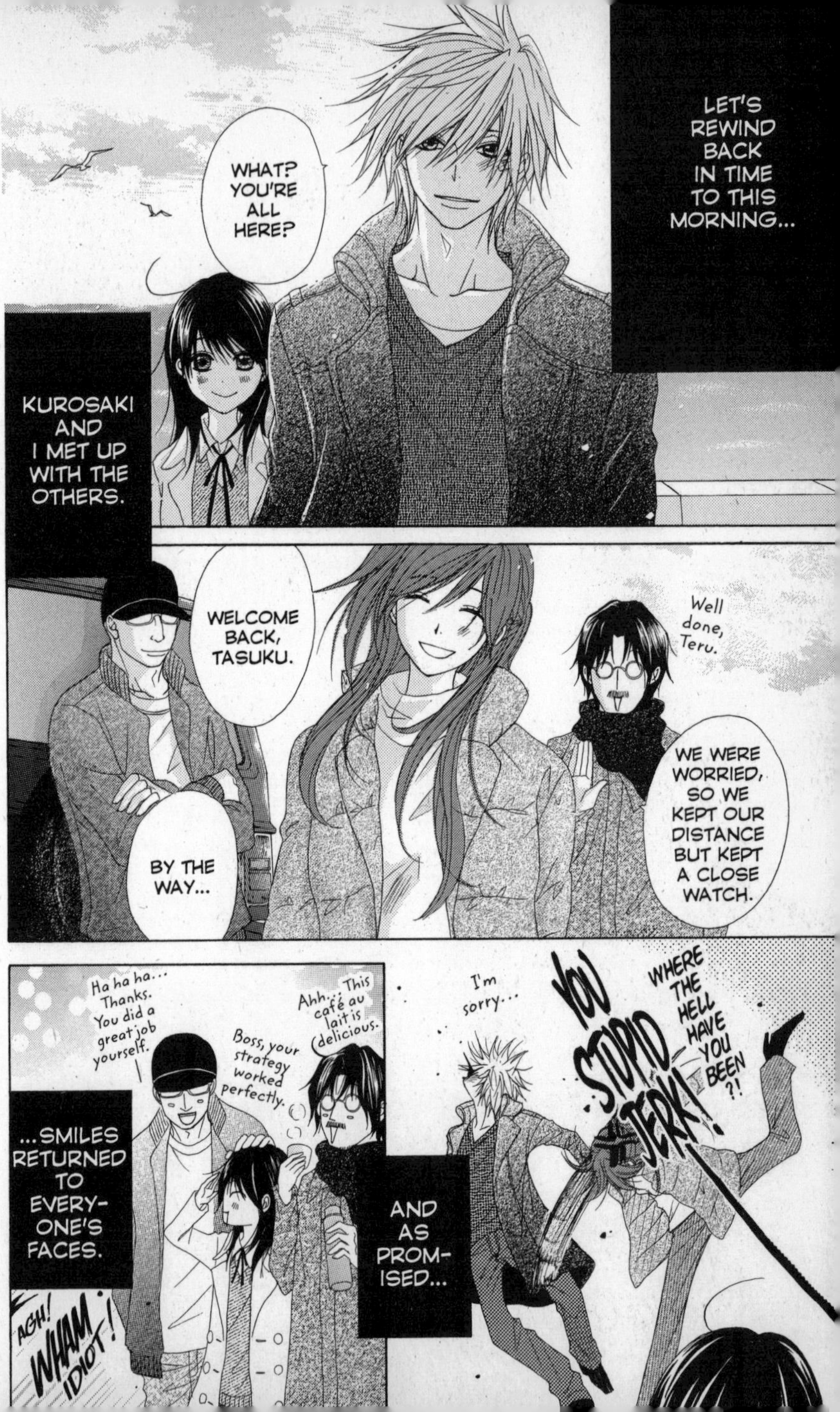
LET'S REWIND BACK IN TIME TO THIS MORNING...
WHAT? YOU'RE ALL HERE?
KUROSAKI AND I MET UP WITH THE OTHERS.
Well done, Teru.
WE WERE WORRIED, SO WE KEPT OUR DISTANCE BUT KEPT A CLOSE WATCH.
WELCOME BACK, TASUKU.
BY THE WAY...
WHERE THE HELL HAVE YOU BEEN?!
YOU STUPID JERK!
I'm sorry...
AND AS PROMISED...
Ahh... This café au lait is delicious.
Boss, your strategy worked perfectly.
Ha ha ha... Thanks. You did a great job yourself.
...SMILES RETURNED TO EVERYONE'S FACES.
AGH!
WHAM
IDIOT!

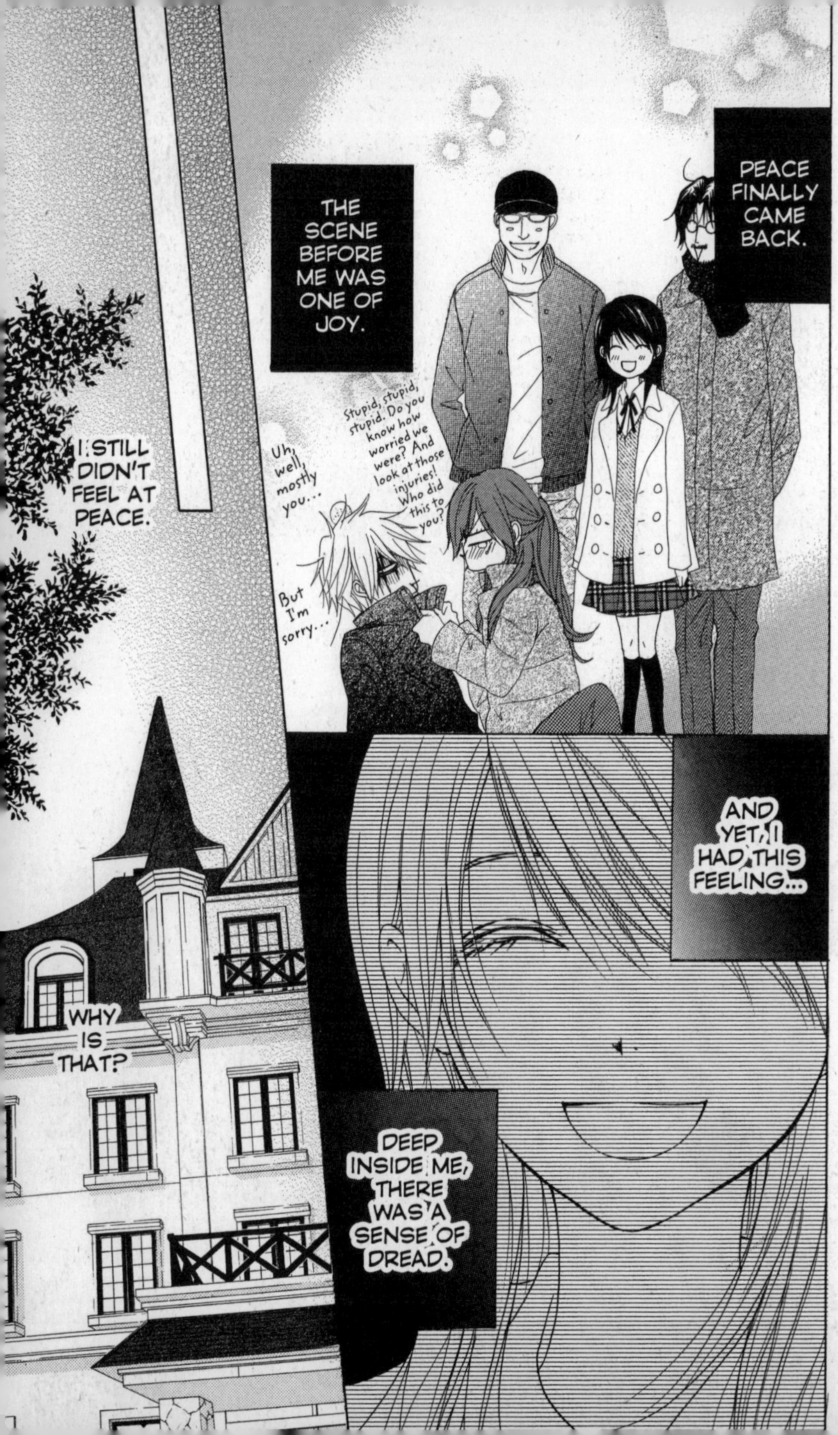
PEACE FINALLY CAME BACK.
THE SCENE BEFORE ME WAS ONE OF JOY.
Stupid, stupid, stupid. Do you know how worried we were? And look at those injuries! Who did this to you?
Uh, well, mostly you...
But I'm sorry...
AND YET, I HAD THIS FEELING...
DEEP INSIDE ME, THERE WAS A SENSE OF DREAD.
I STILL DIDN'T FEEL AT PEACE.
WHY IS THAT?

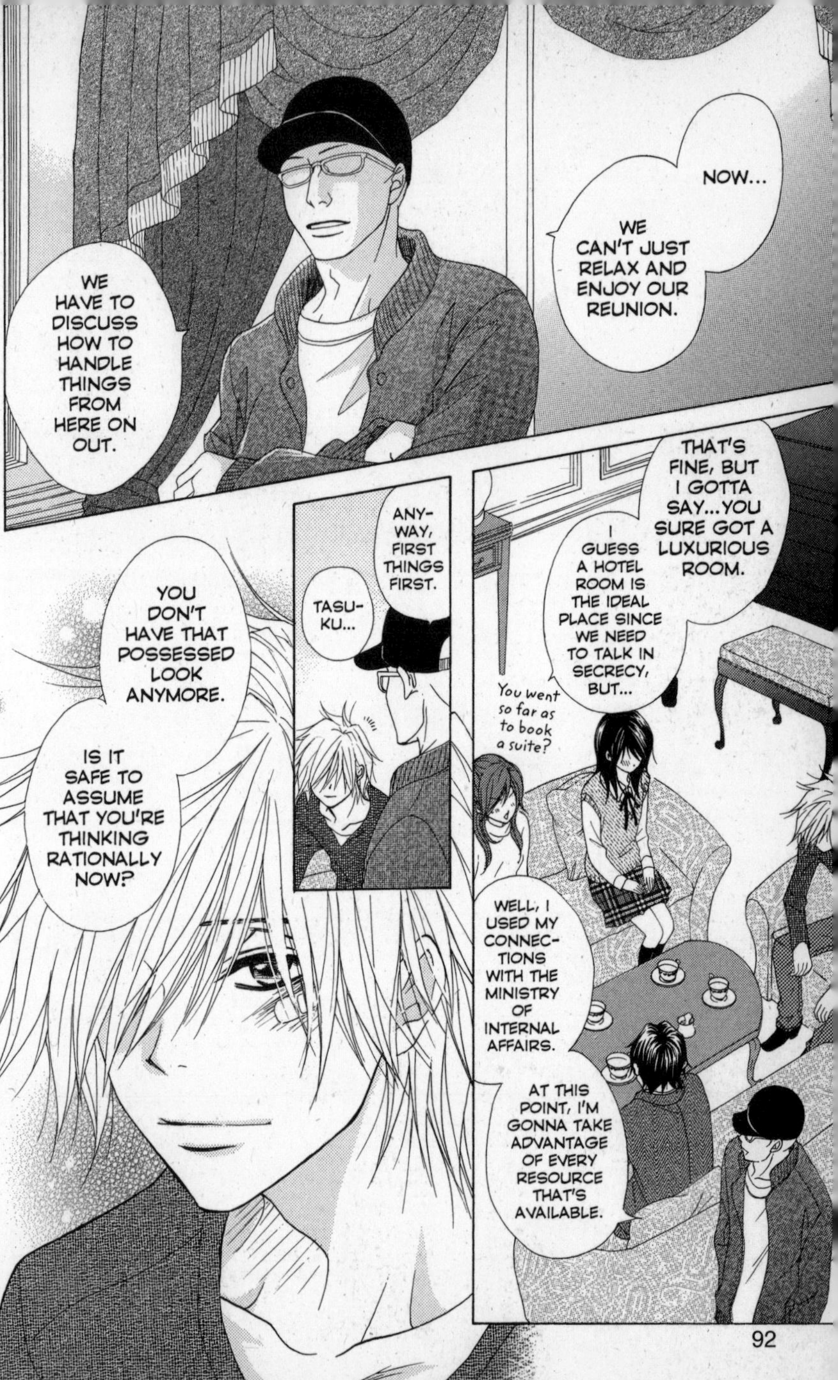
NOW...
WE CAN'T JUST RELAX AND ENJOY OUR REUNION.
WE HAVE TO DISCUSS HOW TO HANDLE THINGS FROM HERE ON OUT.
THAT'S FINE, BUT I GOTTA SAY...YOU SURE GOT A LUXURIOUS ROOM.
I GUESS A HOTEL ROOM IS THE IDEAL PLACE SINCE WE NEED TO TALK IN SECRECY, BUT...
You went so far as to book a suite?
WELL, I USED MY CONNECTIONS WITH THE MINISTRY OF INTERNAL AFFAIRS.
AT THIS POINT, I'M GONNA TAKE ADVANTAGE OF EVERY RESOURCE THAT'S AVAILABLE.
ANYWAY, FIRST THINGS FIRST.
TASUKU...
YOU DON'T HAVE THAT POSSESSED LOOK ANYMORE.
IS IT SAFE TO ASSUME THAT YOU'RE THINKING RATIONALLY NOW?

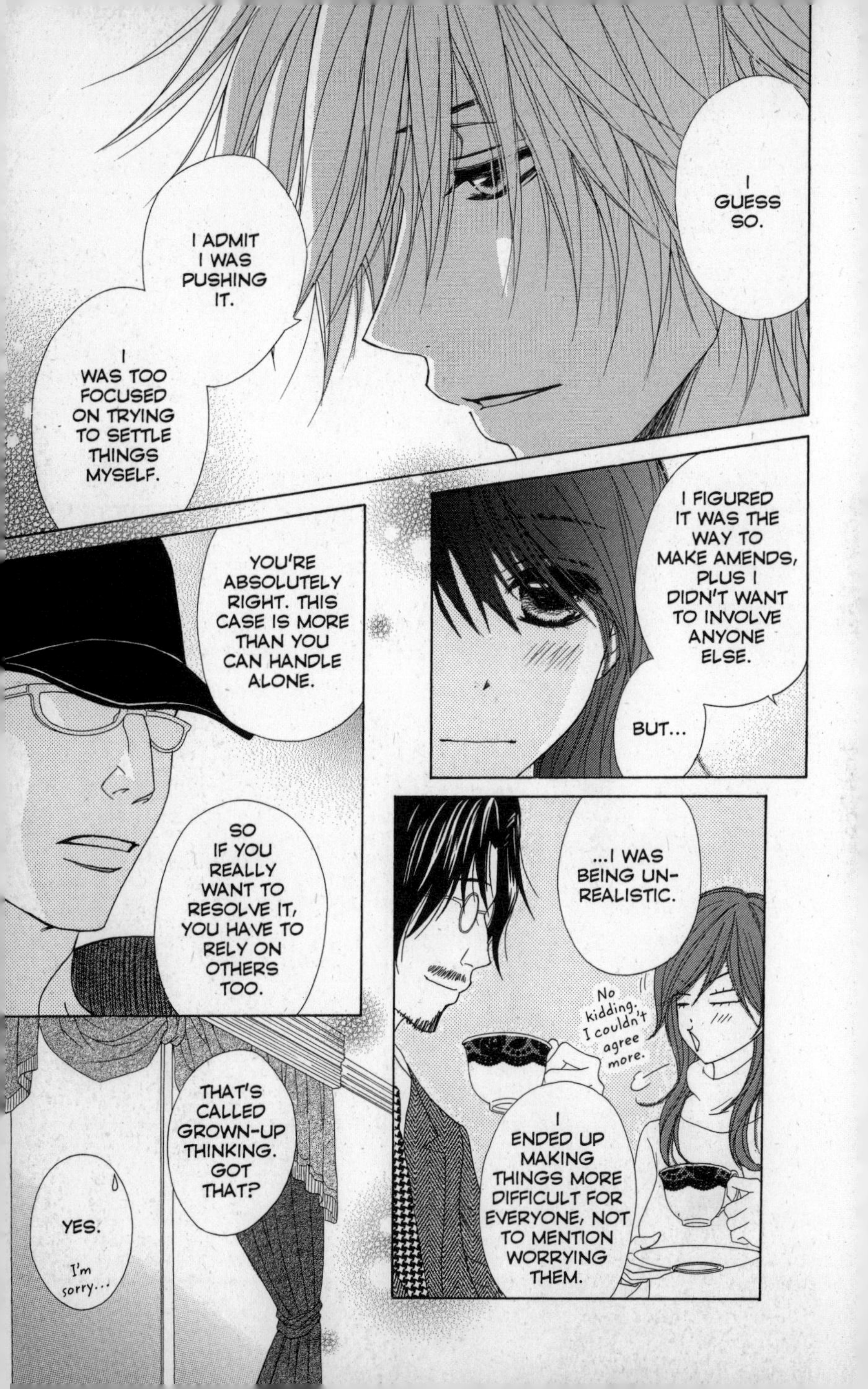
I GUESS SO.
I ADMIT I WAS PUSHING IT.
I WAS TOO FOCUSED ON TRYING TO SETTLE THINGS MYSELF.
I FIGURED IT WAS THE WAY TO MAKE AMENDS, PLUS I DIDN'T WANT TO INVOLVE ANYONE ELSE.
BUT...
...I WAS BEING UN-REALISTIC.
No kidding, I couldn't agree more.
I ENDED UP MAKING THINGS MORE DIFFICULT FOR EVERYONE, NOT TO MENTION WORRYING THEM.
YOU'RE ABSOLUTELY RIGHT. THIS CASE IS MORE THAN YOU CAN HANDLE ALONE.
SO IF YOU REALLY WANT TO RESOLVE IT, YOU HAVE TO RELY ON OTHERS TOO.
THAT'S CALLED GROWN-UP THINKING. GOT THAT?
YES.
I'm sorry...

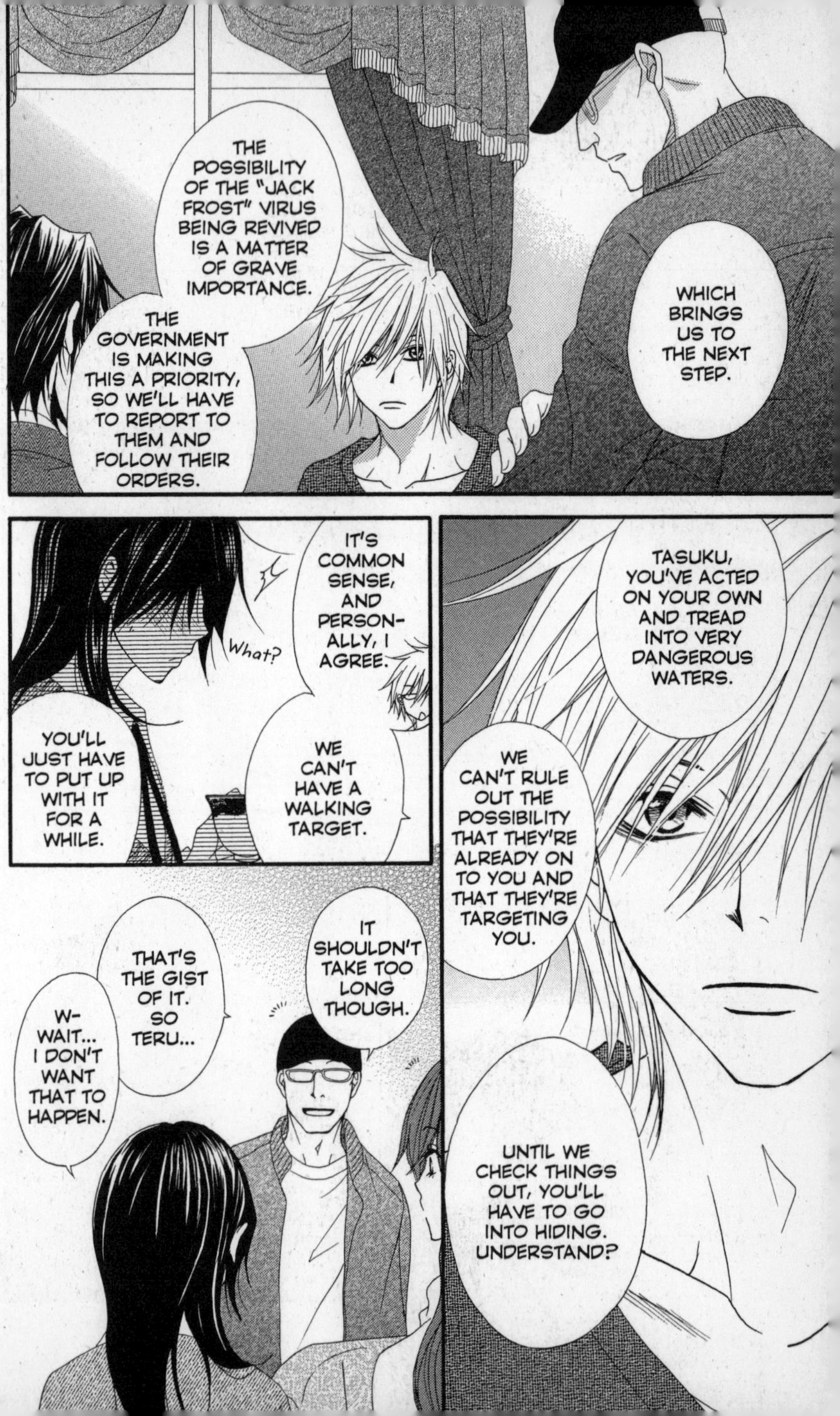
THE POSSIBILITY OF THE "JACK FROST" VIRUS BEING REVIVED IS A MATTER OF GRAVE IMPORTANCE.
THE GOVERNMENT IS MAKING THIS A PRIORITY, SO WE'LL HAVE TO REPORT TO THEM AND FOLLOW THEIR ORDERS.
WHICH BRINGS US TO THE NEXT STEP.
TASUKU, YOU'VE ACTED ON YOUR OWN AND TREAD INTO VERY DANGEROUS WATERS.
WE CAN'T RULE OUT THE POSSIBILITY THAT THEY'RE ALREADY ON TO YOU AND THAT THEY'RE TARGETING YOU.
UNTIL WE CHECK THINGS OUT, YOU'LL HAVE TO GO INTO HIDING. UNDERSTAND?
IT'S COMMON SENSE, AND PERSONALLY, I AGREE.
What?
WE CAN'T HAVE A WALKING TARGET.
YOU'LL JUST HAVE TO PUT UP WITH IT FOR A WHILE.
IT SHOULDN'T TAKE TOO LONG THOUGH.
THAT'S THE GIST OF IT. SO TERU...
W-WAIT... I DON'T WANT THAT TO HAPPEN.

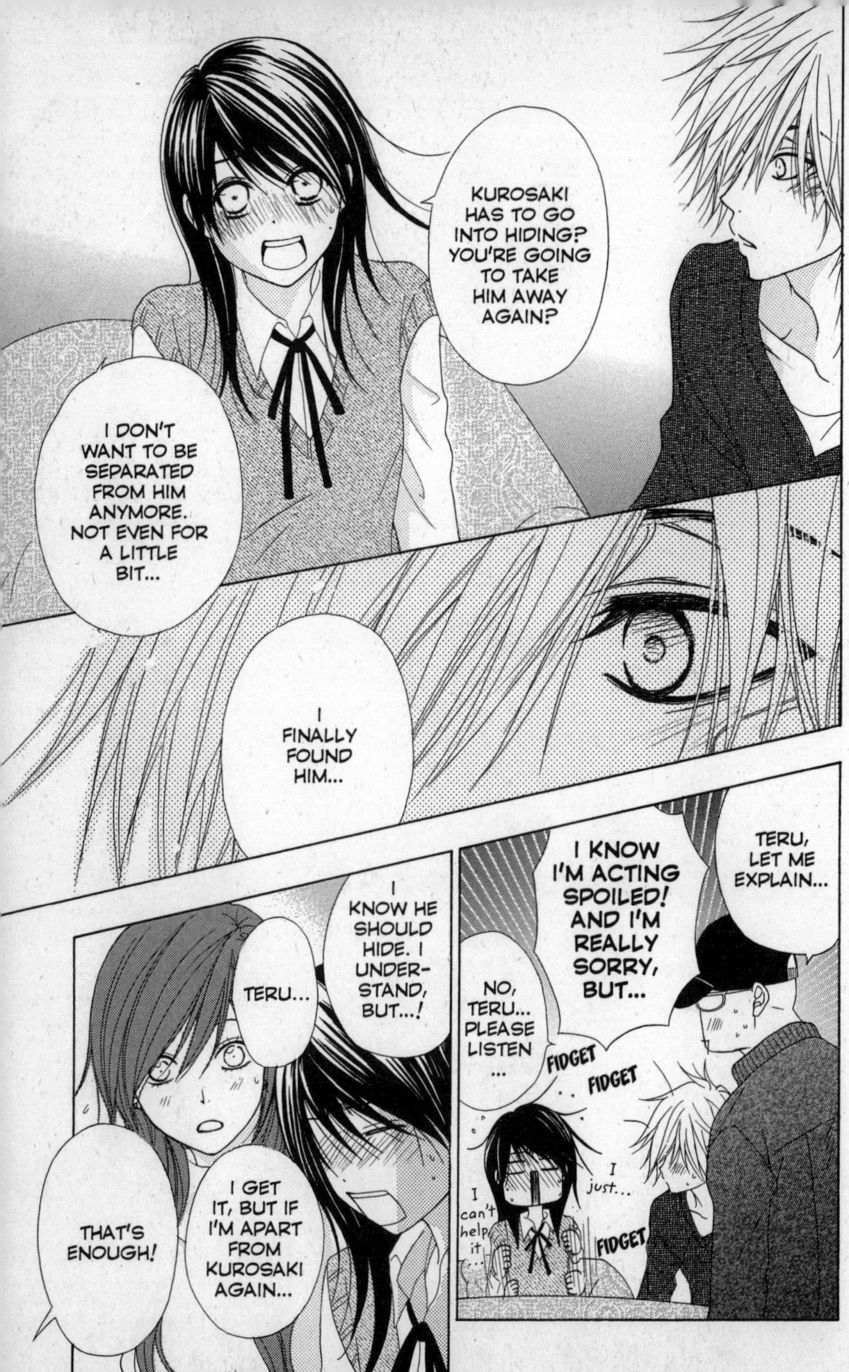
KUROSAKI HAS TO GO INTO HIDING? YOU'RE GOING TO TAKE HIM AWAY AGAIN?
I DON'T WANT TO BE SEPARATED FROM HIM ANYMORE. NOT EVEN FOR A LITTLE BIT...
I FINALLY FOUND HIM...
TERU, LET ME EXPLAIN...
I KNOW I'M ACTING SPOILED! AND I'M REALLY SORRY, BUT...
NO, TERU... PLEASE LISTEN ...
FIDGET
FIDGET
I just...
I can't help it...
FIDGET
I KNOW HE SHOULD HIDE. I UNDER-STAND, BUT...!
TERU...
I GET IT, BUT IF I'M APART FROM KUROSAKI AGAIN...
THAT'S ENOUGH!

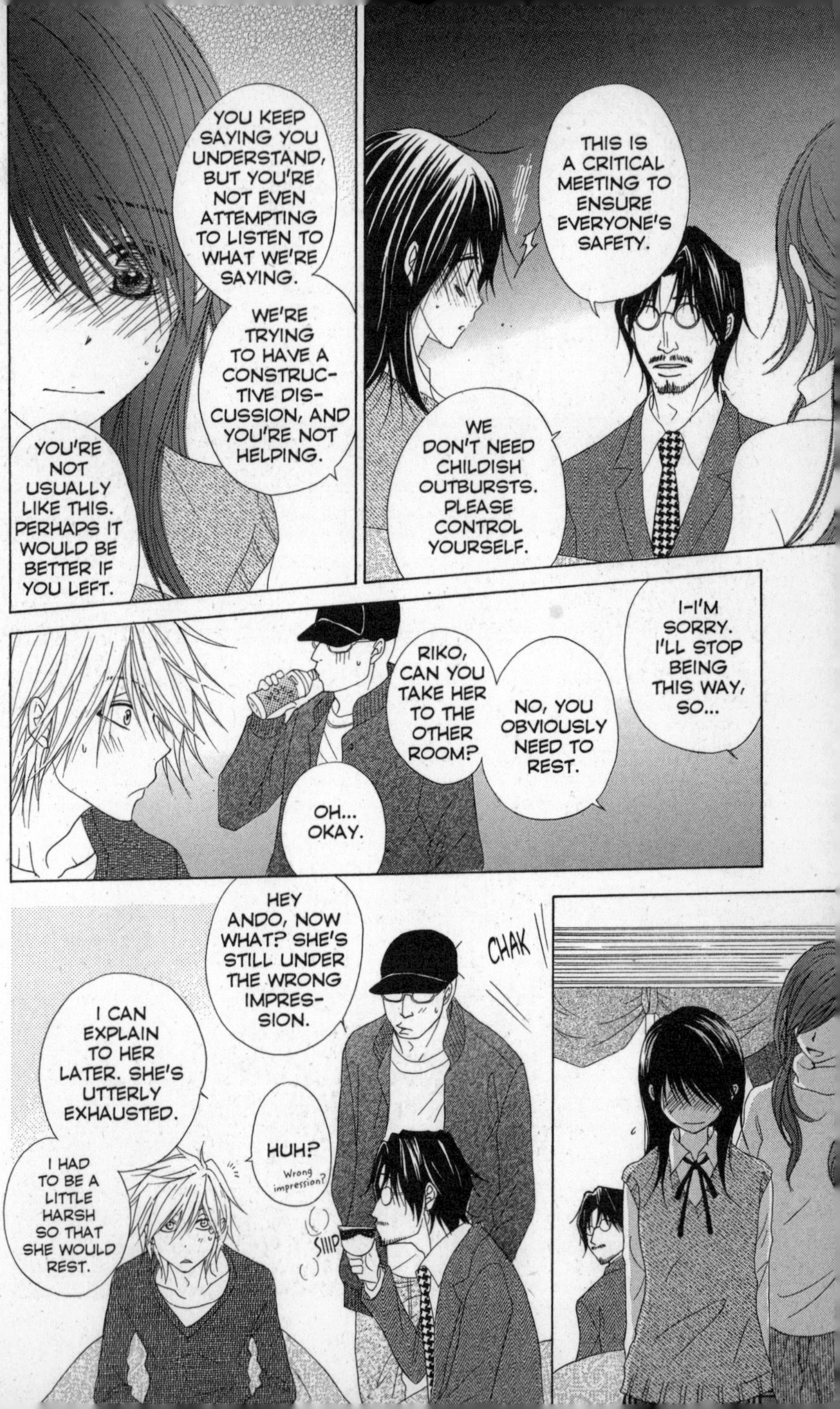
THIS IS A CRITICAL MEETING TO ENSURE EVERYONE'S SAFETY.
WE DON'T NEED CHILDISH OUTBURSTS. PLEASE CONTROL YOURSELF.
YOU KEEP SAYING YOU UNDERSTAND, BUT YOU'RE NOT EVEN ATTEMPTING TO LISTEN TO WHAT WE'RE SAYING.
WE'RE TRYING TO HAVE A CONSTRUCTIVE DISCUSSION, AND YOU'RE NOT HELPING.
YOU'RE NOT USUALLY LIKE THIS. PERHAPS IT WOULD BE BETTER IF YOU LEFT.
I-I'M SORRY. I'LL STOP BEING THIS WAY, SO...
NO, YOU OBVIOUSLY NEED TO REST.
RIKO, CAN YOU TAKE HER TO THE OTHER ROOM?
OH... OKAY.
CHAK
HEY ANDO, NOW WHAT? SHE'S STILL UNDER THE WRONG IMPRESSION.
HUH?
Wrong impression?
I CAN EXPLAIN TO HER LATER. SHE'S UTTERLY EXHAUSTED.
I HAD TO BE A LITTLE HARSH SO THAT SHE WOULD REST.
SIIIP

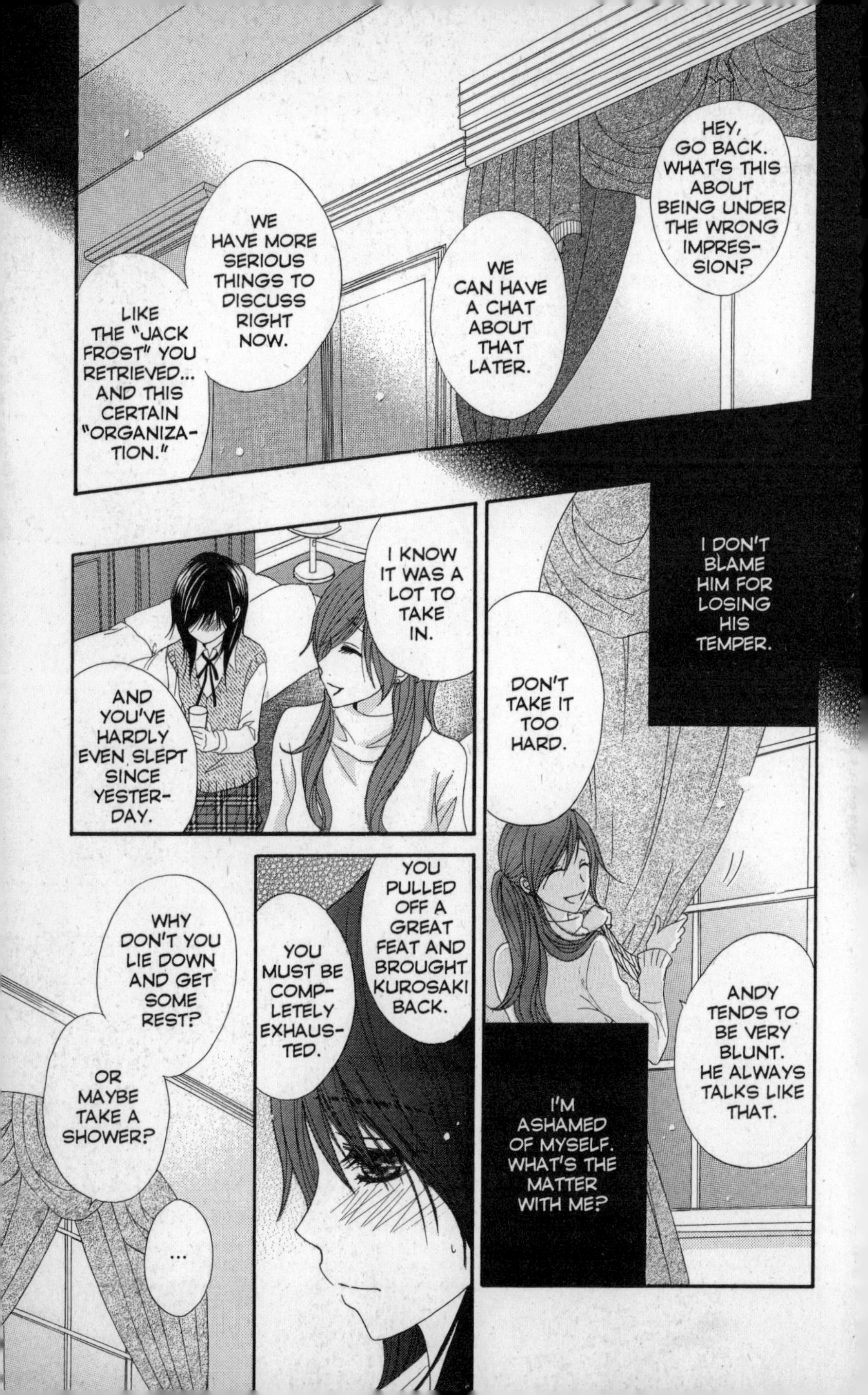
HEY, GO BACK. WHAT'S THIS ABOUT BEING UNDER THE WRONG IMPRES-SION?
WE CAN HAVE A CHAT ABOUT THAT LATER.
WE HAVE MORE SERIOUS THINGS TO DISCUSS RIGHT NOW.
LIKE THE "JACK FROST" YOU RETRIEVED... AND THIS CERTAIN "ORGANIZA-TION."
I DON'T BLAME HIM FOR LOSING HIS TEMPER.
DON'T TAKE IT TOO HARD.
ANDY TENDS TO BE VERY BLUNT. HE ALWAYS TALKS LIKE THAT.
I'M ASHAMED OF MYSELF. WHAT'S THE MATTER WITH ME?
I KNOW IT WAS A LOT TO TAKE IN.
AND YOU'VE HARDLY EVEN SLEPT SINCE YESTER-DAY.
YOU PULLED OFF A GREAT FEAT AND BROUGHT KUROSAKI BACK.
YOU MUST BE COMP-LETELY EXHAUS-TED.
WHY DON'T YOU LIE DOWN AND GET SOME REST?
OR MAYBE TAKE A SHOWER?
...

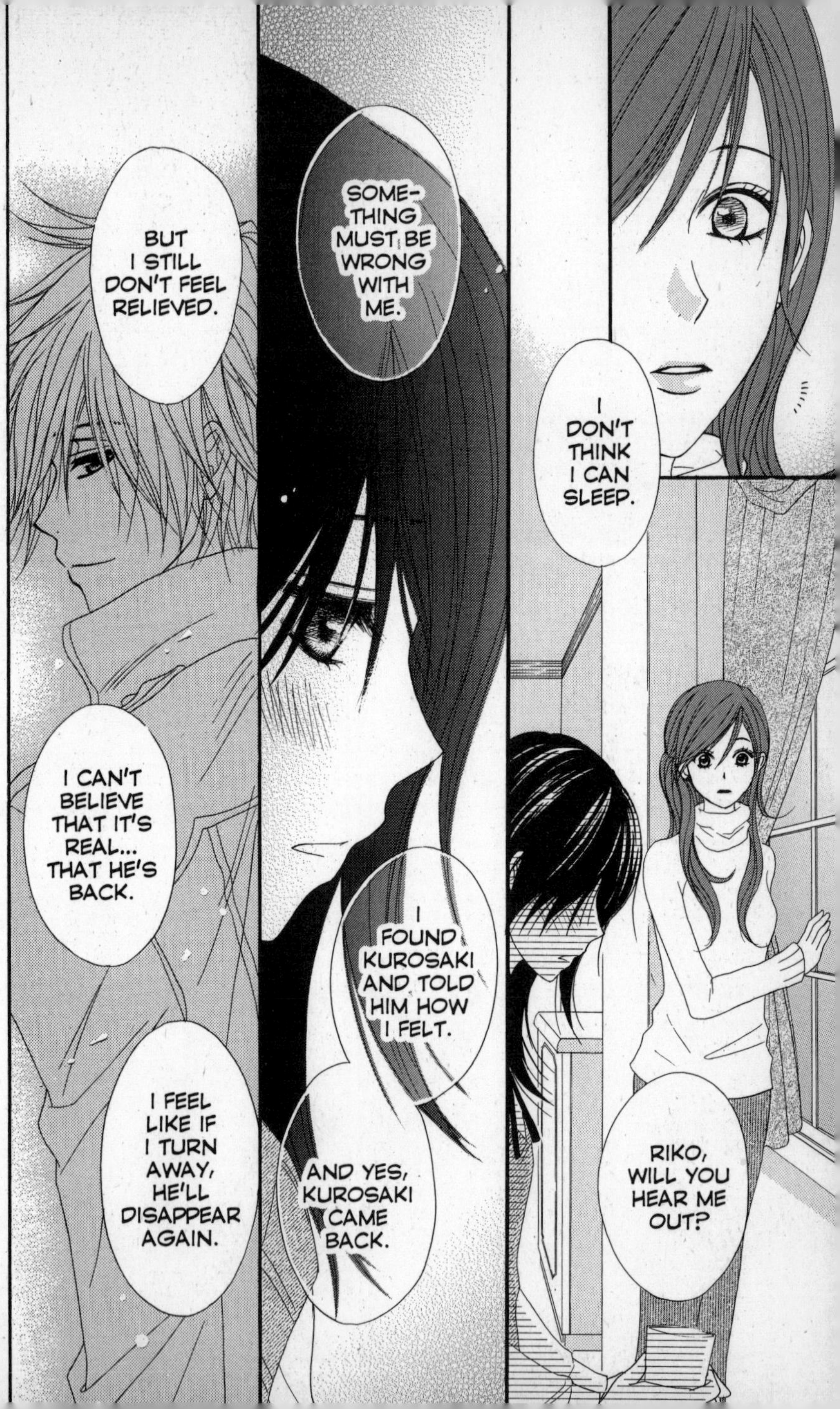
I DON'T THINK I CAN SLEEP.
RIKO, WILL YOU HEAR ME OUT?
SOME-THING MUST BE WRONG WITH ME.
I FOUND KUROSAKI AND TOLD HIM HOW I FELT.
AND YES, KUROSAKI CAME BACK.
BUT I STILL DON'T FEEL RELIEVED.
I CAN'T BELIEVE THAT IT'S REAL... THAT HE'S BACK.
I FEEL LIKE IF I TURN AWAY, HE'LL DISAPPEAR AGAIN.

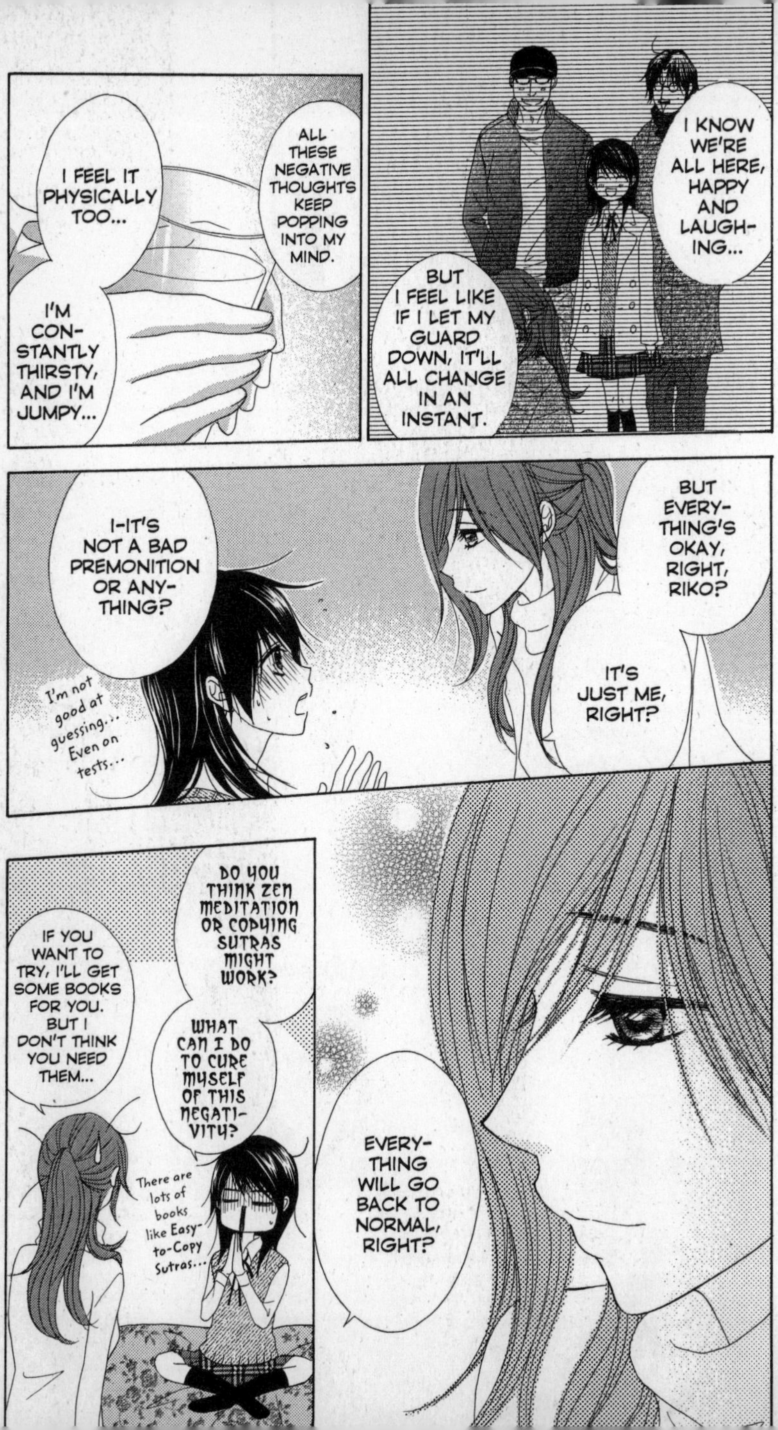
I KNOW WE'RE ALL HERE, HAPPY AND LAUGHING...
BUT I FEEL LIKE IF I LET MY GUARD DOWN, IT'LL ALL CHANGE IN AN INSTANT.
ALL THESE NEGATIVE THOUGHTS KEEP POPPING INTO MY MIND.
I FEEL IT PHYSICALLY TOO...
I'M CONSTANTLY THIRSTY, AND I'M JUMPY...
BUT EVERYTHING'S OKAY, RIGHT, RIKO?
IT'S JUST ME, RIGHT?
I-IT'S NOT A BAD PREMONITION OR ANYTHING?
I'm not good at guessing... Even on tests...
EVERYTHING WILL GO BACK TO NORMAL, RIGHT?
DO YOU THINK ZEN MEDITATION OR COPYING SUTRAS MIGHT WORK?
WHAT CAN I DO TO CURE MYSELF OF THIS NEGATIVITY?
IF YOU WANT TO TRY, I'LL GET SOME BOOKS FOR YOU. BUT I DON'T THINK YOU NEED THEM...
There are lots of books like Easy-to-Copy Sutras...

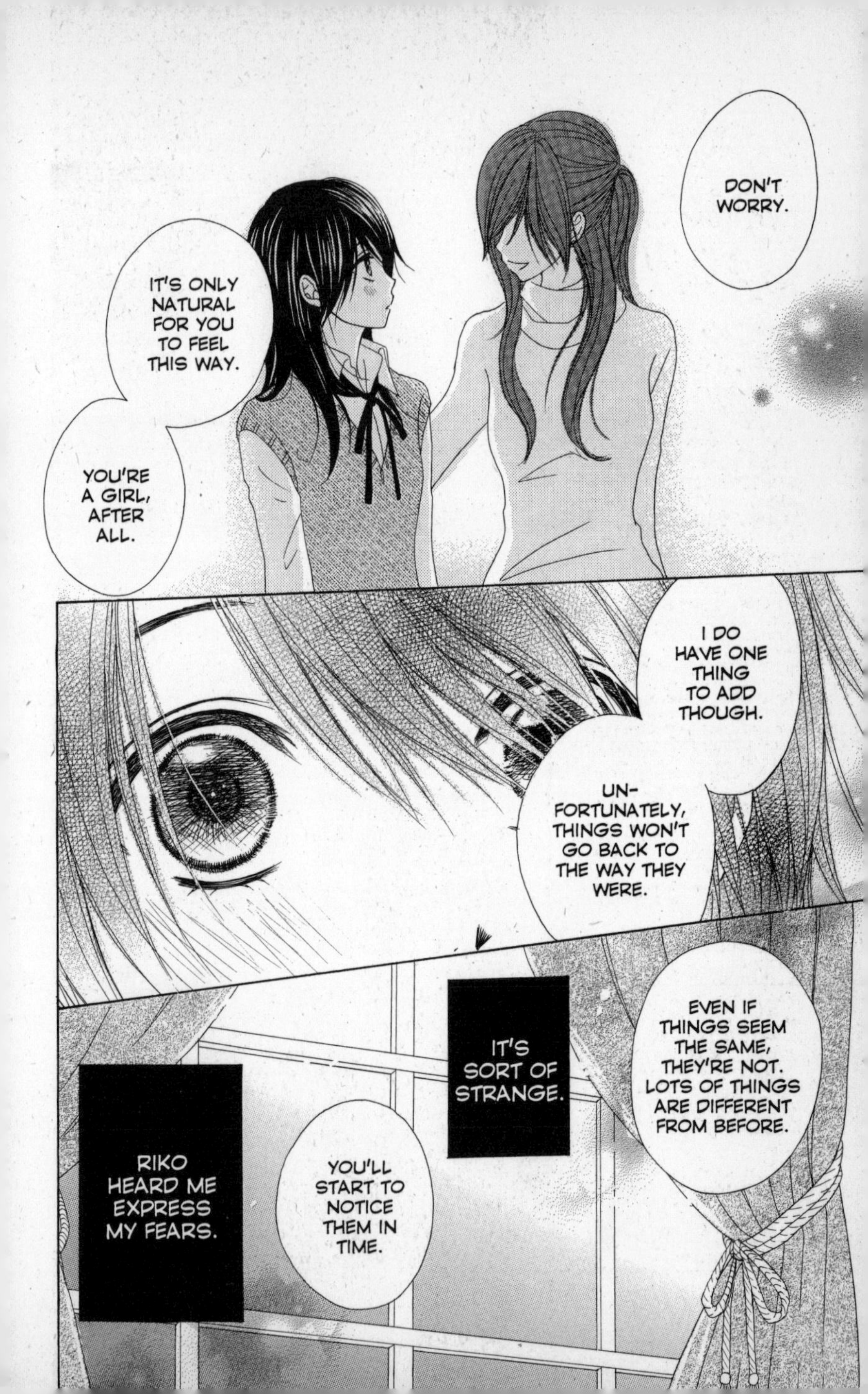
DON'T WORRY.
IT'S ONLY NATURAL FOR YOU TO FEEL THIS WAY.
YOU'RE A GIRL, AFTER ALL.
I DO HAVE ONE THING TO ADD THOUGH.
UN-FORTUNATELY, THINGS WON'T GO BACK TO THE WAY THEY WERE.
EVEN IF THINGS SEEM THE SAME, THEY'RE NOT. LOTS OF THINGS ARE DIFFERENT FROM BEFORE.
IT'S SORT OF STRANGE.
YOU'LL START TO NOTICE THEM IN TIME.
RIKO HEARD ME EXPRESS MY FEARS.

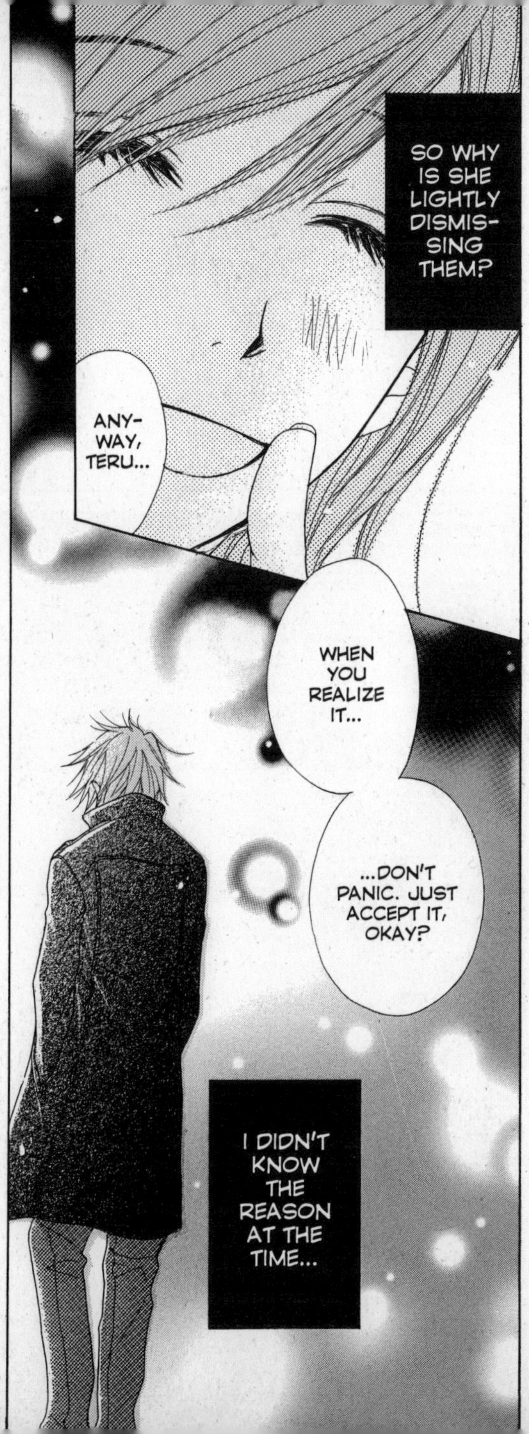
SO WHY IS SHE LIGHTLY DISMIS-SING THEM?
ANY-WAY, TERU...
WHEN YOU REALIZE IT...
...DON'T PANIC. JUST ACCEPT IT, OKAY?
I DIDN'T KNOW THE REASON AT THE TIME...

DENGEKI DAISY QUESTION CORNER

BALDLY ASK!! ③

Q. TERU KNOWS KUROSAKI AND DAISY'S EMAIL ADDRESSES, RIGHT? IF THEY'RE THE SAME, TERU WOULD KNOW THAT THEY'RE THE SAME PERSON. HOW DID YOU HANDLE THIS? I'M SUPER CONCERNED.

(S.T., CHIBA PREFECTURE)

A. YES, THAT MIGHT HAVE BEEN DIFFICULT TO PICK UP ON. SOMEWHERE AROUND VOLUME 3, TERU MISTAKENLY SENDS KUROSAKI HER MESSAGE INSTEAD OF TO DAISY, AND KUROSAKI RETRIEVES HIS EMAIL VIA HIS CELL PHONE AS USUAL. ACTUALLY, KUROSAKI HAD GIVEN TERU THE EMAIL ADDRESS OF HIS COMPUTER ACCOUNT AT HOME. KUROSAKI HAD IT SET UP SO THAT TERU'S EMAIL TO DAISY WOULD GO TO HIS HOME COMPUTER ACCOUNT, WHICH WOULD THEN BE REROUTED TO HIS CELL PHONE. SO YOU HAVE TO HAND IT TO KUROSAKI... HE DIDN'T GIVE TERU THE SAME EMAIL ADDRESS. THAT WAS A GOOD QUESTION.

Q. WHEN TASUKU SMOKES, HE SEEMS SO GROWN-UP AND I LOVE HIM. BUT PRICES HAVE GONE UP, SO DO YOU EVER THINK ABOUT MAKING HIM QUIT?

(M.I., NAGANO PREFECTURE)

A. M.I., YOU ARE SO KIND. TO BE HONEST, THERE IS QUITE A BIT OF PRESSURE ABOUT THAT, BUT HE'LL CONTINUE SMOKING. ALTHOUGH KUROSAKI SEEMS TO BE THINKING ABOUT IT... THAT HE SHOULD JUST QUIT SMOKING ALREADY.

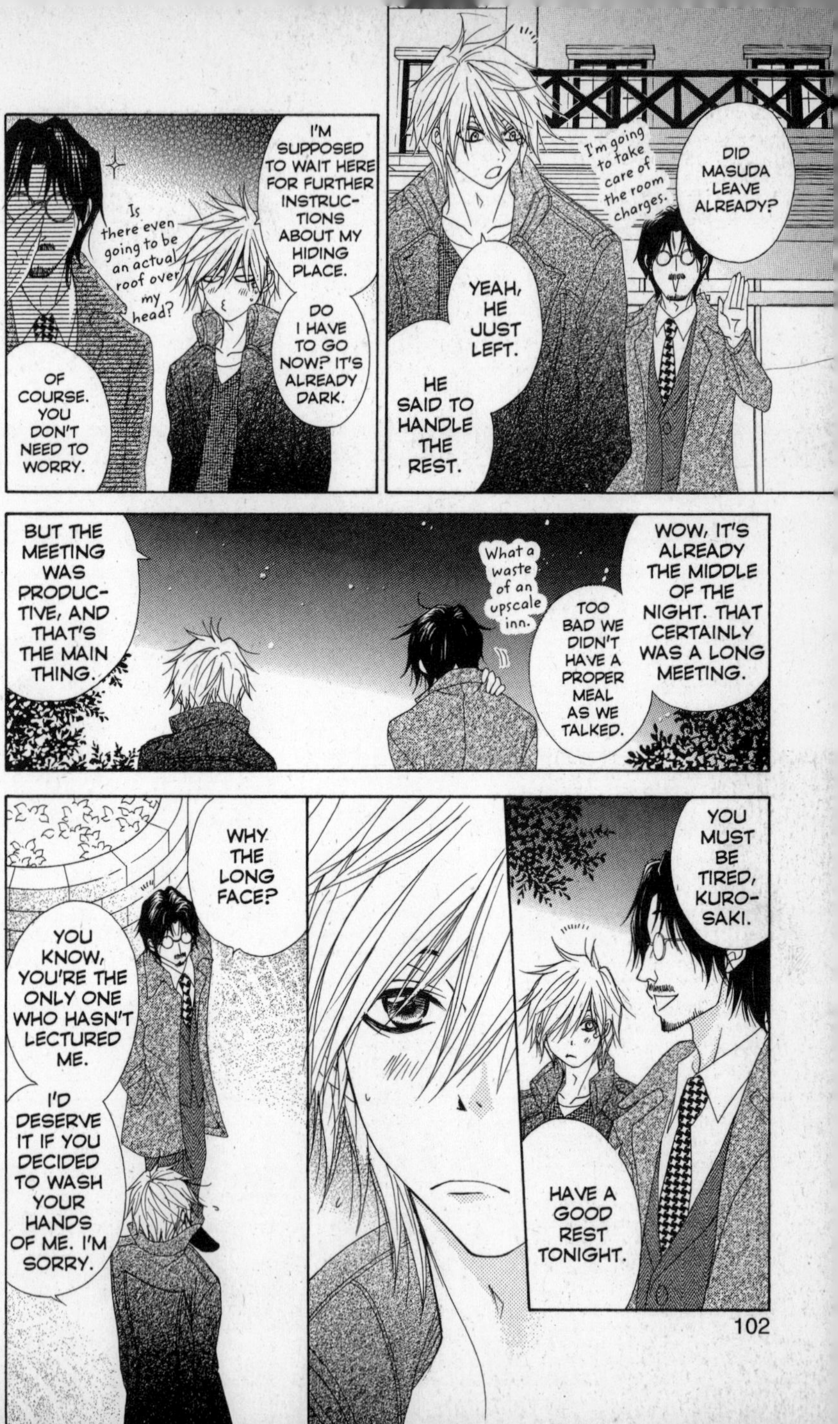
DID MASUDA LEAVE ALREADY?
I'm going to take care of the room charges.
YEAH, HE JUST LEFT.
HE SAID TO HANDLE THE REST.
I'M SUPPOSED TO WAIT HERE FOR FURTHER INSTRUCTIONS ABOUT MY HIDING PLACE.
Is there even going to be an actual roof over my head?
DO I HAVE TO GO NOW? IT'S ALREADY DARK.
OF COURSE. YOU DON'T NEED TO WORRY.
WOW, IT'S ALREADY THE MIDDLE OF THE NIGHT. THAT CERTAINLY WAS A LONG MEETING.
TOO BAD WE DIDN'T HAVE A PROPER MEAL AS WE TALKED.
What a waste of an upscale inn.
BUT THE MEETING WAS PRODUCTIVE, AND THAT'S THE MAIN THING.
YOU MUST BE TIRED, KUROSAKI.
HAVE A GOOD REST TONIGHT.
WHY THE LONG FACE?
YOU KNOW, YOU'RE THE ONLY ONE WHO HASN'T LECTURED ME.
I'D DESERVE IT IF YOU DECIDED TO WASH YOUR HANDS OF ME. I'M SORRY.

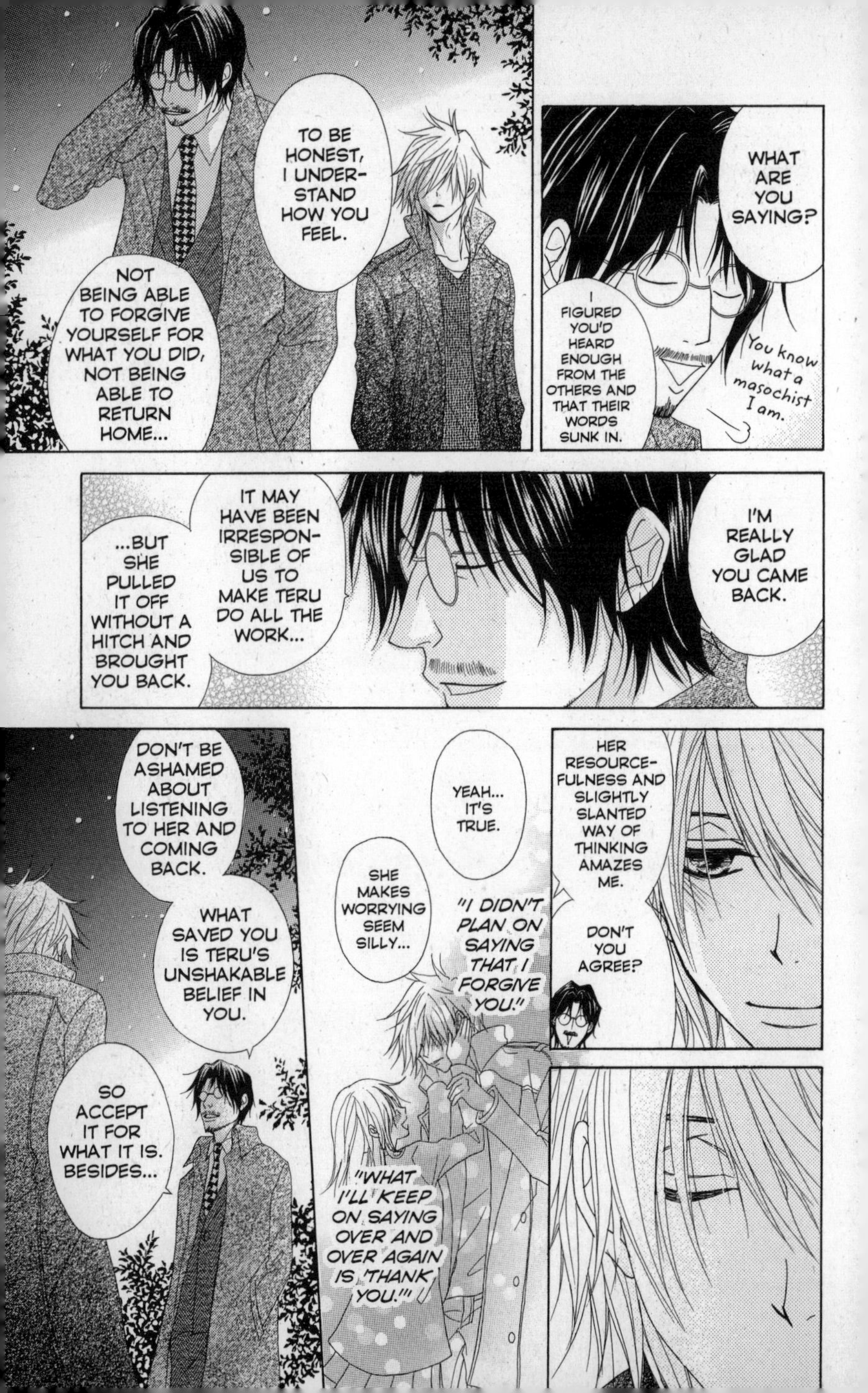
TO BE HONEST, I UNDER-STAND HOW YOU FEEL.
NOT BEING ABLE TO FORGIVE YOURSELF FOR WHAT YOU DID, NOT BEING ABLE TO RETURN HOME...
WHAT ARE YOU SAYING?
I FIGURED YOU'D HEARD ENOUGH FROM THE OTHERS AND THAT THEIR WORDS SUNK IN.
You know what a masochist I am.
IT MAY HAVE BEEN IRRESPON-SIBLE OF US TO MAKE TERU DO ALL THE WORK...
...BUT SHE PULLED IT OFF WITHOUT A HITCH AND BROUGHT YOU BACK.
I'M REALLY GLAD YOU CAME BACK.
DON'T BE ASHAMED ABOUT LISTENING TO HER AND COMING BACK.
WHAT SAVED YOU IS TERU'S UNSHAKABLE BELIEF IN YOU.
SO ACCEPT IT FOR WHAT IT IS. BESIDES...
HER RESOURCE-FULNESS AND SLIGHTLY SLANTED WAY OF THINKING AMAZES ME.
DON'T YOU AGREE?
YEAH... IT'S TRUE.
SHE MAKES WORRYING SEEM SILLY...
"I DIDN'T PLAN ON SAYING THAT I FORGIVE YOU."
"WHAT I'LL KEEP ON SAYING OVER AND OVER AGAIN IS 'THANK YOU.'"

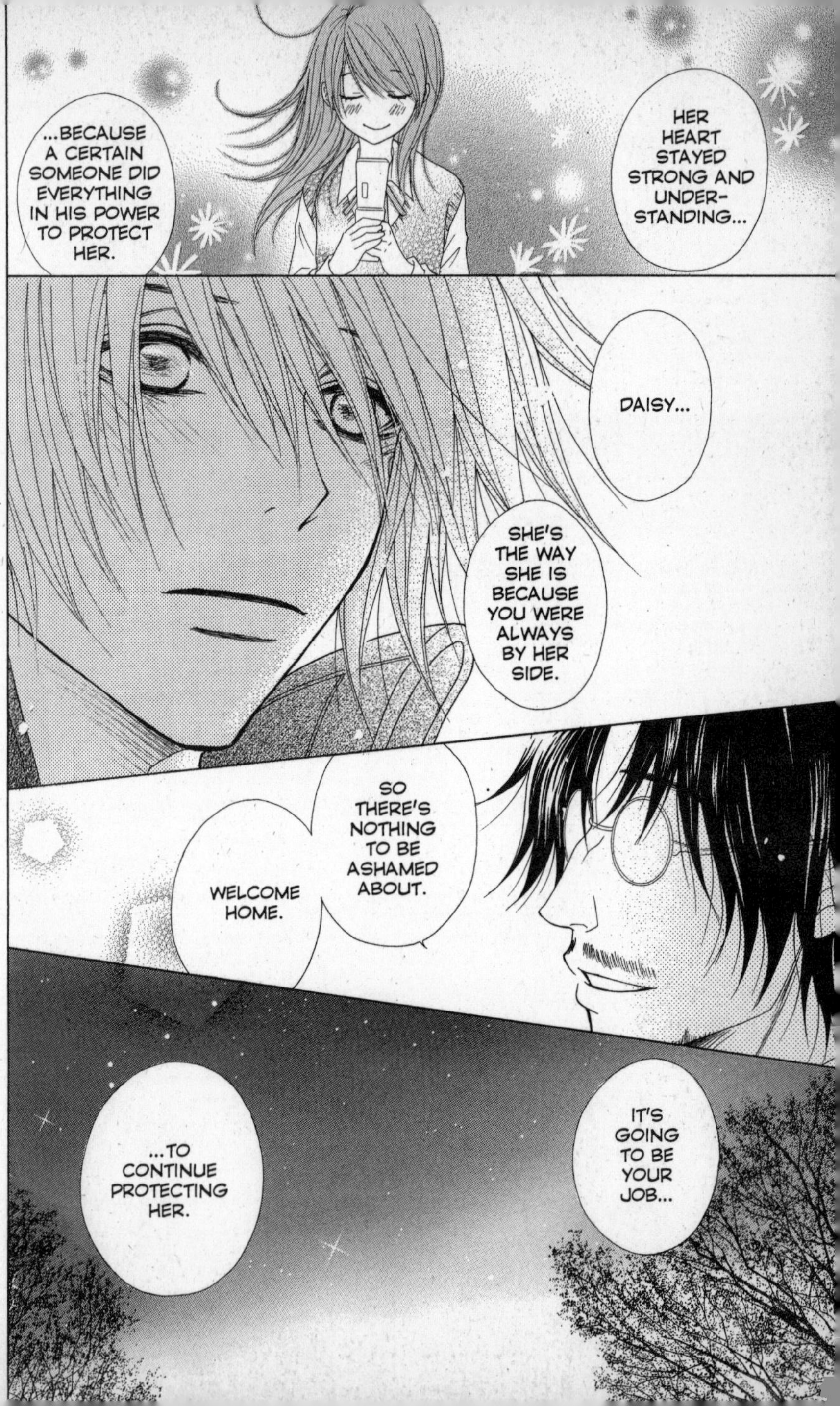
HER HEART STAYED STRONG AND UNDER-STANDING...
...BECAUSE A CERTAIN SOMEONE DID EVERYTHING IN HIS POWER TO PROTECT HER.
DAISY...
SHE'S THE WAY SHE IS BECAUSE YOU WERE ALWAYS BY HER SIDE.
SO THERE'S NOTHING TO BE ASHAMED ABOUT.
WELCOME HOME.
IT'S GOING TO BE YOUR JOB...
...TO CONTINUE PROTECTING HER.

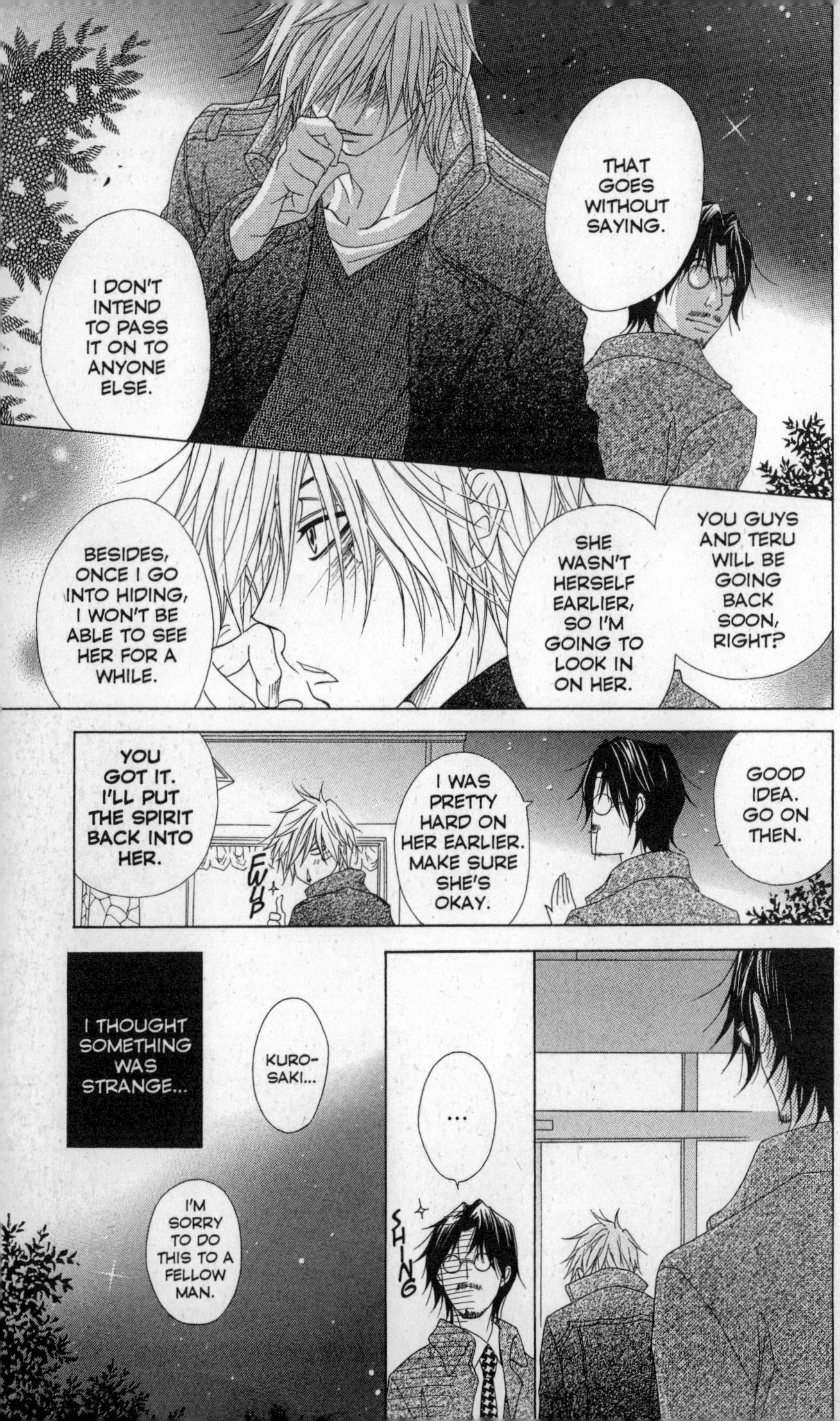
THAT GOES WITHOUT SAYING.
I DON'T INTEND TO PASS IT ON TO ANYONE ELSE.
YOU GUYS AND TERU WILL BE GOING BACK SOON, RIGHT?
SHE WASN'T HERSELF EARLIER, SO I'M GOING TO LOOK IN ON HER.
BESIDES, ONCE I GO INTO HIDING, I WON'T BE ABLE TO SEE HER FOR A WHILE.
GOOD IDEA. GO ON THEN.
I WAS PRETTY HARD ON HER EARLIER. MAKE SURE SHE'S OKAY.
FWUP
YOU GOT IT. I'LL PUT THE SPIRIT BACK INTO HER.
...
SHING
I THOUGHT SOMETHING WAS STRANGE...
KURO-SAKI...
I'M SORRY TO DO THIS TO A FELLOW MAN.

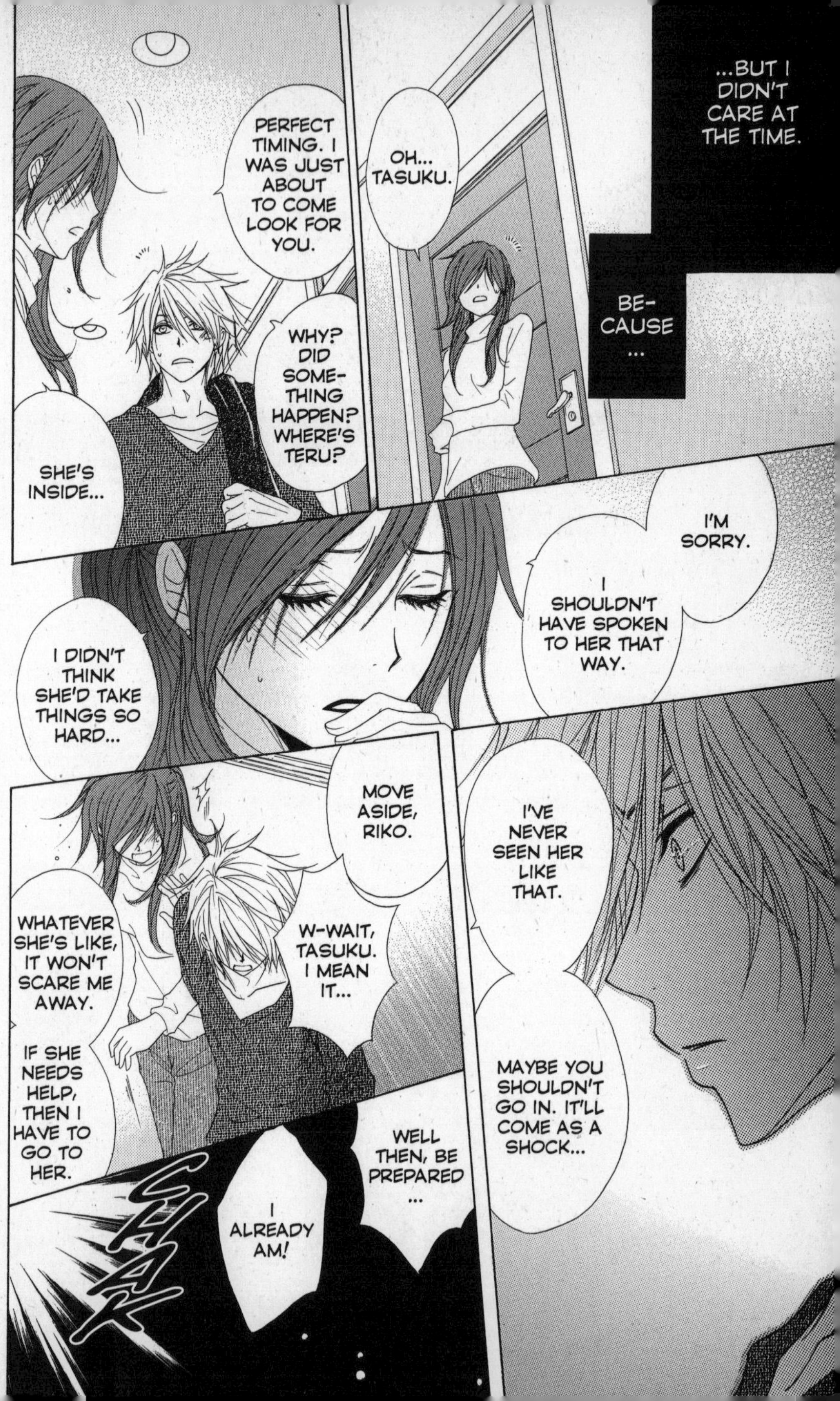
...BUT I DIDN'T CARE AT THE TIME.
BE-CAUSE ...
OH... TASUKU.
PERFECT TIMING. I WAS JUST ABOUT TO COME LOOK FOR YOU.
WHY? DID SOMETHING HAPPEN? WHERE'S TERU?
SHE'S INSIDE...
I'M SORRY.
I SHOULDN'T HAVE SPOKEN TO HER THAT WAY.
I DIDN'T THINK SHE'D TAKE THINGS SO HARD...
I'VE NEVER SEEN HER LIKE THAT.
MAYBE YOU SHOULDN'T GO IN. IT'LL COME AS A SHOCK...
MOVE ASIDE, RIKO.
W-WAIT, TASUKU. I MEAN IT...
WHATEVER SHE'S LIKE, IT WON'T SCARE ME AWAY.
IF SHE NEEDS HELP, THEN I HAVE TO GO TO HER.
WELL THEN, BE PREPARED ...
I ALREADY AM!
CHAK

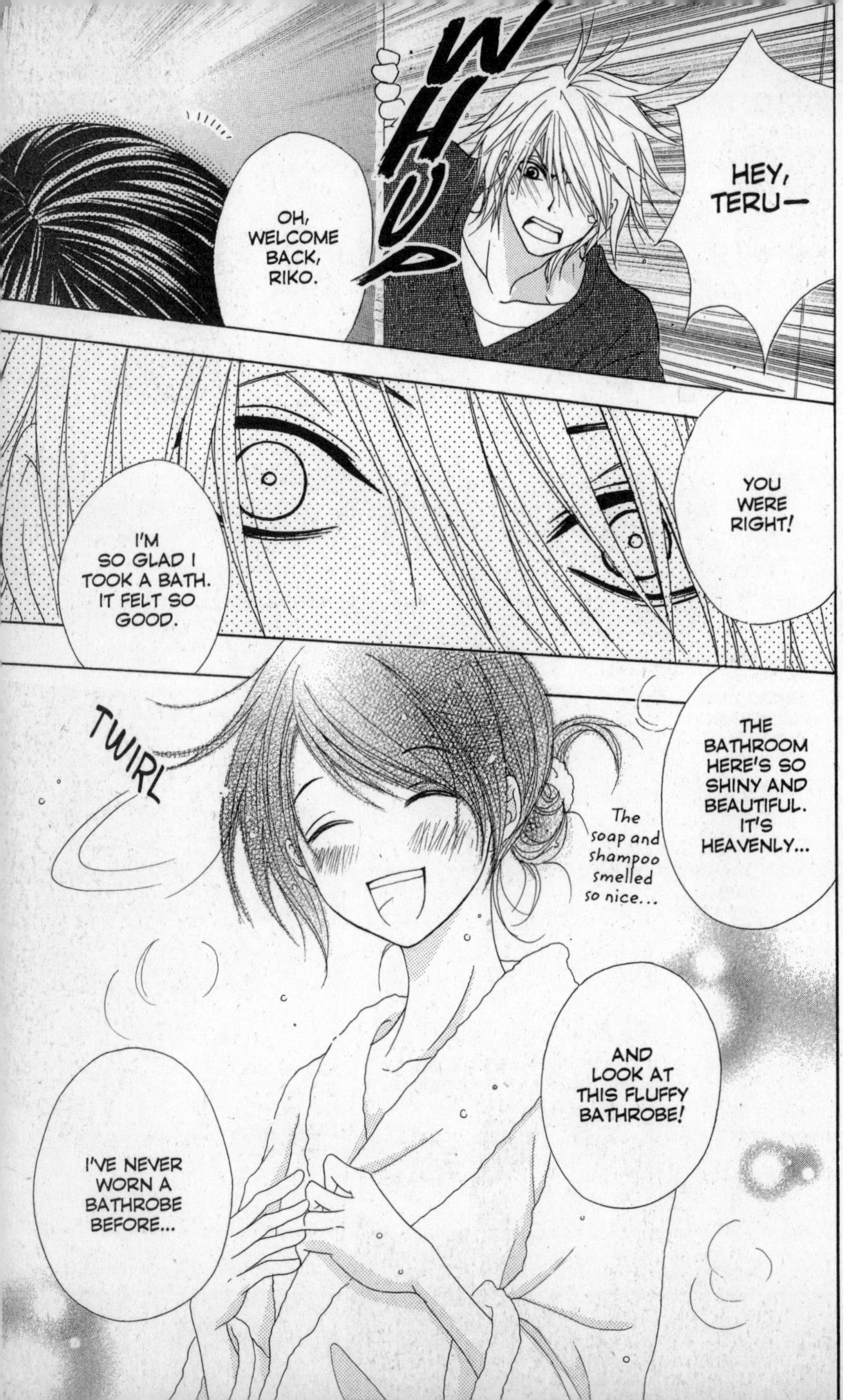
HEY, TERU—
WHIP
OH, WELCOME BACK, RIKO.
YOU WERE RIGHT!
I'M SO GLAD I TOOK A BATH. IT FELT SO GOOD.
THE BATHROOM HERE'S SO SHINY AND BEAUTIFUL. IT'S HEAVENLY...
The soap and shampoo smelled so nice...
TWIRL
AND LOOK AT THIS FLUFFY BATHROBE!
I'VE NEVER WORN A BATHROBE BEFORE...

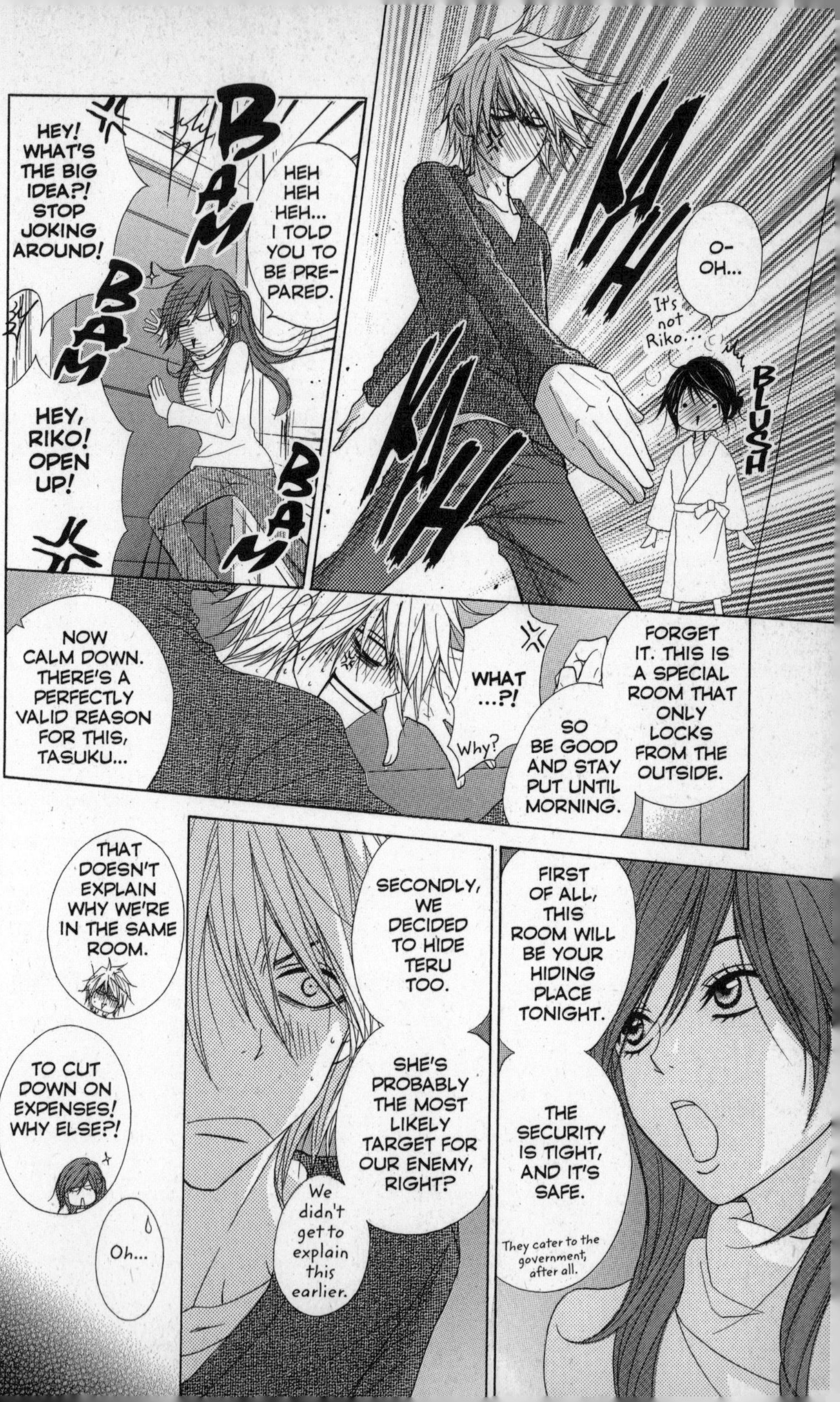
WAH
WAH
O-OH...
It's not Riko...
BLUSH
BAM
HEH HEH HEH... I TOLD YOU TO BE PRE-PARED.
HEY! WHAT'S THE BIG IDEA?! STOP JOKING AROUND!
BAM
BAM
HEY, RIKO! OPEN UP!
BAM
FORGET IT. THIS IS A SPECIAL ROOM THAT ONLY LOCKS FROM THE OUTSIDE.
SO BE GOOD AND STAY PUT UNTIL MORNING.
WHAT ...?!
Why?
NOW CALM DOWN. THERE'S A PERFECTLY VALID REASON FOR THIS, TASUKU...
FIRST OF ALL, THIS ROOM WILL BE YOUR HIDING PLACE TONIGHT.
THE SECURITY IS TIGHT, AND IT'S SAFE.
They cater to the government, after all.
SECONDLY, WE DECIDED TO HIDE TERU TOO.
SHE'S PROBABLY THE MOST LIKELY TARGET FOR OUR ENEMY, RIGHT?
We didn't get to explain this earlier.
THAT DOESN'T EXPLAIN WHY WE'RE IN THE SAME ROOM.
TO CUT DOWN ON EXPENSES! WHY ELSE?!
Oh...

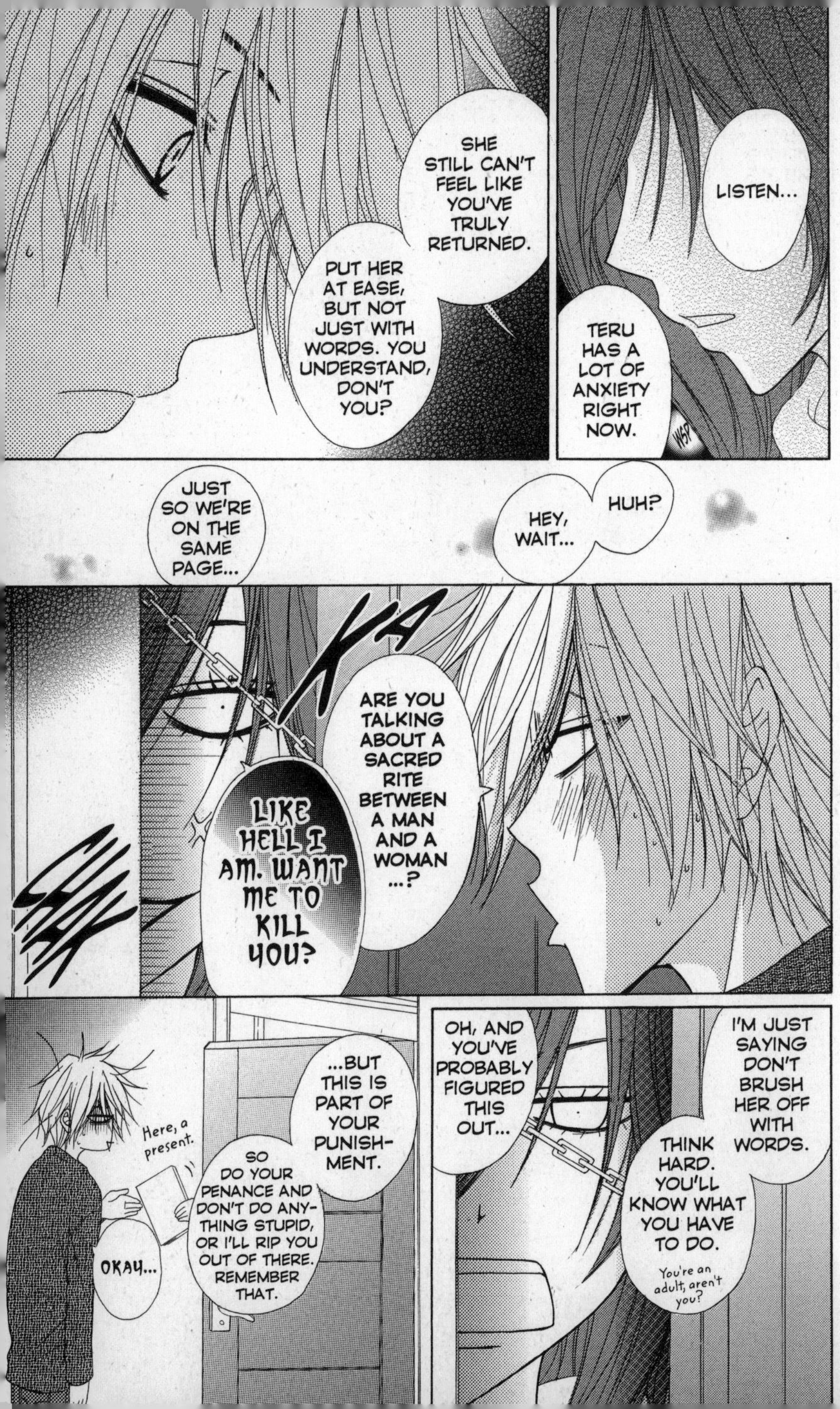
LISTEN...
TERU HAS A LOT OF ANXIETY RIGHT NOW.
WSP
SHE STILL CAN'T FEEL LIKE YOU'VE TRULY RETURNED.
PUT HER AT EASE, BUT NOT JUST WITH WORDS. YOU UNDERSTAND, DON'T YOU?
HUH?
HEY, WAIT...
JUST SO WE'RE ON THE SAME PAGE...
KA
ARE YOU TALKING ABOUT A SACRED RITE BETWEEN A MAN AND A WOMAN ...?
LIKE HELL I AM. WANT ME TO KILL YOU?
CHAK
I'M JUST SAYING DON'T BRUSH HER OFF WITH WORDS.
OH, AND YOU'VE PROBABLY FIGURED THIS OUT...
THINK HARD. YOU'LL KNOW WHAT YOU HAVE TO DO.
You're an adult, aren't you?
...BUT THIS IS PART OF YOUR PUNISH- MENT.
SO DO YOUR PENANCE AND DON'T DO ANY- THING STUPID, OR I'LL RIP YOU OUT OF THERE. REMEMBER THAT.
Here, a present.
OKAY...

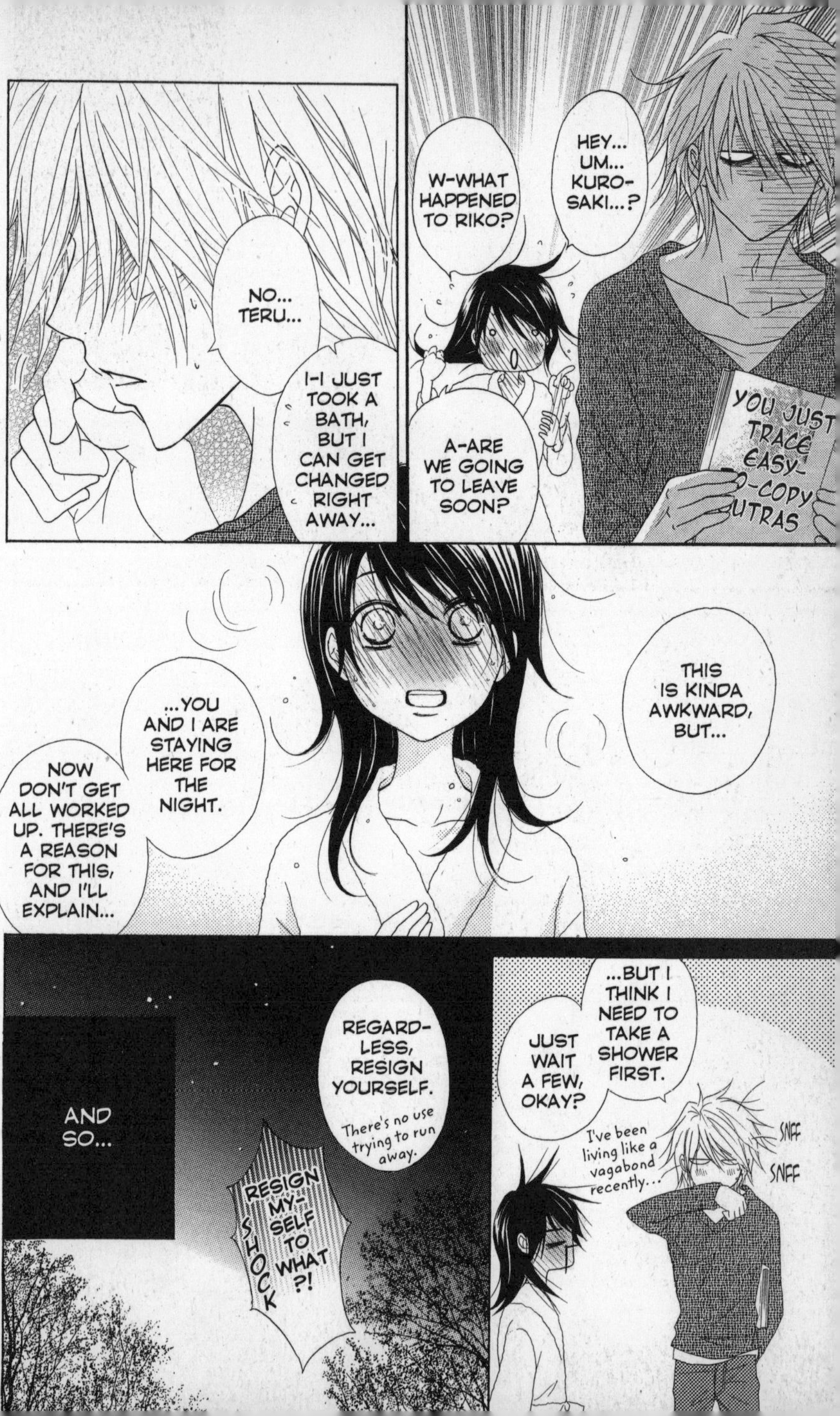
HEY... UM... KURO-SAKI...?
W-WHAT HAPPENED TO RIKO?
YOU JUST TRACE EASY-
O-COPY
UTRAS
A-ARE WE GOING TO LEAVE SOON?
NO... TERU...
I-I JUST TOOK A BATH, BUT I CAN GET CHANGED RIGHT AWAY...
THIS IS KINDA AWKWARD, BUT...
...YOU AND I ARE STAYING HERE FOR THE NIGHT.
NOW DON'T GET ALL WORKED UP. THERE'S A REASON FOR THIS, AND I'LL EXPLAIN...
...BUT I THINK I NEED TO TAKE A SHOWER FIRST.
JUST WAIT A FEW, OKAY?
SNFF
SNFF
I've been living like a vagabond recently...
REGARD-LESS, RESIGN YOURSELF.
There's no use trying to run away.
RESIGN MY-SELF TO WHAT?!
SHOCK
AND SO...

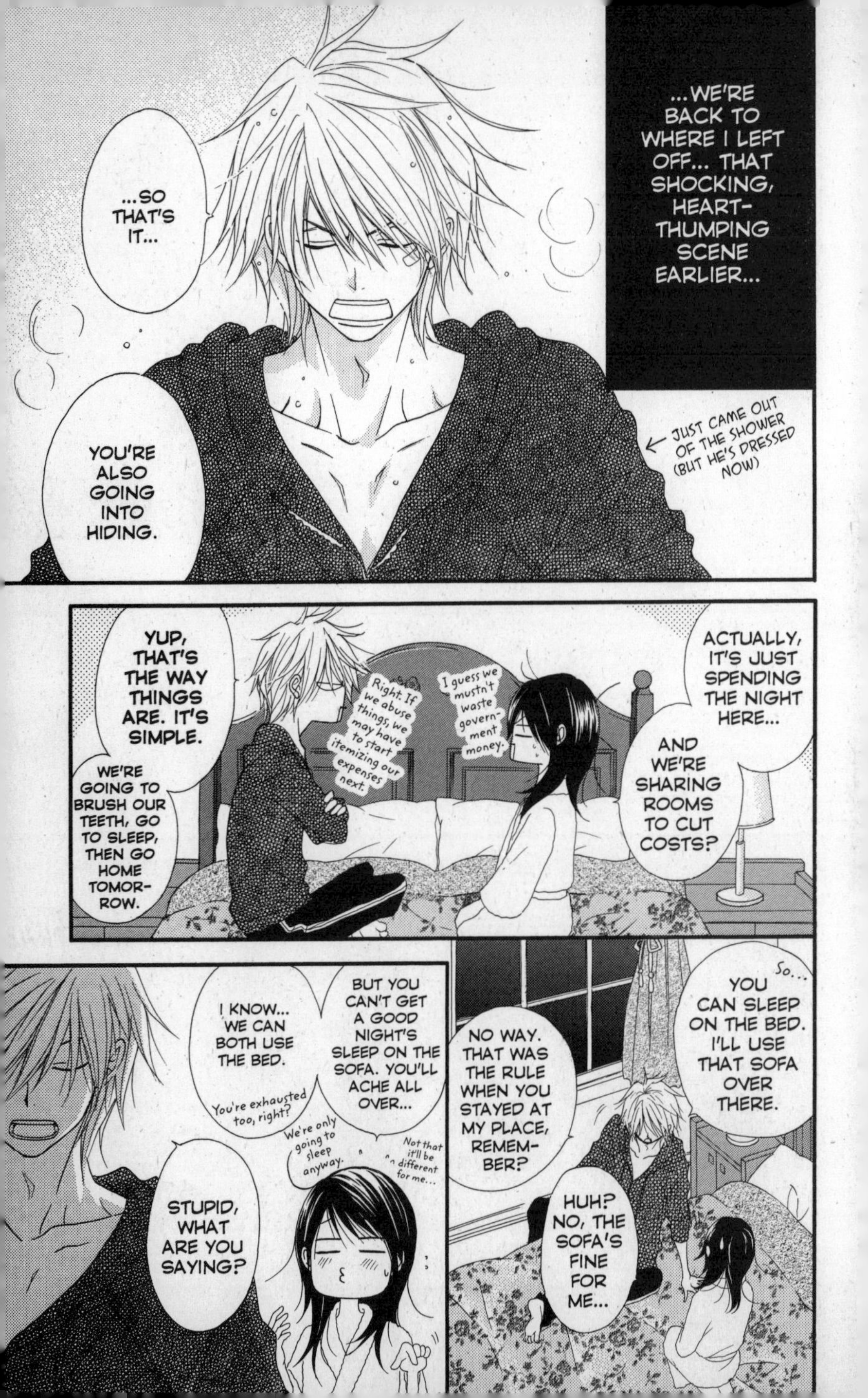
...WE'RE BACK TO WHERE I LEFT OFF... THAT SHOCKING, HEART-THUMPING SCENE EARLIER...
...SO THAT'S IT...
JUST CAME OUT OF THE SHOWER (BUT HE'S DRESSED NOW)
YOU'RE ALSO GOING INTO HIDING.
ACTUALLY, IT'S JUST SPENDING THE NIGHT HERE...
AND WE'RE SHARING ROOMS TO CUT COSTS?
I guess we mustn't waste government money.
YUP, THAT'S THE WAY THINGS ARE. IT'S SIMPLE.
Right. If we abuse things, we may have to start itemizing our expenses next.
WE'RE GOING TO BRUSH OUR TEETH, GO TO SLEEP, THEN GO HOME TOMORROW.
So...
YOU CAN SLEEP ON THE BED. I'LL USE THAT SOFA OVER THERE.
NO WAY. THAT WAS THE RULE WHEN YOU STAYED AT MY PLACE, REMEMBER?
HUH? NO, THE SOFA'S FINE FOR ME...
BUT YOU CAN'T GET A GOOD NIGHT'S SLEEP ON THE SOFA. YOU'LL ACHE ALL OVER...
I KNOW... WE CAN BOTH USE THE BED.
You're exhausted too, right?
Not that it'll be different for me...
We're only going to sleep anyway.
STUPID, WHAT ARE YOU SAYING?

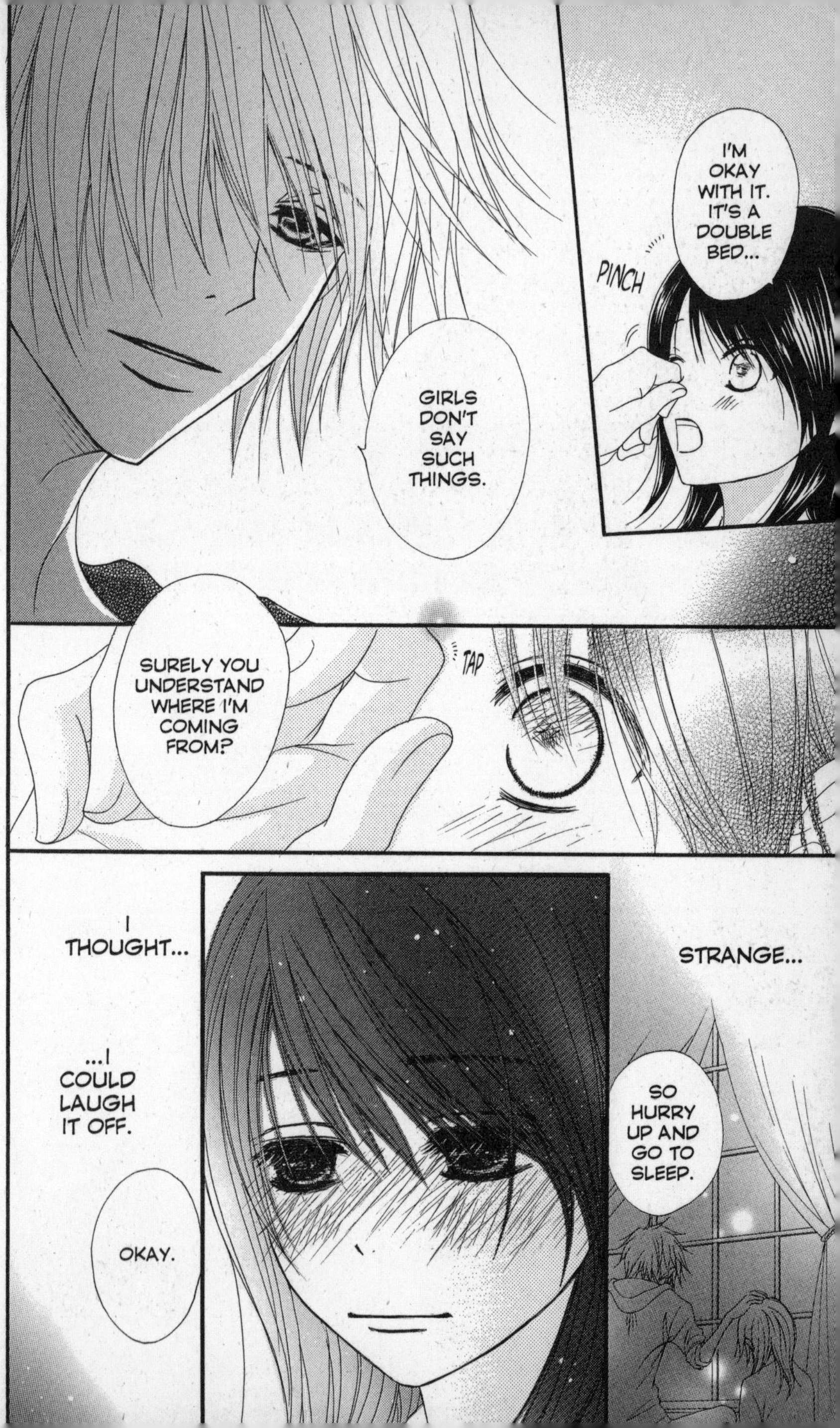
PINCH
I'M OKAY WITH IT. IT'S A DOUBLE BED...
GIRLS DON'T SAY SUCH THINGS.
TAP
SURELY YOU UNDERSTAND WHERE I'M COMING FROM?
STRANGE...
SO HURRY UP AND GO TO SLEEP.
I THOUGHT...
...I COULD LAUGH IT OFF.
OKAY.

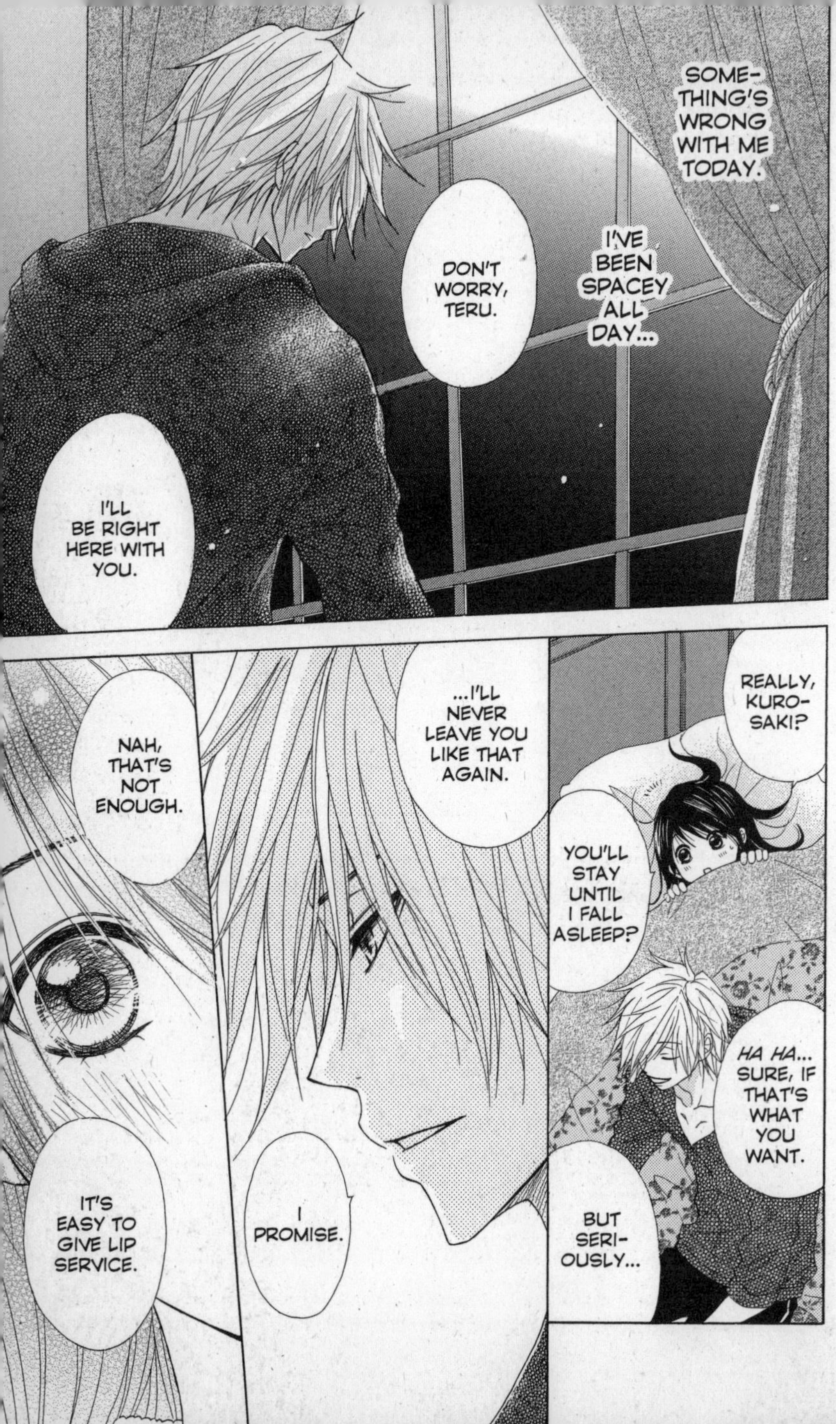
SOMETHING'S WRONG WITH ME TODAY.
I'VE BEEN SPACEY ALL DAY...
DON'T WORRY, TERU.
I'LL BE RIGHT HERE WITH YOU.
REALLY, KUROSAKI?
YOU'LL STAY UNTIL I FALL ASLEEP?
HA HA... SURE, IF THAT'S WHAT YOU WANT.
BUT SERIOUSLY...
...I'LL NEVER LEAVE YOU LIKE THAT AGAIN.
I PROMISE.
NAH, THAT'S NOT ENOUGH.
IT'S EASY TO GIVE LIP SERVICE.

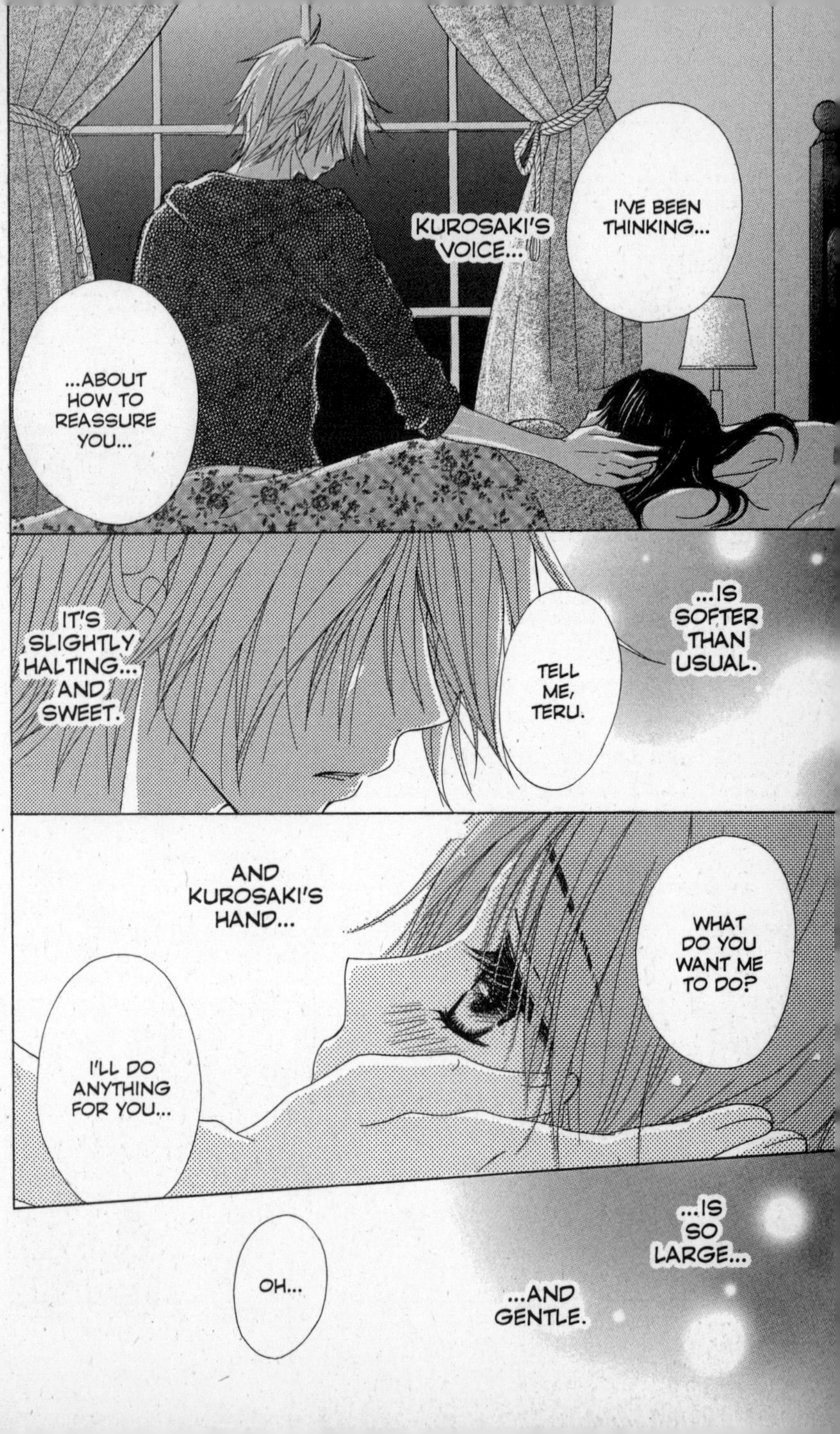
I'VE BEEN THINKING...
KUROSAKI'S VOICE...
...ABOUT HOW TO REASSURE YOU...
...IS SOFTER THAN USUAL.
TELL ME, TERU.
IT'S SLIGHTLY HALTING... AND SWEET.
WHAT DO YOU WANT ME TO DO?
AND KUROSAKI'S HAND...
I'LL DO ANYTHING FOR YOU...
...IS SO LARGE...
...AND GENTLE.
OH...

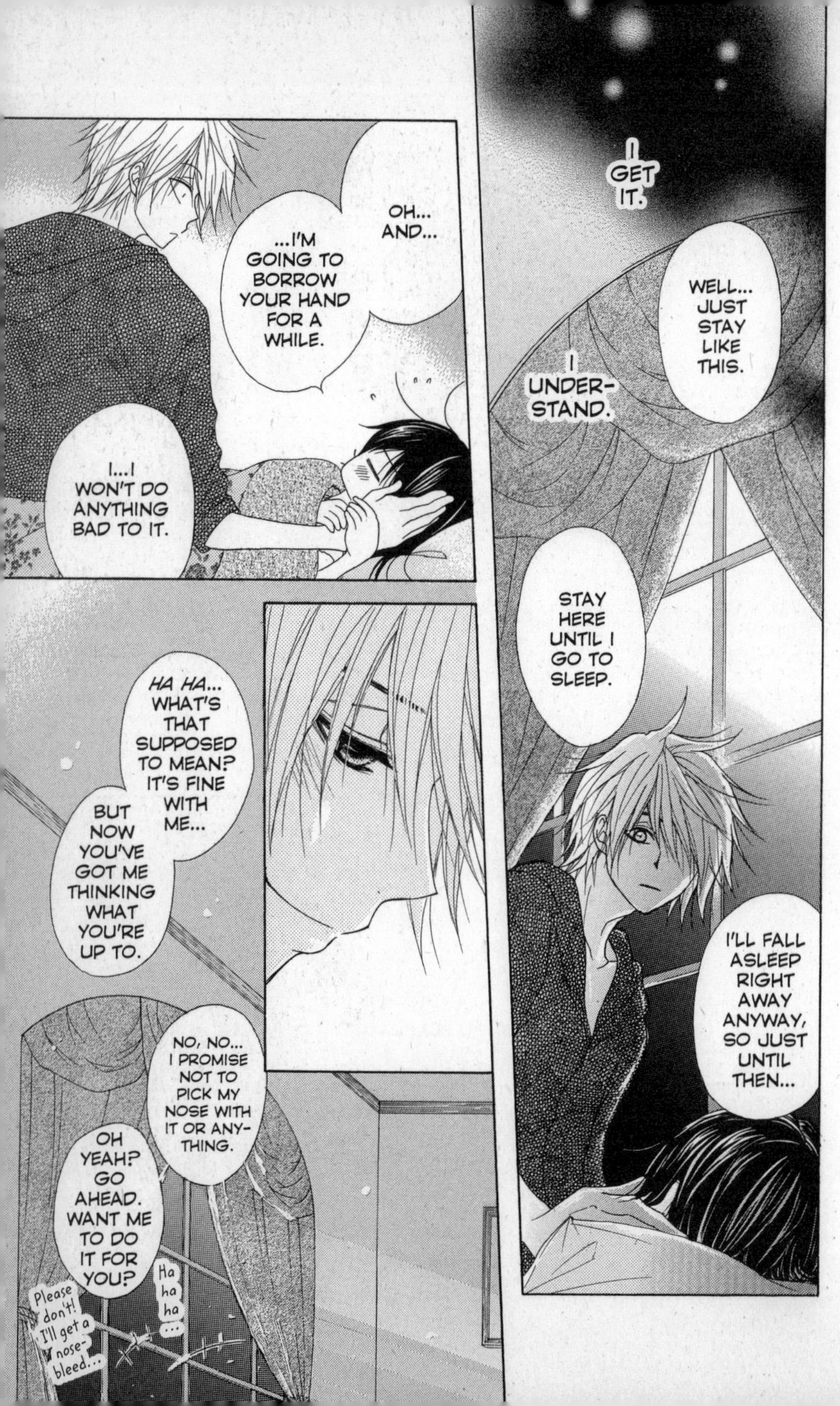
I GET IT.
WELL... JUST STAY LIKE THIS.
I UNDERSTAND.
STAY HERE UNTIL I GO TO SLEEP.
I'LL FALL ASLEEP RIGHT AWAY ANYWAY, SO JUST UNTIL THEN...
OH... AND...
...I'M GOING TO BORROW YOUR HAND FOR A WHILE.
I...I WON'T DO ANYTHING BAD TO IT.
HA HA... WHAT'S THAT SUPPOSED TO MEAN? IT'S FINE WITH ME...
BUT NOW YOU'VE GOT ME THINKING WHAT YOU'RE UP TO.
NO, NO... I PROMISE NOT TO PICK MY NOSE WITH IT OR ANYTHING.
OH YEAH? GO AHEAD. WANT ME TO DO IT FOR YOU?
Ha ha ha...
Please don't! I'll get a nosebleed...

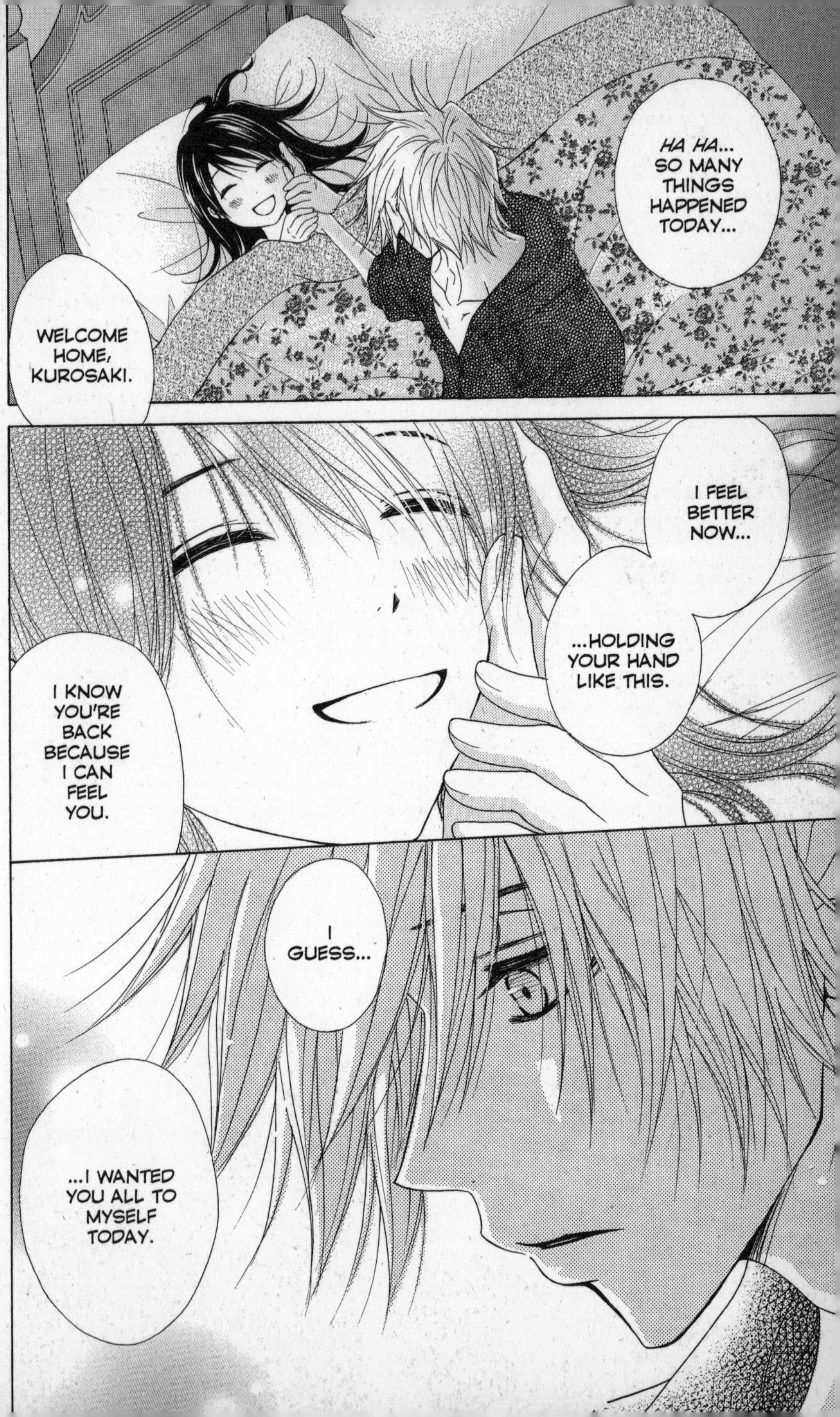
HA HA... SO MANY THINGS HAPPENED TODAY...
WELCOME HOME, KUROSAKI.
I FEEL BETTER NOW...
...HOLDING YOUR HAND LIKE THIS.
I KNOW YOU'RE BACK BECAUSE I CAN FEEL YOU.
I GUESS...
...I WANTED YOU ALL TO MYSELF TODAY.

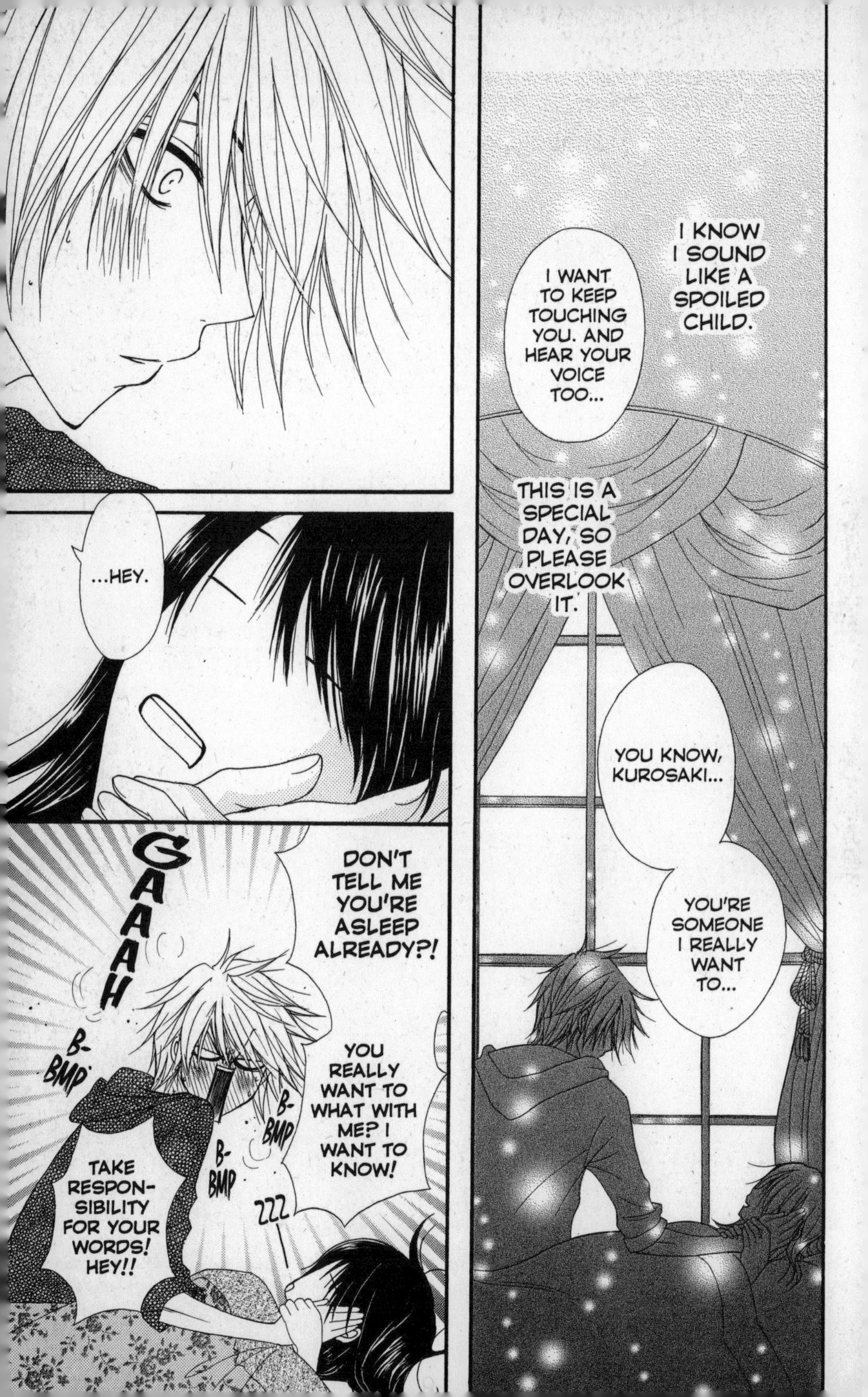
I KNOW I SOUND LIKE A SPOILED CHILD.
I WANT TO KEEP TOUCHING YOU. AND HEAR YOUR VOICE TOO...
THIS IS A SPECIAL DAY, SO PLEASE OVERLOOK IT.
YOU KNOW, KUROSAKI...
YOU'RE SOMEONE I REALLY WANT TO...
...HEY.
DON'T TELL ME YOU'RE ASLEEP ALREADY?!
GAAAH
YOU REALLY WANT TO WHAT WITH ME? I WANT TO KNOW!
B-BMP
B-BMP
B-BMP
ZZZ
TAKE RESPON-SIBILITY FOR YOUR WORDS! HEY!!

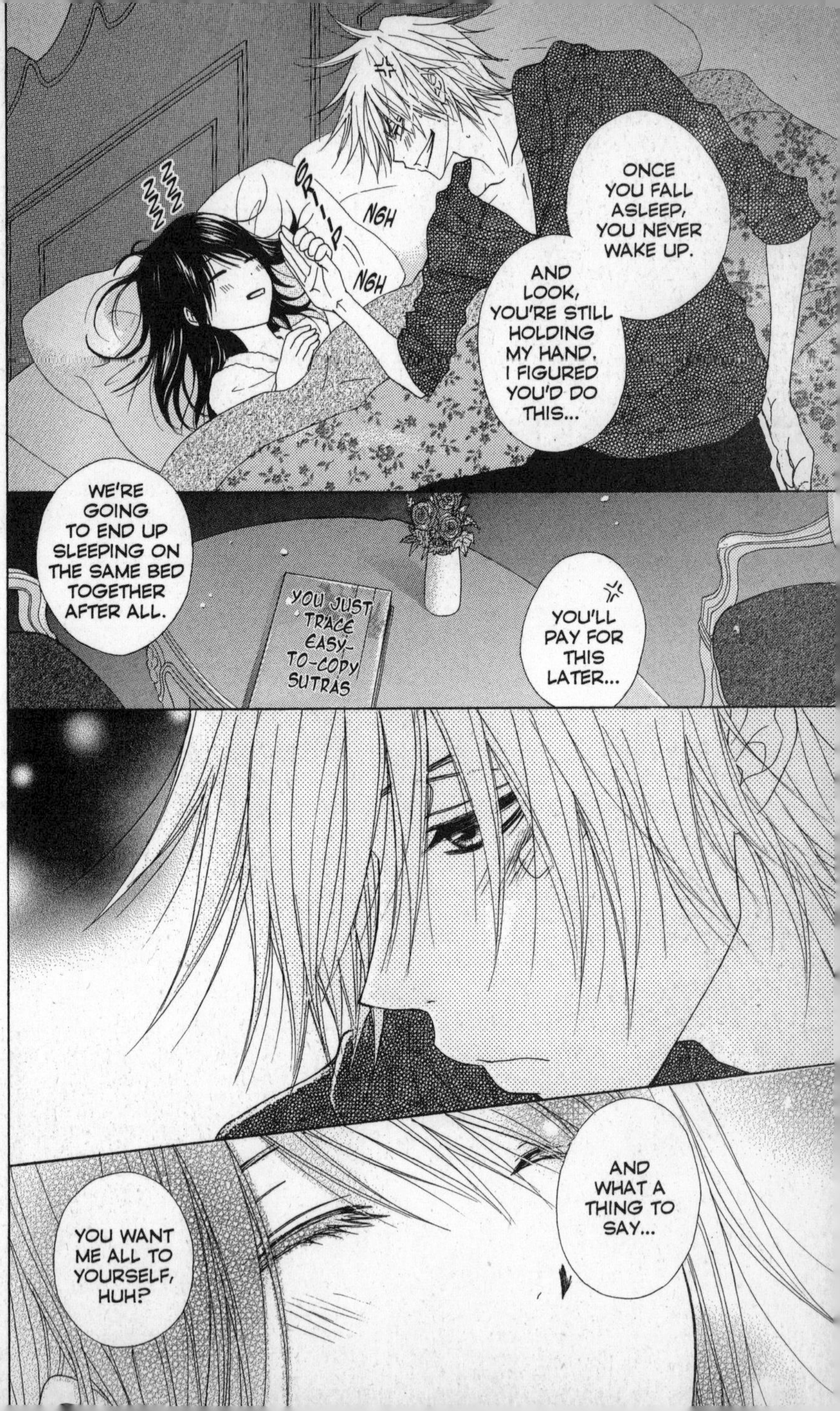
ONCE YOU FALL ASLEEP, YOU NEVER WAKE UP.
AND LOOK, YOU'RE STILL HOLDING MY HAND. I FIGURED YOU'D DO THIS...
NGH
NGH
ZZZ
ZZZ
YOU'LL PAY FOR THIS LATER...
YOU JUST TRACE EASY-TO-COPY SUTRAS
WE'RE GOING TO END UP SLEEPING ON THE SAME BED TOGETHER AFTER ALL.
AND WHAT A THING TO SAY...
YOU WANT ME ALL TO YOURSELF, HUH?

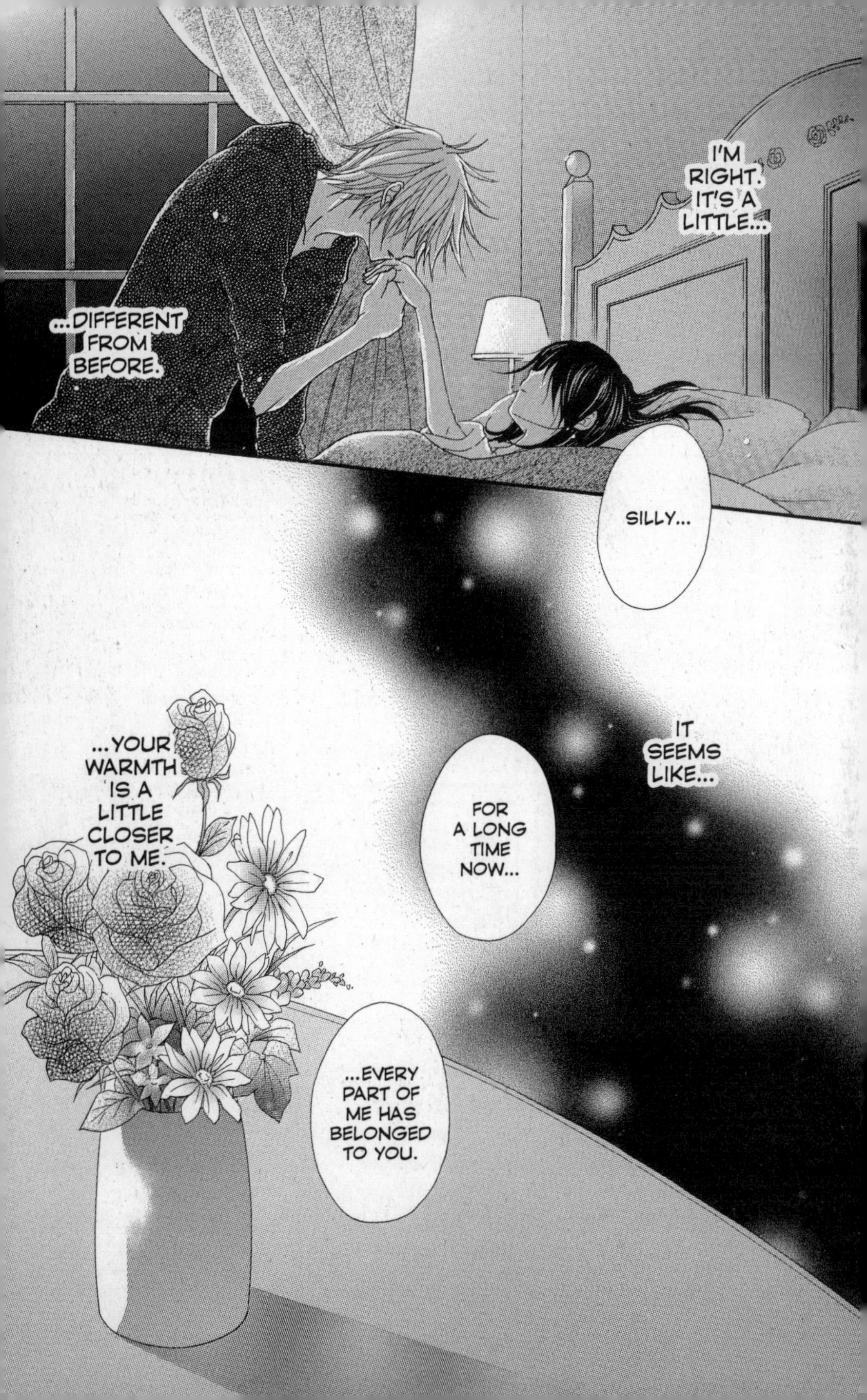
I'M RIGHT. IT'S A LITTLE...
...DIFFERENT FROM BEFORE.
SILLY...
IT SEEMS LIKE...
FOR A LONG TIME NOW...
...YOUR WARMTH IS A LITTLE CLOSER TO ME.
...EVERY PART OF ME HAS BELONGED TO YOU.

THE BEST ☆ OF ☆ THE SECRET SCHOOL CUSTODIAN OFFICE ♥

THE 4TH OF THIS SUPER POPULAR SECTION ♥

THERE IS A *DENGEKI DAISY* FAN SEGMENT BOLDLY FEATURED IN *BETSUCOMI* THAT IS APTLY TITLED "THE SECRET SCHOOL CUSTODIAN OFFICE ♥"!
WITH ARBITRARY EYES, WE EXAMINED ALL THE GREAT WORK FEATURED THERE AND PICKED THE "BEST" AMONG THEM THAT WE WANTED TO LEAVE FOR POSTERITY!

THE "BEST OF" FOR VOLUME 9...ARE THE *DAISY* ACROSTICS!

THE IDEA IS TO USE THE LETTERS OF NAMES OR THINGS IN *DENGEKI DAISY* AND CREATE AN ACROSTIC. WE RECEIVED MANY ENTRIES, BUT JUST AS WE EXPECTED, THE OVERWHELMING MAJORITY USED THE NAME "KUROSAKI." AND WITHOUT FAIL, THEY WERE ALL PERVERTED LINES! THE PRINCE REMAINS FIRMLY IN HIS THRONE!

★★★ DAISY ACROSTICS REVEALED! ★★★

(TA) THE SUNLIGHT
(SU) SHONE THROUGH AND YOU COULD SEE
(KU) KUROSAKI'S BOXERS! (HA HA)

-MIKAN, TOKYO

NO WAY! MY WORK PANTS ARE THICK. YOU CAN'T SEE THROUGH THEM...CAN YOU?

(KU) KUROSAKI CAME OVER TO MY
(RO) ROOM AND
(SA) SPOKE SOFTLY INTO MY EAR...
(KI) KYAAAA!

GIRAFFE, SAITAMA PREFECTURE

I WONDER WHAT I WHISPERED TO GIRAFFE?

WINS AN AUTOGRAPH!

(SO) SIDE BY SIDE IS HOW WE SLEEP.
(I) I'M THE KID SISTER HE'S CRAZY ABOUT.
(CHI) CHESTS CAN BE FLAT ON WOMEN, BECAUSE I'M FLAT-CHESTED TOO.
(RO) RECOGNIZE THAT HE HAS A LOLITA COMPLEX.

-RAKKO, CHIBA PREFECTURE

TERU IS TRULY AN ANGEL. ♡ SHE'S A BROTHER'S DREAM. HEH HEH HEH.

(H) HOPE HE GOES BALD,
(A) A
(C) CURSE FOR BEING A
(K) KINKY LOLITA COMPLEX GUY WITH
(E) EYES THAT SQUINT WITH
(R) REAL INTENT.

-ASUKA, AICHI PREFECTURE

I'VE BECOME IMMUNE TO THESE KINDS OF WORDS. THAT'S GOOD...RIGHT?

(TA) TAMORI (A COMEDIAN)
(SU) SEEMS TO HAVE TAKEN A LIKING TO
(KU) KUROSAKI.

-FUMINA OBA, AICHI PREFECTURE

IS IT BECAUSE OF THE OLD-MAN SHADES...?

THAT'S AMAZING! YOU'RE THE SUBJECT OF SO MANY ENTRIES!

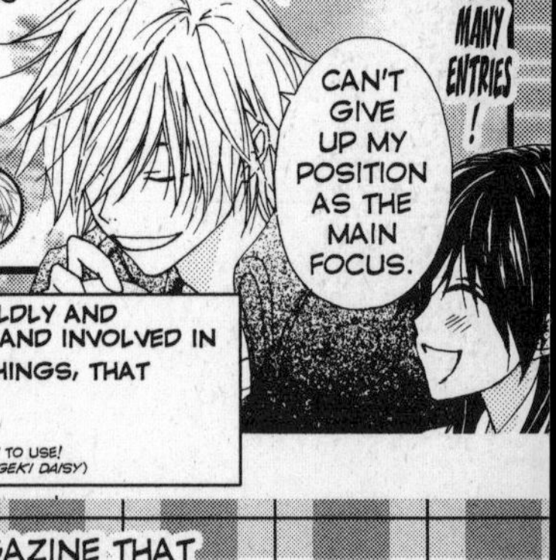
CAN'T GIVE UP MY POSITION AS THE MAIN FOCUS.

JUDGES' COMMENTS

(TA) THANK YOU FOR YOUR
(SU) SUPER CREATIVE AND
(KU) KNOWLEDGEABLE ENTRIES!

WE CAN SEE HOW EASY IT IS TO USE "TASUKU" IN ACROSTICS. (HEAD JUDGE: KYOUSUKE MOTOMI)

(TA) TRULY WORLDLY AND PERVERTED AND INVOLVED IN
(SU) SO MANY THINGS, THAT
(KU) KUROSAKI.

"TASUKU" REALLY IS EASY TO USE! (JUDGE: EDITOR FOR *DENGEKI DAISY*)

BETSUCOMI, THE MAGAZINE THAT SERIALIZES *DAISY*, GOES ON SALE EVERY MONTH AROUND THE 13TH!
PLEASE LOOK FOR IT IF YOU WANT TO READ "THE SECRET SCHOOL CUSTODIAN OFFICE"! ♥

CHAPTER 43: YOU'VE GOT MAIL

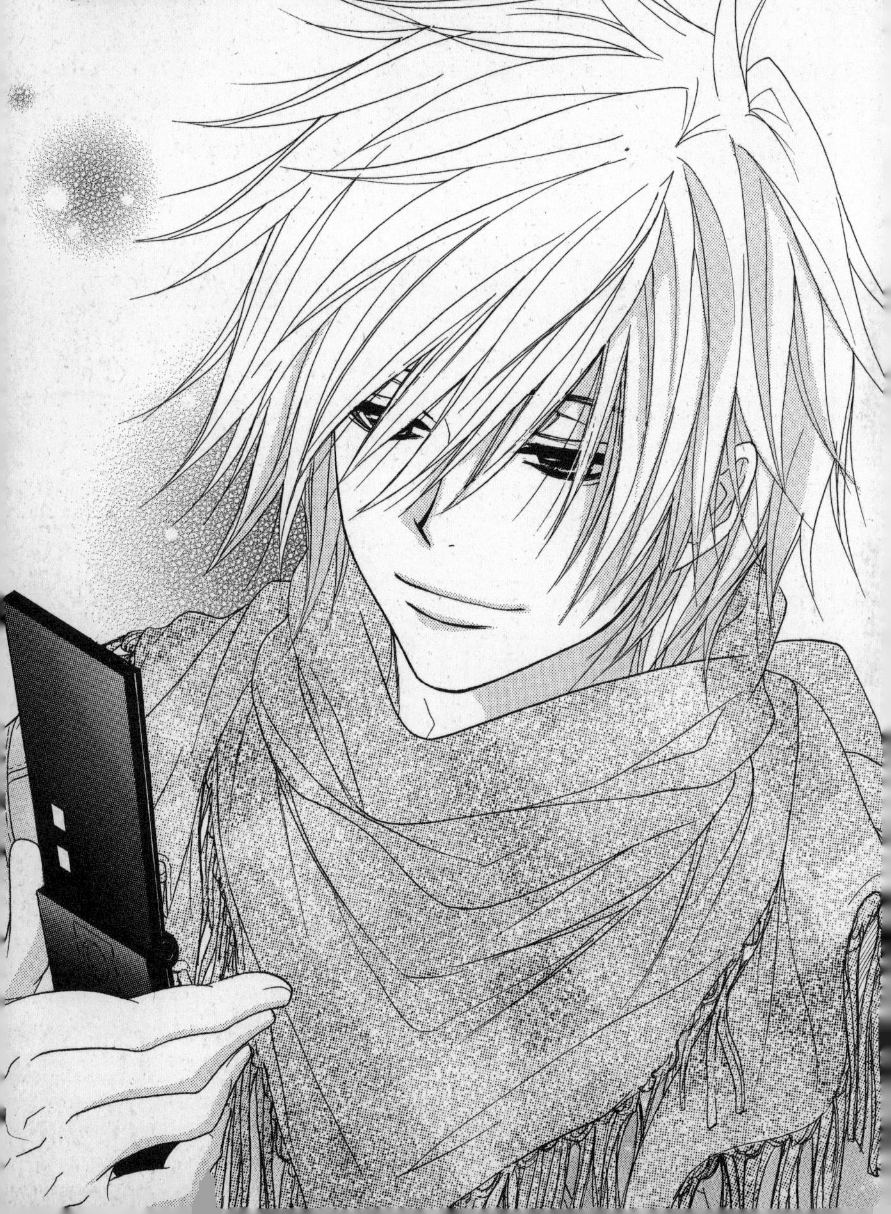

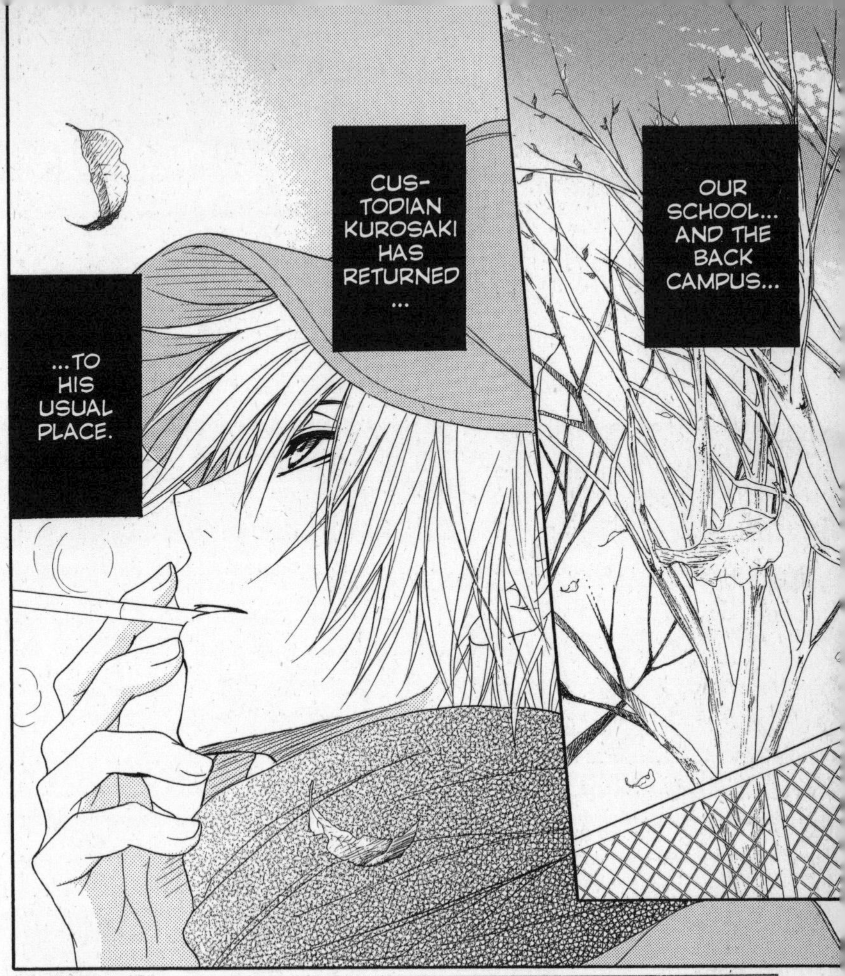
OUR SCHOOL... AND THE BACK CAMPUS...
CUS-TODIAN KUROSAKI HAS RETURNED...
...TO HIS USUAL PLACE.

IN CHAPTER 42, IT MAY SEEM STRANGE THAT KUROSAKI IS WEARING HIS HOODIE AFTER HIS BATH FOR SOME REASON... (THE ISSUE WAS WHETHER HE WOULD SEEM TOO WELL PREPARED FOR THIS SCENE.) WE CONSIDERED THE FACT THAT PROBABLY NO ONE WOULD BE INTERESTED IN SEEING KUROSAKI IN A BATHROBE. NO MATTER HOW IT WAS PRESENTED, A PICTURE OF KUROSAKI IN A BATHROBE WOULD BE COMEDIC. I MEAN, KUROSAKI IN A BATHROBE. THE WORDS ALONE ARE FUNNY.

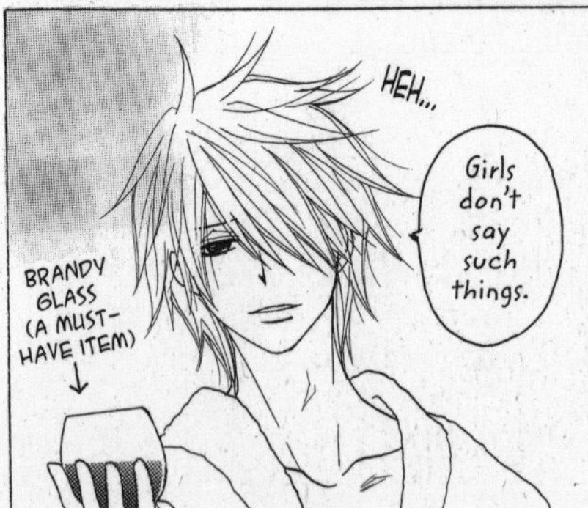
HEH...
Girls don't say such things.
BRANDY GLASS (A MUST-HAVE ITEM)

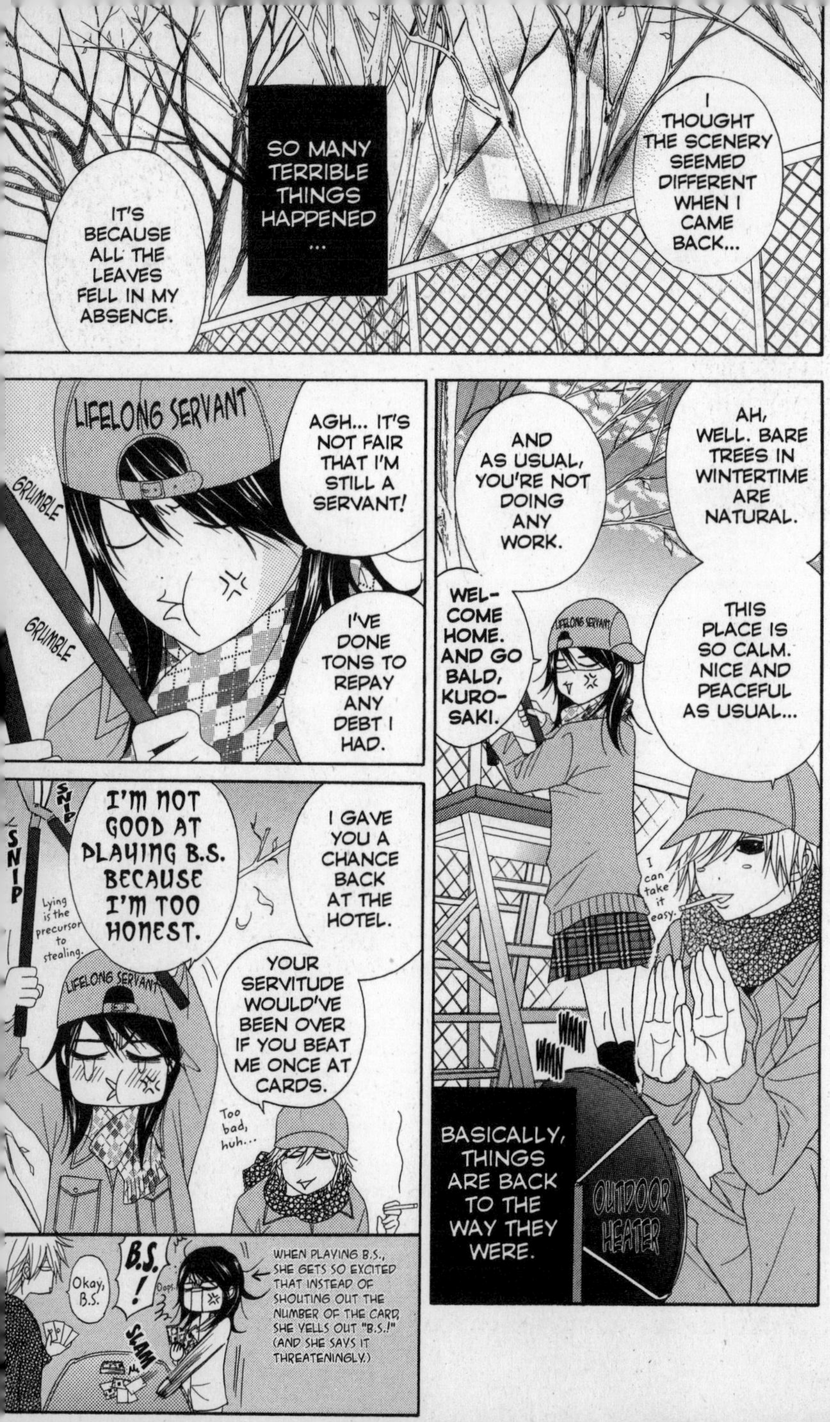
I THOUGHT THE SCENERY SEEMED DIFFERENT WHEN I CAME BACK...
SO MANY TERRIBLE THINGS HAPPENED ...
IT'S BECAUSE ALL THE LEAVES FELL IN MY ABSENCE.
AH, WELL. BARE TREES IN WINTERTIME ARE NATURAL.
AND AS USUAL, YOU'RE NOT DOING ANY WORK.
THIS PLACE IS SO CALM. NICE AND PEACEFUL AS USUAL...
WEL-COME HOME. AND GO BALD, KURO-SAKI.
LIFELONG SERVANT
I can take it easy.
WMN WMN
BASICALLY, THINGS ARE BACK TO THE WAY THEY WERE.
OUTDOOR HEATER
LIFELONG SERVANT
AGH... IT'S NOT FAIR THAT I'M STILL A SERVANT!
I'VE DONE TONS TO REPAY ANY DEBT I HAD.
GRUMBLE
GRUMBLE
I GAVE YOU A CHANCE BACK AT THE HOTEL.
YOUR SERVITUDE WOULD'VE BEEN OVER IF YOU BEAT ME ONCE AT CARDS.
I'M NOT GOOD AT PLAYING B.S. BECAUSE I'M TOO HONEST.
SNIP
SNIP
Lying is the precursor to stealing.
LIFELONG SERVANT
Too bad, huh...
WHEN PLAYING B.S., SHE GETS SO EXCITED THAT INSTEAD OF SHOUTING OUT THE NUMBER OF THE CARD, SHE YELLS OUT "B.S.!" (AND SHE SAYS IT THREATENINGLY.)
B.S. !
Oops
SLAM
Okay, B.S.

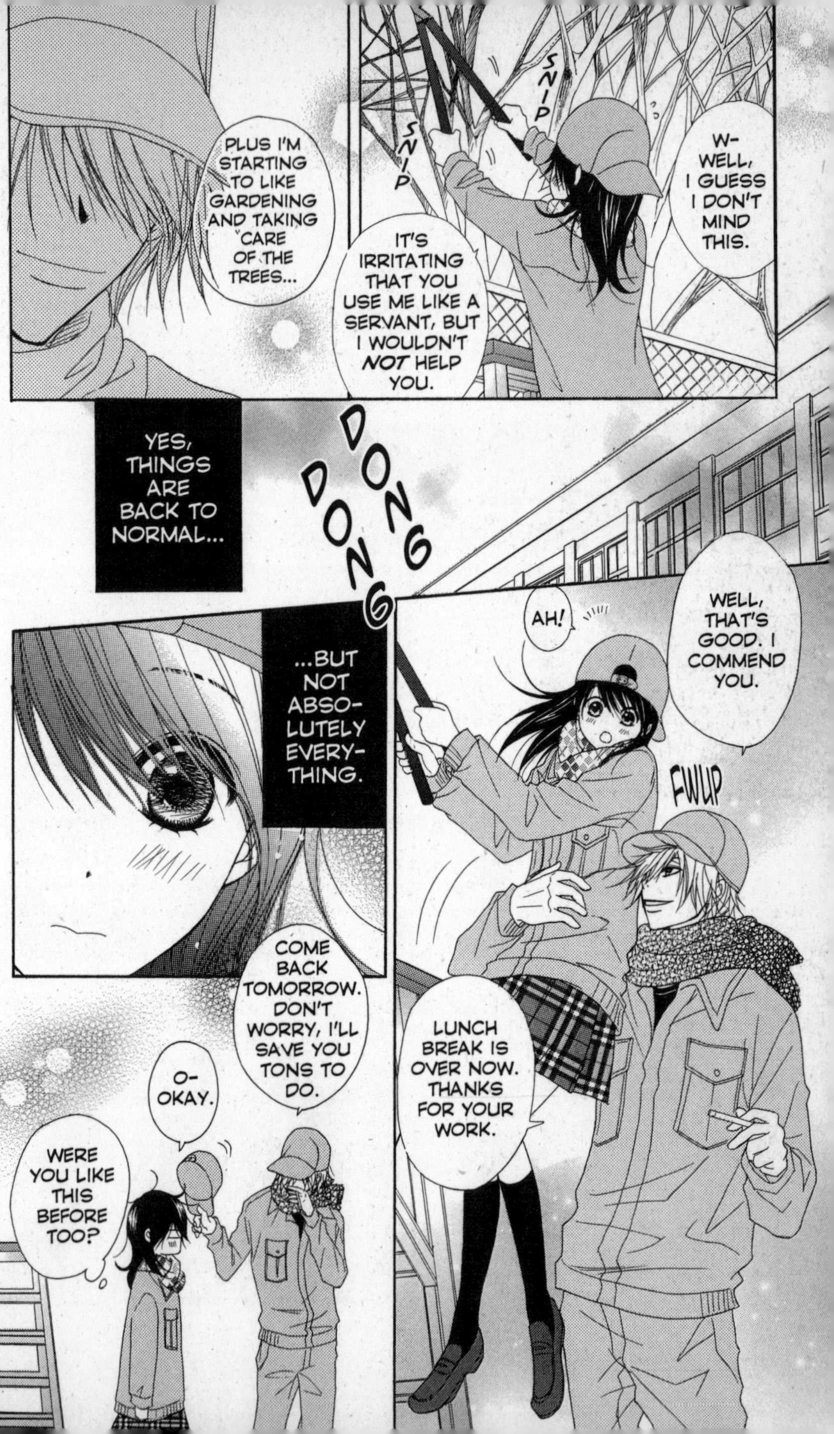
SNIP
SNIP
W-WELL, I GUESS I DON'T MIND THIS.
IT'S IRRITATING THAT YOU USE ME LIKE A SERVANT, BUT I WOULDN'T *NOT* HELP YOU.
PLUS I'M STARTING TO LIKE GARDENING AND TAKING CARE OF THE TREES...
WELL, THAT'S GOOD. I COMMEND YOU.
YES, THINGS ARE BACK TO NORMAL...
DONG DONG
AH!
FWUP
LUNCH BREAK IS OVER NOW. THANKS FOR YOUR WORK.
...BUT NOT ABSOLUTELY EVERYTHING.
COME BACK TOMORROW. DON'T WORRY, I'LL SAVE YOU TONS TO DO.
O-OKAY.
WERE YOU LIKE THIS BEFORE TOO?

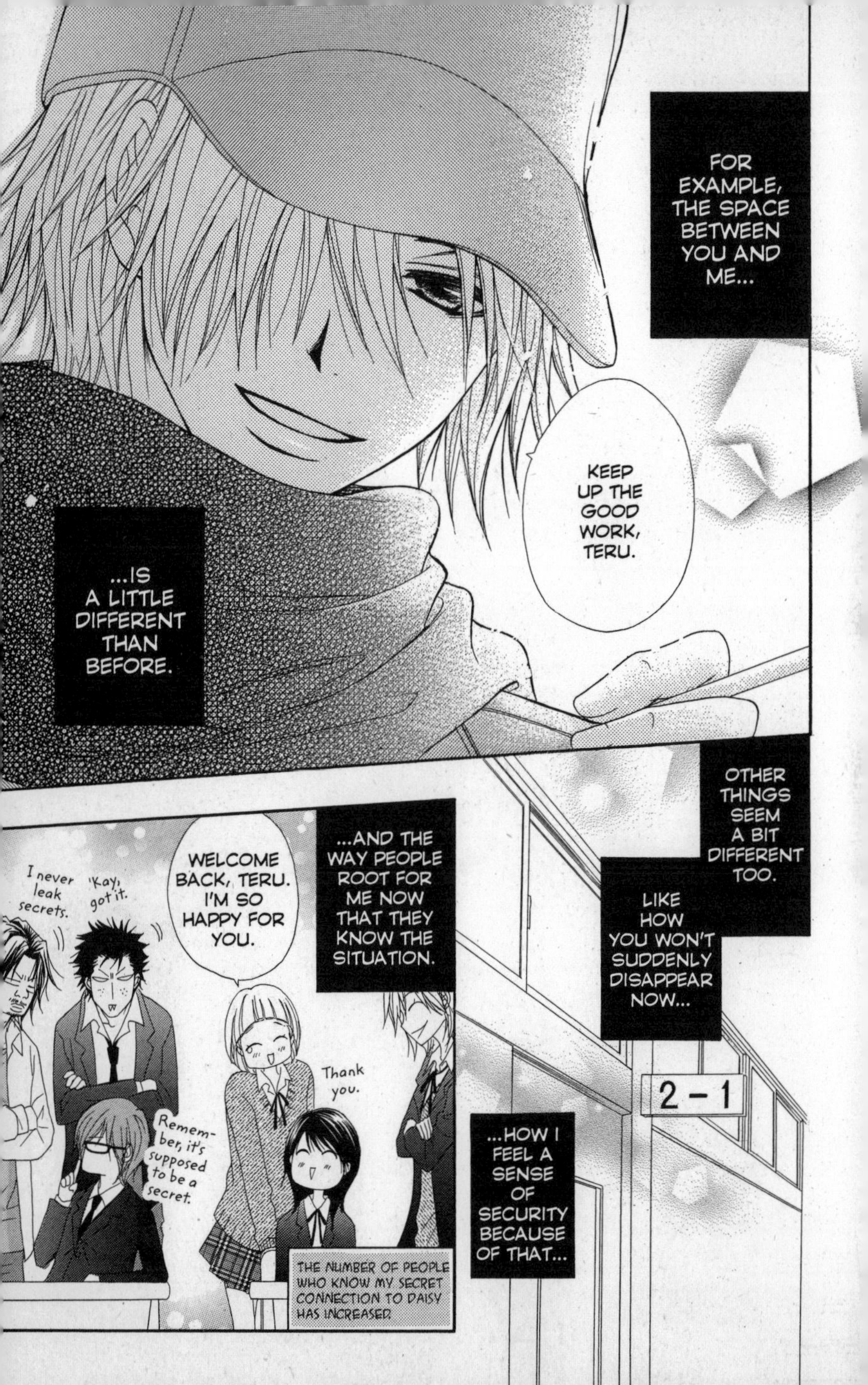
FOR EXAMPLE, THE SPACE BETWEEN YOU AND ME...
KEEP UP THE GOOD WORK, TERU.
...IS A LITTLE DIFFERENT THAN BEFORE.
OTHER THINGS SEEM A BIT DIFFERENT TOO.
LIKE HOW YOU WON'T SUDDENLY DISAPPEAR NOW...
2-1
...HOW I FEEL A SENSE OF SECURITY BECAUSE OF THAT...
...AND THE WAY PEOPLE ROOT FOR ME NOW THAT THEY KNOW THE SITUATION.
WELCOME BACK, TERU. I'M SO HAPPY FOR YOU.
Thank you.
'Kay, got it.
I never leak secrets.
Remember, it's supposed to be a secret.
THE NUMBER OF PEOPLE WHO KNOW MY SECRET CONNECTION TO DAISY HAS INCREASED.

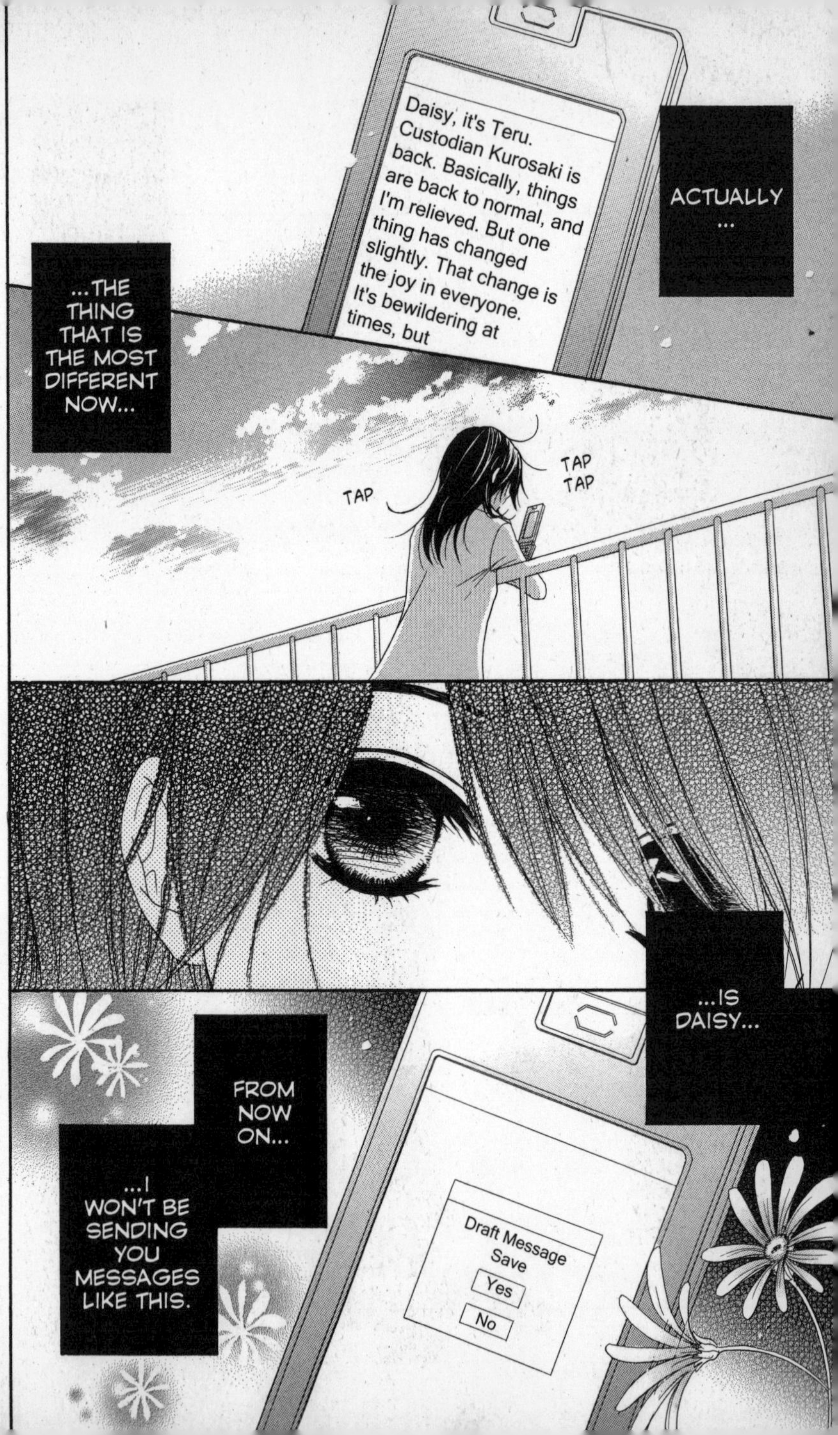
ACTUALLY ...
Daisy, it's Teru. Custodian Kurosaki is back. Basically, things are back to normal, and I'm relieved. But one thing has changed slightly. That change is the joy in everyone. It's bewildering at times, but
...THE THING THAT IS THE MOST DIFFERENT NOW...
TAP TAP
TAP
...IS DAISY...
FROM NOW ON...
...I WON'T BE SENDING YOU MESSAGES LIKE THIS.
Draft Message Save
Yes
No

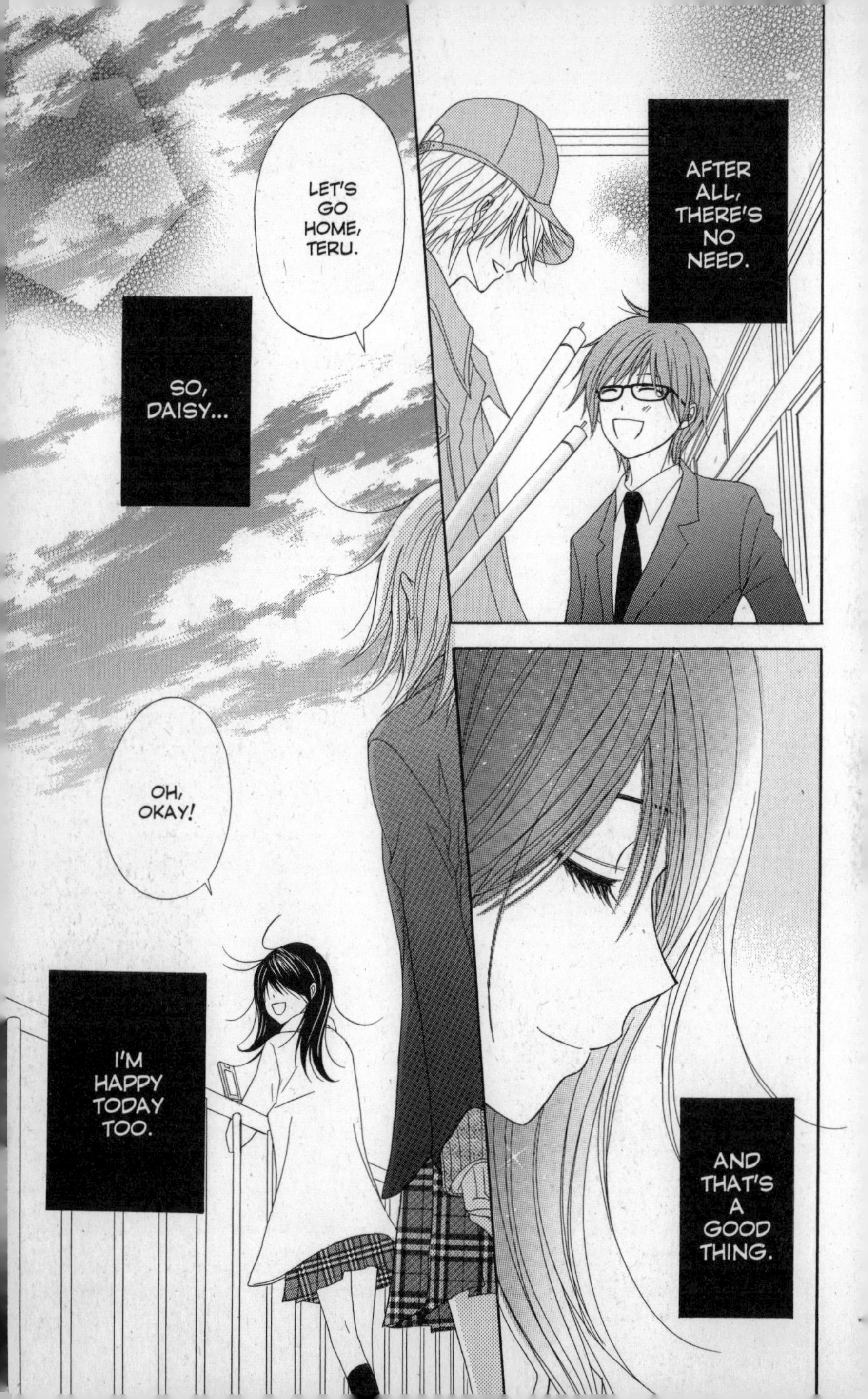
AFTER ALL, THERE'S NO NEED.
AND THAT'S A GOOD THING.
LET'S GO HOME, TERU.
SO, DAISY...
OH, OKAY!
I'M HAPPY TODAY TOO.

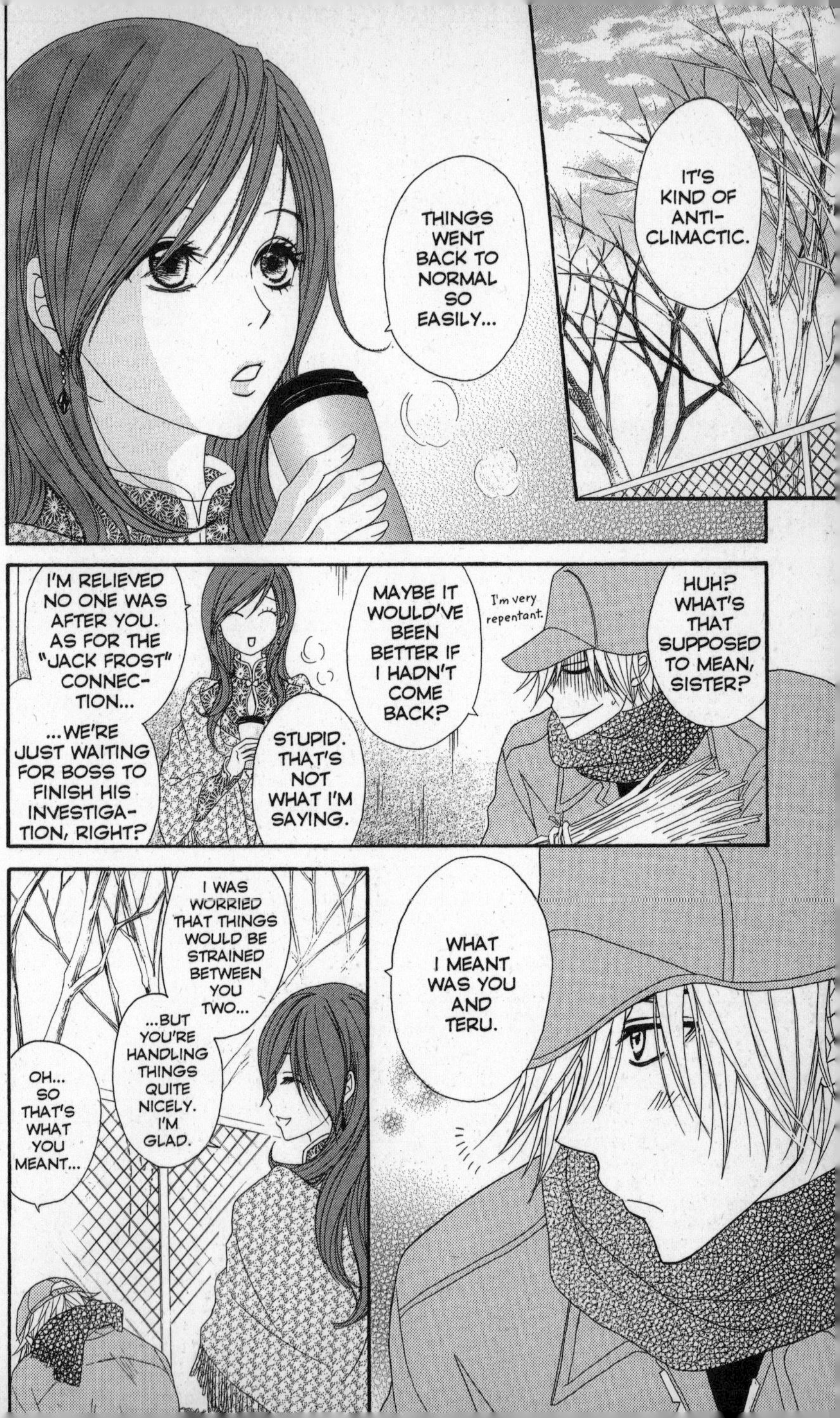
IT'S KIND OF ANTI-CLIMACTIC.
THINGS WENT BACK TO NORMAL SO EASILY...
HUH? WHAT'S THAT SUPPOSED TO MEAN, SISTER?
I'm very repentant.
MAYBE IT WOULD'VE BEEN BETTER IF I HADN'T COME BACK?
STUPID. THAT'S NOT WHAT I'M SAYING.
I'M RELIEVED NO ONE WAS AFTER YOU. AS FOR THE "JACK FROST" CONNECTION...
...WE'RE JUST WAITING FOR BOSS TO FINISH HIS INVESTIGATION, RIGHT?
WHAT I MEANT WAS YOU AND TERU.
I WAS WORRIED THAT THINGS WOULD BE STRAINED BETWEEN YOU TWO...
...BUT YOU'RE HANDLING THINGS QUITE NICELY. I'M GLAD.
OH... SO THAT'S WHAT YOU MEANT...

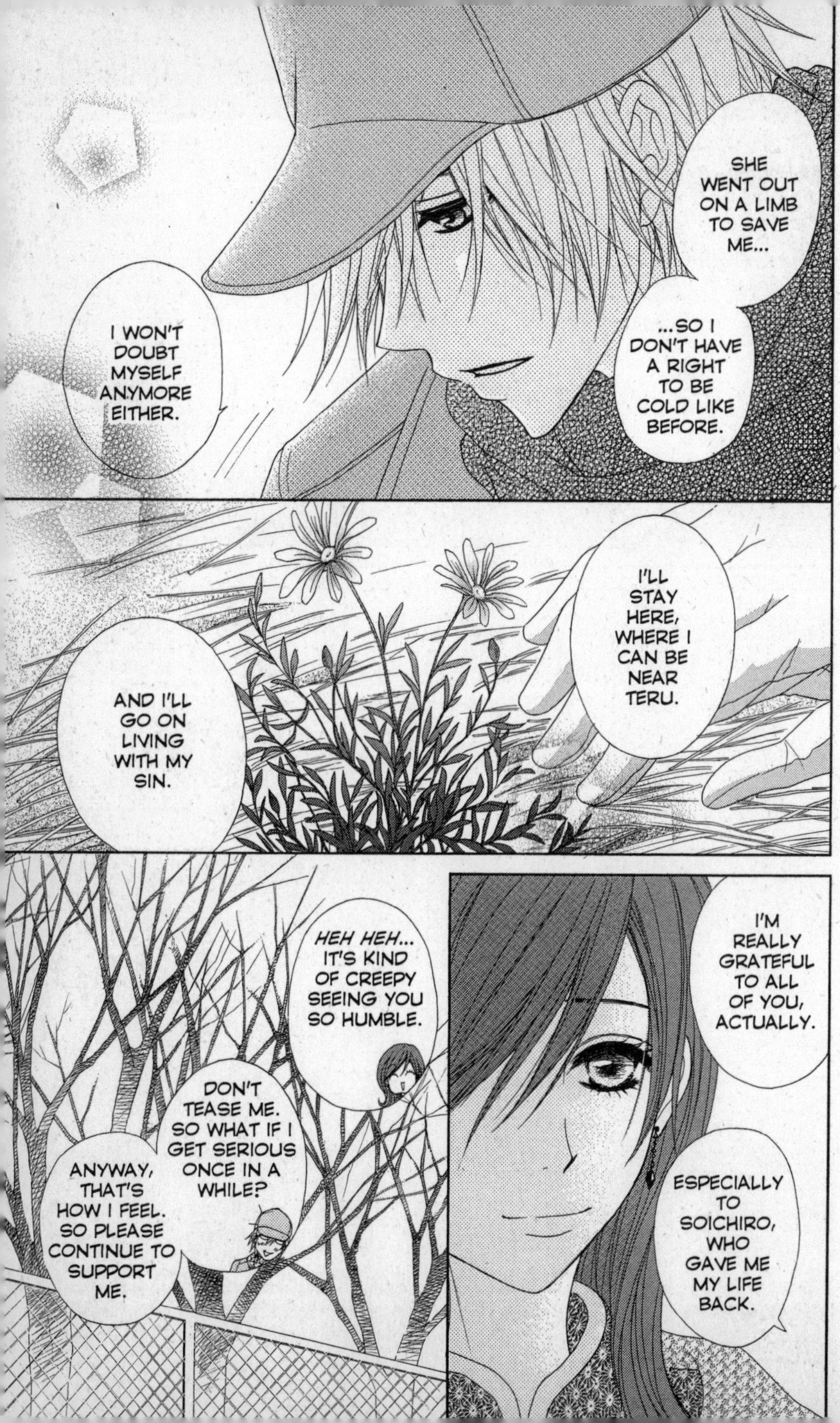
SHE WENT OUT ON A LIMB TO SAVE ME...
...SO I DON'T HAVE A RIGHT TO BE COLD LIKE BEFORE.
I WON'T DOUBT MYSELF ANYMORE EITHER.
I'LL STAY HERE, WHERE I CAN BE NEAR TERU.
AND I'LL GO ON LIVING WITH MY SIN.
I'M REALLY GRATEFUL TO ALL OF YOU, ACTUALLY.
ESPECIALLY TO SOICHIRO, WHO GAVE ME MY LIFE BACK.
HEH HEH... IT'S KIND OF CREEPY SEEING YOU SO HUMBLE.
DON'T TEASE ME. SO WHAT IF I GET SERIOUS ONCE IN A WHILE?
ANYWAY, THAT'S HOW I FEEL. SO PLEASE CONTINUE TO SUPPORT ME.

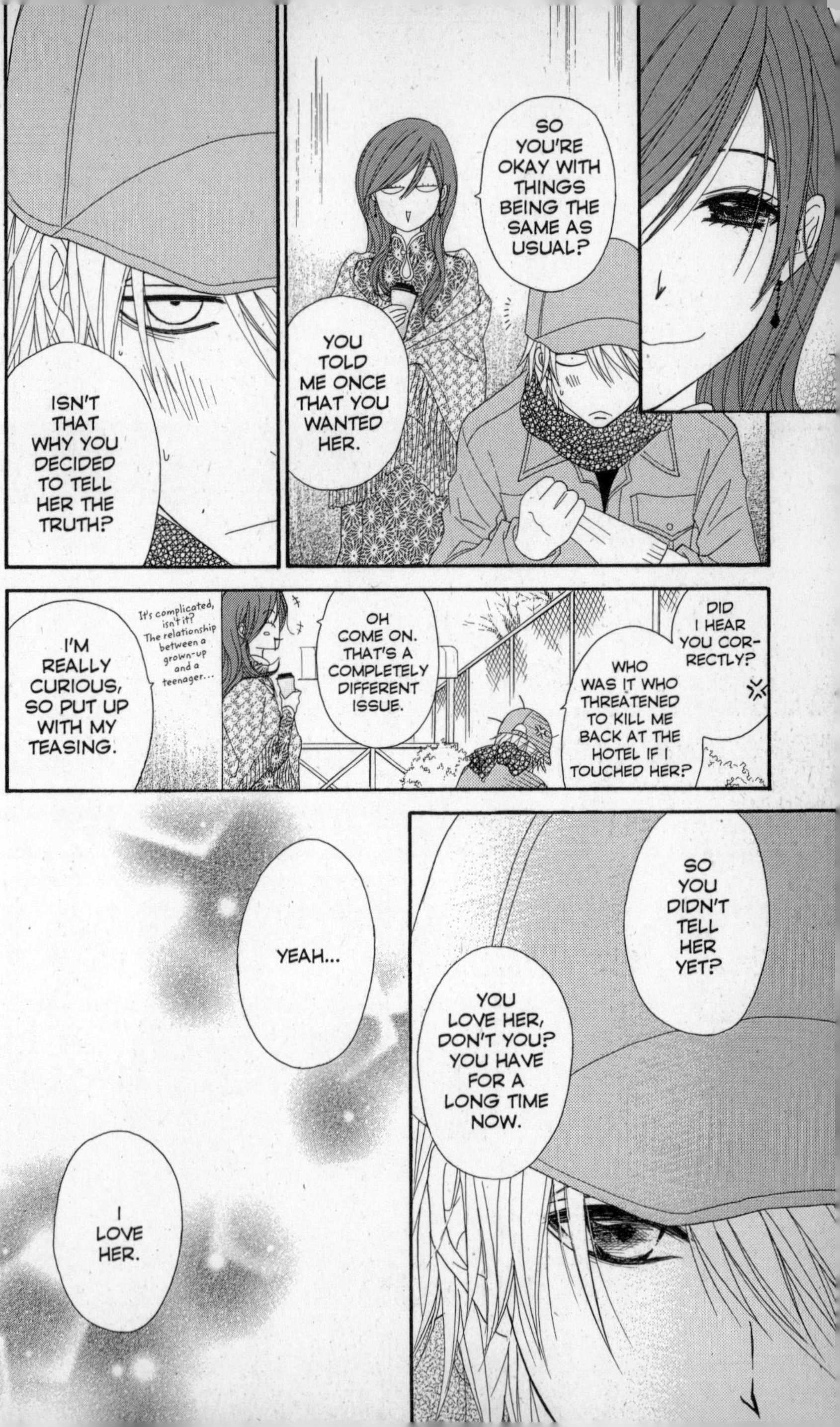
SO YOU'RE OKAY WITH THINGS BEING THE SAME AS USUAL?
YOU TOLD ME ONCE THAT YOU WANTED HER.
ISN'T THAT WHY YOU DECIDED TO TELL HER THE TRUTH?
DID I HEAR YOU CORRECTLY?
WHO WAS IT WHO THREATENED TO KILL ME BACK AT THE HOTEL IF I TOUCHED HER?
OH COME ON. THAT'S A COMPLETELY DIFFERENT ISSUE.
It's complicated, isn't it? The relationship between a grown-up and a teenager...
I'M REALLY CURIOUS, SO PUT UP WITH MY TEASING.
SO YOU DIDN'T TELL HER YET?
YOU LOVE HER, DON'T YOU? YOU HAVE FOR A LONG TIME NOW.
YEAH...
I LOVE HER.

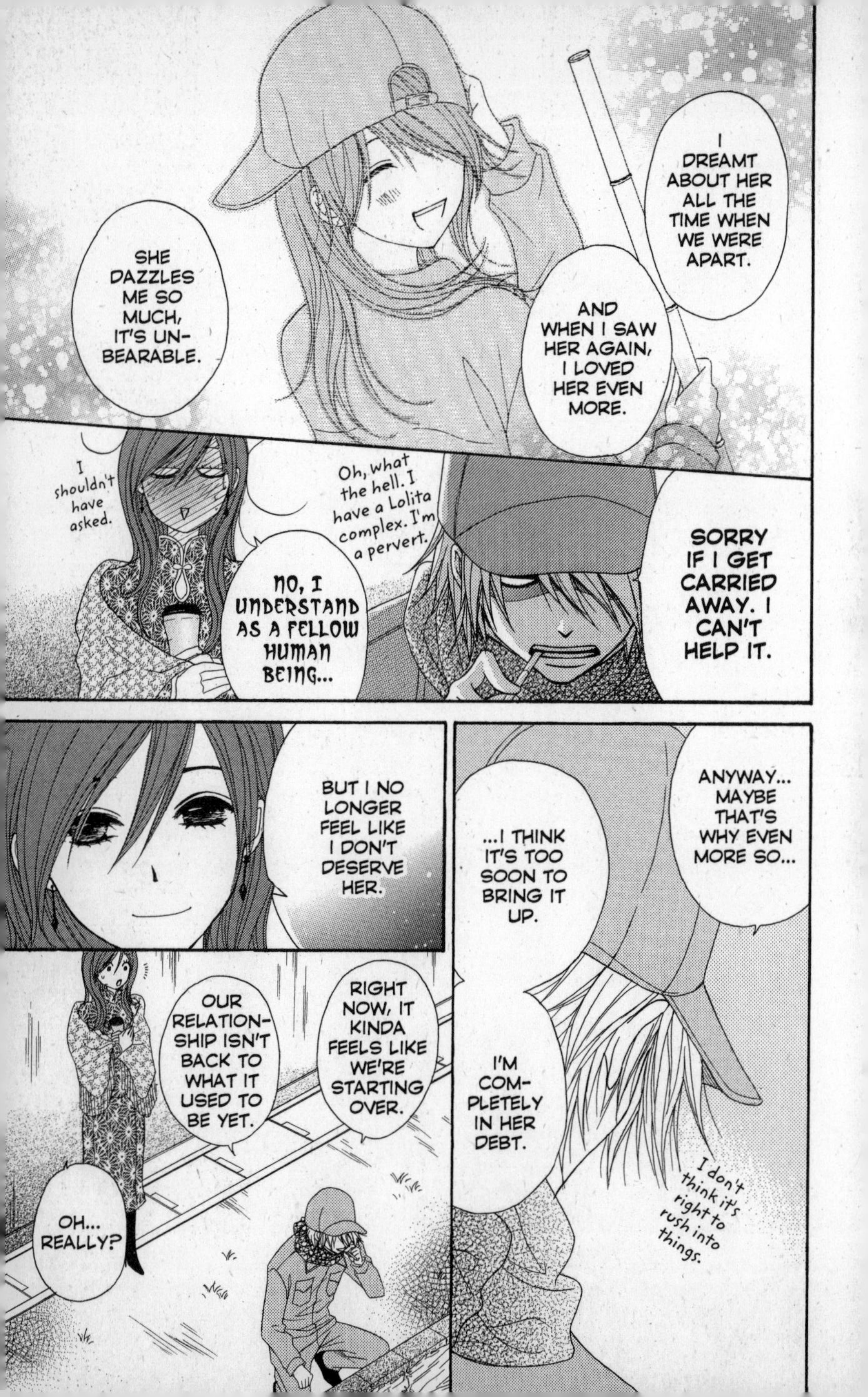
I DREAMT ABOUT HER ALL THE TIME WHEN WE WERE APART.
AND WHEN I SAW HER AGAIN, I LOVED HER EVEN MORE.
SHE DAZZLES ME SO MUCH, IT'S UN-BEARABLE.
SORRY IF I GET CARRIED AWAY. I CAN'T HELP IT.
Oh, what the hell. I have a Lolita complex. I'm a pervert.
NO, I UNDERSTAND AS A FELLOW HUMAN BEING...
I shouldn't have asked.
ANYWAY... MAYBE THAT'S WHY EVEN MORE SO...
...I THINK IT'S TOO SOON TO BRING IT UP.
I'M COM-PLETELY IN HER DEBT.
I don't think it's right to rush into things.
BUT I NO LONGER FEEL LIKE I DON'T DESERVE HER.
RIGHT NOW, IT KINDA FEELS LIKE WE'RE STARTING OVER.
OUR RELATION-SHIP ISN'T BACK TO WHAT IT USED TO BE YET.
OH... REALLY?

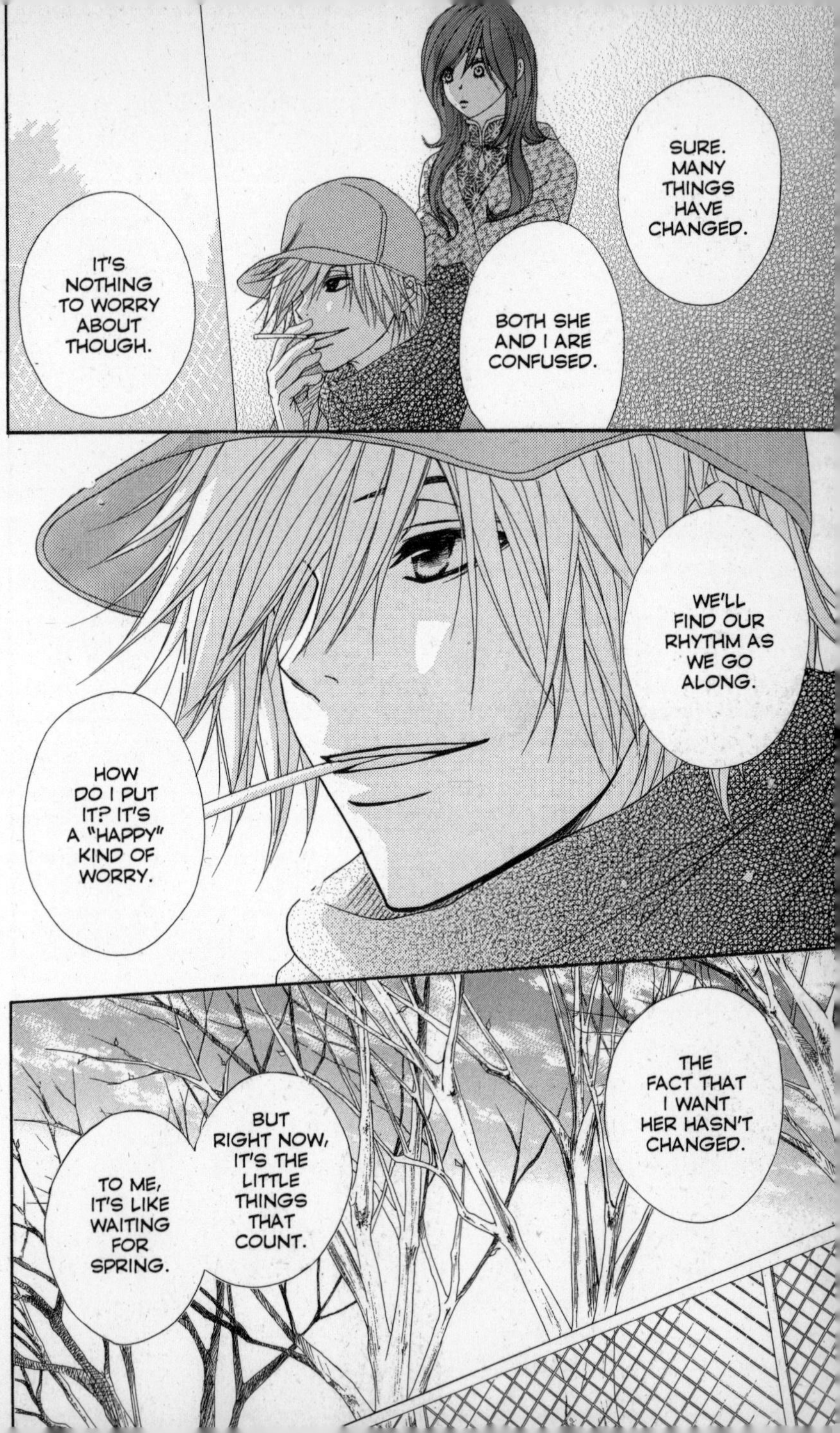
SURE. MANY THINGS HAVE CHANGED.
BOTH SHE AND I ARE CONFUSED.
IT'S NOTHING TO WORRY ABOUT THOUGH.
WE'LL FIND OUR RHYTHM AS WE GO ALONG.
HOW DO I PUT IT? IT'S A "HAPPY" KIND OF WORRY.
THE FACT THAT I WANT HER HASN'T CHANGED.
BUT RIGHT NOW, IT'S THE LITTLE THINGS THAT COUNT.
TO ME, IT'S LIKE WAITING FOR SPRING.

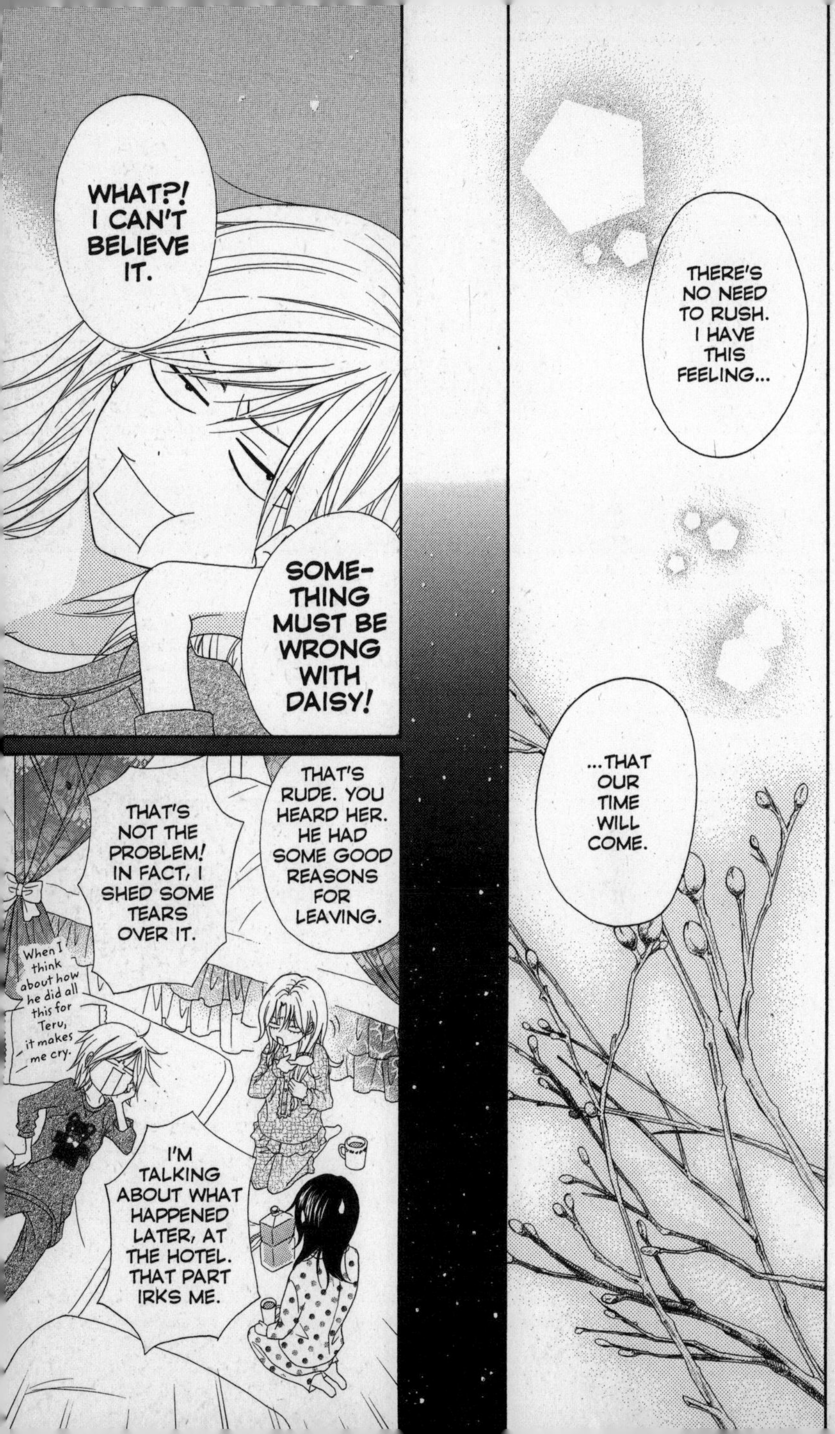
THERE'S NO NEED TO RUSH. I HAVE THIS FEELING...
...THAT OUR TIME WILL COME.
WHAT?! I CAN'T BELIEVE IT.
SOME-THING MUST BE WRONG WITH DAISY!
THAT'S RUDE. YOU HEARD HER. HE HAD SOME GOOD REASONS FOR LEAVING.
THAT'S NOT THE PROBLEM! IN FACT, I SHED SOME TEARS OVER IT.
When I think about how he did all this for Teru, it makes me cry.
I'M TALKING ABOUT WHAT HAPPENED LATER, AT THE HOTEL. THAT PART IRKS ME.

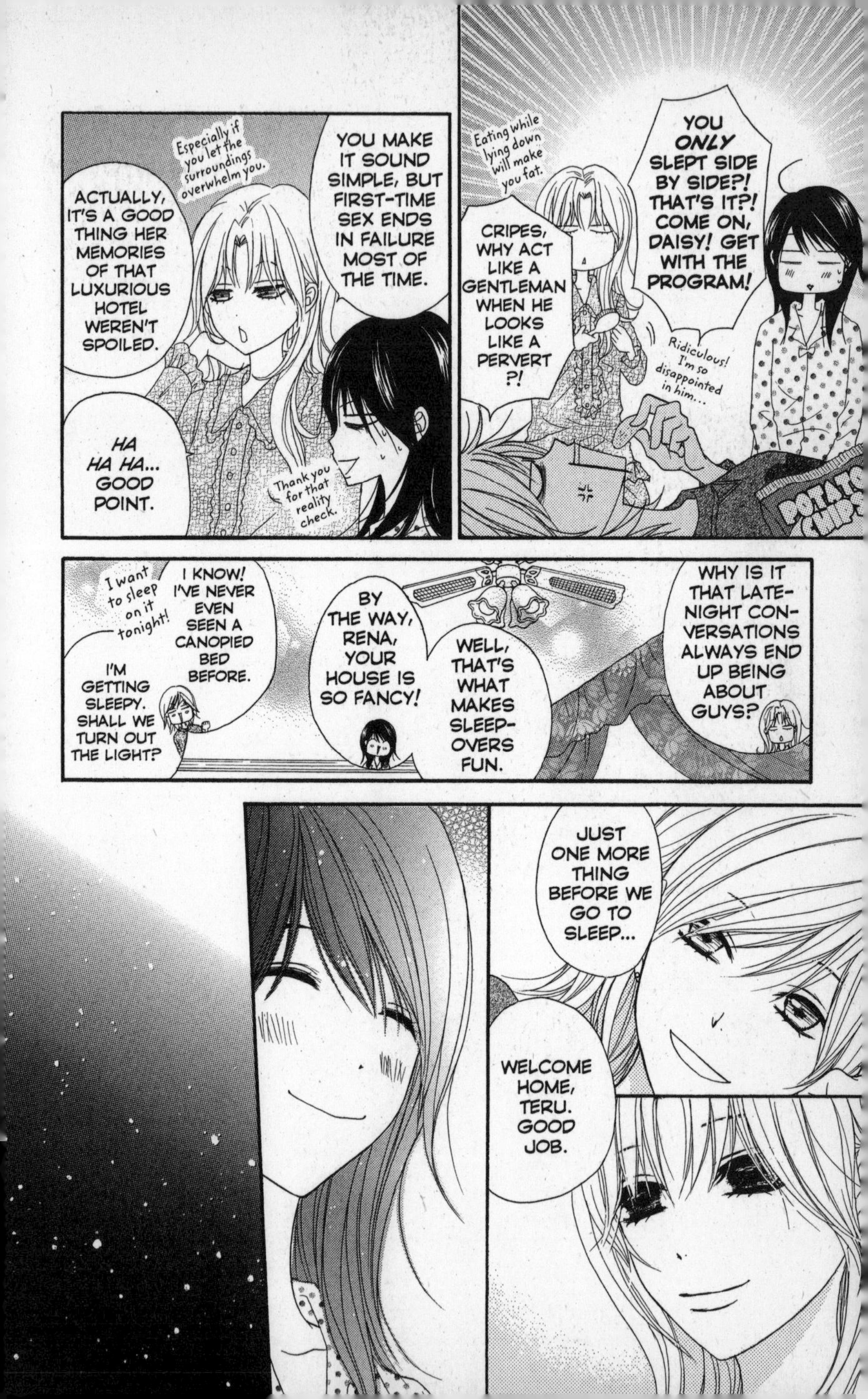
YOU *ONLY* SLEPT SIDE BY SIDE?! THAT'S IT?! COME ON, DAISY! GET WITH THE PROGRAM!
Ridiculous! I'm so disappointed in him...
Eating while lying down will make you fat.
CRIPES, WHY ACT LIKE A GENTLEMAN WHEN HE LOOKS LIKE A PERVERT?!
YOU MAKE IT SOUND SIMPLE, BUT FIRST-TIME SEX ENDS IN FAILURE MOST OF THE TIME.
Especially if you let the surroundings overwhelm you.
ACTUALLY, IT'S A GOOD THING HER MEMORIES OF THAT LUXURIOUS HOTEL WEREN'T SPOILED.
Thank you for that reality check.
HA HA HA... GOOD POINT.
WHY IS IT THAT LATE-NIGHT CONVERSATIONS ALWAYS END UP BEING ABOUT GUYS?
WELL, THAT'S WHAT MAKES SLEEPOVERS FUN.
BY THE WAY, RENA, YOUR HOUSE IS SO FANCY!
I KNOW! I'VE NEVER EVEN SEEN A CANOPIED BED BEFORE.
I want to sleep on it tonight!
I'M GETTING SLEEPY. SHALL WE TURN OUT THE LIGHT?
JUST ONE MORE THING BEFORE WE GO TO SLEEP...
WELCOME HOME, TERU. GOOD JOB.

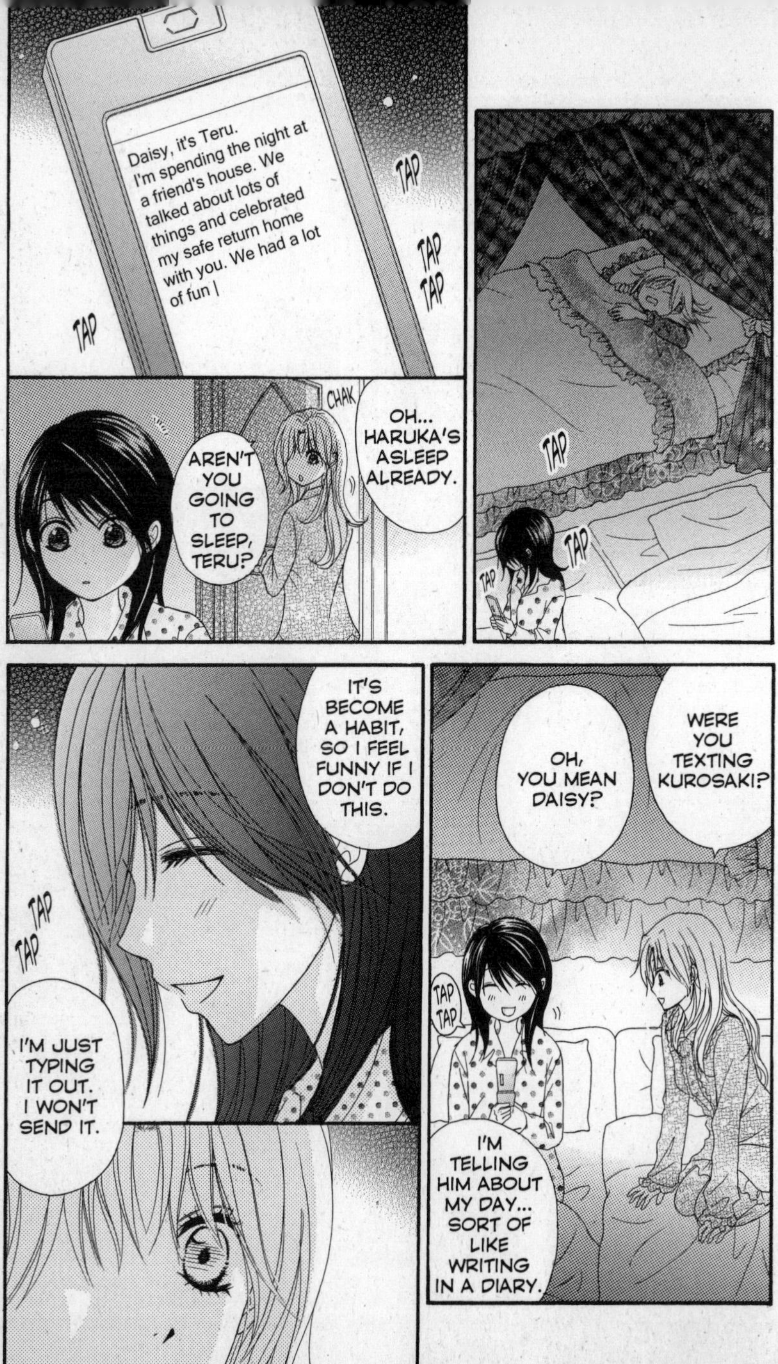
TAP
TAP
TAP
Daisy, it's Teru. I'm spending the night at a friend's house. We talked about lots of things and celebrated my safe return home with you. We had a lot of fun |
TAP
TAP
TAP
TAP
CHAK
OH... HARUKA'S ASLEEP ALREADY.
AREN'T YOU GOING TO SLEEP, TERU?
WERE YOU TEXTING KUROSAKI?
OH, YOU MEAN DAISY?
TAP TAP
I'M TELLING HIM ABOUT MY DAY... SORT OF LIKE WRITING IN A DIARY.
IT'S BECOME A HABIT, SO I FEEL FUNNY IF I DON'T DO THIS.
TAP TAP
I'M JUST TYPING IT OUT. I WON'T SEND IT.

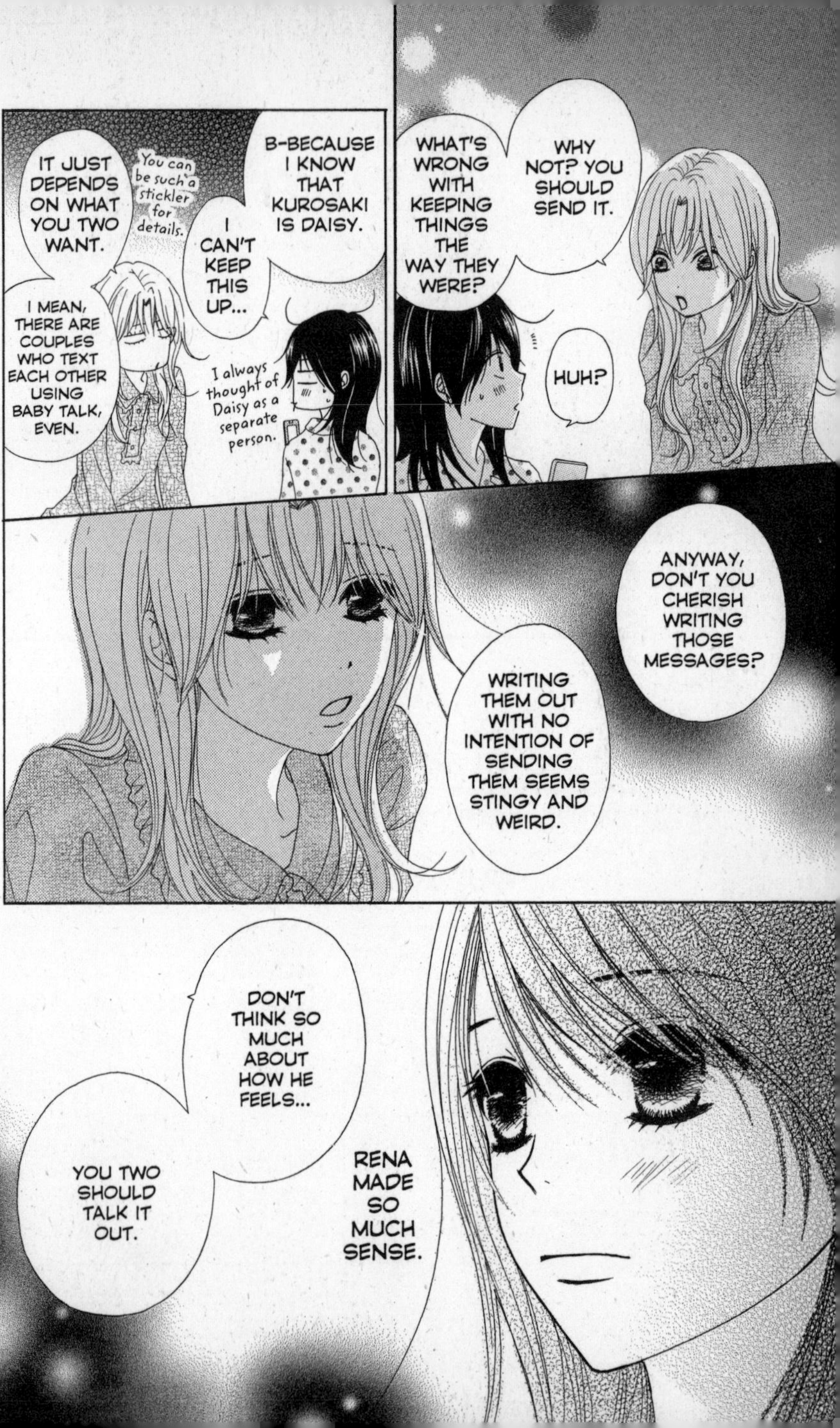
WHY NOT? YOU SHOULD SEND IT.
WHAT'S WRONG WITH KEEPING THINGS THE WAY THEY WERE?
HUH?
B-BECAUSE I KNOW THAT KUROSAKI IS DAISY.
I CAN'T KEEP THIS UP...
You can be such a stickler for details.
IT JUST DEPENDS ON WHAT YOU TWO WANT.
I always thought of Daisy as a separate person.
I MEAN, THERE ARE COUPLES WHO TEXT EACH OTHER USING BABY TALK, EVEN.
ANYWAY, DON'T YOU CHERISH WRITING THOSE MESSAGES?
WRITING THEM OUT WITH NO INTENTION OF SENDING THEM SEEMS STINGY AND WEIRD.
DON'T THINK SO MUCH ABOUT HOW HE FEELS...
YOU TWO SHOULD TALK IT OUT.
RENA MADE SO MUCH SENSE.

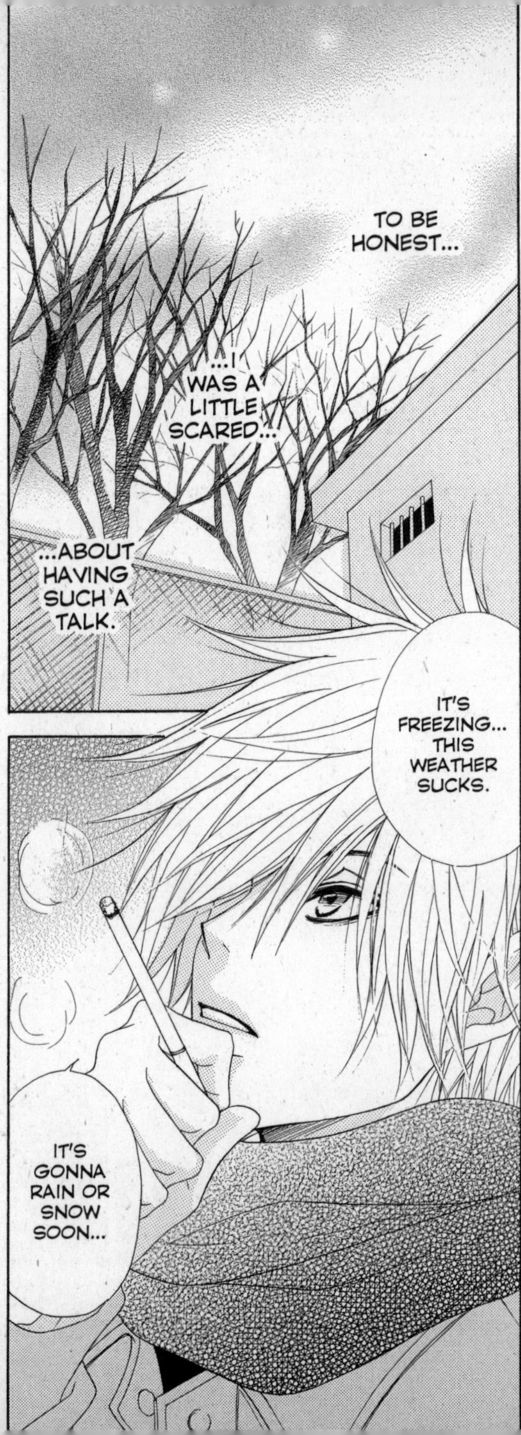
TO BE HONEST...
...I WAS A LITTLE SCARED...
...ABOUT HAVING SUCH A TALK.
IT'S FREEZING... THIS WEATHER SUCKS.
IT'S GONNA RAIN OR SNOW SOON...

DENGEKI DAISY QUESTION CORNER

BALDLY ASK!! ④

Q. DO THE DAISY CHARACTERS LIKE BREAD WITH THE CRUST ON? OR THE CRUST CUT OFF?

(Y.K., HOKKAIDO)

A. KUROSAKI AND SOICHIRO ARE LAZY AND DON'T LIKE TO CHEW SO MUCH, SO THEY PREFER BREAD WITHOUT THE CRUST. THE REST OF THE CHARACTERS LIKE TO EAT THE CRUST. OH, BUT IF IT'S TERU'S, KUROSAKI WOULDN'T MIND AT ALL— (OMITTED)

Q. IN THE PAST, KUROSAKI TENDED TO HAVE STRAIGHT HAIR. LATELY THOUGH, HAS HIS HAIR BECOME MORE OUT OF CONTROL?

(MINSS, HOKKAIDO)

A. ...YOU'RE RIGHT... MAYBE KUROSAKI'S HAIR IS LIKE A BAROMETER THAT MEASURES HIS LEVEL OF AGITATION. WHEN HE WAS FEELING HEARTBROKEN, HIS HAIR TENDED TO BE VERY DOCILE.

Q. WHAT WERE THE CHILDHOOD DREAMS OF TERU AND COMPANY?

(A.T., KAGOSHIMA PREFECTURE)

A. KUROSAKI WANTED TO BECOME A PILOT. TERU, A NINJA. RIKO WANTED TO BECOME A BRIDE. SOICHIRO WANTED TO BECOME A RHINOCEROS BEETLE.

THAT'S IT FOR THIS VOLUME!! THIS MAY CONTINUE IN THE NEXT!!!

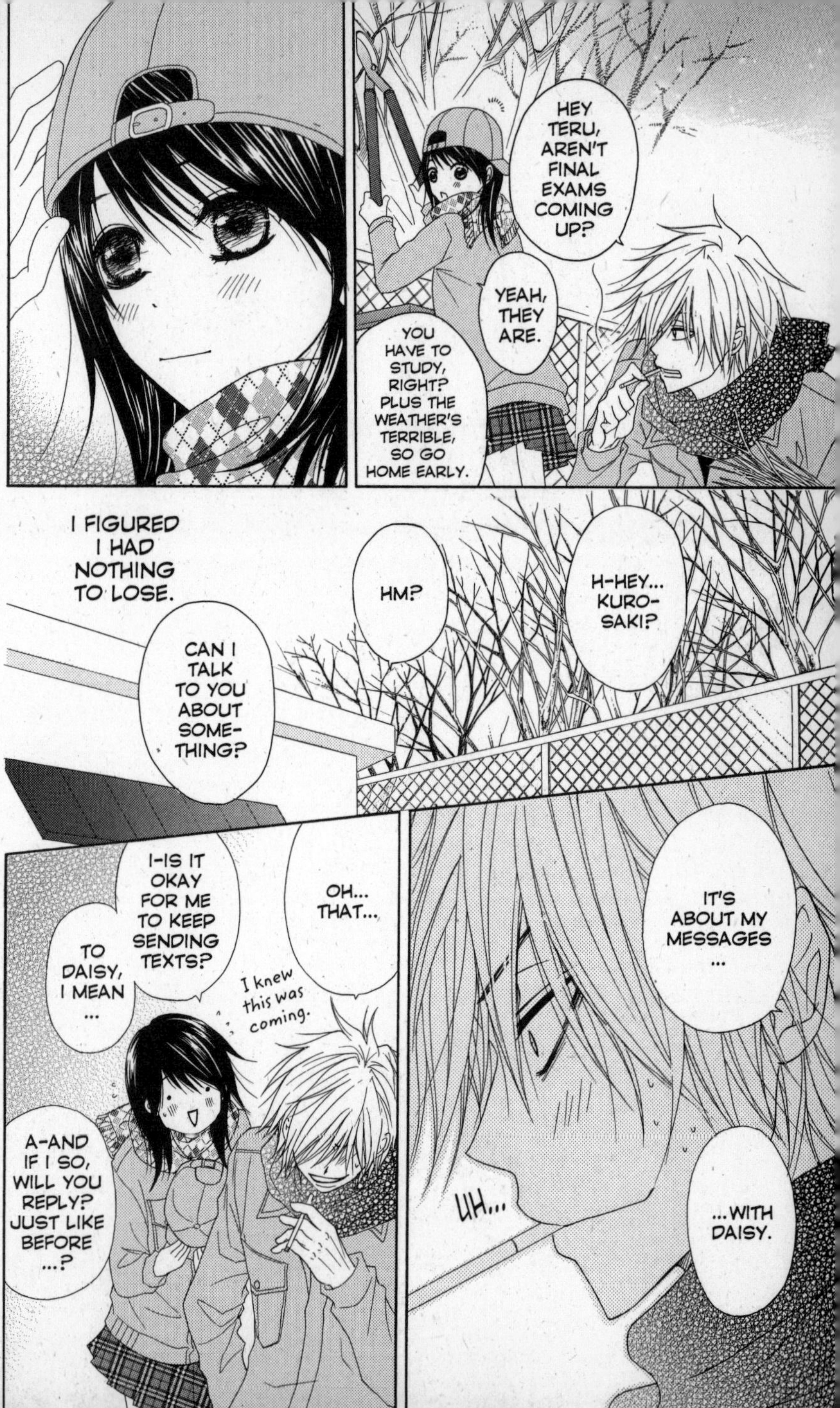
HEY TERU, AREN'T FINAL EXAMS COMING UP?
YEAH, THEY ARE.
YOU HAVE TO STUDY, RIGHT? PLUS THE WEATHER'S TERRIBLE, SO GO HOME EARLY.
H-HEY... KURO-SAKI?
HM?
I FIGURED I HAD NOTHING TO LOSE.
CAN I TALK TO YOU ABOUT SOME-THING?
IT'S ABOUT MY MESSAGES ...
...WITH DAISY.
UH...
OH... THAT...
I knew this was coming.
I-IS IT OKAY FOR ME TO KEEP SENDING TEXTS?
TO DAISY, I MEAN ...
A-AND IF I SO, WILL YOU REPLY? JUST LIKE BEFORE ...?

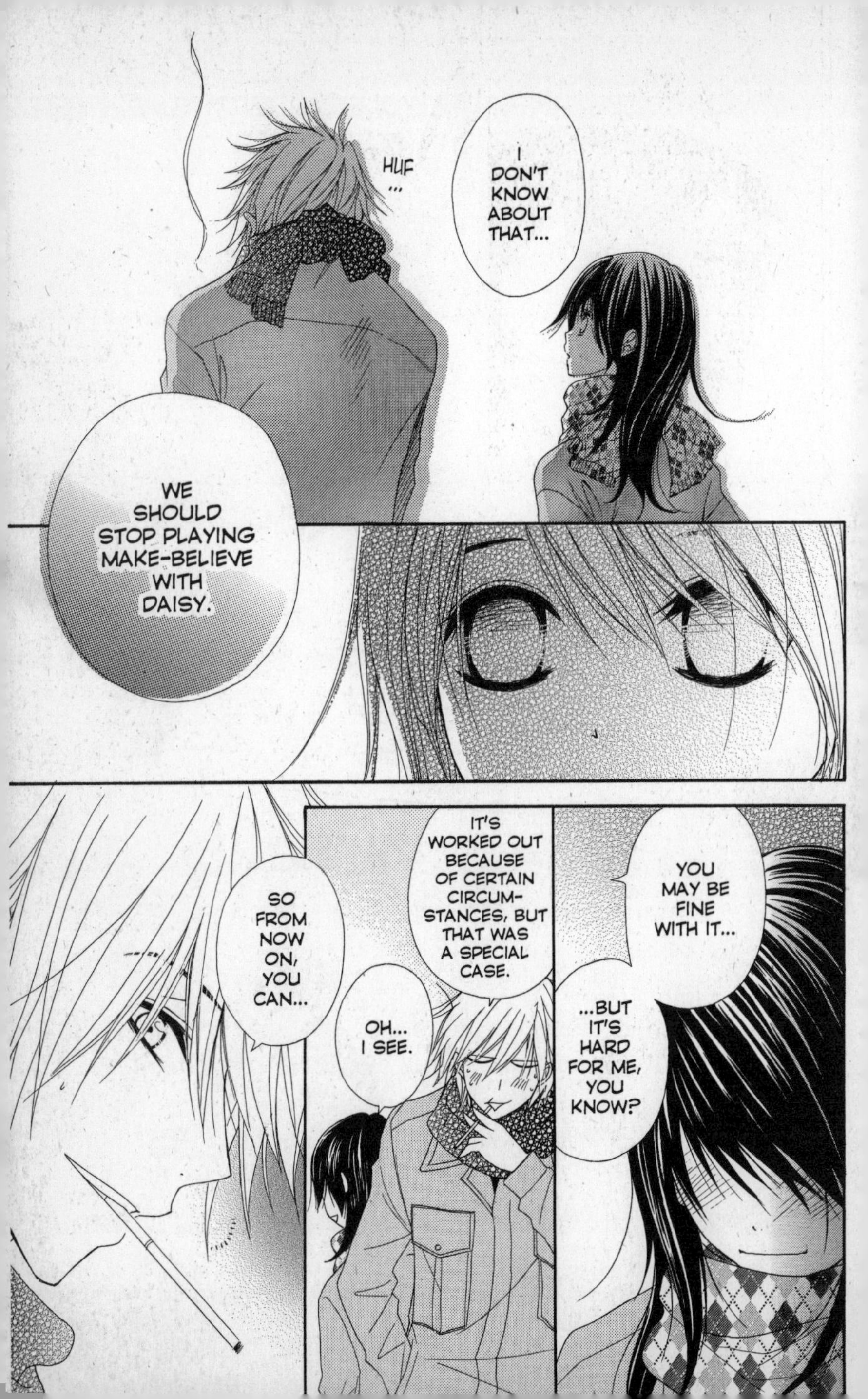
I DON'T KNOW ABOUT THAT...
HUF...
WE SHOULD STOP PLAYING MAKE-BELIEVE WITH DAISY.
YOU MAY BE FINE WITH IT...
...BUT IT'S HARD FOR ME, YOU KNOW?
IT'S WORKED OUT BECAUSE OF CERTAIN CIRCUM-STANCES, BUT THAT WAS A SPECIAL CASE.
OH... I SEE.
SO FROM NOW ON, YOU CAN...

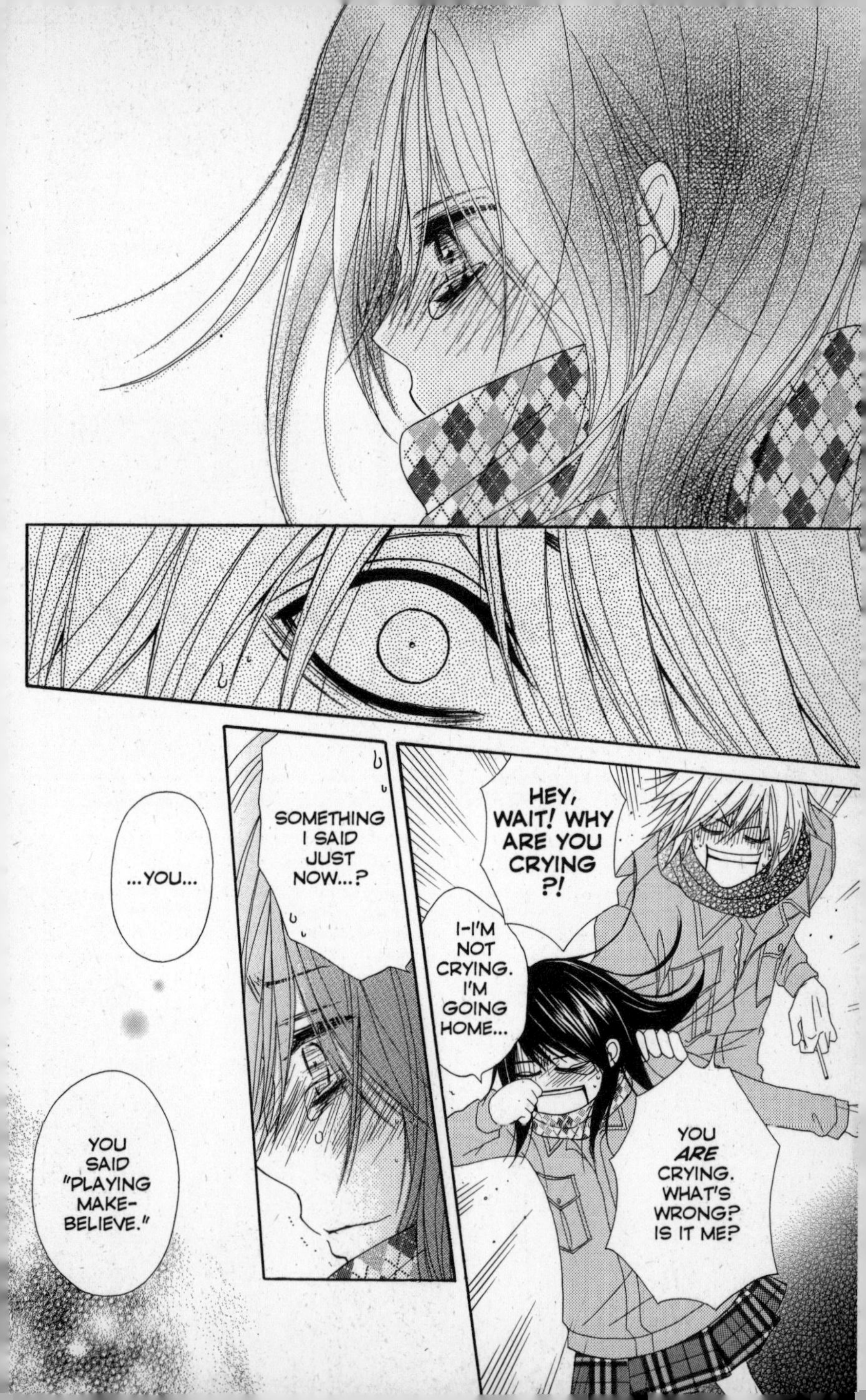
HEY, WAIT! WHY ARE YOU CRYING?!
I-I'M NOT CRYING. I'M GOING HOME...
YOU *ARE* CRYING. WHAT'S WRONG? IS IT ME?
SOMETHING I SAID JUST NOW...?
...YOU...
YOU SAID "PLAYING MAKE-BELIEVE."

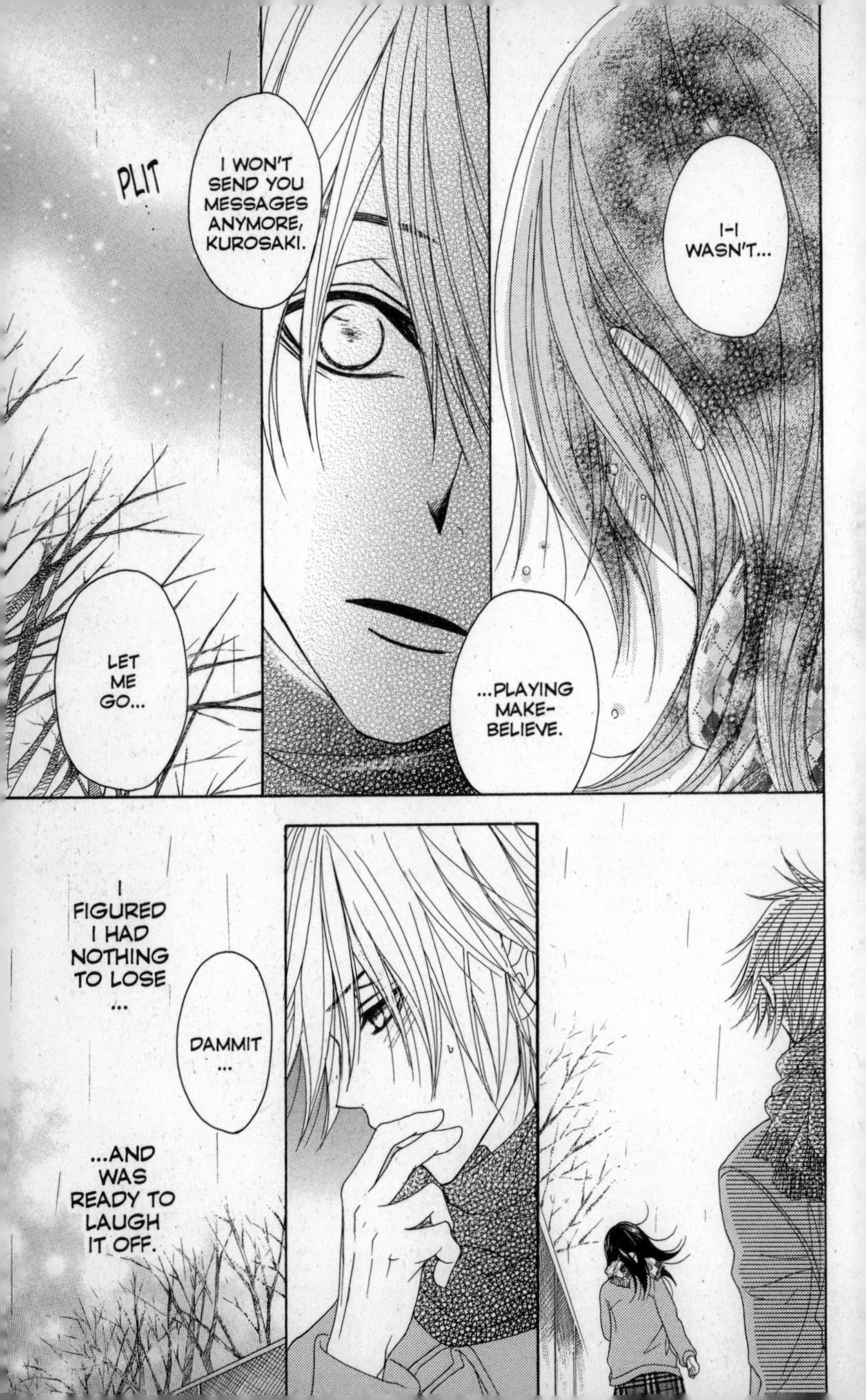
I-I WASN'T...
...PLAYING MAKE-BELIEVE.
I WON'T SEND YOU MESSAGES ANYMORE, KUROSAKI.
PLIT
LET ME GO...
DAMMIT...
I FIGURED I HAD NOTHING TO LOSE...
...AND WAS READY TO LAUGH IT OFF.

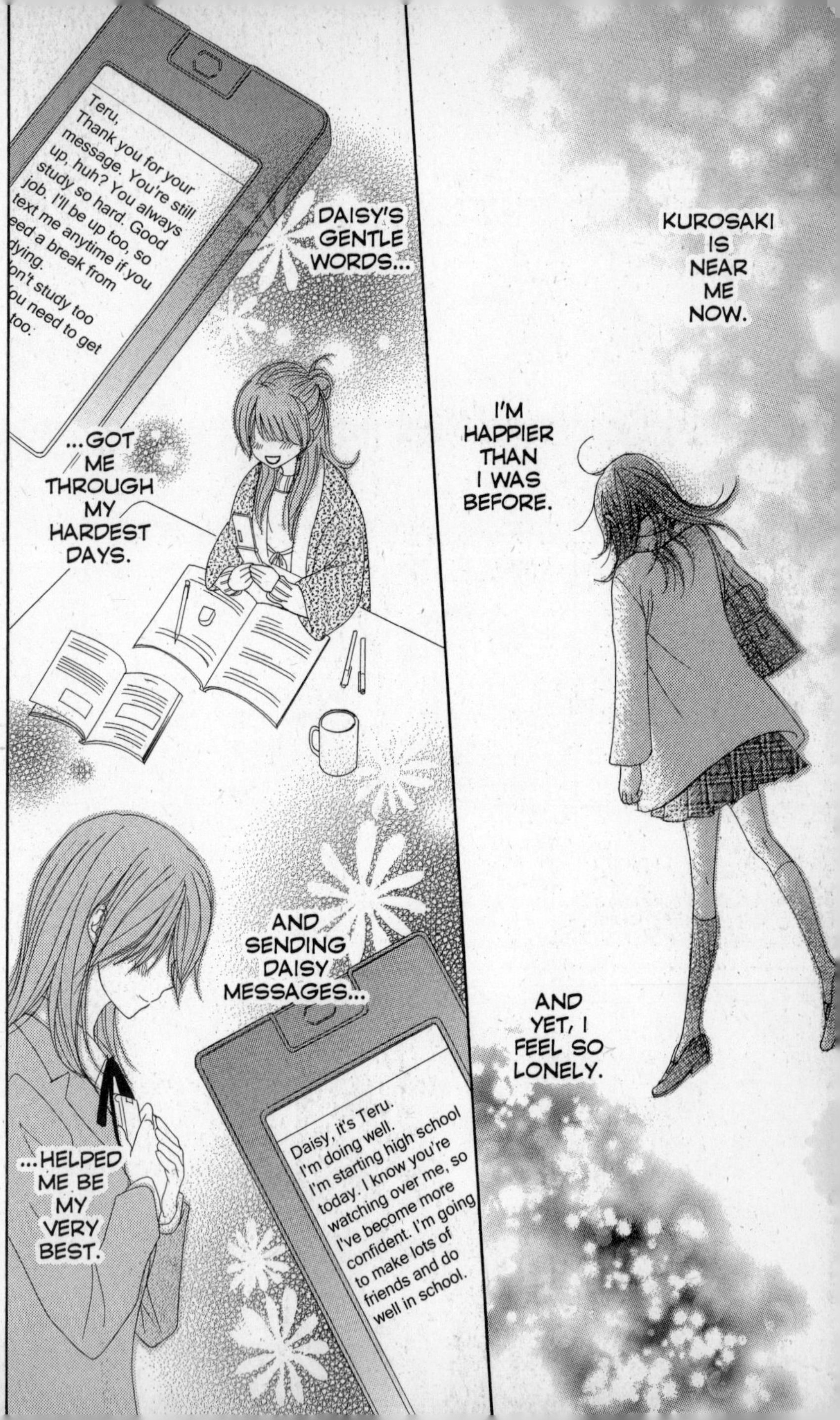
KUROSAKI IS NEAR ME NOW.
I'M HAPPIER THAN I WAS BEFORE.
AND YET, I FEEL SO LONELY.
Teru, Thank you for your message. You're still up, huh? You always study so hard. Good job. I'll be up too, so text me anytime if you eed a break from dying. on't study too ou need to get too.
DAISY'S GENTLE WORDS...
...GOT ME THROUGH MY HARDEST DAYS.
AND SENDING DAISY MESSAGES...
Daisy, it's Teru. I'm doing well. I'm starting high school today. I know you're watching over me, so I've become more confident. I'm going to make lots of friends and do well in school.
...HELPED ME BE MY VERY BEST.

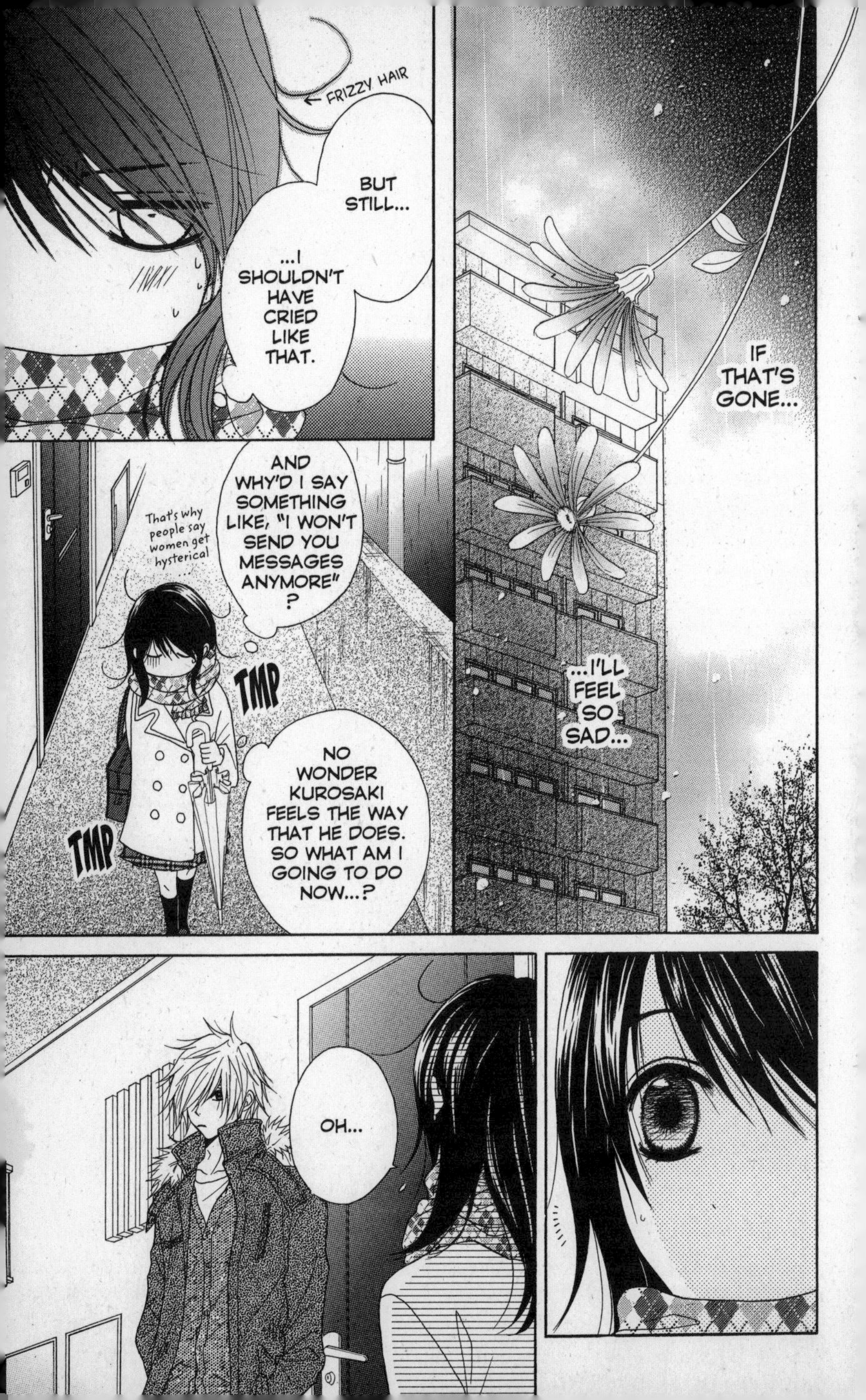
IF THAT'S GONE...
...I'LL FEEL SO SAD...
BUT STILL...
...I SHOULDN'T HAVE CRIED LIKE THAT.
← FRIZZY HAIR
AND WHY'D I SAY SOMETHING LIKE, "I WON'T SEND YOU MESSAGES ANYMORE"?
That's why people say women get hysterical...
TMP
TMP
NO WONDER KUROSAKI FEELS THE WAY THAT HE DOES. SO WHAT AM I GOING TO DO NOW...?
OH...

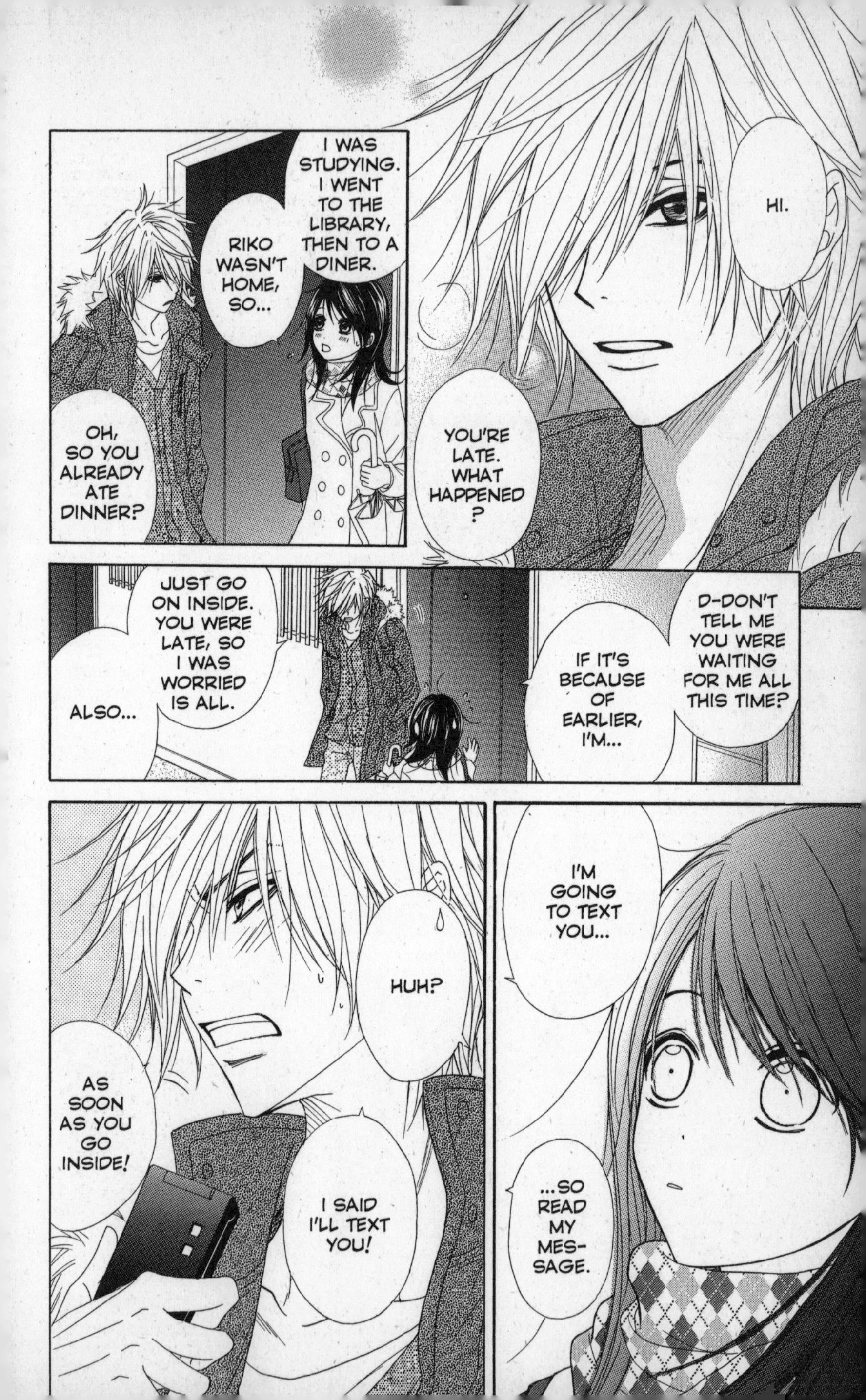
HI.
YOU'RE LATE. WHAT HAPPENED?
I WAS STUDYING. I WENT TO THE LIBRARY, THEN TO A DINER.
RIKO WASN'T HOME, SO...
OH, SO YOU ALREADY ATE DINNER?
D-DON'T TELL ME YOU WERE WAITING FOR ME ALL THIS TIME?
IF IT'S BECAUSE OF EARLIER, I'M...
JUST GO ON INSIDE. YOU WERE LATE, SO I WAS WORRIED IS ALL.
ALSO...
I'M GOING TO TEXT YOU...
...SO READ MY MES-SAGE.
HUH?
I SAID I'LL TEXT YOU!
AS SOON AS YOU GO INSIDE!

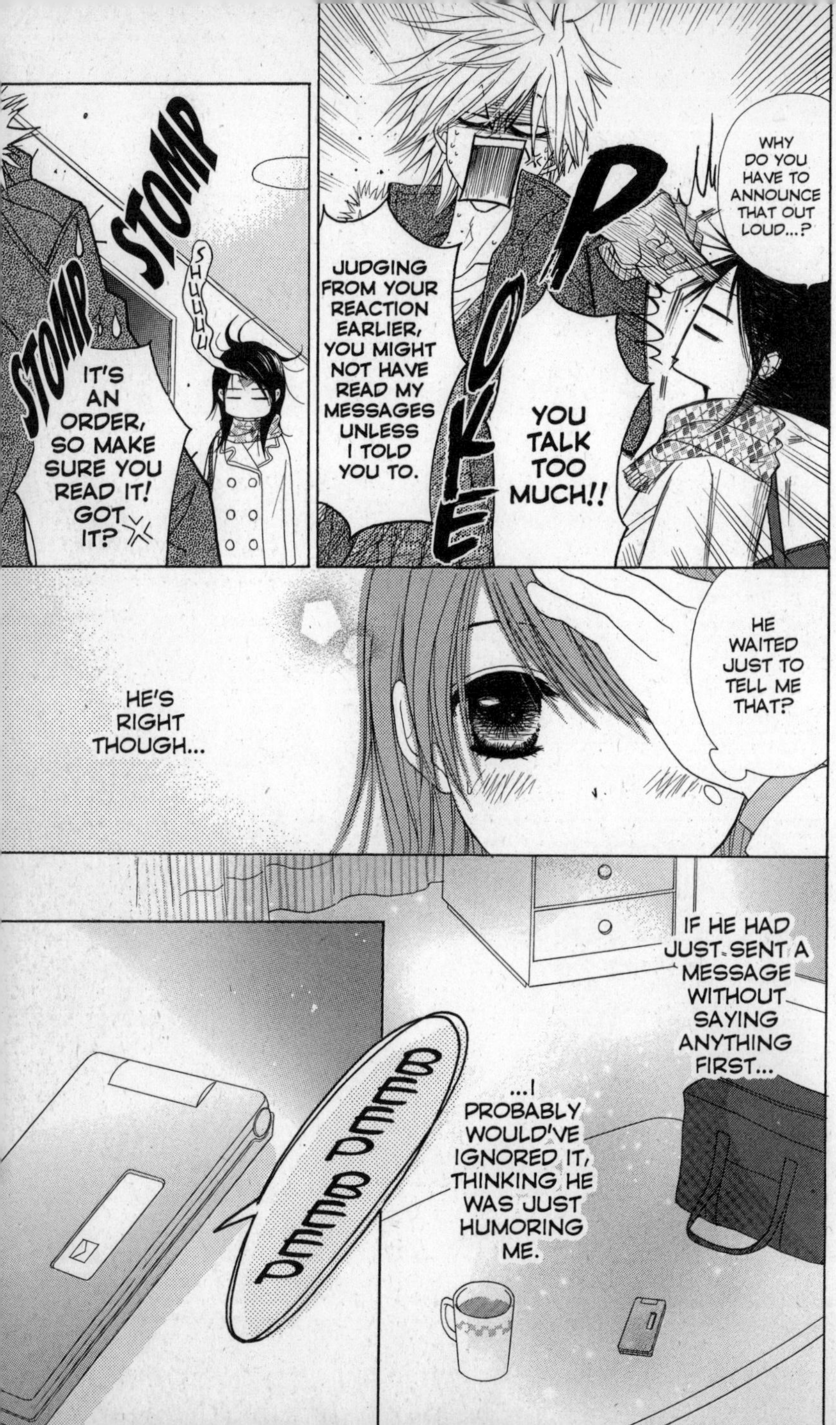
WHY DO YOU HAVE TO ANNOUNCE THAT OUT LOUD...?
POKE
YOU TALK TOO MUCH!!
JUDGING FROM YOUR REACTION EARLIER, YOU MIGHT NOT HAVE READ MY MESSAGES UNLESS I TOLD YOU TO.
STOMP
STOMP
STOMP
SHUUUU
IT'S AN ORDER, SO MAKE SURE YOU READ IT! GOT IT?
HE WAITED JUST TO TELL ME THAT?
HE'S RIGHT THOUGH...
IF HE HAD JUST SENT A MESSAGE WITHOUT SAYING ANYTHING FIRST...
...I PROBABLY WOULD'VE IGNORED IT, THINKING HE WAS JUST HUMORING ME.
BEEP BEEP

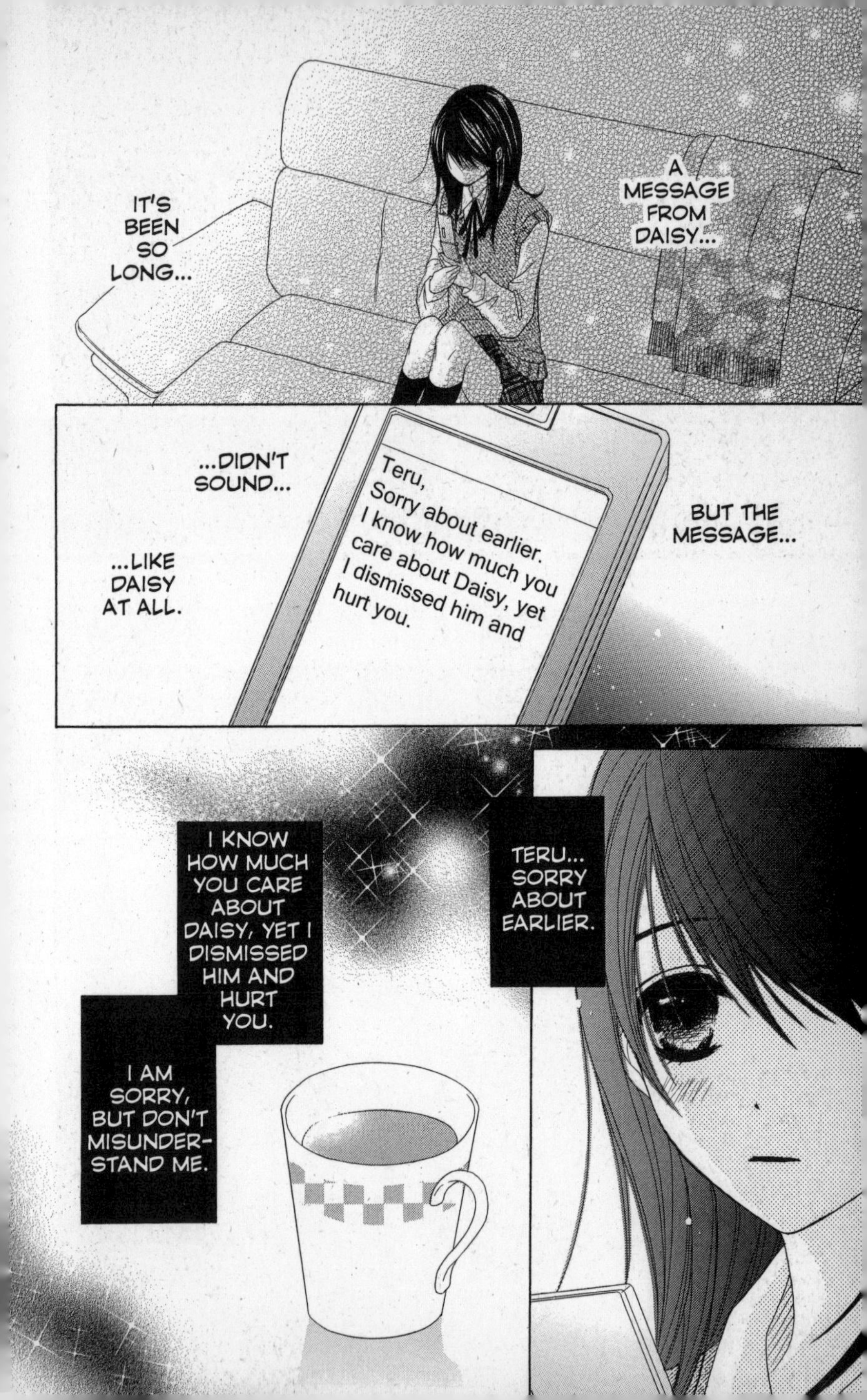
A MESSAGE FROM DAISY...
IT'S BEEN SO LONG...
BUT THE MESSAGE...
Teru,
Sorry about earlier.
I know how much you care about Daisy, yet I dismissed him and hurt you.
...DIDN'T SOUND...
...LIKE DAISY AT ALL.
TERU... SORRY ABOUT EARLIER.
I KNOW HOW MUCH YOU CARE ABOUT DAISY, YET I DISMISSED HIM AND HURT YOU.
I AM SORRY, BUT DON'T MISUNDER-STAND ME.

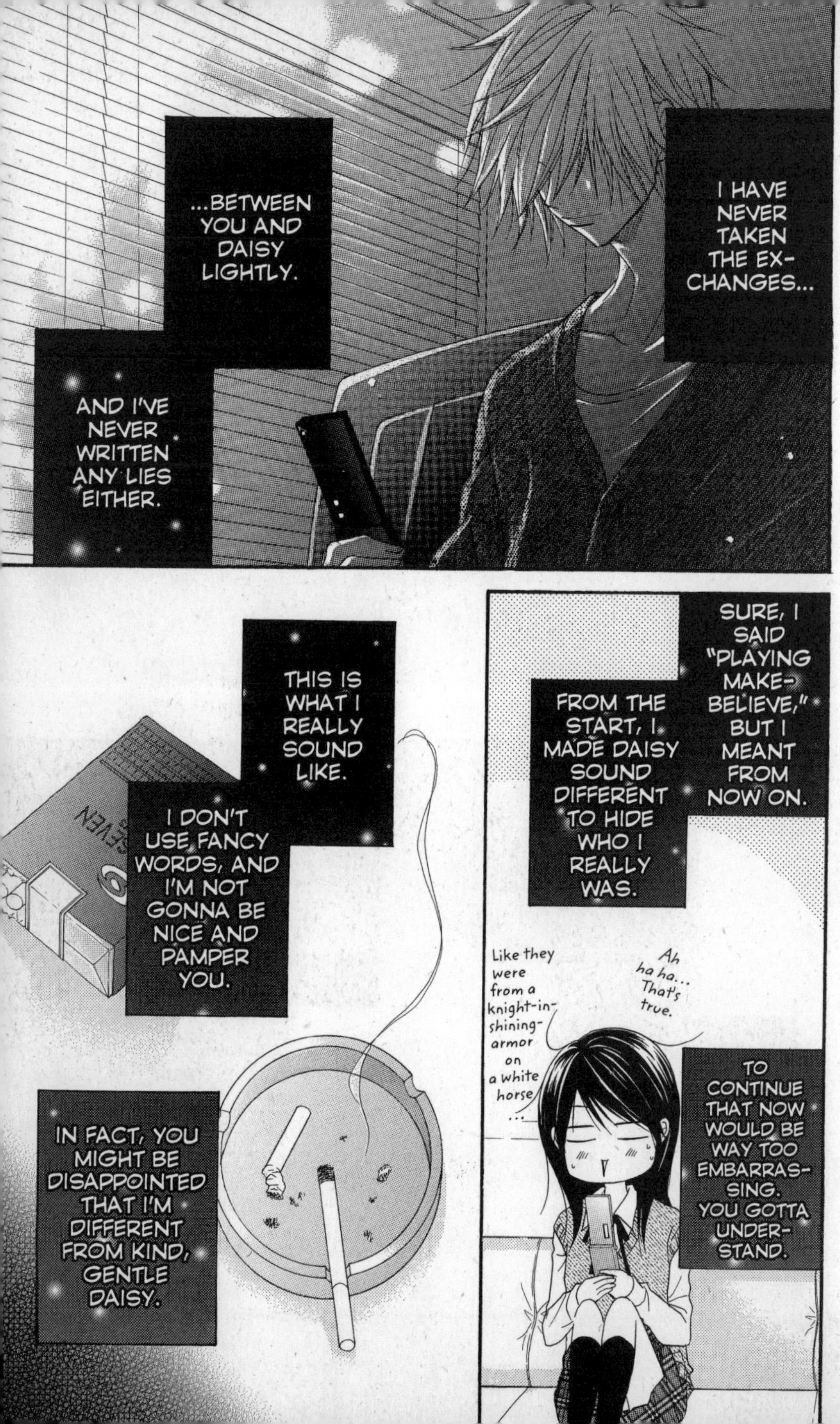
I HAVE NEVER TAKEN THE EX-CHANGES...
...BETWEEN YOU AND DAISY LIGHTLY.
AND I'VE NEVER WRITTEN ANY LIES EITHER.
SURE, I SAID "PLAYING MAKE-BELIEVE," BUT I MEANT FROM NOW ON.
FROM THE START, I MADE DAISY SOUND DIFFERENT TO HIDE WHO I REALLY WAS.
Ah ha ha... That's true.
Like they were from a knight-in-shining-armor on a white horse...
TO CONTINUE THAT NOW WOULD BE WAY TOO EMBARRAS-SING. YOU GOTTA UNDER-STAND.
THIS IS WHAT I REALLY SOUND LIKE.
I DON'T USE FANCY WORDS, AND I'M NOT GONNA BE NICE AND PAMPER YOU.
IN FACT, YOU MIGHT BE DISAPPOINTED THAT I'M DIFFERENT FROM KIND, GENTLE DAISY.

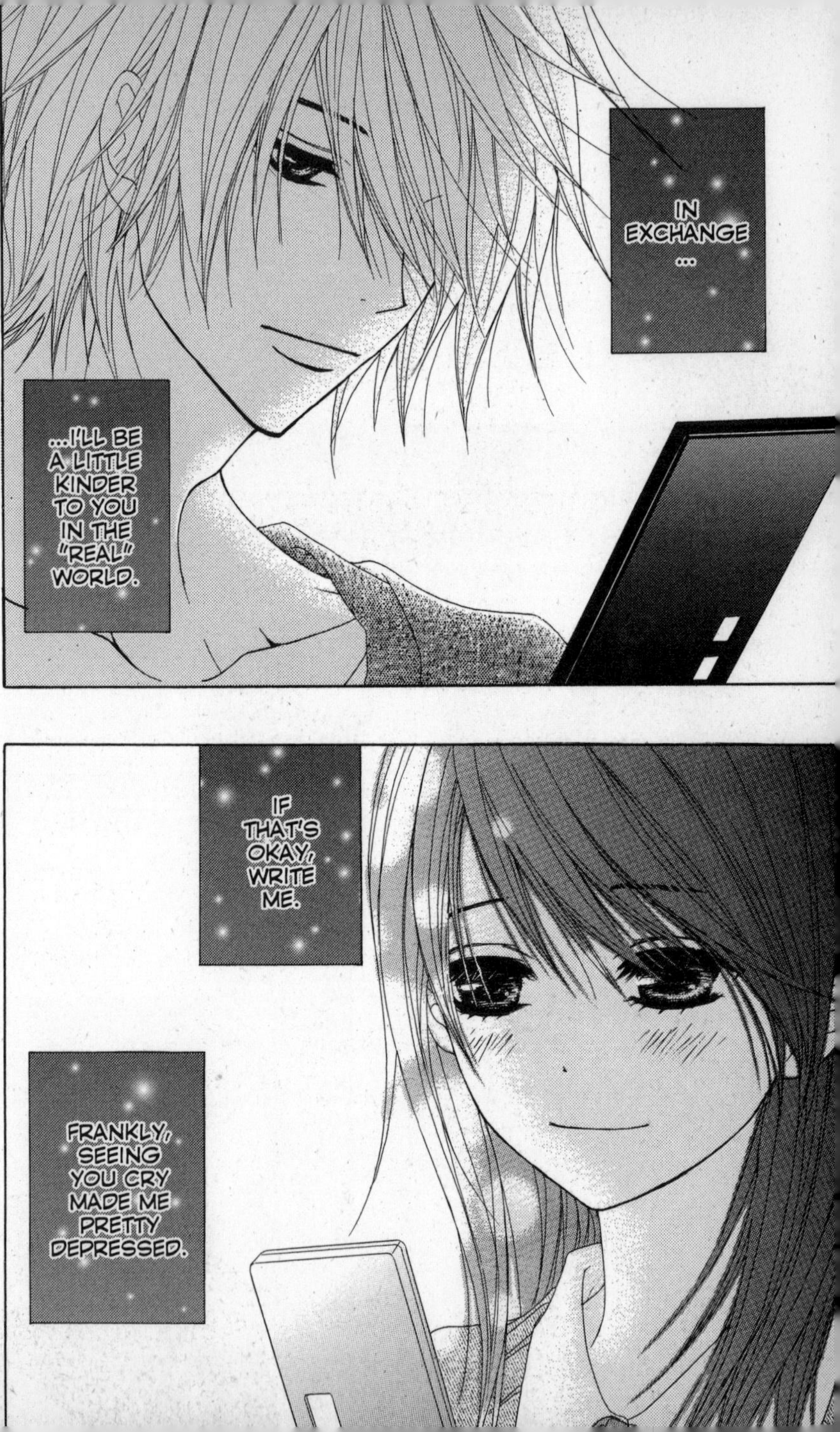
IN EXCHANGE ...
...I'LL BE A LITTLE KINDER TO YOU IN THE "REAL" WORLD.
IF THAT'S OKAY, WRITE ME.
FRANKLY, SEEING YOU CRY MADE ME PRETTY DEPRESSED.

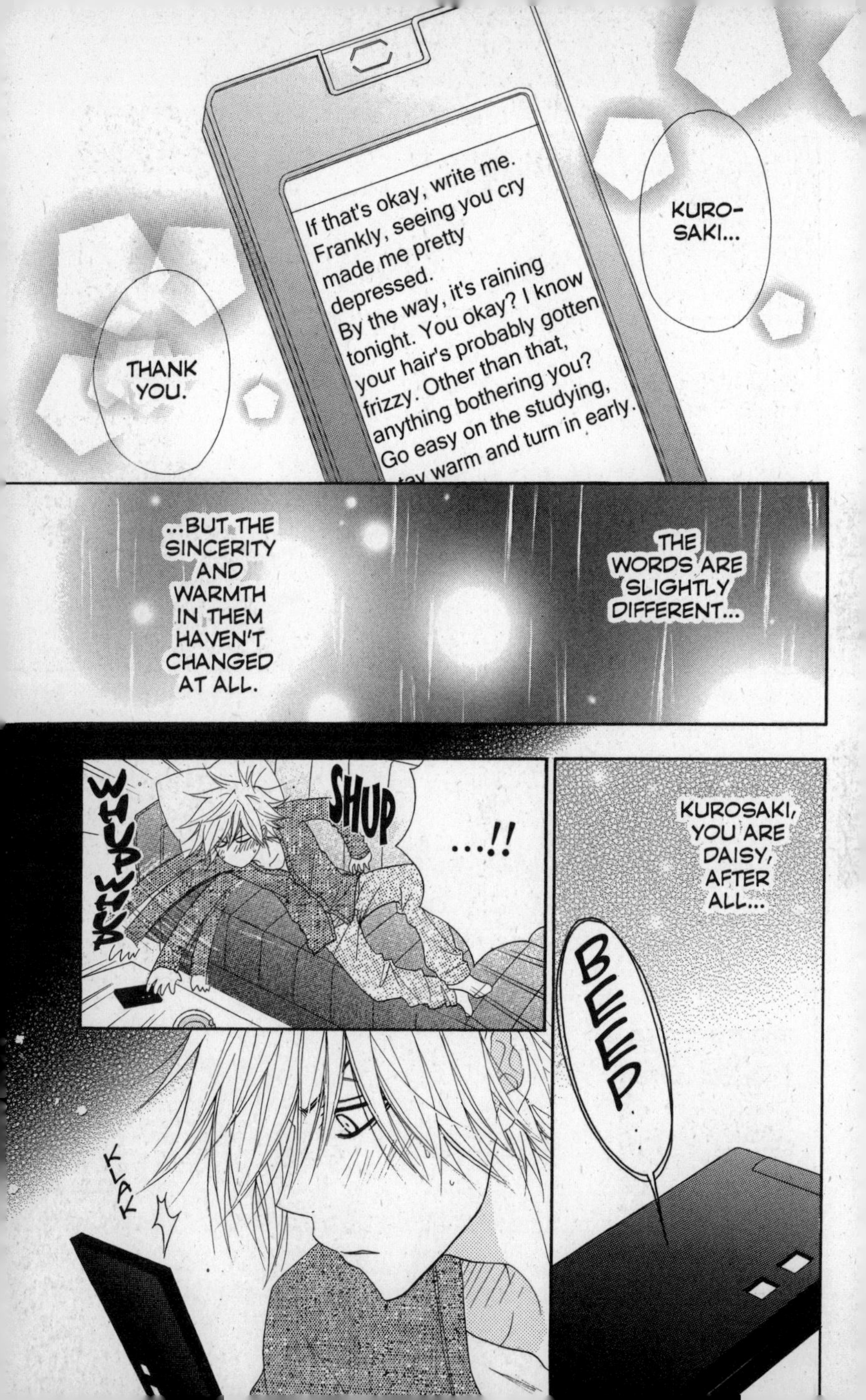
KURO-SAKI...
If that's okay, write me.
Frankly, seeing you cry made me pretty depressed.
By the way, it's raining tonight. You okay? I know your hair's probably gotten frizzy. Other than that, anything bothering you?
Go easy on the studying,
warm and turn in early.
THANK YOU.
THE WORDS ARE SLIGHTLY DIFFERENT...
...BUT THE SINCERITY AND WARMTH IN THEM HAVEN'T CHANGED AT ALL.
KUROSAKI, YOU ARE DAISY, AFTER ALL...
BEEP
SHUP
...!!
KLAK

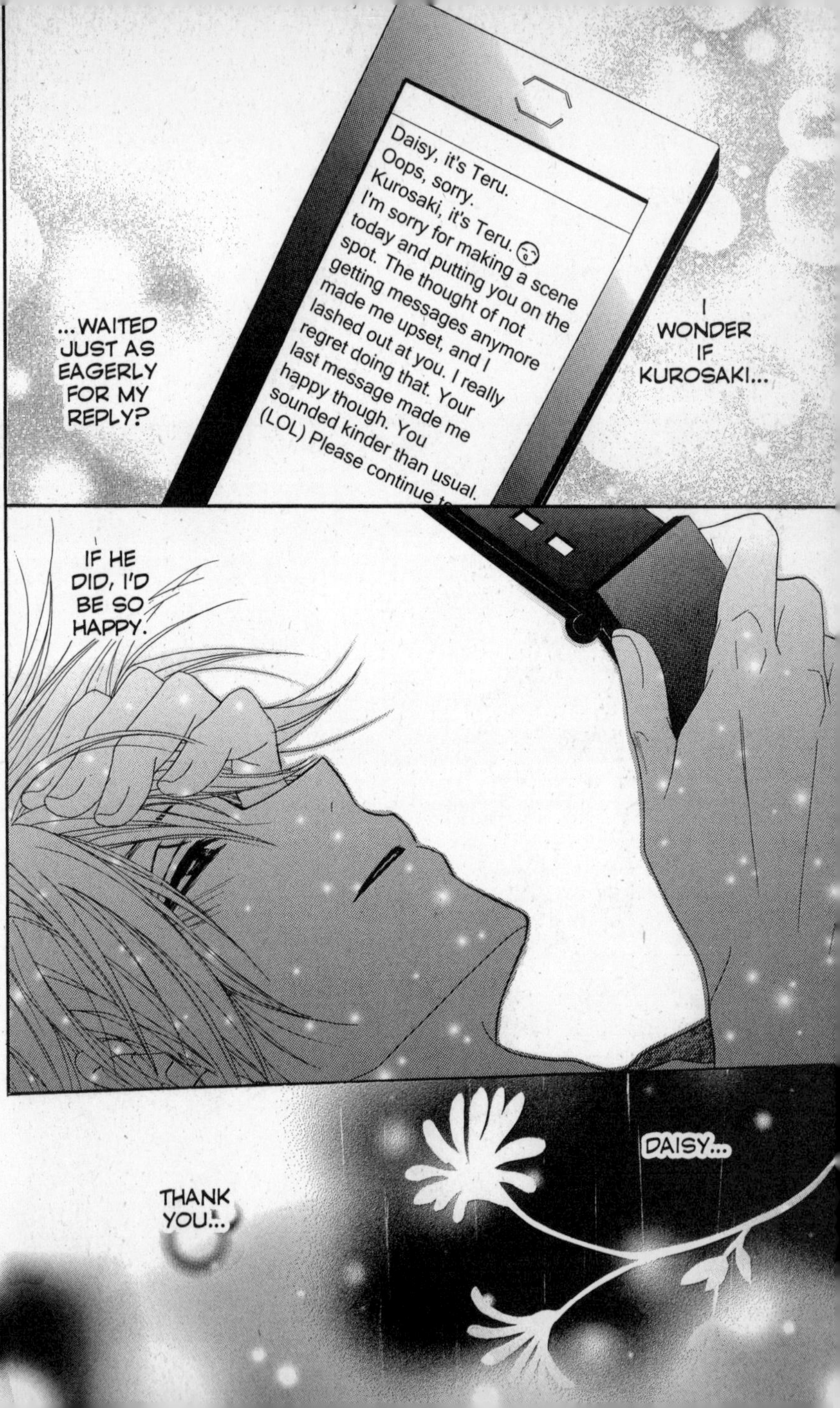
I WONDER IF KUROSAKI...
Daisy, it's Teru. Oops, sorry. Kurosaki, it's Teru. I'm sorry for making a scene today and putting you on the spot. The thought of not getting messages anymore made me upset, and I lashed out at you. I really regret doing that. Your last message made me happy though. You sounded kinder than usual. (LOL) Please continue
...WAITED JUST AS EAGERLY FOR MY REPLY?
IF HE DID, I'D BE SO HAPPY.
DAISY...
THANK YOU...

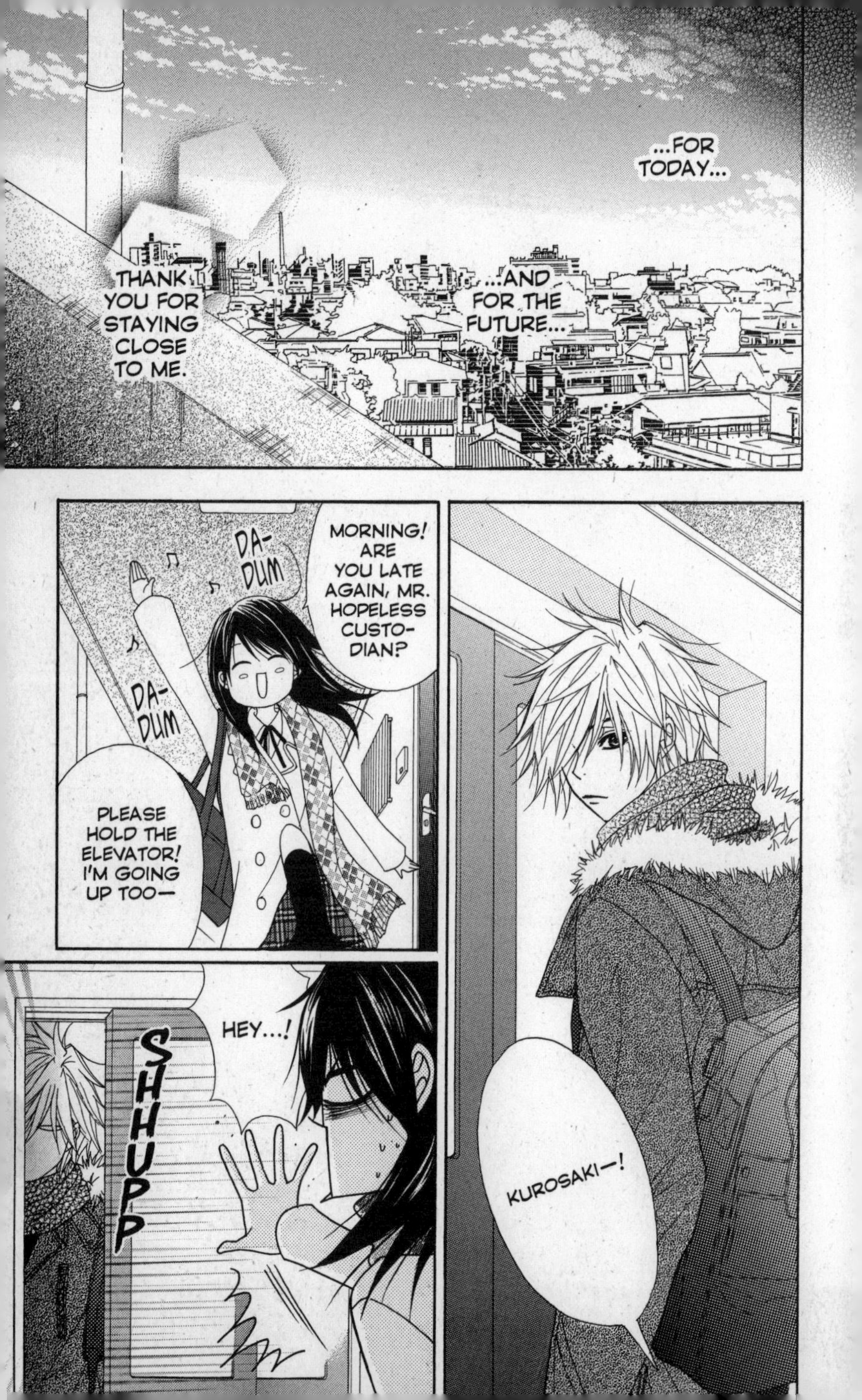
...FOR TODAY...
...AND FOR THE FUTURE...
THANK YOU FOR STAYING CLOSE TO ME.
KUROSAKI—!
MORNING! ARE YOU LATE AGAIN, MR. HOPELESS CUSTODIAN?
DA-DUM
DA-DUM
PLEASE HOLD THE ELEVATOR! I'M GOING UP TOO—
HEY...!
SHHUPP

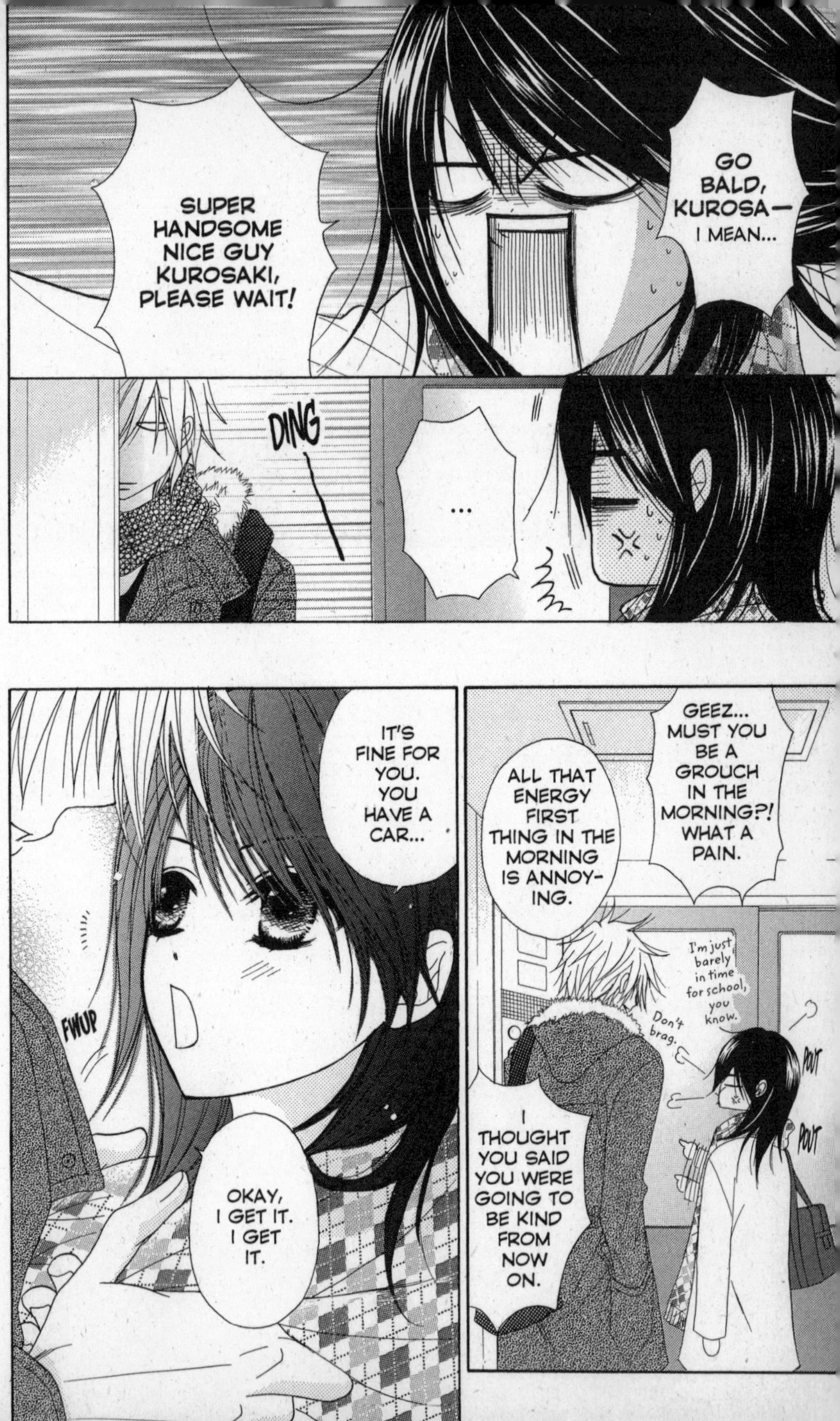
GO BALD, KUROSA— I MEAN...
SUPER HANDSOME NICE GUY KUROSAKI, PLEASE WAIT!
...
DING
GEEZ... MUST YOU BE A GROUCH IN THE MORNING?! WHAT A PAIN.
ALL THAT ENERGY FIRST THING IN THE MORNING IS ANNOY-ING.
I'm just barely in time for school, you know.
Don't brag.
POUT
POUT
I THOUGHT YOU SAID YOU WERE GOING TO BE KIND FROM NOW ON.
IT'S FINE FOR YOU. YOU HAVE A CAR...
FWUP
OKAY, I GET IT. I GET IT.

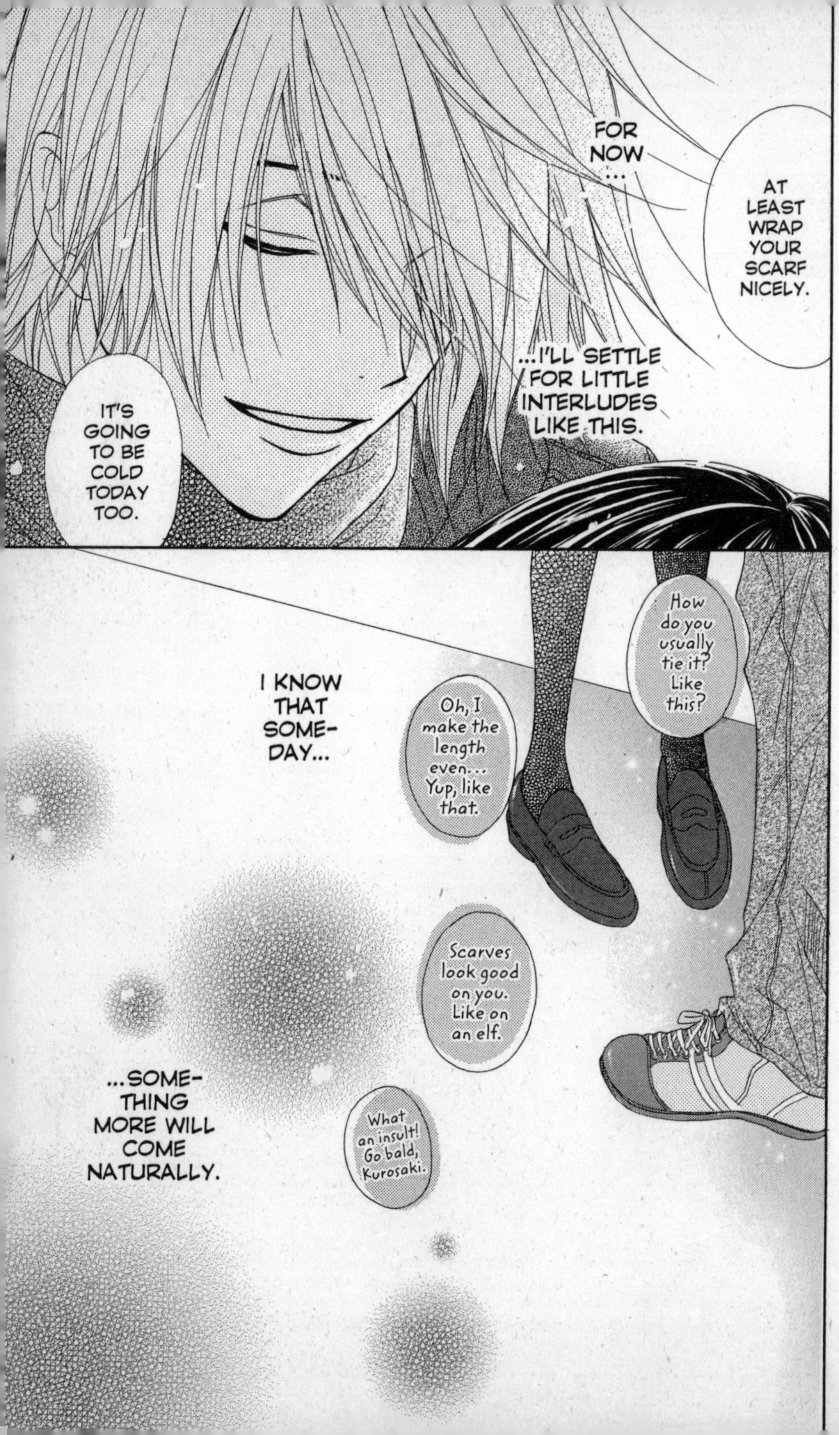
AT LEAST WRAP YOUR SCARF NICELY.
FOR NOW...
...I'LL SETTLE FOR LITTLE INTERLUDES LIKE THIS.
IT'S GOING TO BE COLD TODAY TOO.
How do you usually tie it? Like this?
Oh, I make the length even... Yup, like that.
I KNOW THAT SOME-DAY...
Scarves look good on you. Like on an elf.
What an insult! Go bald, Kurosaki.
...SOME-THING MORE WILL COME NATURALLY.

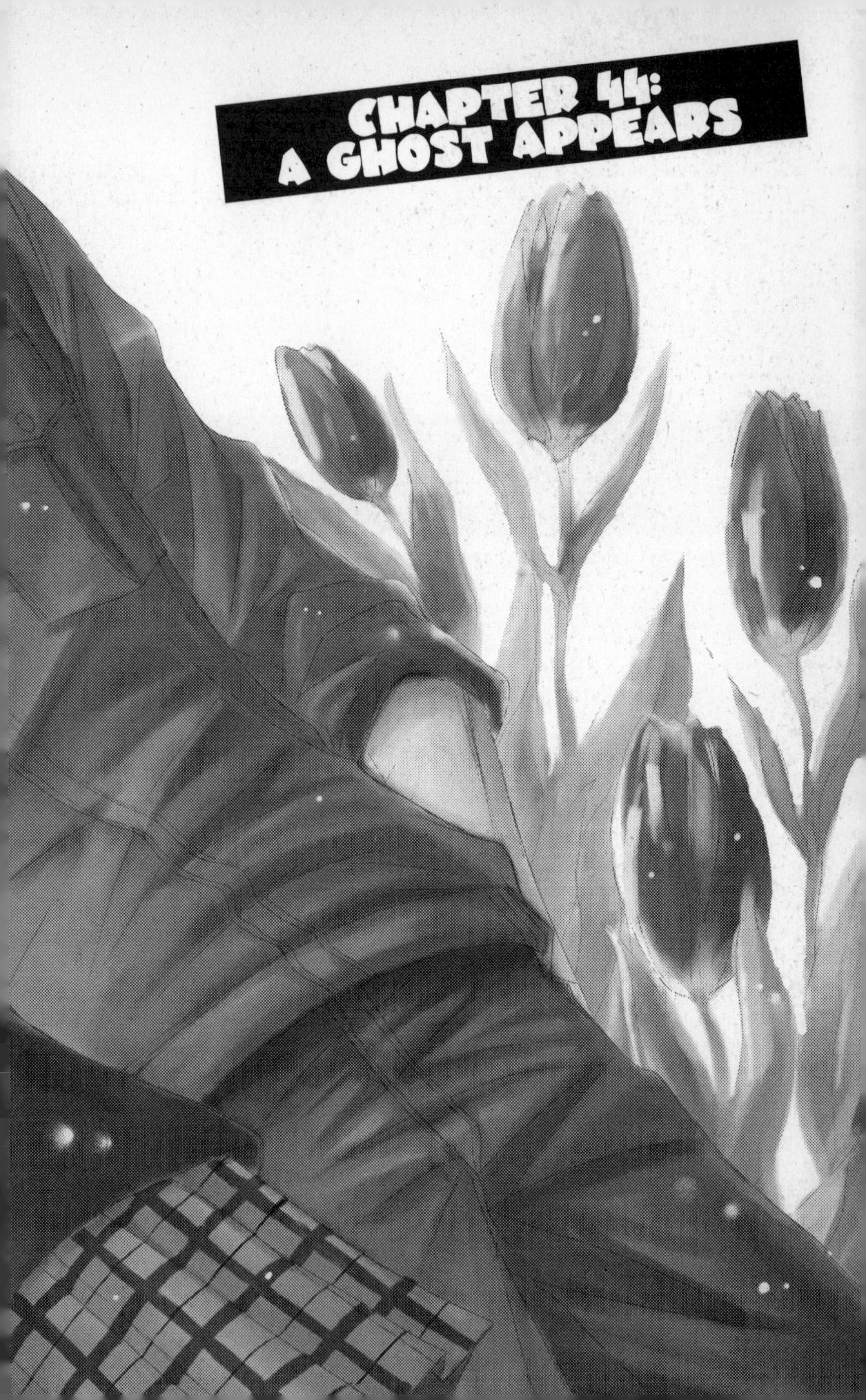
CHAPTER 44:
A GHOST APPEARS

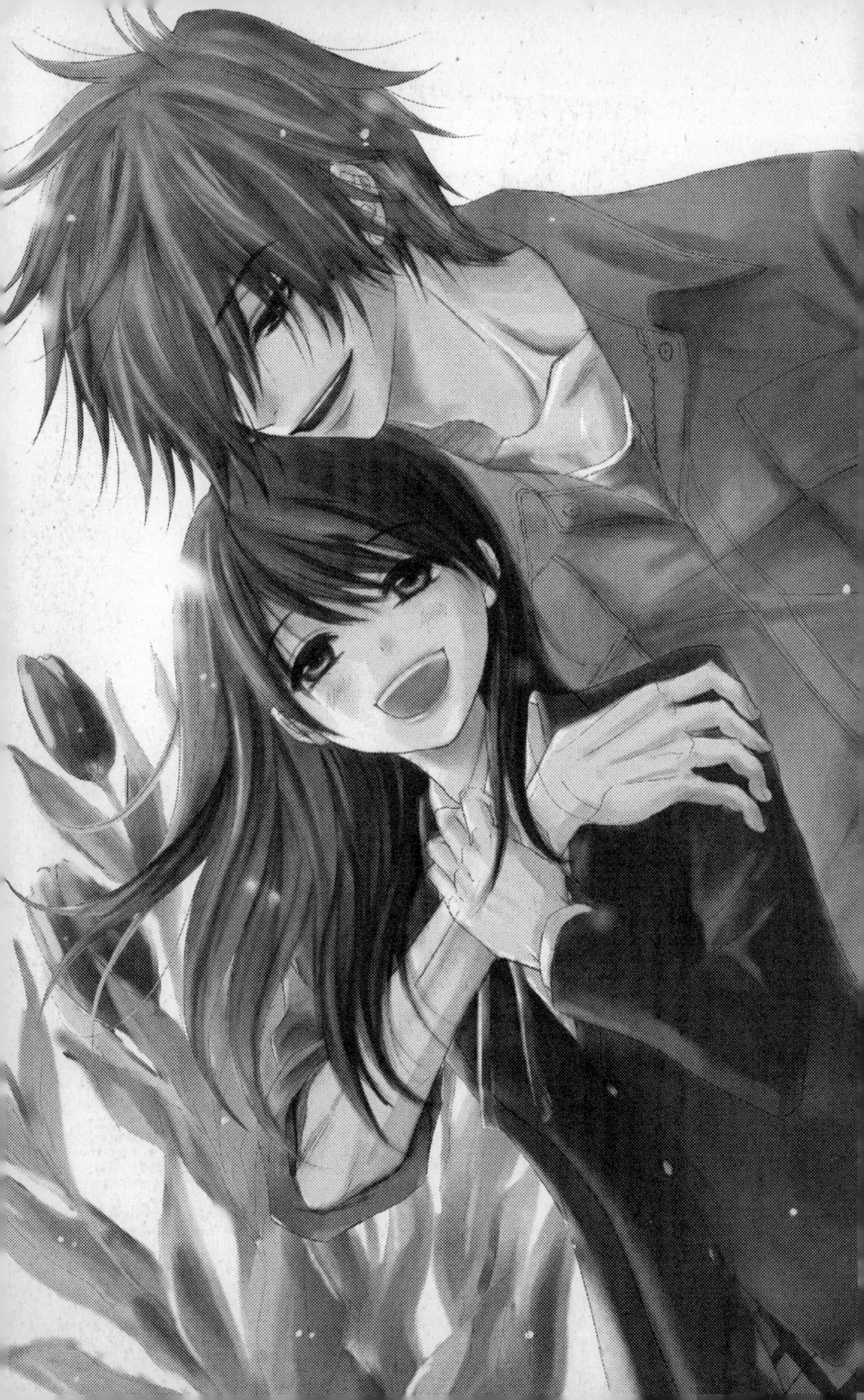

AFTERWORD

THE MORNING AFTER
AT THE HOTEL

My Huh?!

All the sutras have been copied in this book.

YOU JUST TRACE EASY-TO-COPY

BRSH BRSH

...HI! THANK YOU FOR READING *DENGEKI DAISY* VOLUME 9.
(WE HAD A BLANK PAGE HERE, SO THIS BECAME
THE AFTERWORD.)

WELL, *DAISY* IS BACK TO NORMAL SPEED AT LAST. ACTUALLY, I THOUGHT
THAT KUROSAKI WOULD RETURN MUCH SOONER. (AND HAVE PEOPLE
SNICKERING, "THERE WAS SUCH A FUSS ABOUT HIS DISAPPEARANCE,
AND HE'S BACK ALREADY! HAHAHA...") BUT IT TOOK QUITE A BIT OF
TIME. MY APOLOGIES. SO TO THE READERS WHO WAITED PATIENTLY
DESPITE THIS, MY SINCERE THANKS.

...NOW THEN, LIFE IS BACK TO THE WAY IT WAS, BUT MANY THINGS ARE
LEFT UNSOLVED IN *DENGEKI DAISY*. GRATEFULLY, THE STORY CONTINUES
ON. TERU, KUROSAKI, ALL THE OTHERS, AND I, THE AUTHOR, WILL
AIMLESSLY CONTINUE TO DO OUR BEST. IT WILL PLEASE ME SO
MUCH IF WE CAN MEET AGAIN IN THE NEXT VOLUME. THANK YOU.

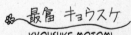

最富 キョウスケ
KYOUSUKE MOTOMI

DENGEKI DAISY
C/O DENGEKI DAISY EDITOR
VIZ MEDIA
P.O. BOX 77010
SAN FRANCISCO, CA 94107

IF YOU HAVE ANY QUESTIONS, PLEASE
SEND THEM HERE. FOR REGULAR FAN MAIL,
PLEASE SEND THEM TO THE SAME ADDRESS
BUT CHANGE THE ADDRESSEE TO:

KYOUSUKE MOTOMI
C/O DENGEKI DAISY EDITOR

...AND THAT'S IT. THANK YOU
VERY MUCH!!!

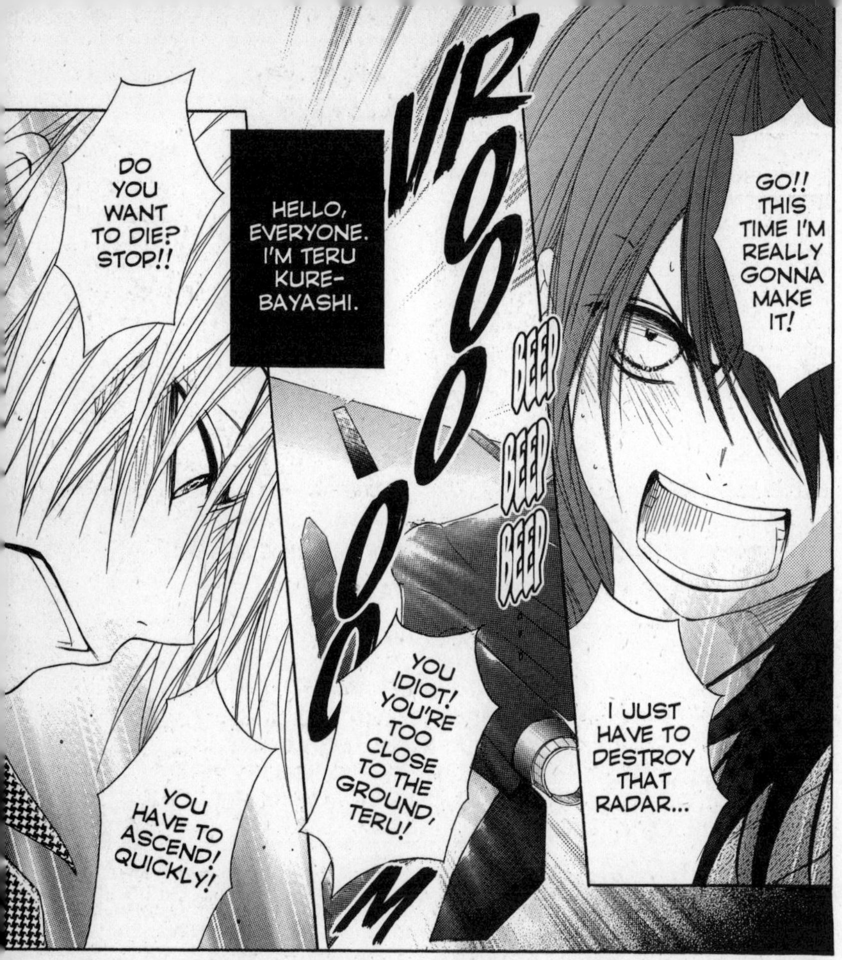
GO!! THIS TIME I'M REALLY GONNA MAKE IT!
I JUST HAVE TO DESTROY THAT RADAR...
BEEP BEEP BEEP
VROOOOOOM
HELLO, EVERYONE. I'M TERU KURE-BAYASHI.
YOU IDIOT! YOU'RE TOO CLOSE TO THE GROUND, TERU!
DO YOU WANT TO DIE? STOP!!
YOU HAVE TO ASCEND! QUICKLY!

IT HAD BEEN QUITE SOME TIME SINCE I HAD USED THE SCREEN TONE KNOWN AS NUMBER 41 (←).

THEN SUDDENLY WITH THIS VOLUME, I RESUMED USING IT, AND I HAD THIS STRONG SENSE THAT THINGS WERE BACK TO NORMAL. NUMBER 41 IS THE COLOR OF THEIR WORK UNIFORMS. AND IT REINFORCED MY OPINION THAT KUROSAKI LOOKS BEST IN A WORK UNIFORM. NEXT TO HER SCHOOL UNIFORM, I THINK THIS LOOKS BEST ON TERU TOO. WHEN THEY'RE IN THEIR WORK CLOTHES, I FEEL A SENSE OF RELIEF. (PLUS, I DON'T HAVE TO THINK ABOUT WHAT THEY WEAR.)

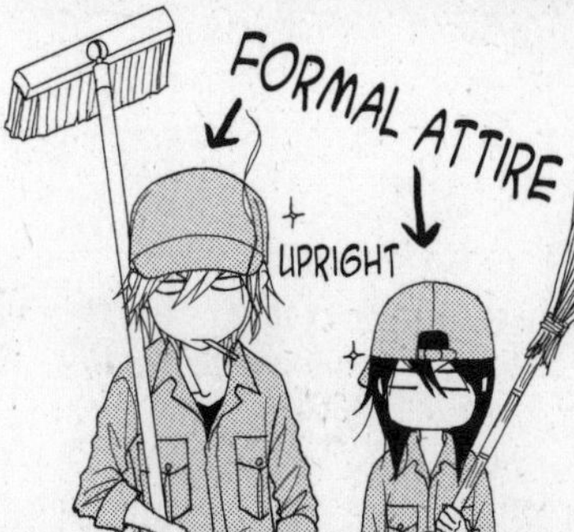
FORMAL ATTIRE
UPRIGHT

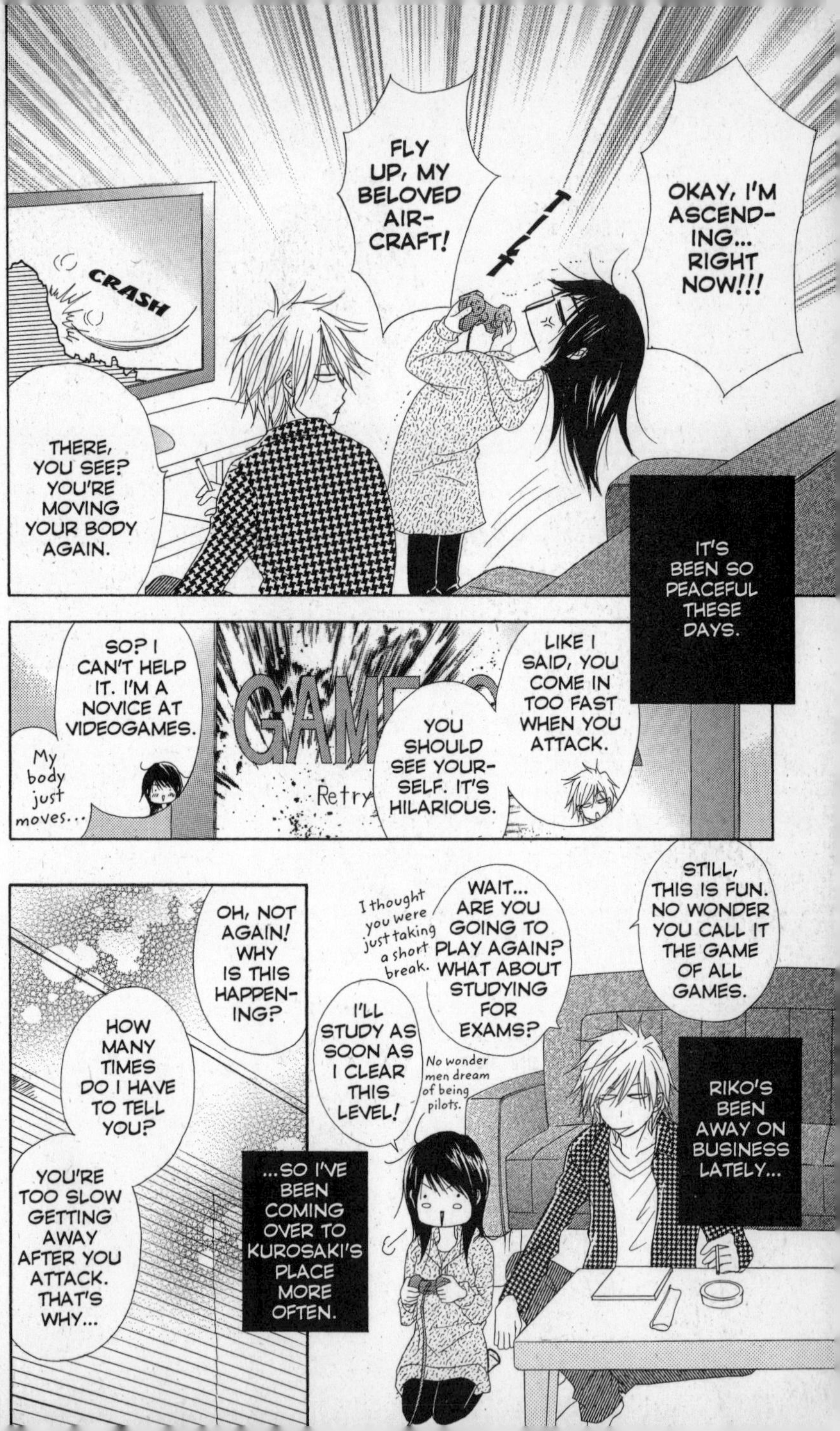
OKAY, I'M ASCEND-ING... RIGHT NOW!!!
FLY UP, MY BELOVED AIR-CRAFT!
TILT
CRASH
THERE, YOU SEE? YOU'RE MOVING YOUR BODY AGAIN.
IT'S BEEN SO PEACEFUL THESE DAYS.
LIKE I SAID, YOU COME IN TOO FAST WHEN YOU ATTACK.
YOU SHOULD SEE YOUR-SELF. IT'S HILARIOUS.
Retry
SO? I CAN'T HELP IT. I'M A NOVICE AT VIDEOGAMES.
My body just moves...
STILL, THIS IS FUN. NO WONDER YOU CALL IT THE GAME OF ALL GAMES.
RIKO'S BEEN AWAY ON BUSINESS LATELY...
WAIT... ARE YOU GOING TO PLAY AGAIN? WHAT ABOUT STUDYING FOR EXAMS?
I thought you were just taking a short break.
I'LL STUDY AS SOON AS I CLEAR THIS LEVEL!
No wonder men dream of being pilots.
...SO I'VE BEEN COMING OVER TO KUROSAKI'S PLACE MORE OFTEN.
OH, NOT AGAIN! WHY IS THIS HAPPEN-ING?
HOW MANY TIMES DO I HAVE TO TELL YOU?
YOU'RE TOO SLOW GETTING AWAY AFTER YOU ATTACK. THAT'S WHY...

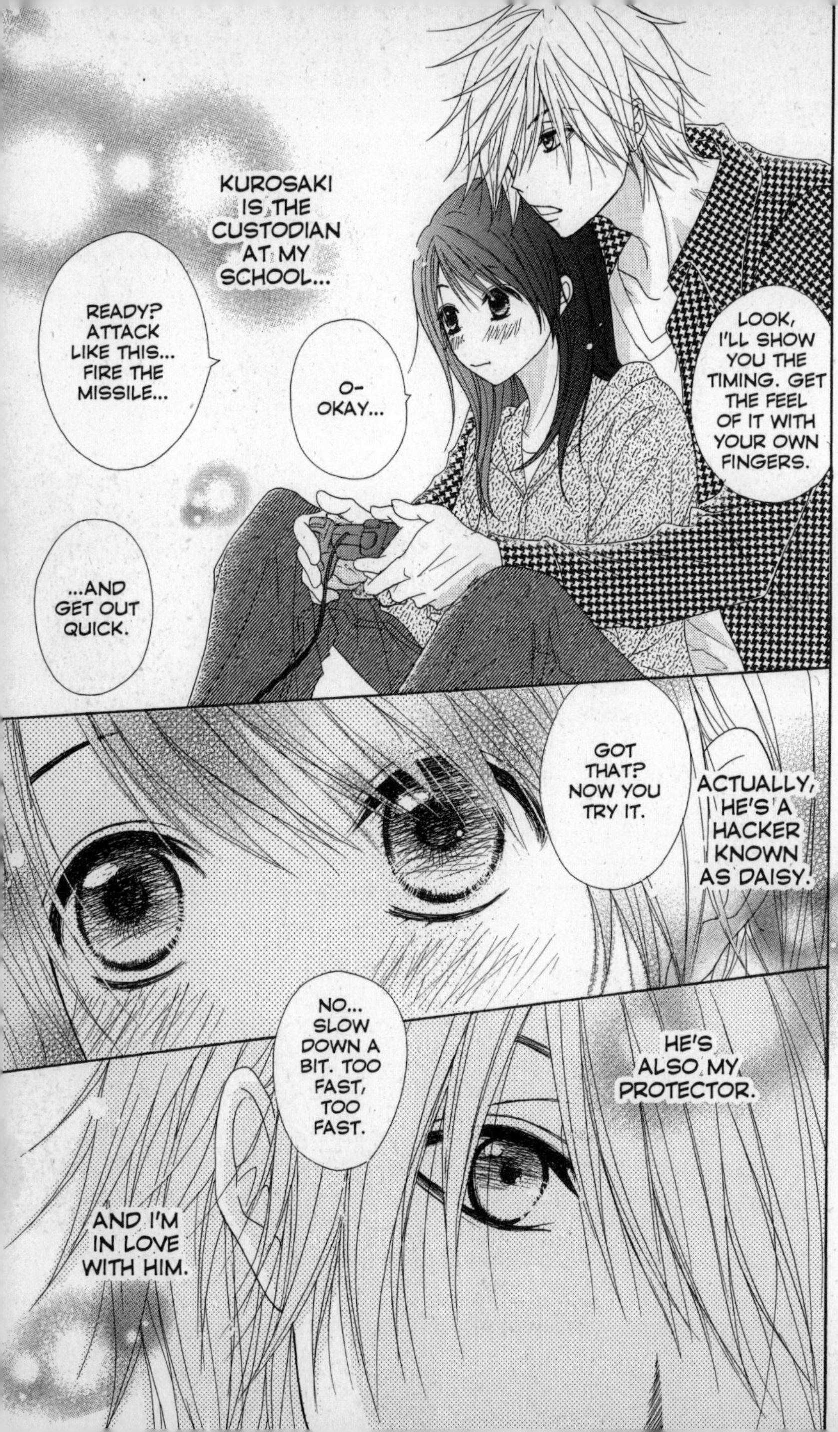
KUROSAKI IS THE CUSTODIAN AT MY SCHOOL...
LOOK, I'LL SHOW YOU THE TIMING. GET THE FEEL OF IT WITH YOUR OWN FINGERS.
READY? ATTACK LIKE THIS... FIRE THE MISSILE...
O-OKAY...
...AND GET OUT QUICK.
ACTUALLY, HE'S A HACKER KNOWN AS DAISY.
GOT THAT? NOW YOU TRY IT.
HE'S ALSO MY PROTECTOR.
NO... SLOW DOWN A BIT. TOO FAST, TOO FAST.
AND I'M IN LOVE WITH HIM.

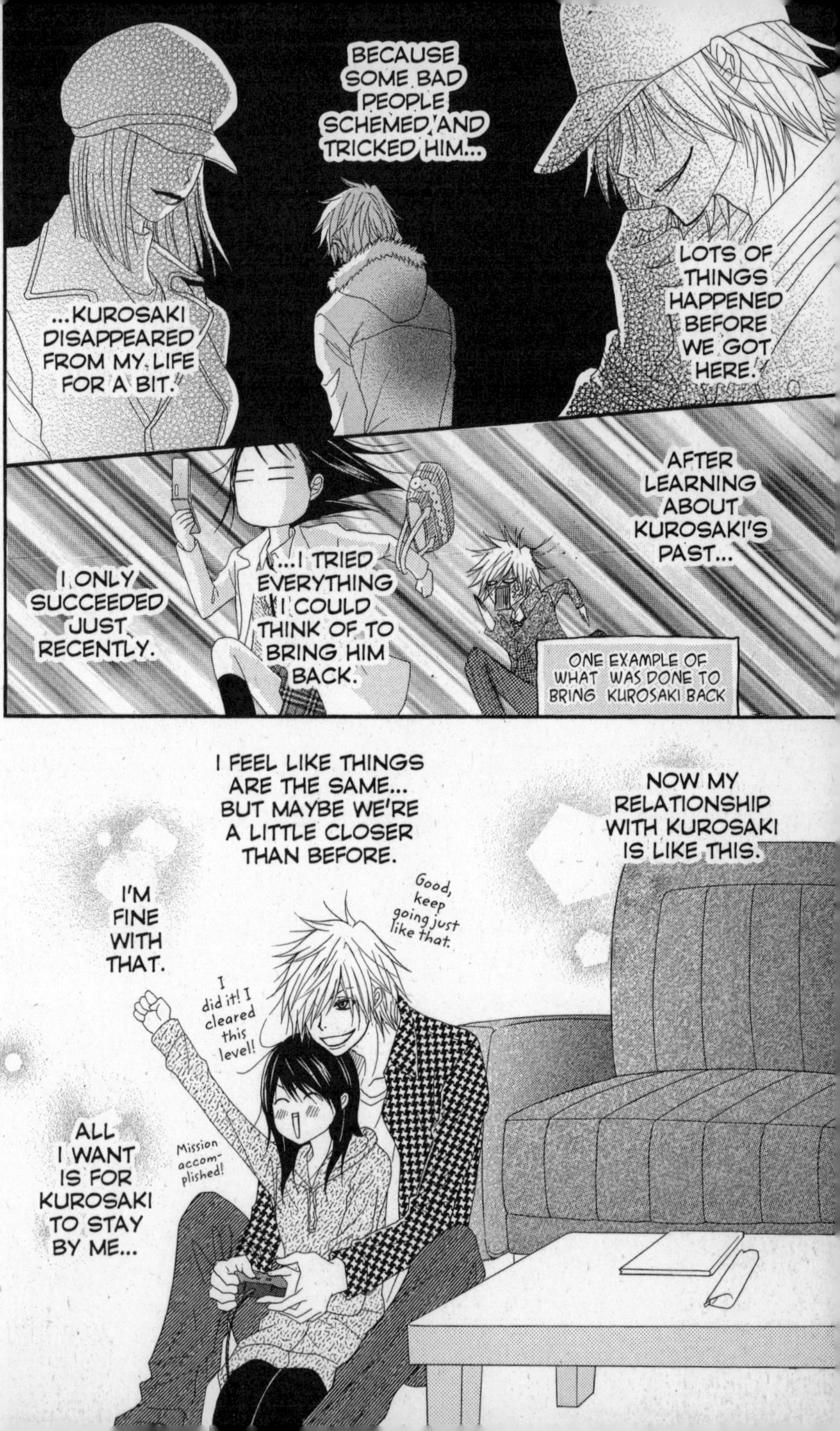
LOTS OF THINGS HAPPENED BEFORE WE GOT HERE.
BECAUSE SOME BAD PEOPLE SCHEMED AND TRICKED HIM...
...KUROSAKI DISAPPEARED FROM MY LIFE FOR A BIT.
AFTER LEARNING ABOUT KUROSAKI'S PAST...
...I TRIED EVERYTHING I COULD THINK OF TO BRING HIM BACK.
ONE EXAMPLE OF WHAT WAS DONE TO BRING KUROSAKI BACK
I ONLY SUCCEEDED JUST RECENTLY.
NOW MY RELATIONSHIP WITH KUROSAKI IS LIKE THIS.
I FEEL LIKE THINGS ARE THE SAME... BUT MAYBE WE'RE A LITTLE CLOSER THAN BEFORE.
Good, keep going just like that.
I'M FINE WITH THAT.
I did it! I cleared this level!
Mission accomplished!
ALL I WANT IS FOR KUROSAKI TO STAY BY ME...

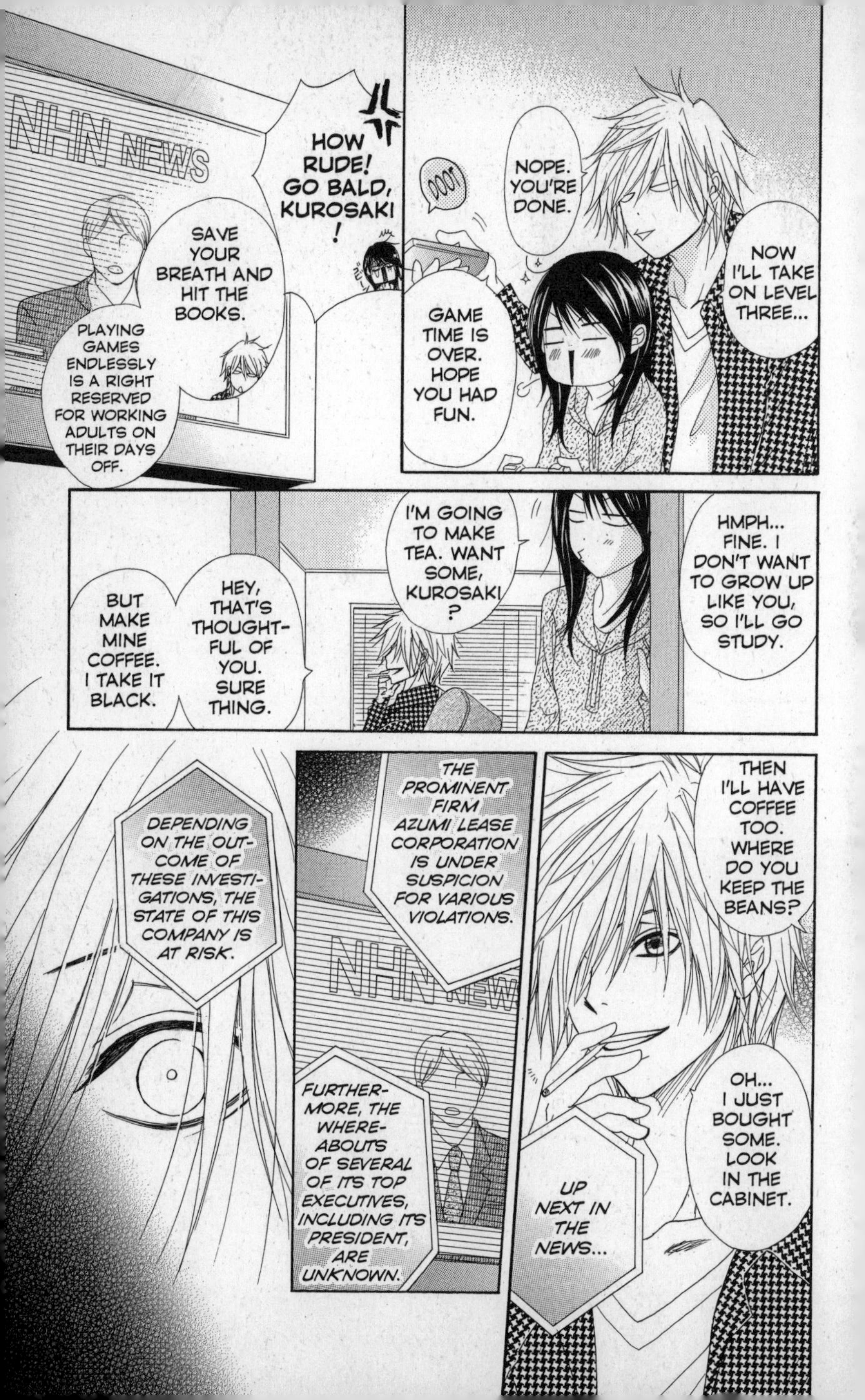
NOW I'LL TAKE ON LEVEL THREE...
NOPE. YOU'RE DONE.
GAME TIME IS OVER. HOPE YOU HAD FUN.
HOW RUDE! GO BALD, KUROSAKI!
NHN NEWS
SAVE YOUR BREATH AND HIT THE BOOKS.
PLAYING GAMES ENDLESSLY IS A RIGHT RESERVED FOR WORKING ADULTS ON THEIR DAYS OFF.
HMPH... FINE. I DON'T WANT TO GROW UP LIKE YOU, SO I'LL GO STUDY.
I'M GOING TO MAKE TEA. WANT SOME, KUROSAKI?
HEY, THAT'S THOUGHTFUL OF YOU. SURE THING.
BUT MAKE MINE COFFEE. I TAKE IT BLACK.
THEN I'LL HAVE COFFEE TOO. WHERE DO YOU KEEP THE BEANS?
OH... I JUST BOUGHT SOME. LOOK IN THE CABINET.
UP NEXT IN THE NEWS...
THE PROMINENT FIRM AZUMI LEASE CORPORATION IS UNDER SUSPICION FOR VARIOUS VIOLATIONS.
NHN NEWS
FURTHERMORE, THE WHEREABOUTS OF SEVERAL OF ITS TOP EXECUTIVES, INCLUDING ITS PRESIDENT, ARE UNKNOWN.
DEPENDING ON THE OUTCOME OF THESE INVESTIGATIONS, THE STATE OF THIS COMPANY IS AT RISK.

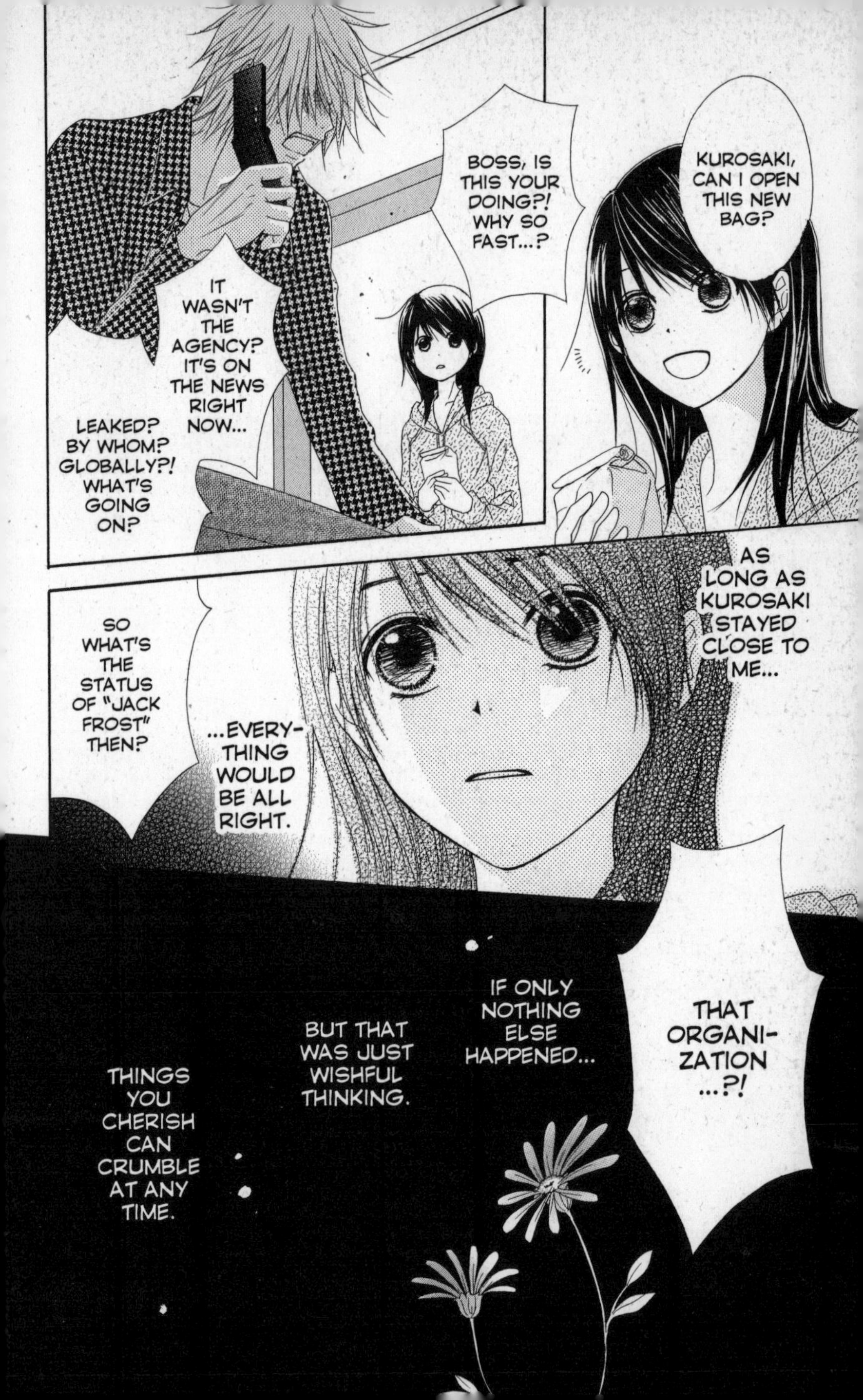
KUROSAKI, CAN I OPEN THIS NEW BAG?
BOSS, IS THIS YOUR DOING?! WHY SO FAST...?
IT WASN'T THE AGENCY? IT'S ON THE NEWS RIGHT NOW...
LEAKED? BY WHOM? GLOBALLY?! WHAT'S GOING ON?
AS LONG AS KUROSAKI STAYED CLOSE TO ME...
...EVERYTHING WOULD BE ALL RIGHT.
SO WHAT'S THE STATUS OF "JACK FROST" THEN?
THAT ORGANIZATION...?!
IF ONLY NOTHING ELSE HAPPENED...
BUT THAT WAS JUST WISHFUL THINKING.
THINGS YOU CHERISH CAN CRUMBLE AT ANY TIME.

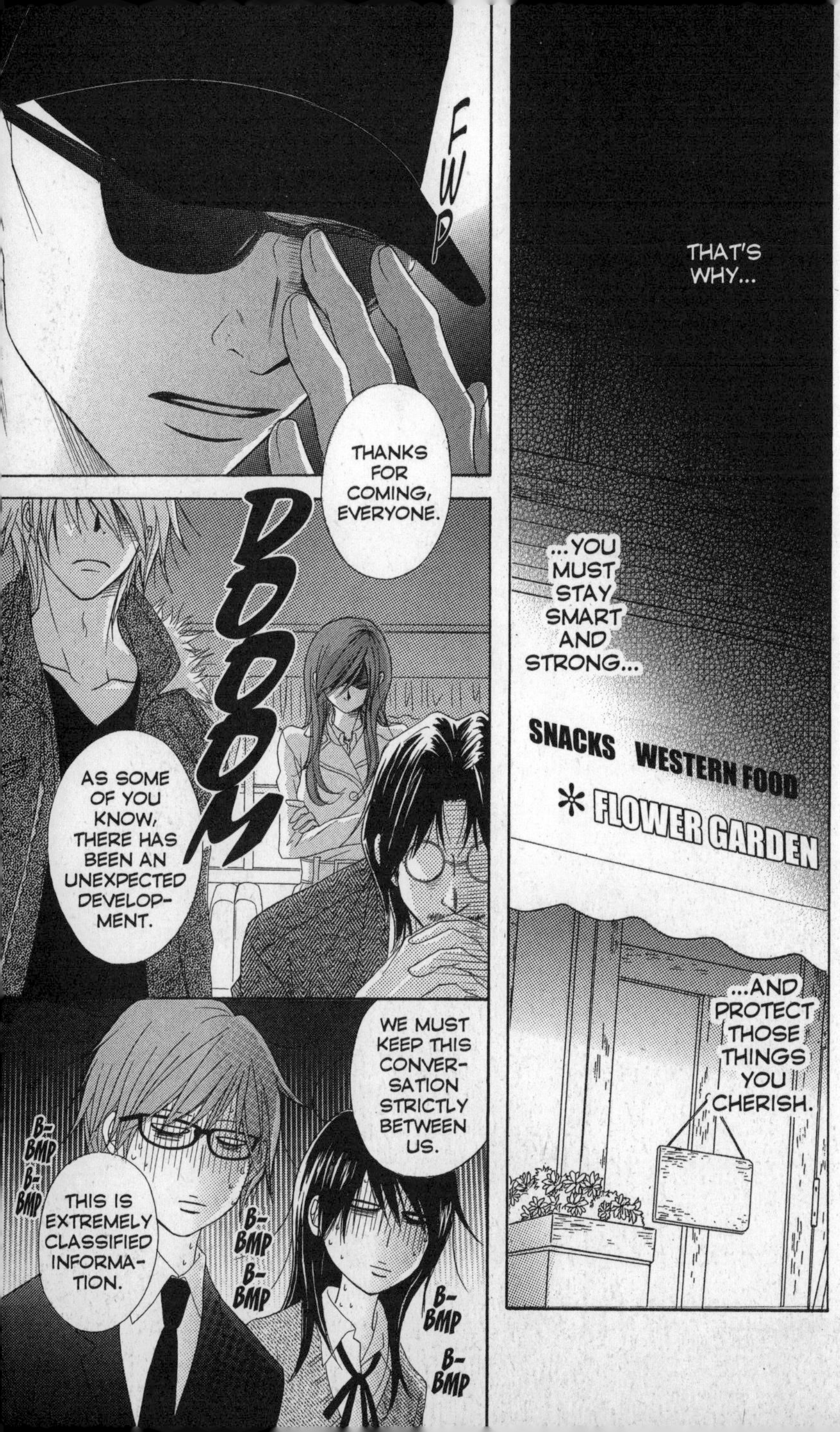
THAT'S WHY...
...YOU MUST STAY SMART AND STRONG...
SNACKS WESTERN FOOD
* FLOWER GARDEN
...AND PROTECT THOSE THINGS YOU CHERISH.
FWP
THANKS FOR COMING, EVERYONE.
BOOOM
AS SOME OF YOU KNOW, THERE HAS BEEN AN UNEXPECTED DEVELOPMENT.
WE MUST KEEP THIS CONVERSATION STRICTLY BETWEEN US.
B-BMP B-BMP
THIS IS EXTREMELY CLASSIFIED INFORMATION.
B-BMP B-BMP
B-BMP B-BMP

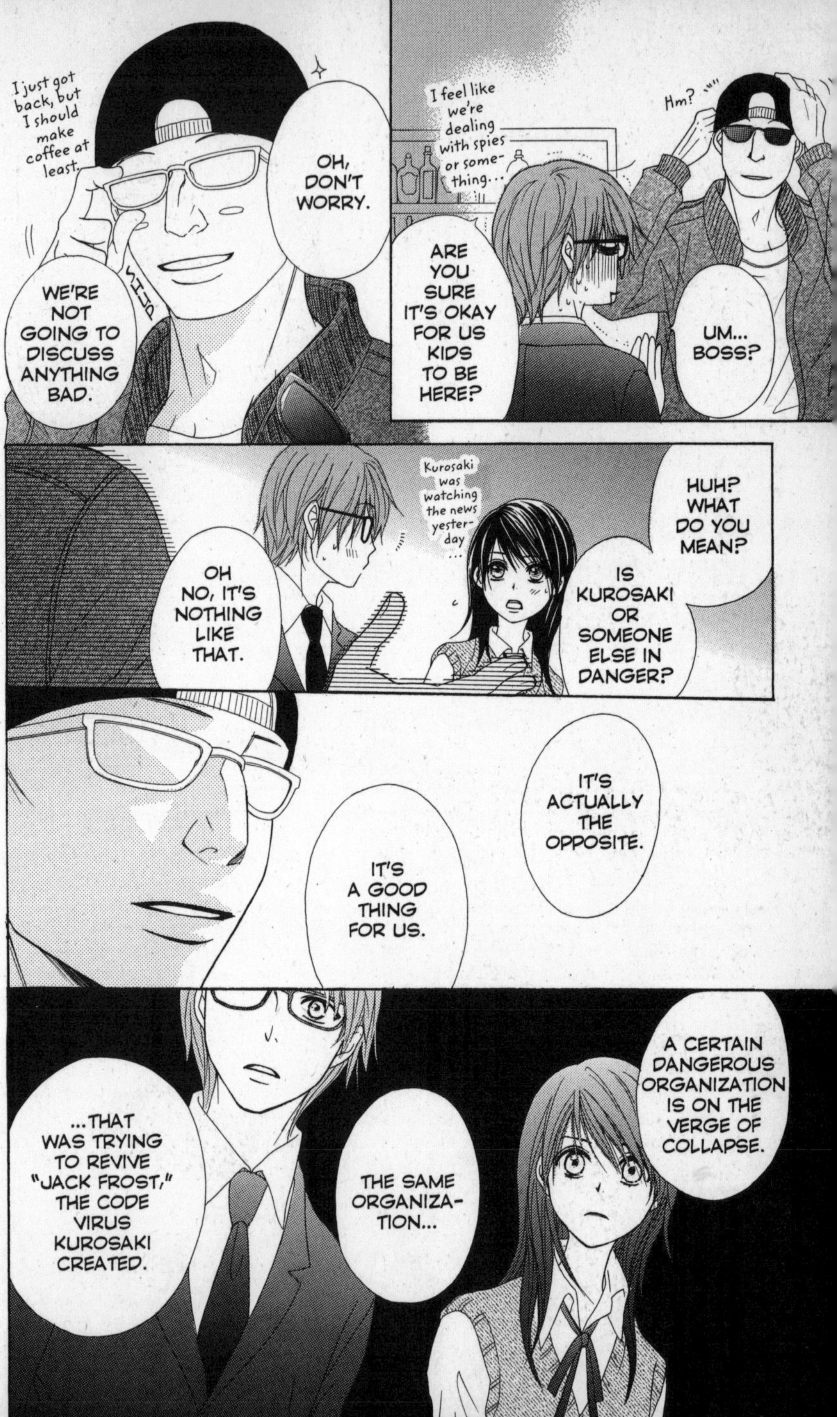
Hm?
UM... BOSS?
I feel like we're dealing with spies or something...
ARE YOU SURE IT'S OKAY FOR US KIDS TO BE HERE?
OH, DON'T WORRY.
I just got back, but I should make coffee at least.
WE'RE NOT GOING TO DISCUSS ANYTHING BAD.
HUH? WHAT DO YOU MEAN?
IS KUROSAKI OR SOMEONE ELSE IN DANGER?
Kurosaki was watching the news yesterday...
OH NO, IT'S NOTHING LIKE THAT.
IT'S ACTUALLY THE OPPOSITE.
IT'S A GOOD THING FOR US.
A CERTAIN DANGEROUS ORGANIZATION IS ON THE VERGE OF COLLAPSE.
THE SAME ORGANIZATION...
...THAT WAS TRYING TO REVIVE "JACK FROST," THE CODE VIRUS KUROSAKI CREATED.

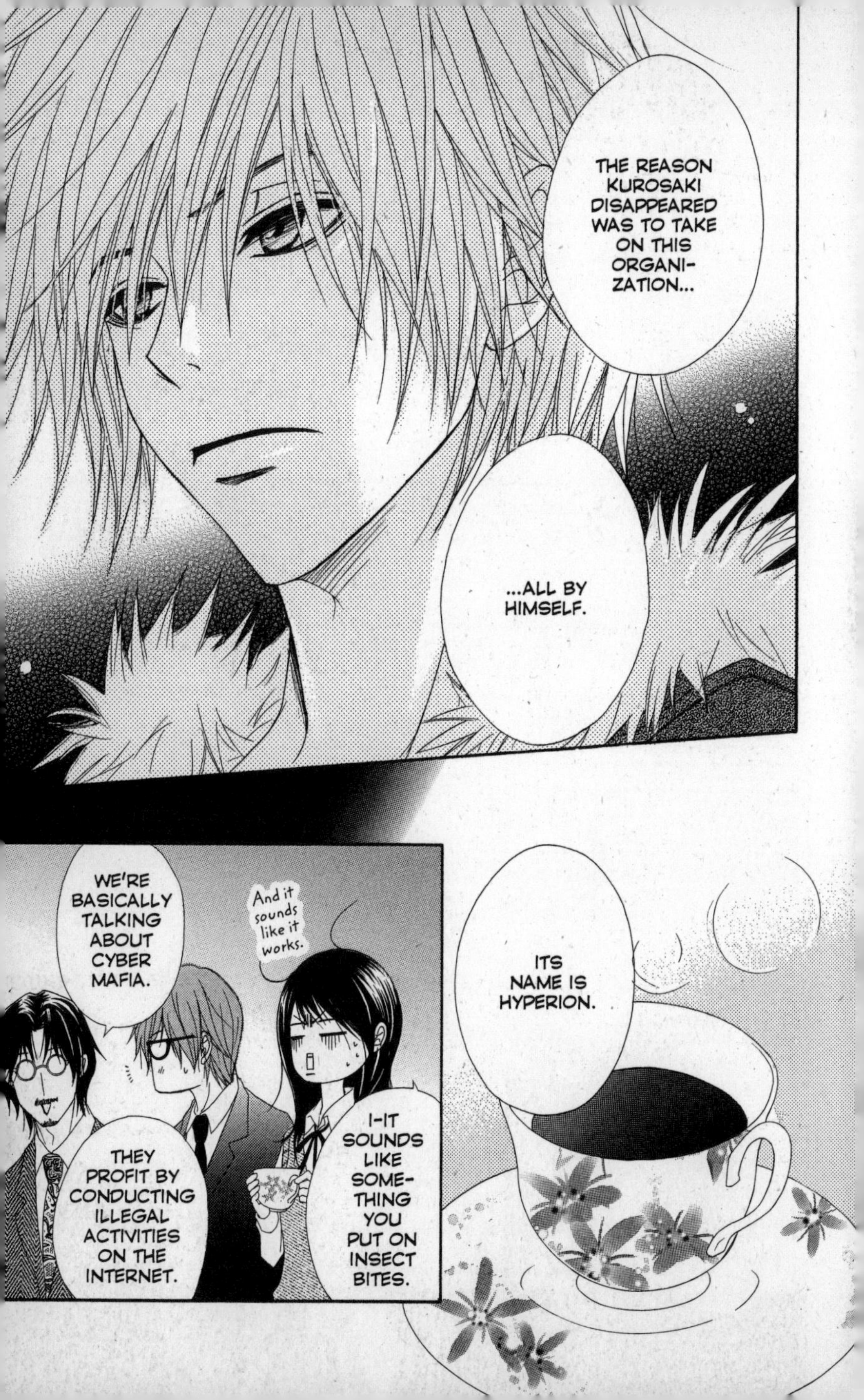
THE REASON KUROSAKI DISAPPEARED WAS TO TAKE ON THIS ORGANI-ZATION...
...ALL BY HIMSELF.
ITS NAME IS HYPERION.
I-IT SOUNDS LIKE SOME-THING YOU PUT ON INSECT BITES.
And it sounds like it works.
WE'RE BASICALLY TALKING ABOUT CYBER MAFIA.
THEY PROFIT BY CONDUCTING ILLEGAL ACTIVITIES ON THE INTERNET.

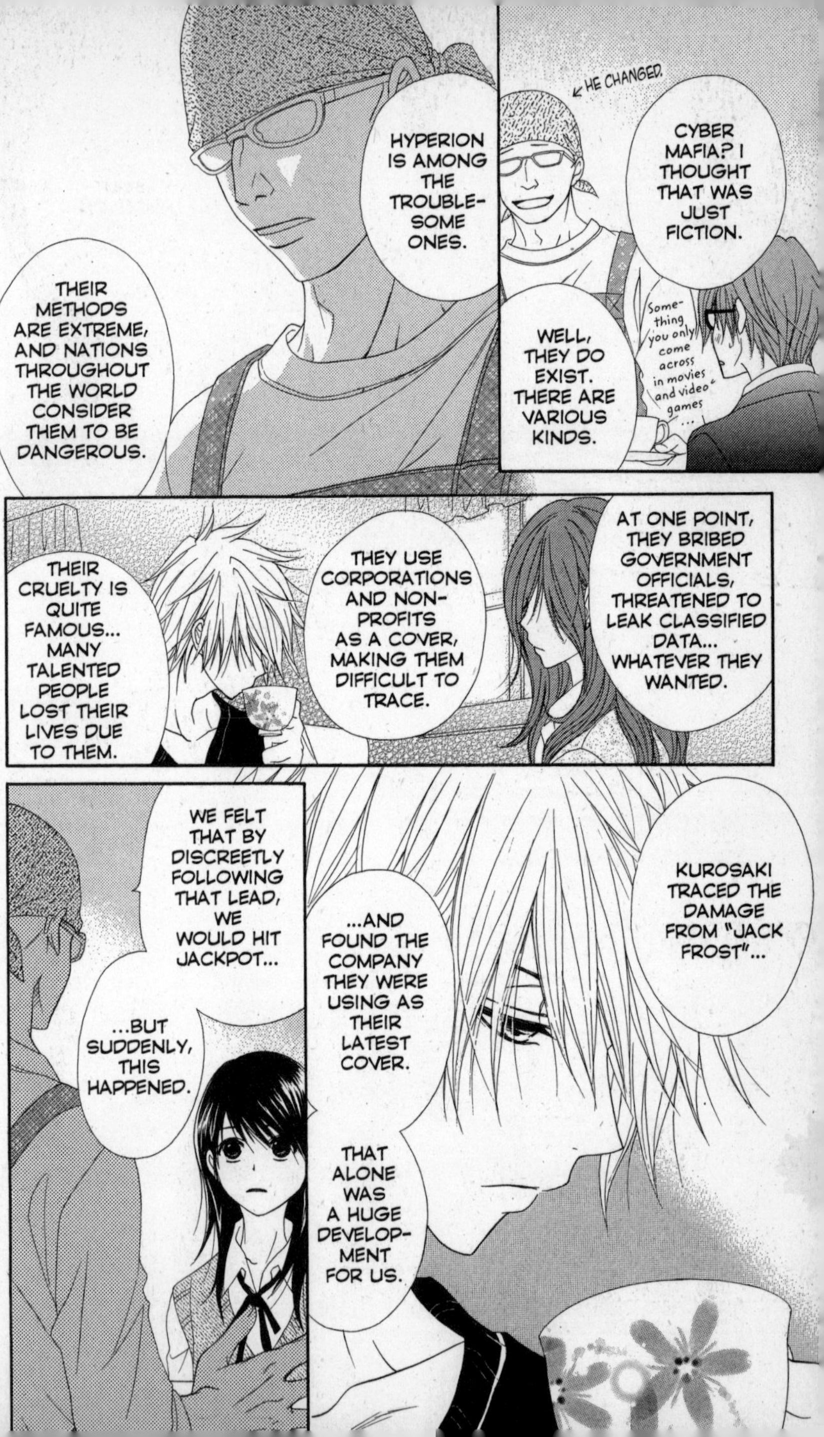
HE CHANGED.
CYBER MAFIA? I THOUGHT THAT WAS JUST FICTION.
Some-thing you only come across in movies and video games...
WELL, THEY DO EXIST. THERE ARE VARIOUS KINDS.
HYPERION IS AMONG THE TROUBLE-SOME ONES.
THEIR METHODS ARE EXTREME, AND NATIONS THROUGHOUT THE WORLD CONSIDER THEM TO BE DANGEROUS.
AT ONE POINT, THEY BRIBED GOVERNMENT OFFICIALS, THREATENED TO LEAK CLASSIFIED DATA... WHATEVER THEY WANTED.
THEY USE CORPORATIONS AND NON-PROFITS AS A COVER, MAKING THEM DIFFICULT TO TRACE.
THEIR CRUELTY IS QUITE FAMOUS... MANY TALENTED PEOPLE LOST THEIR LIVES DUE TO THEM.
KUROSAKI TRACED THE DAMAGE FROM "JACK FROST"...
...AND FOUND THE COMPANY THEY WERE USING AS THEIR LATEST COVER.
THAT ALONE WAS A HUGE DEVELOP-MENT FOR US.
WE FELT THAT BY DISCREETLY FOLLOWING THAT LEAD, WE WOULD HIT JACKPOT...
...BUT SUDDENLY, THIS HAPPENED.

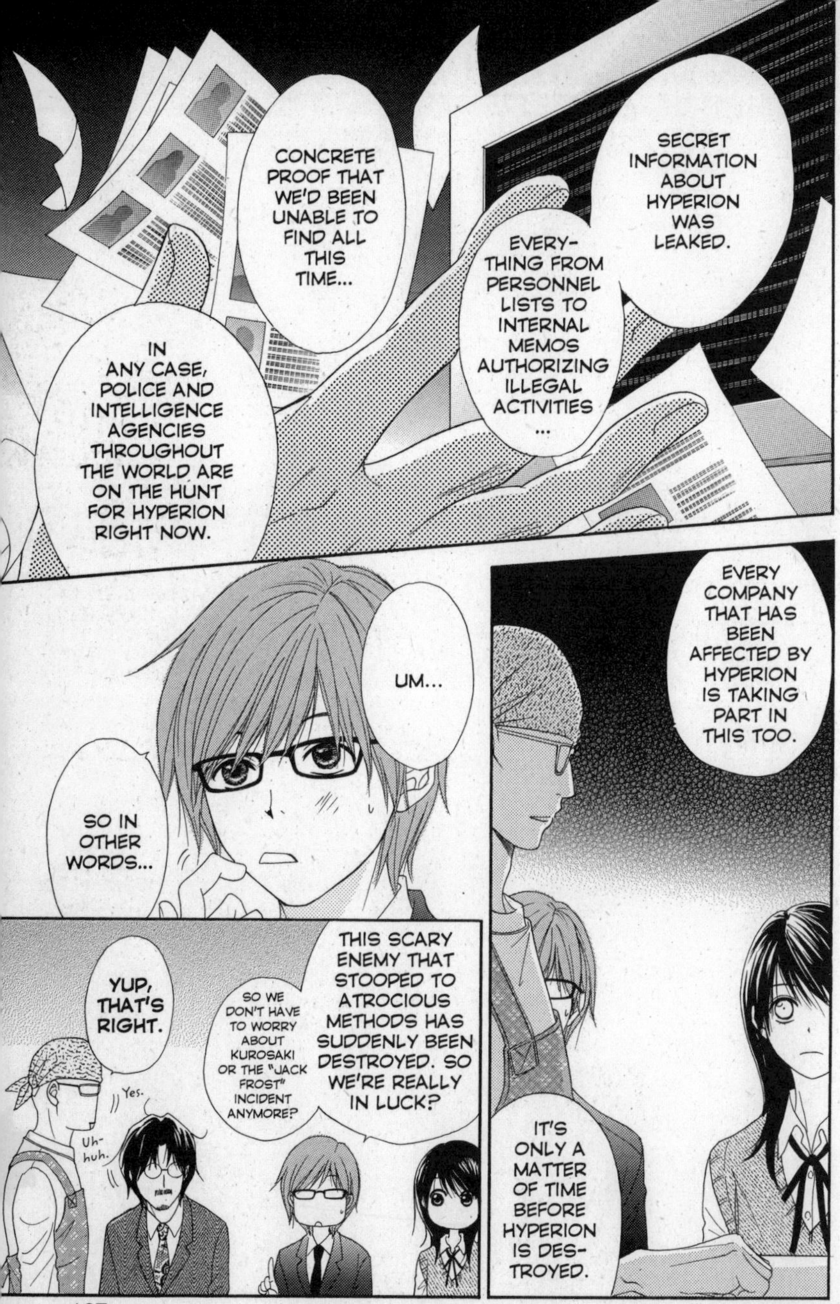
SECRET INFORMATION ABOUT HYPERION WAS LEAKED.
EVERY-THING FROM PERSONNEL LISTS TO INTERNAL MEMOS AUTHORIZING ILLEGAL ACTIVITIES ...
CONCRETE PROOF THAT WE'D BEEN UNABLE TO FIND ALL THIS TIME...
IN ANY CASE, POLICE AND INTELLIGENCE AGENCIES THROUGHOUT THE WORLD ARE ON THE HUNT FOR HYPERION RIGHT NOW.
EVERY COMPANY THAT HAS BEEN AFFECTED BY HYPERION IS TAKING PART IN THIS TOO.
IT'S ONLY A MATTER OF TIME BEFORE HYPERION IS DES-TROYED.
UM...
SO IN OTHER WORDS...
THIS SCARY ENEMY THAT STOOPED TO ATROCIOUS METHODS HAS SUDDENLY BEEN DESTROYED. SO WE'RE REALLY IN LUCK?
SO WE DON'T HAVE TO WORRY ABOUT KUROSAKI OR THE "JACK FROST" INCIDENT ANYMORE?
YUP, THAT'S RIGHT.
Yes.
Uh-huh.

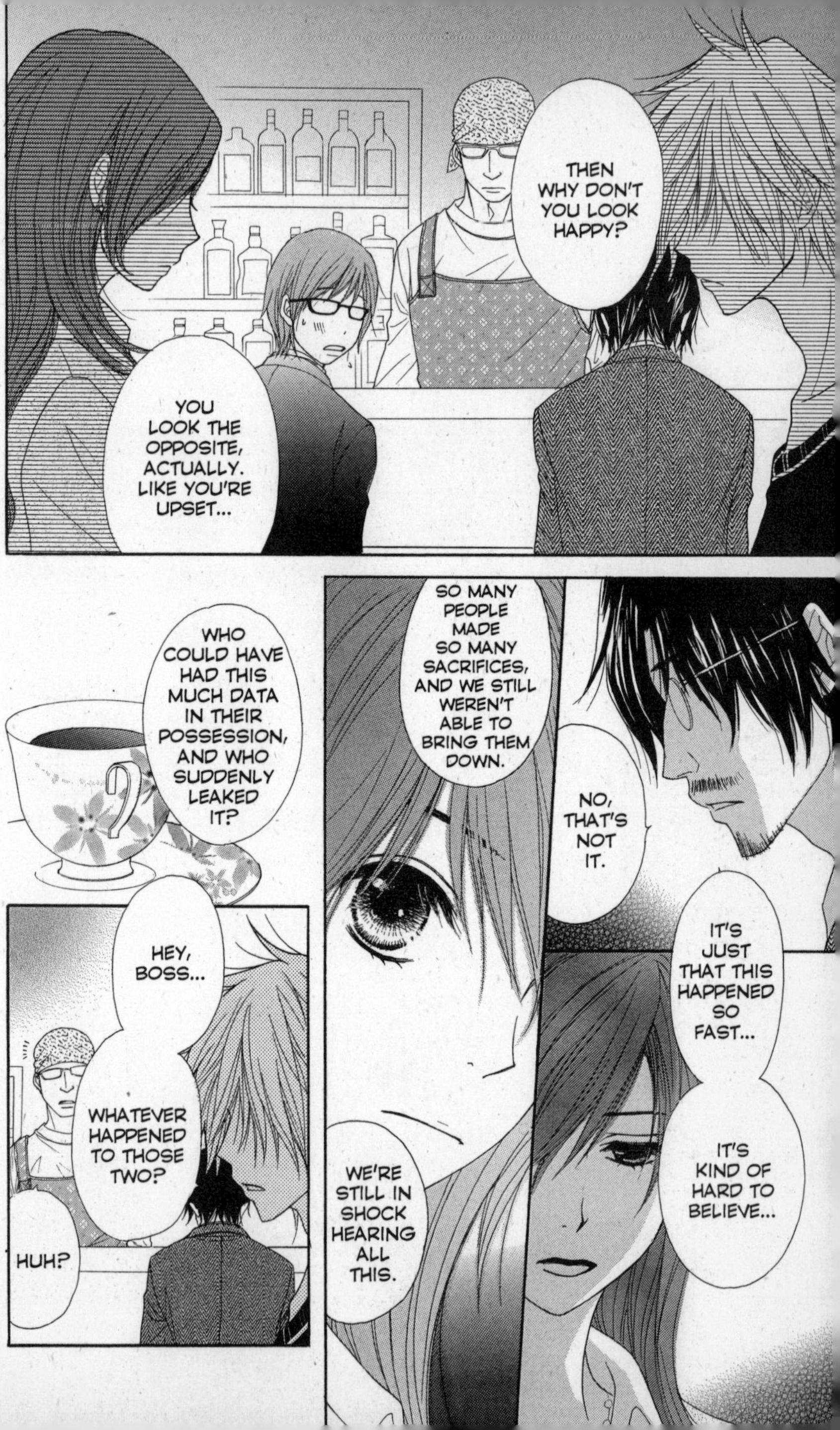
THEN WHY DON'T YOU LOOK HAPPY?
YOU LOOK THE OPPOSITE, ACTUALLY. LIKE YOU'RE UPSET...
NO, THAT'S NOT IT.
IT'S JUST THAT THIS HAPPENED SO FAST...
IT'S KIND OF HARD TO BELIEVE...
SO MANY PEOPLE MADE SO MANY SACRIFICES, AND WE STILL WEREN'T ABLE TO BRING THEM DOWN.
WE'RE STILL IN SHOCK HEARING ALL THIS.
WHO COULD HAVE HAD THIS MUCH DATA IN THEIR POSSESSION, AND WHO SUDDENLY LEAKED IT?
HEY, BOSS...
WHATEVER HAPPENED TO THOSE TWO?
HUH?

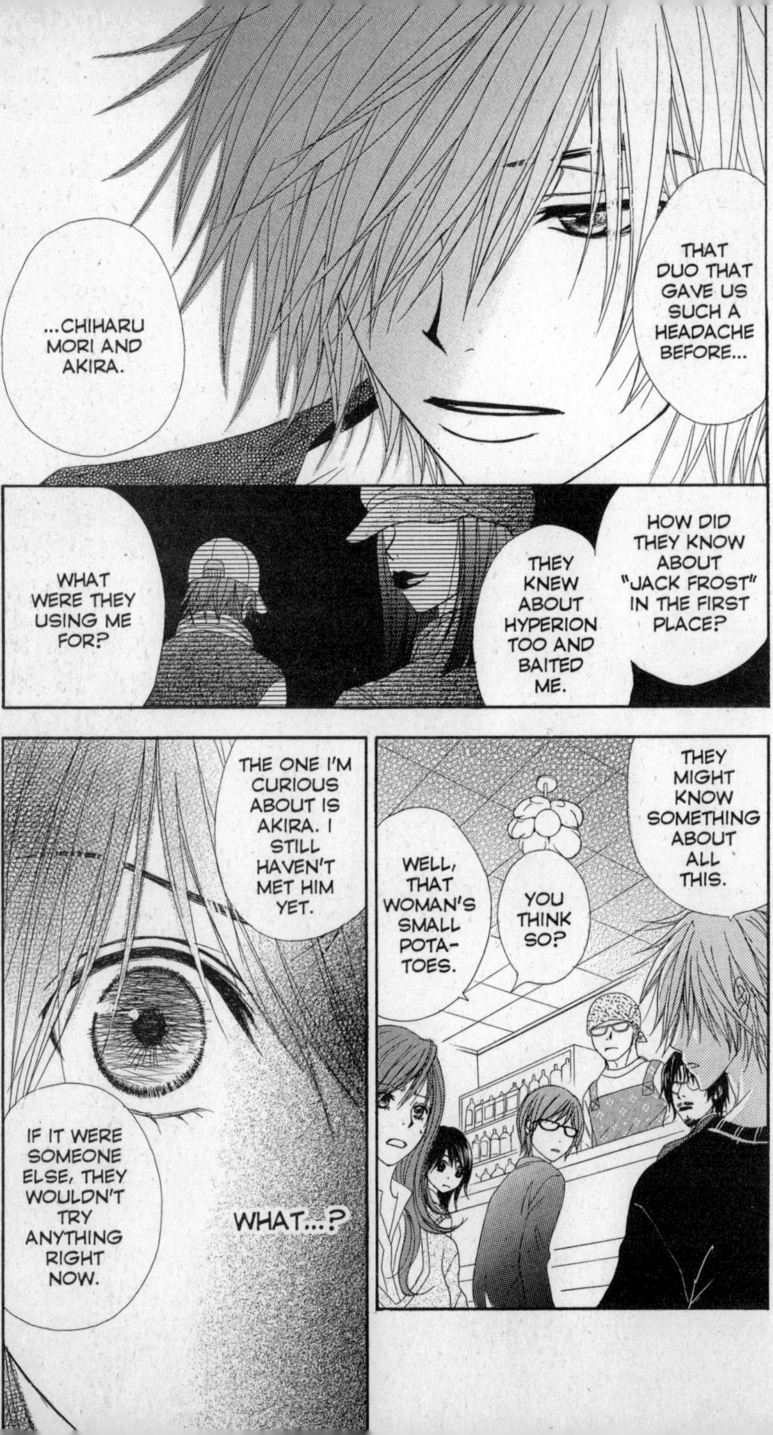
THAT DUO THAT GAVE US SUCH A HEADACHE BEFORE...
...CHIHARU MORI AND AKIRA.
HOW DID THEY KNOW ABOUT "JACK FROST" IN THE FIRST PLACE?
THEY KNEW ABOUT HYPERION TOO AND BAITED ME.
WHAT WERE THEY USING ME FOR?
THEY MIGHT KNOW SOMETHING ABOUT ALL THIS.
YOU THINK SO?
WELL, THAT WOMAN'S SMALL POTA-TOES.
THE ONE I'M CURIOUS ABOUT IS AKIRA. I STILL HAVEN'T MET HIM YET.
IF IT WERE SOMEONE ELSE, THEY WOULDN'T TRY ANYTHING RIGHT NOW.
WHAT...?

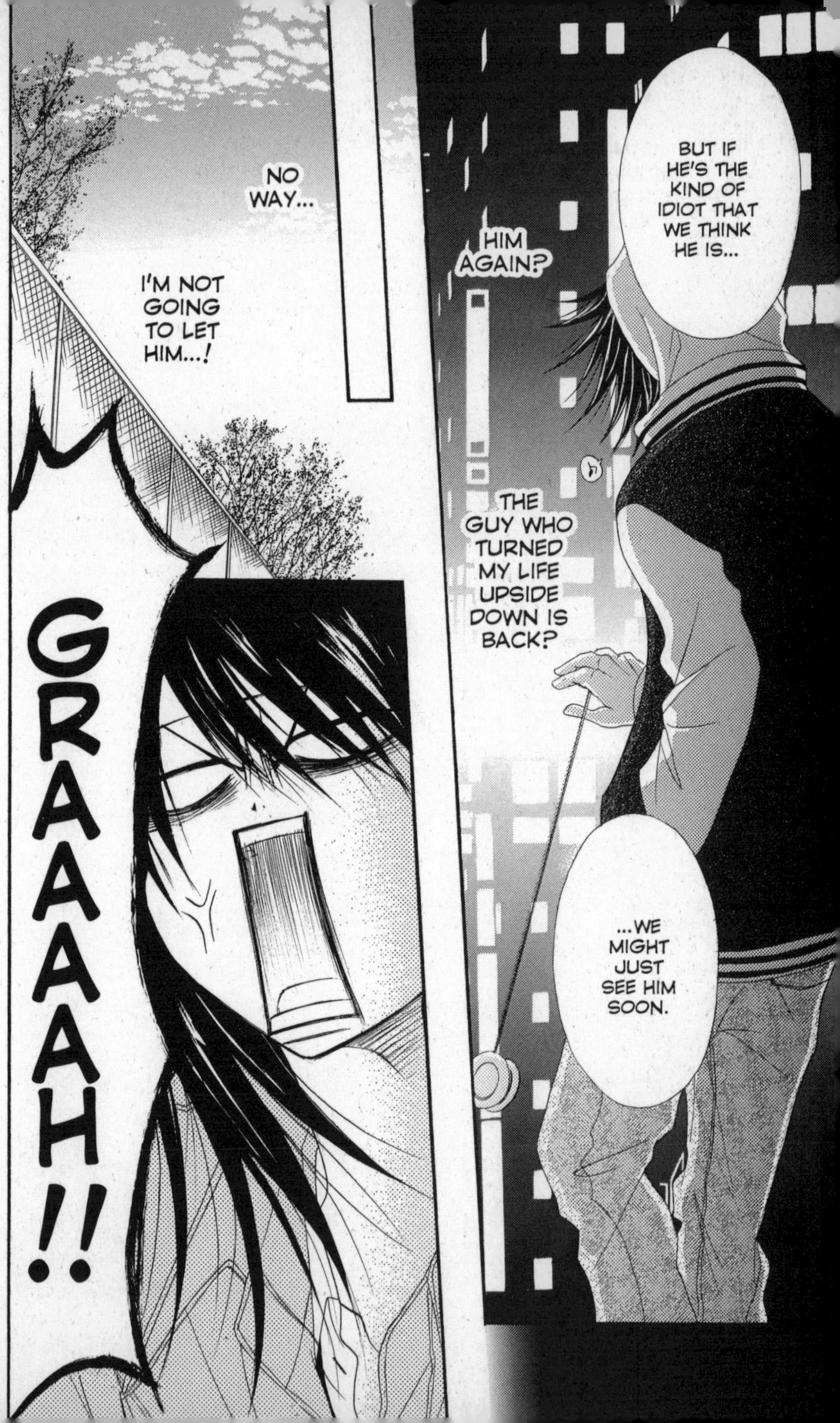
BUT IF HE'S THE KIND OF IDIOT THAT WE THINK HE IS...
HIM AGAIN?
THE GUY WHO TURNED MY LIFE UPSIDE DOWN IS BACK?
...WE MIGHT JUST SEE HIM SOON.
NO WAY...
I'M NOT GOING TO LET HIM...!
GRAAAAH!!

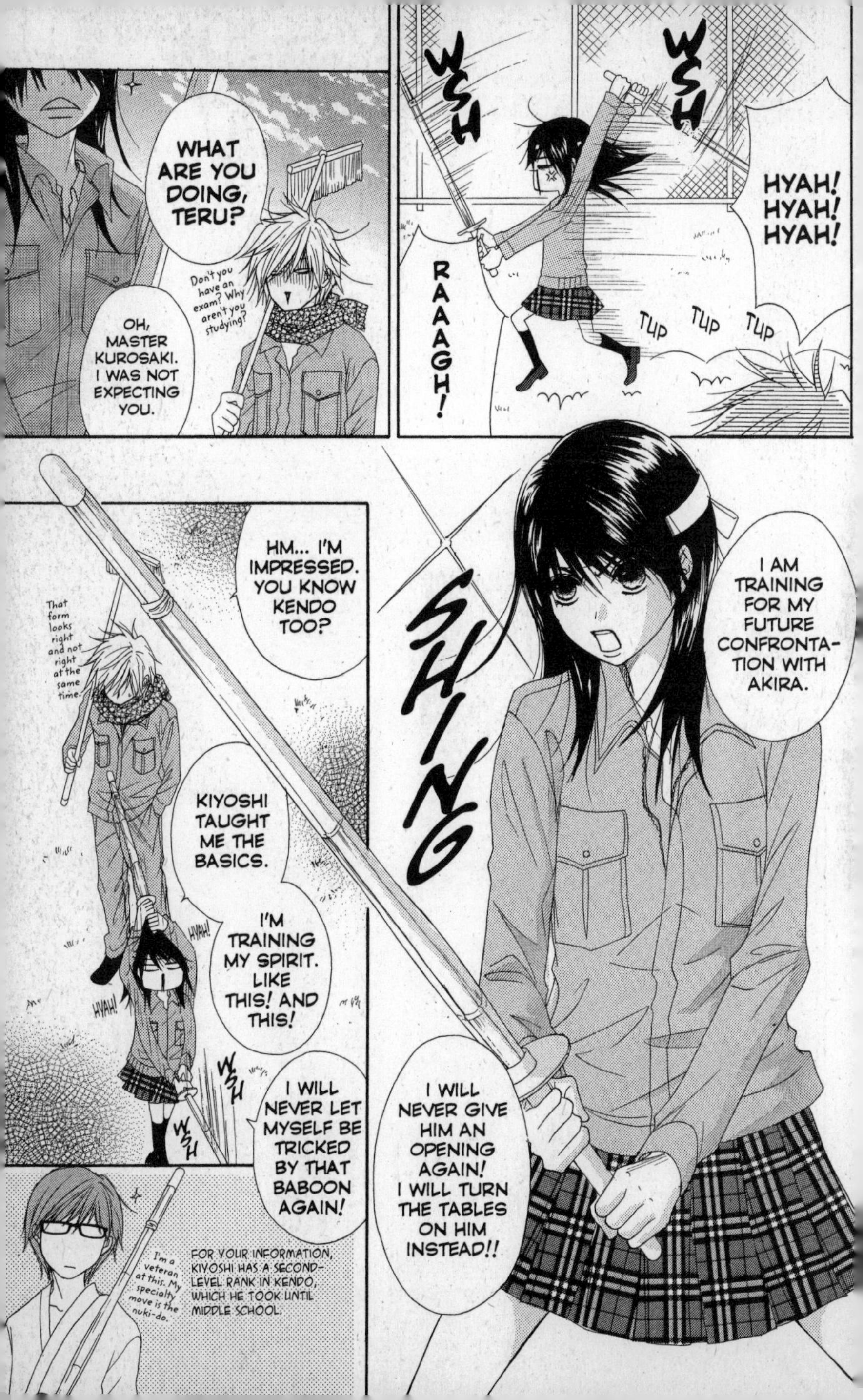
WSH
WSH
HYAH! HYAH! HYAH!
RAAAGH!
TUP TUP TUP
WHAT ARE YOU DOING, TERU?
Don't you have an exam? Why aren't you studying?
OH, MASTER KUROSAKI. I WAS NOT EXPECTING YOU.
I AM TRAINING FOR MY FUTURE CONFRONTATION WITH AKIRA.
SHING
I WILL NEVER GIVE HIM AN OPENING AGAIN! I WILL TURN THE TABLES ON HIM INSTEAD!!
HM... I'M IMPRESSED. YOU KNOW KENDO TOO?
That form looks right and not right at the same time.
KIYOSHI TAUGHT ME THE BASICS.
I'M TRAINING MY SPIRIT. LIKE THIS! AND THIS!
HYAH!
HYAH!
WSH
WSH
I WILL NEVER LET MYSELF BE TRICKED BY THAT BABOON AGAIN!
FOR YOUR INFORMATION, KIYOSHI HAS A SECOND-LEVEL RANK IN KENDO, WHICH HE TOOK UNTIL MIDDLE SCHOOL.
I'm a veteran at this. My specialty move is the nuki-do.

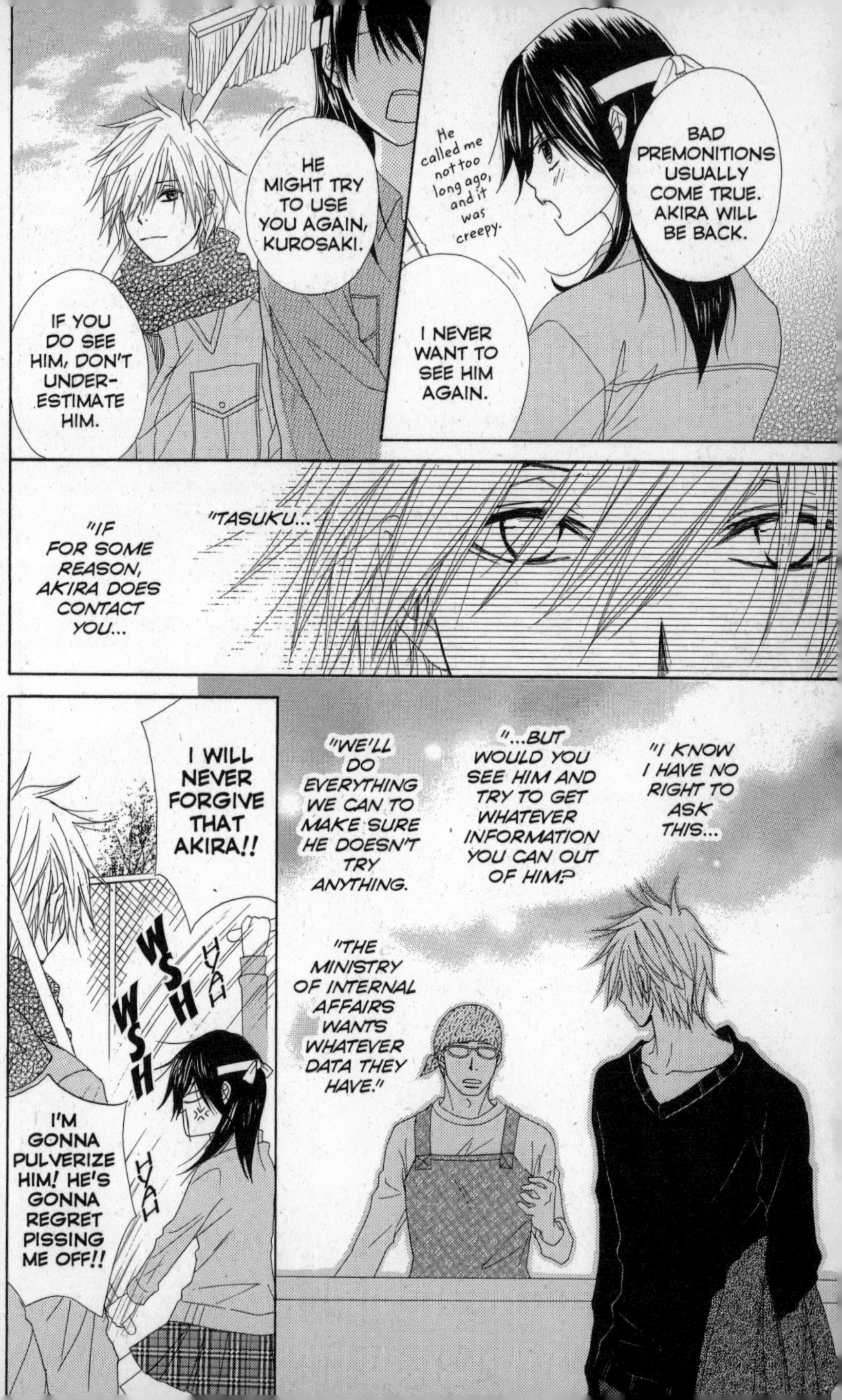
BAD PREMONITIONS USUALLY COME TRUE. AKIRA WILL BE BACK.
He called me not too long ago, and it was creepy.
I NEVER WANT TO SEE HIM AGAIN.
HE MIGHT TRY TO USE YOU AGAIN, KUROSAKI.
IF YOU DO SEE HIM, DON'T UNDER-ESTIMATE HIM.
"TASUKU...
"IF FOR SOME REASON, AKIRA DOES CONTACT YOU...
"I KNOW I HAVE NO RIGHT TO ASK THIS...
"...BUT WOULD YOU SEE HIM AND TRY TO GET WHATEVER INFORMATION YOU CAN OUT OF HIM?
"WE'LL DO EVERYTHING WE CAN TO MAKE SURE HE DOESN'T TRY ANYTHING.
"THE MINISTRY OF INTERNAL AFFAIRS WANTS WHATEVER DATA THEY HAVE."
I WILL NEVER FORGIVE THAT AKIRA!!
WSH
WSH
HYAH
HYAH
I'M GONNA PULVERIZE HIM! HE'S GONNA REGRET PISSING ME OFF!!

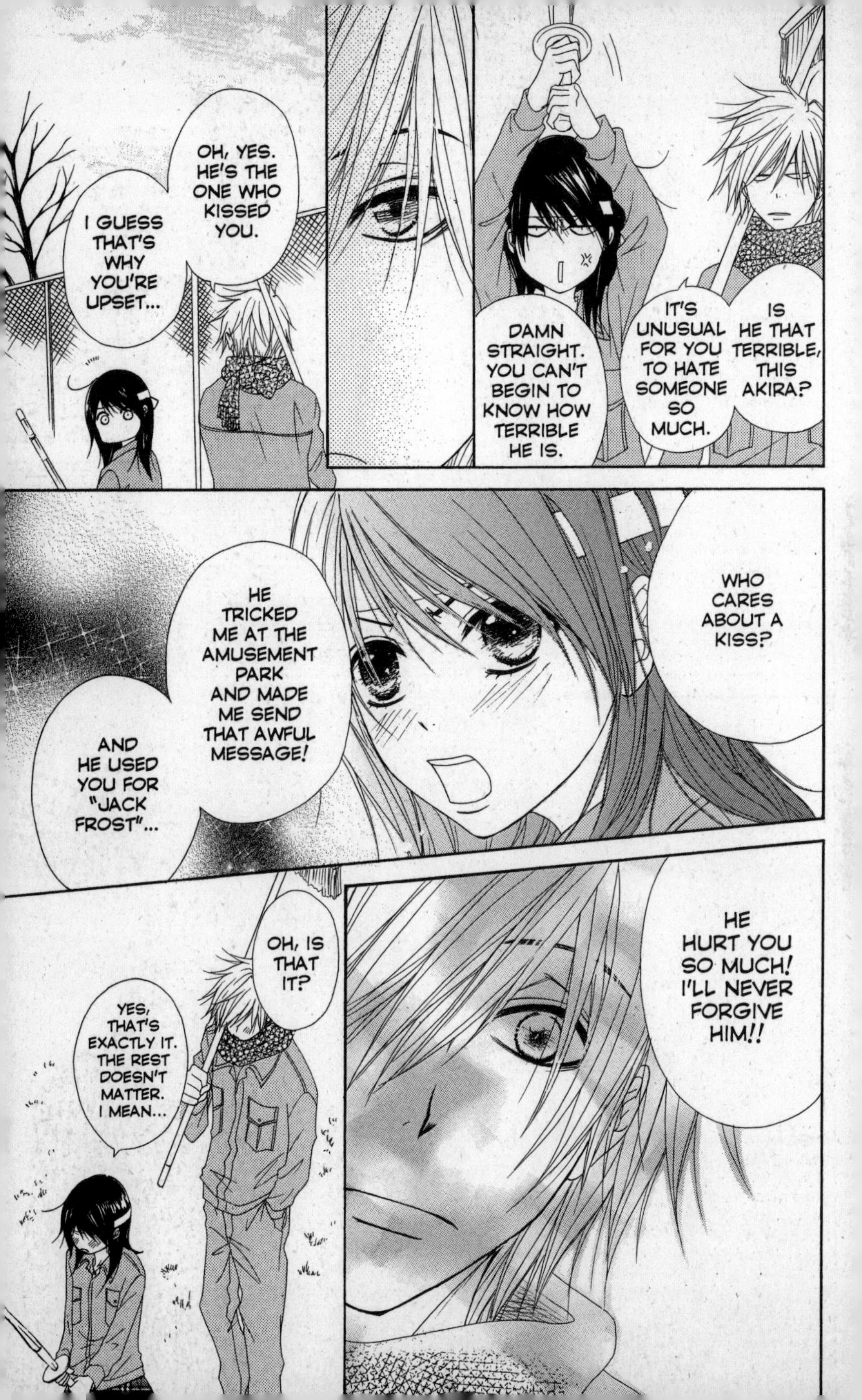
IS HE THAT TERRIBLE, THIS AKIRA?
IT'S UNUSUAL FOR YOU TO HATE SOMEONE SO MUCH.
DAMN STRAIGHT. YOU CAN'T BEGIN TO KNOW HOW TERRIBLE HE IS.
OH, YES. HE'S THE ONE WHO KISSED YOU.
I GUESS THAT'S WHY YOU'RE UPSET...
WHO CARES ABOUT A KISS?
HE TRICKED ME AT THE AMUSEMENT PARK AND MADE ME SEND THAT AWFUL MESSAGE!
AND HE USED YOU FOR "JACK FROST"...
HE HURT YOU SO MUCH! I'LL NEVER FORGIVE HIM!!
OH, IS THAT IT?
YES, THAT'S EXACTLY IT. THE REST DOESN'T MATTER. I MEAN...

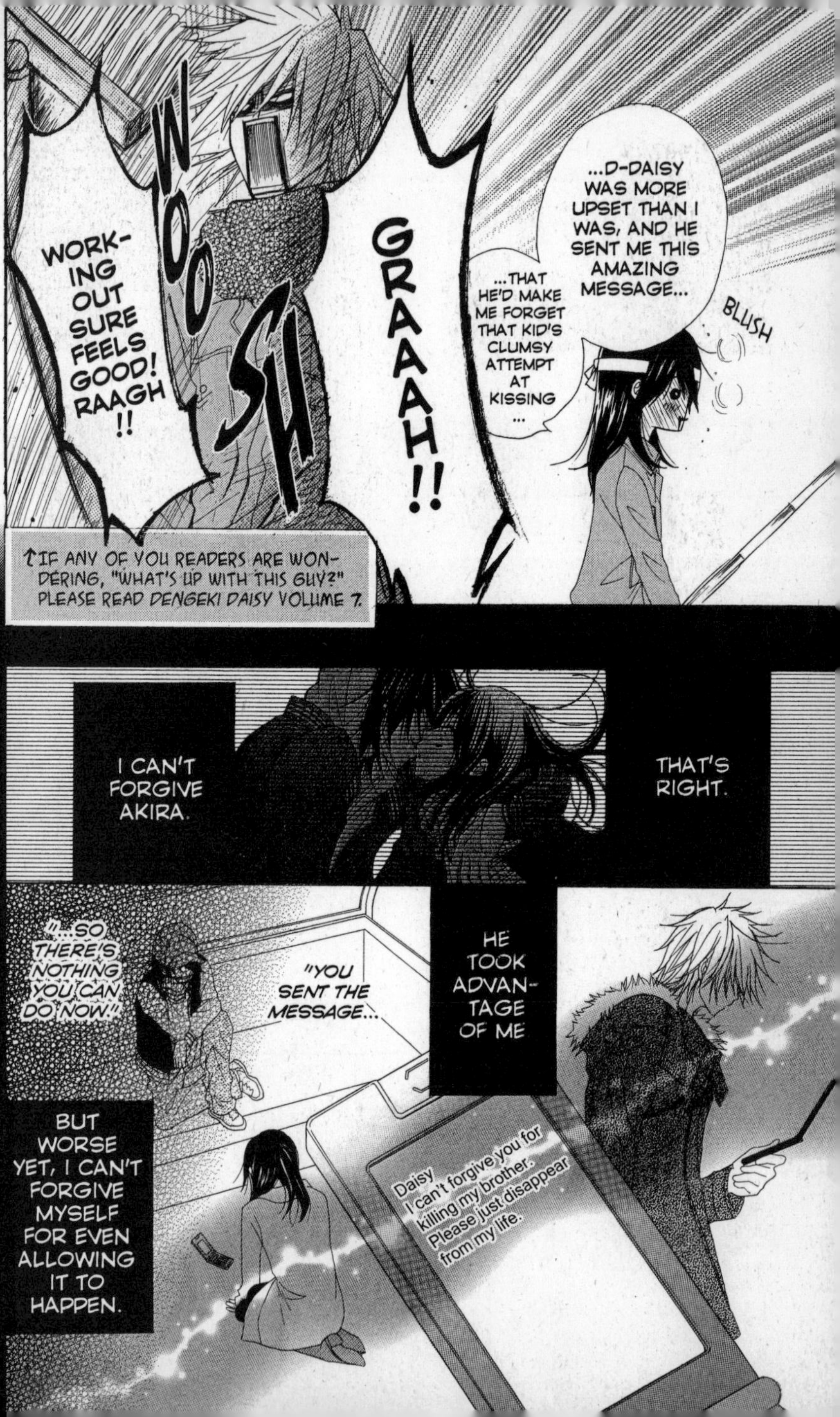
...D-DAISY WAS MORE UPSET THAN I WAS, AND HE SENT ME THIS AMAZING MESSAGE...
...THAT HE'D MAKE ME FORGET THAT KID'S CLUMSY ATTEMPT AT KISSING...
BLUSH
GRAAAH!!
WOOSH
WORKING OUT SURE FEELS GOOD! RAAGH!!
↑IF ANY OF YOU READERS ARE WONDERING, "WHAT'S UP WITH THIS GUY?" PLEASE READ DENGEKI DAISY VOLUME 7.
THAT'S RIGHT.
I CAN'T FORGIVE AKIRA.
HE TOOK ADVANTAGE OF ME
"YOU SENT THE MESSAGE...
"...SO THERE'S NOTHING YOU CAN DO NOW."
Daisy
I can't forgive you for killing my brother.
Please just disappear from my life.
BUT WORSE YET, I CAN'T FORGIVE MYSELF FOR EVEN ALLOWING IT TO HAPPEN.

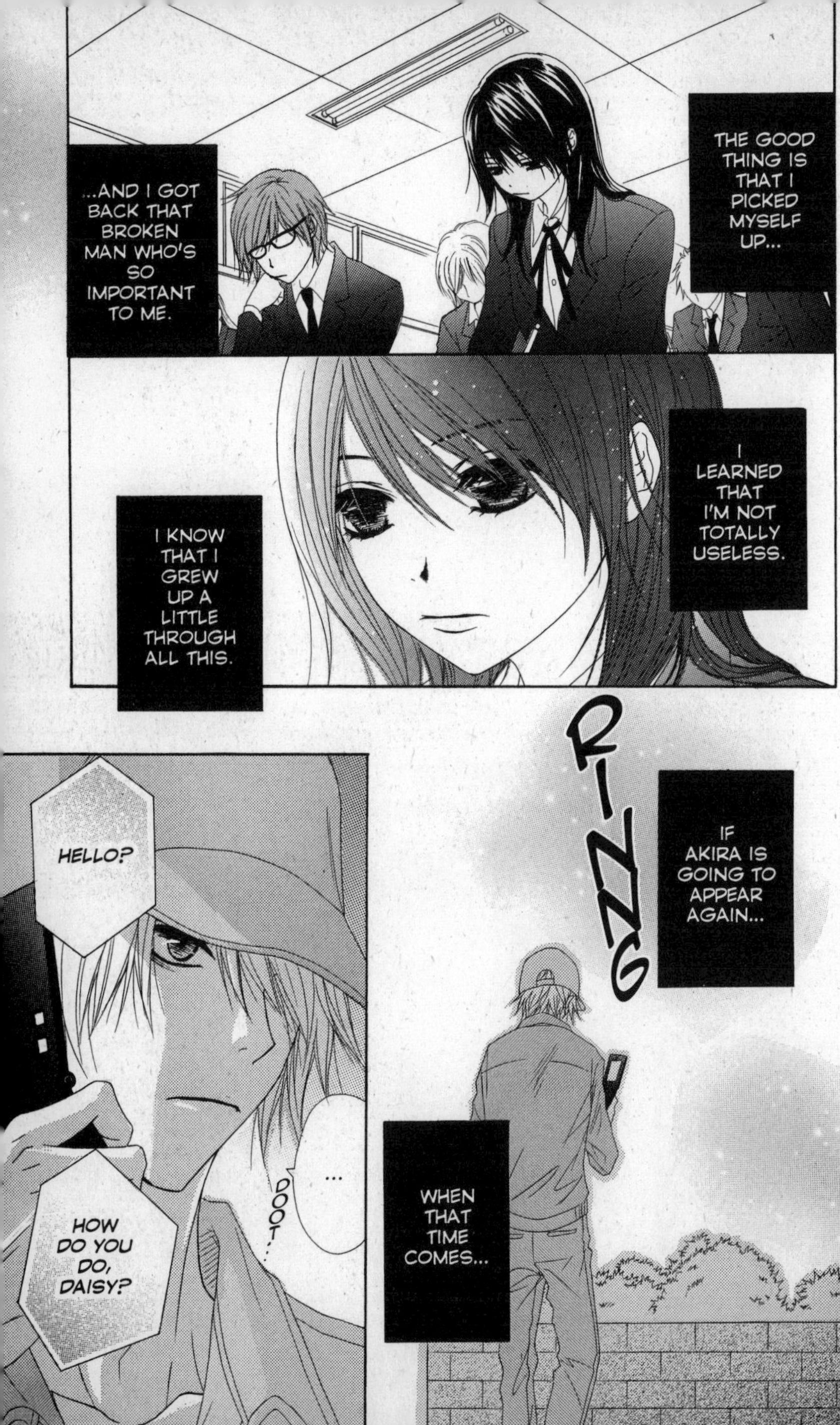
THE GOOD THING IS THAT I PICKED MYSELF UP...
...AND I GOT BACK THAT BROKEN MAN WHO'S SO IMPORTANT TO ME.
I LEARNED THAT I'M NOT TOTALLY USELESS.
I KNOW THAT I GREW UP A LITTLE THROUGH ALL THIS.
RING
IF AKIRA IS GOING TO APPEAR AGAIN...
WHEN THAT TIME COMES...
HELLO?
...
DOOT...
HOW DO YOU DO, DAISY?

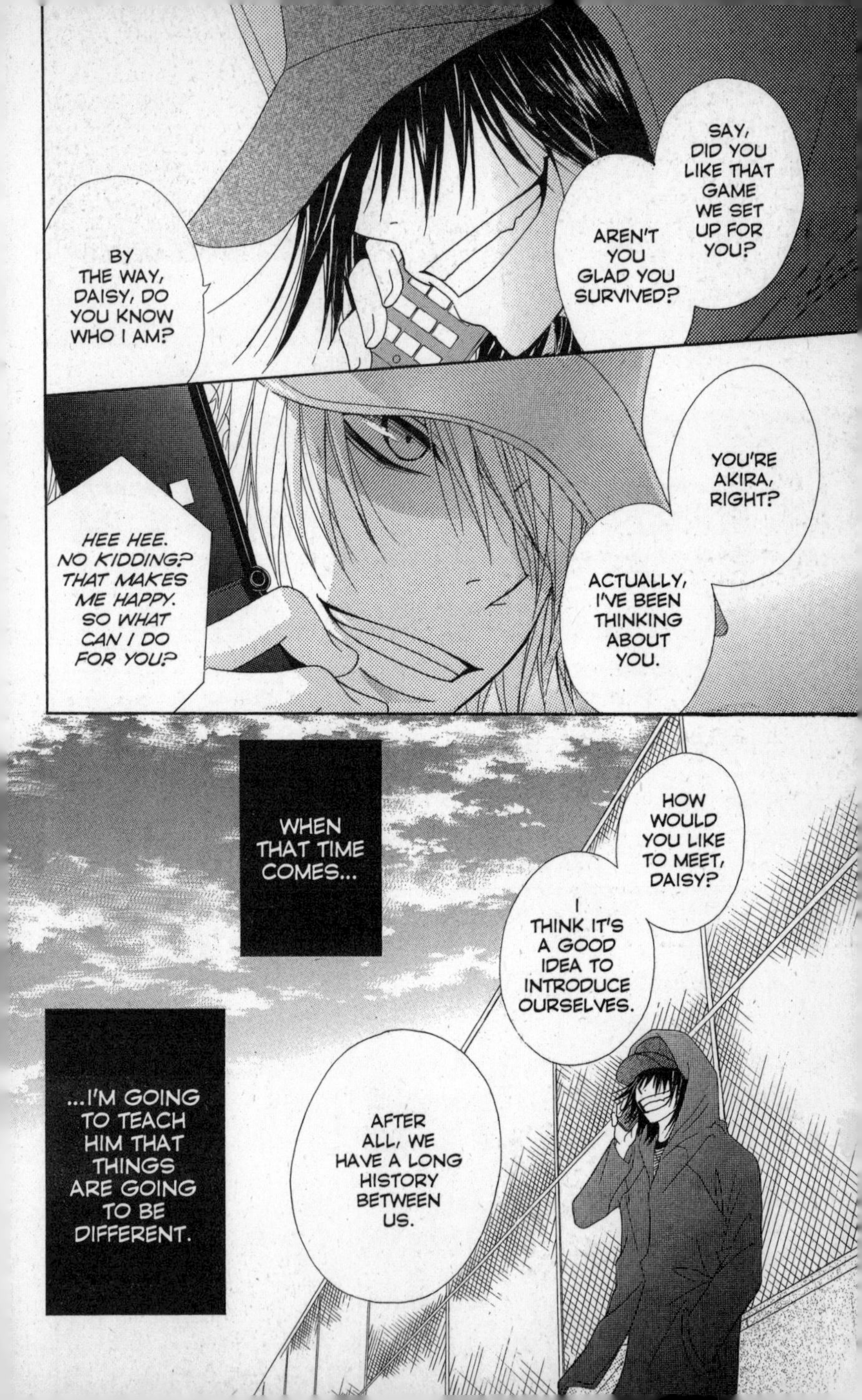
SAY, DID YOU LIKE THAT GAME WE SET UP FOR YOU?
AREN'T YOU GLAD YOU SURVIVED?
BY THE WAY, DAISY, DO YOU KNOW WHO I AM?
YOU'RE AKIRA, RIGHT?
ACTUALLY, I'VE BEEN THINKING ABOUT YOU.
HEE HEE. NO KIDDING? THAT MAKES ME HAPPY. SO WHAT CAN I DO FOR YOU?
HOW WOULD YOU LIKE TO MEET, DAISY?
WHEN THAT TIME COMES...
I THINK IT'S A GOOD IDEA TO INTRODUCE OURSELVES.
AFTER ALL, WE HAVE A LONG HISTORY BETWEEN US.
...I'M GOING TO TEACH HIM THAT THINGS ARE GOING TO BE DIFFERENT.

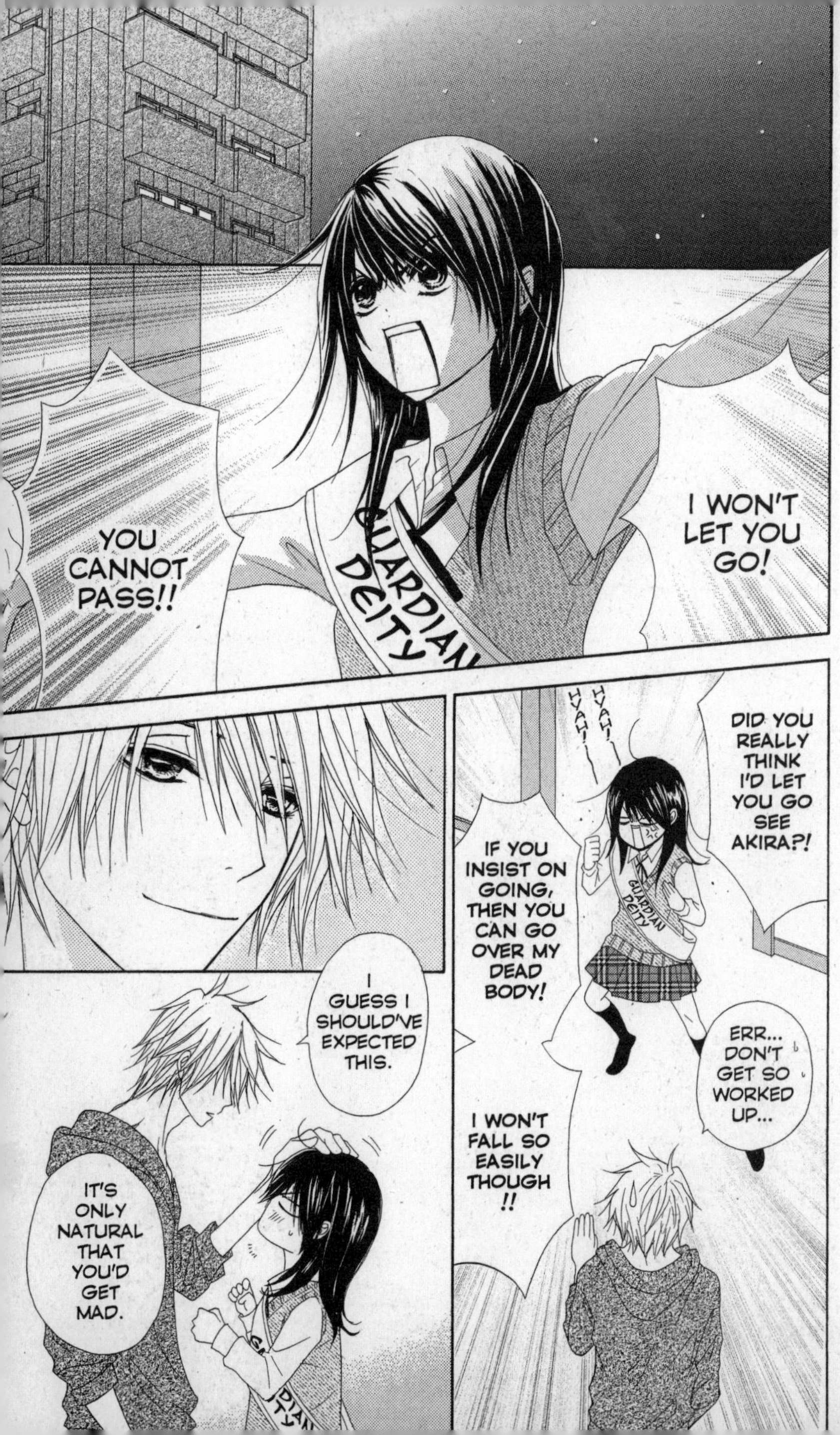
I WON'T LET YOU GO!
GUARDIAN DEITY
YOU CANNOT PASS!!
DID YOU REALLY THINK I'D LET YOU GO SEE AKIRA?!
HYAH! HYAH!
GUARDIAN DEITY
IF YOU INSIST ON GOING, THEN YOU CAN GO OVER MY DEAD BODY!
ERR... DON'T GET SO WORKED UP...
I WON'T FALL SO EASILY THOUGH!!
I GUESS I SHOULD'VE EXPECTED THIS.
IT'S ONLY NATURAL THAT YOU'D GET MAD.

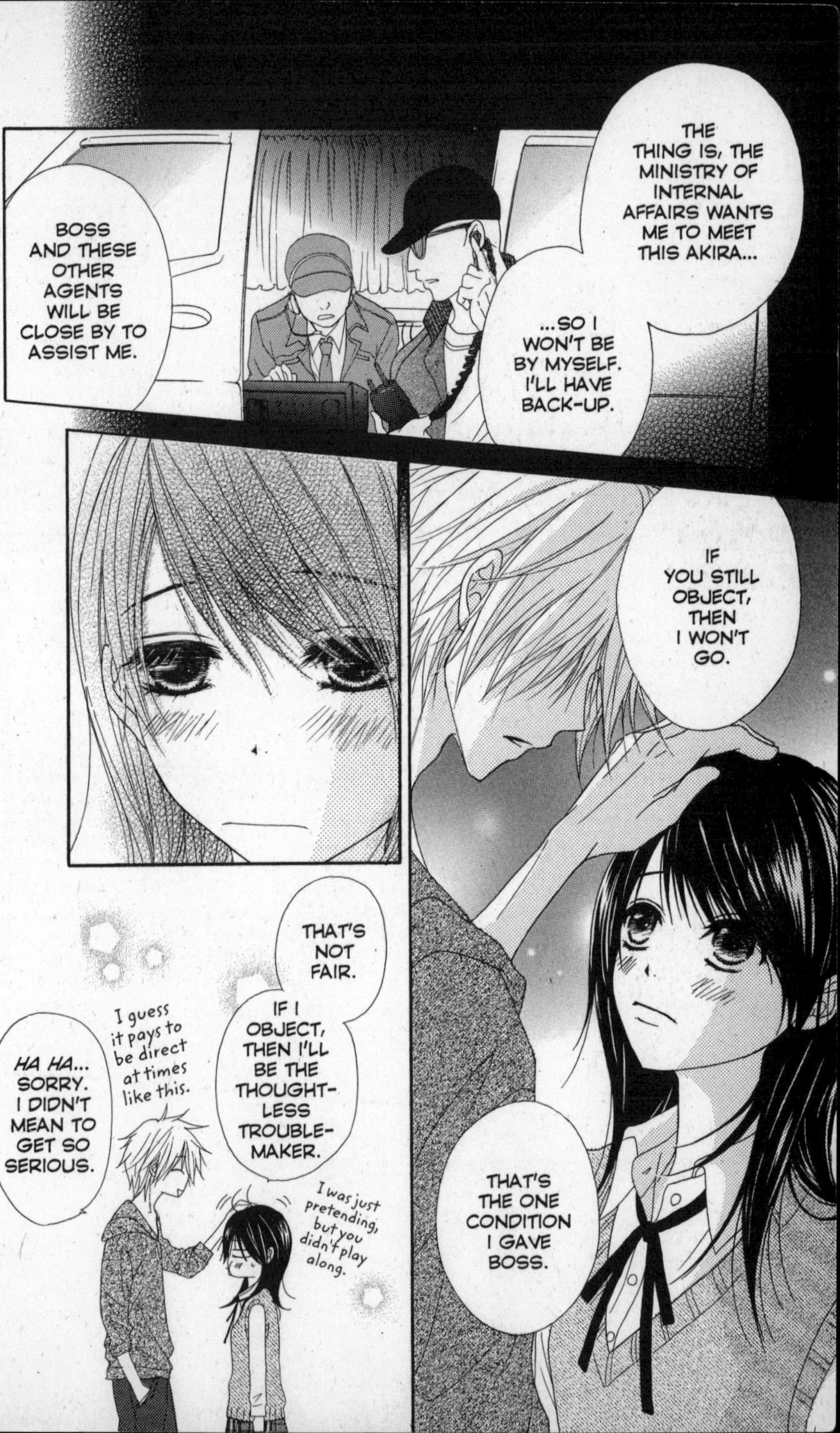
THE THING IS, THE MINISTRY OF INTERNAL AFFAIRS WANTS ME TO MEET THIS AKIRA...
...SO I WON'T BE BY MYSELF. I'LL HAVE BACK-UP.
BOSS AND THESE OTHER AGENTS WILL BE CLOSE BY TO ASSIST ME.
IF YOU STILL OBJECT, THEN I WON'T GO.
THAT'S THE ONE CONDITION I GAVE BOSS.
THAT'S NOT FAIR.
IF I OBJECT, THEN I'LL BE THE THOUGHT-LESS TROUBLE-MAKER.
I was just pretending, but you didn't play along.
HA HA... SORRY. I DIDN'T MEAN TO GET SO SERIOUS.
I guess it pays to be direct at times like this.

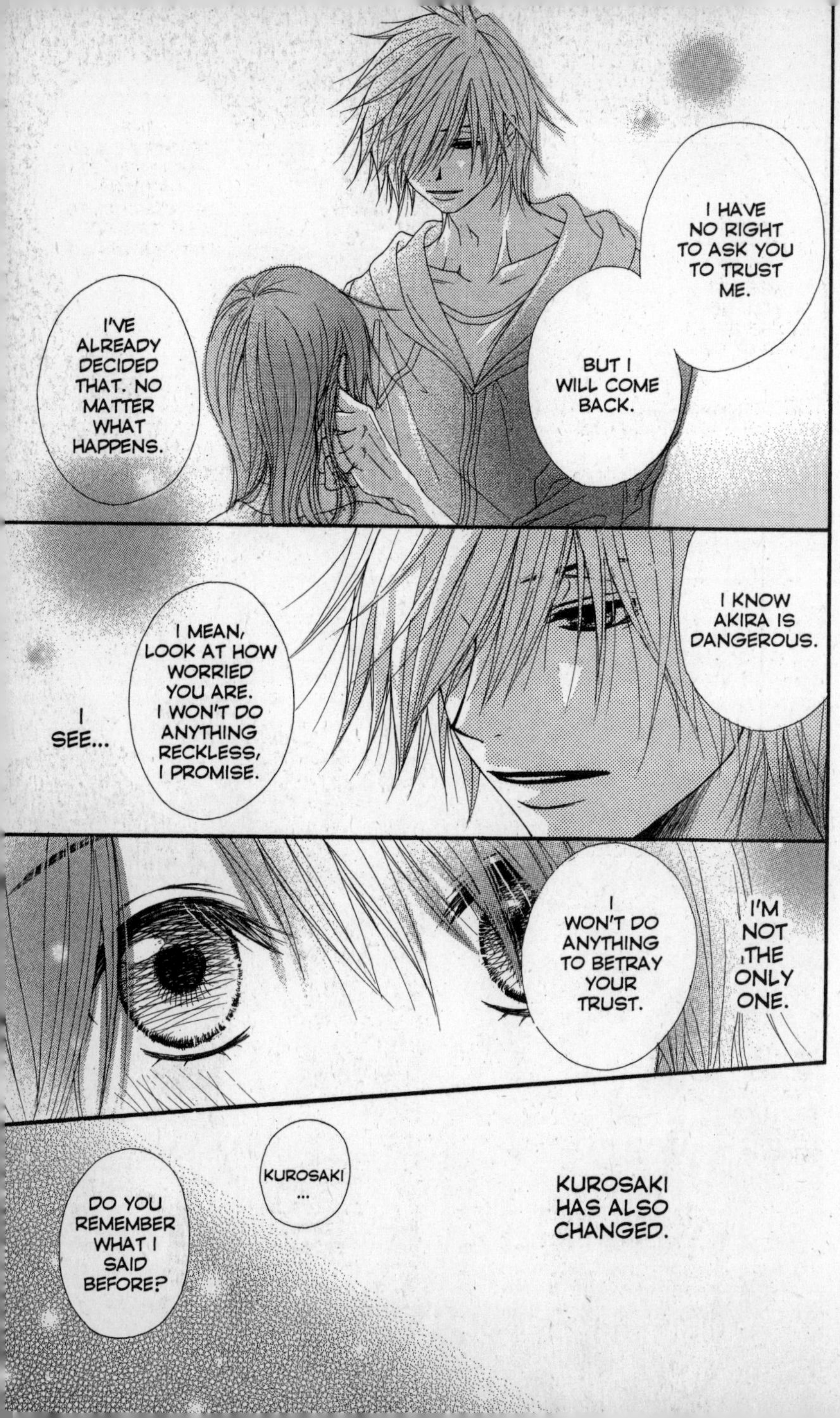
I HAVE NO RIGHT TO ASK YOU TO TRUST ME.
BUT I WILL COME BACK.
I'VE ALREADY DECIDED THAT. NO MATTER WHAT HAPPENS.
I KNOW AKIRA IS DANGEROUS.
I MEAN, LOOK AT HOW WORRIED YOU ARE. I WON'T DO ANYTHING RECKLESS, I PROMISE.
I SEE...
I'M NOT THE ONLY ONE.
I WON'T DO ANYTHING TO BETRAY YOUR TRUST.
KUROSAKI HAS ALSO CHANGED.
KUROSAKI...
DO YOU REMEMBER WHAT I SAID BEFORE?

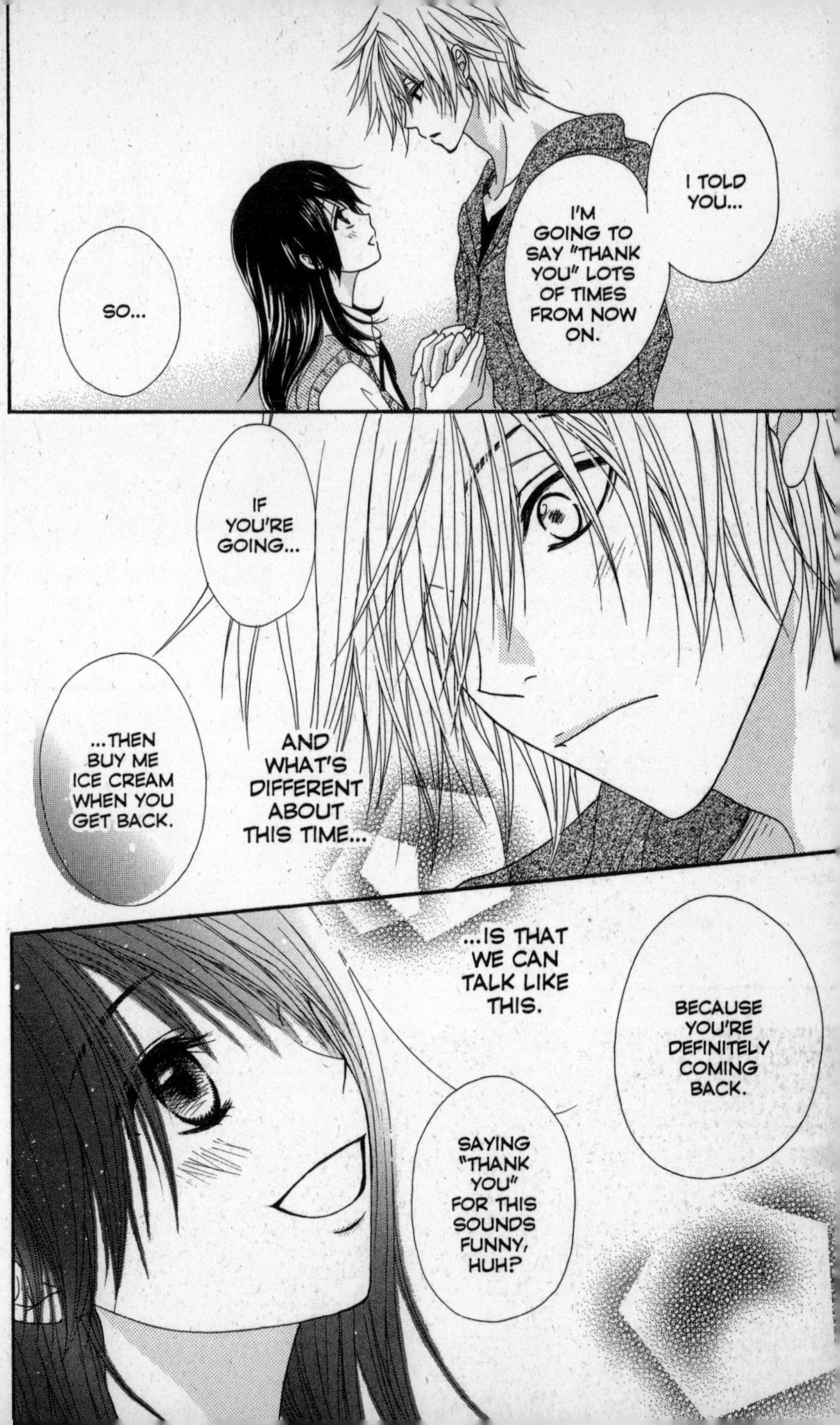
I TOLD YOU...
I'M GOING TO SAY "THANK YOU" LOTS OF TIMES FROM NOW ON.
SO...
IF YOU'RE GOING...
...THEN BUY ME ICE CREAM WHEN YOU GET BACK.
AND WHAT'S DIFFERENT ABOUT THIS TIME...
...IS THAT WE CAN TALK LIKE THIS.
BECAUSE YOU'RE DEFINITELY COMING BACK.
SAYING "THANK YOU" FOR THIS SOUNDS FUNNY, HUH?

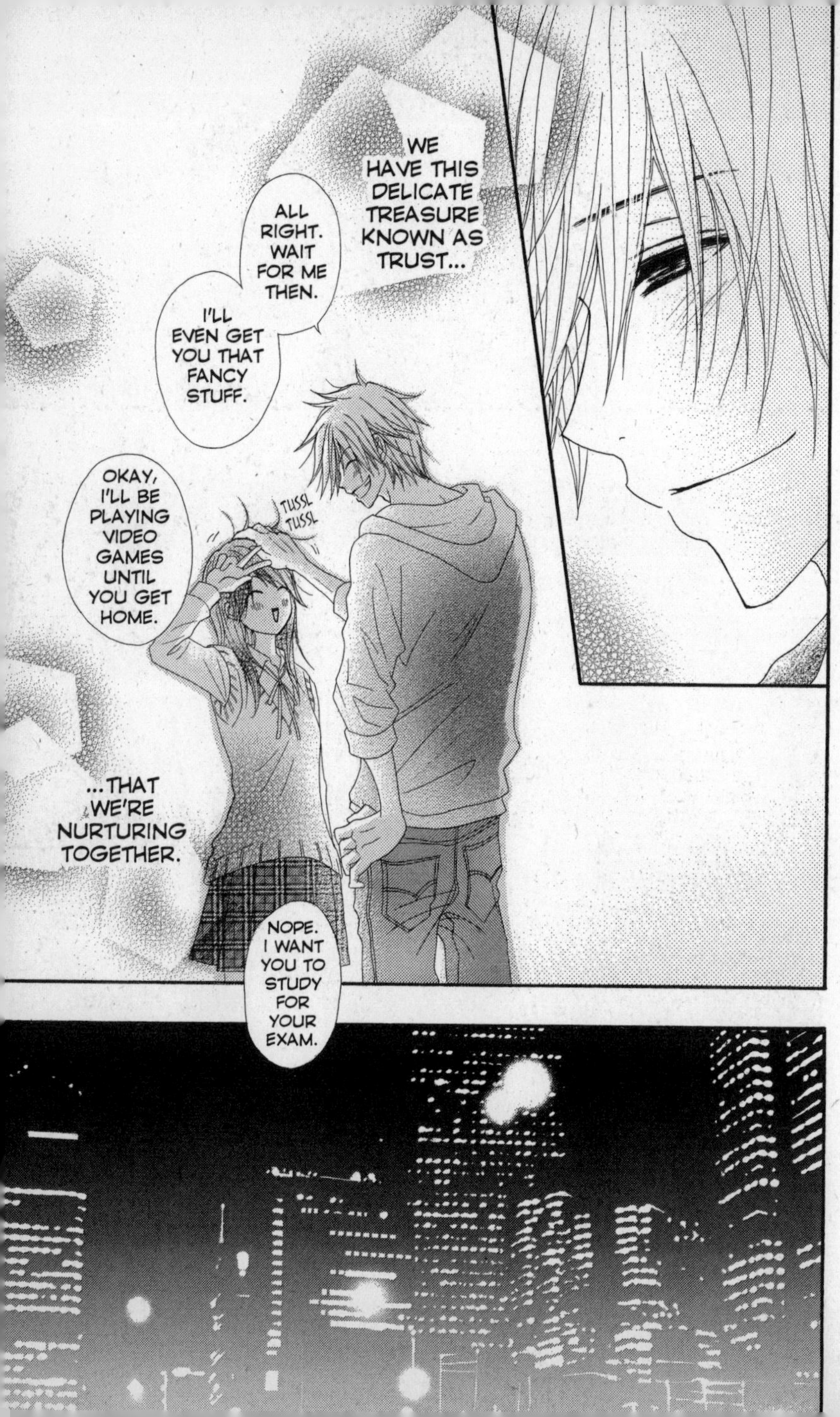
WE HAVE THIS DELICATE TREASURE KNOWN AS TRUST...
ALL RIGHT. WAIT FOR ME THEN.
I'LL EVEN GET YOU THAT FANCY STUFF.
OKAY, I'LL BE PLAYING VIDEO GAMES UNTIL YOU GET HOME.
TUSSL TUSSL
...THAT WE'RE NURTURING TOGETHER.
NOPE. I WANT YOU TO STUDY FOR YOUR EXAM.

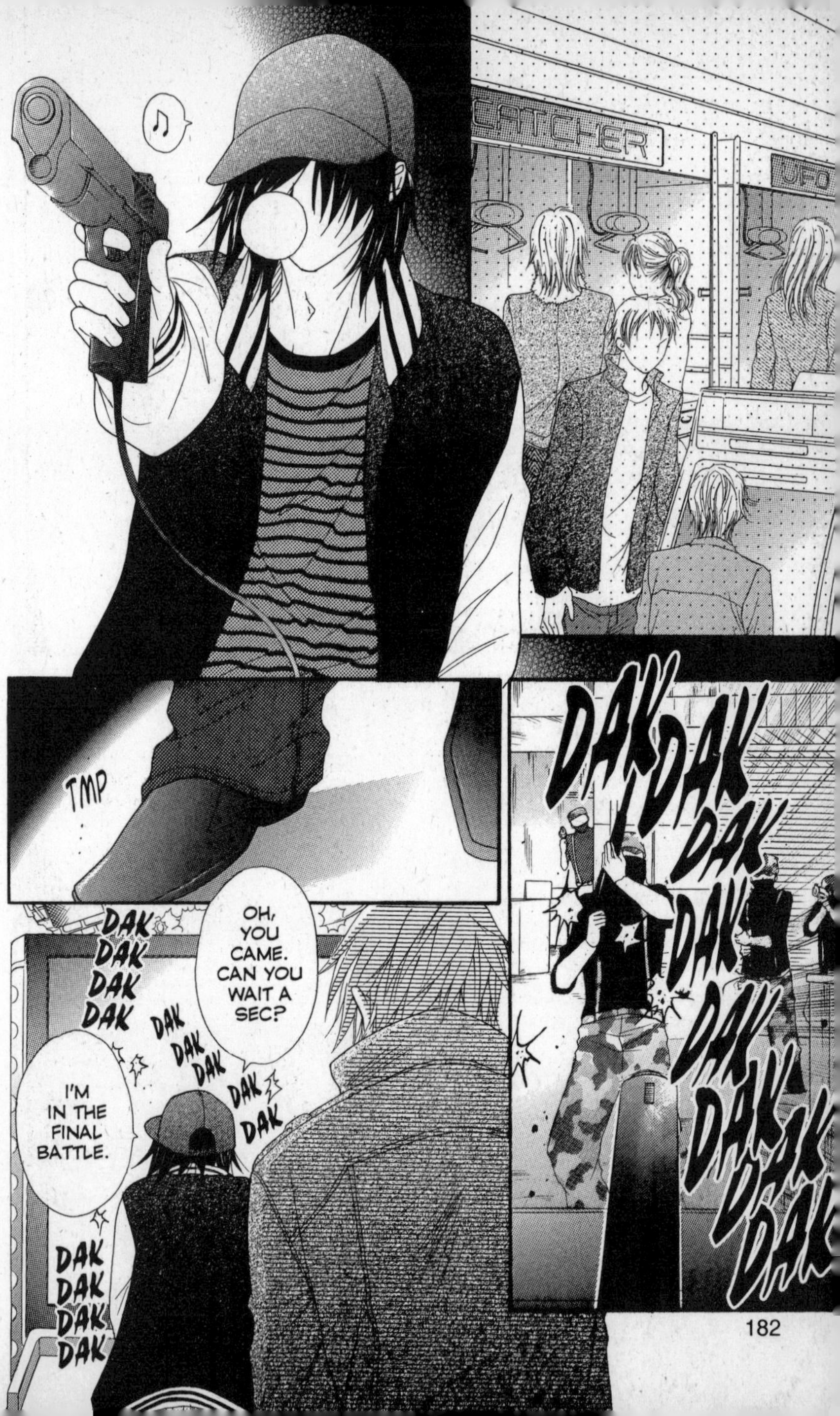
CATCHER
UFO
♪
DAK DAK DAK DAK DAK DAK DAK DAK DAK DAK
TMP
OH, YOU CAME. CAN YOU WAIT A SEC?
I'M IN THE FINAL BATTLE.
DAK DAK DAK DAK
DAK DAK DAK
DAK DAK
DAK DAK DAK DAK

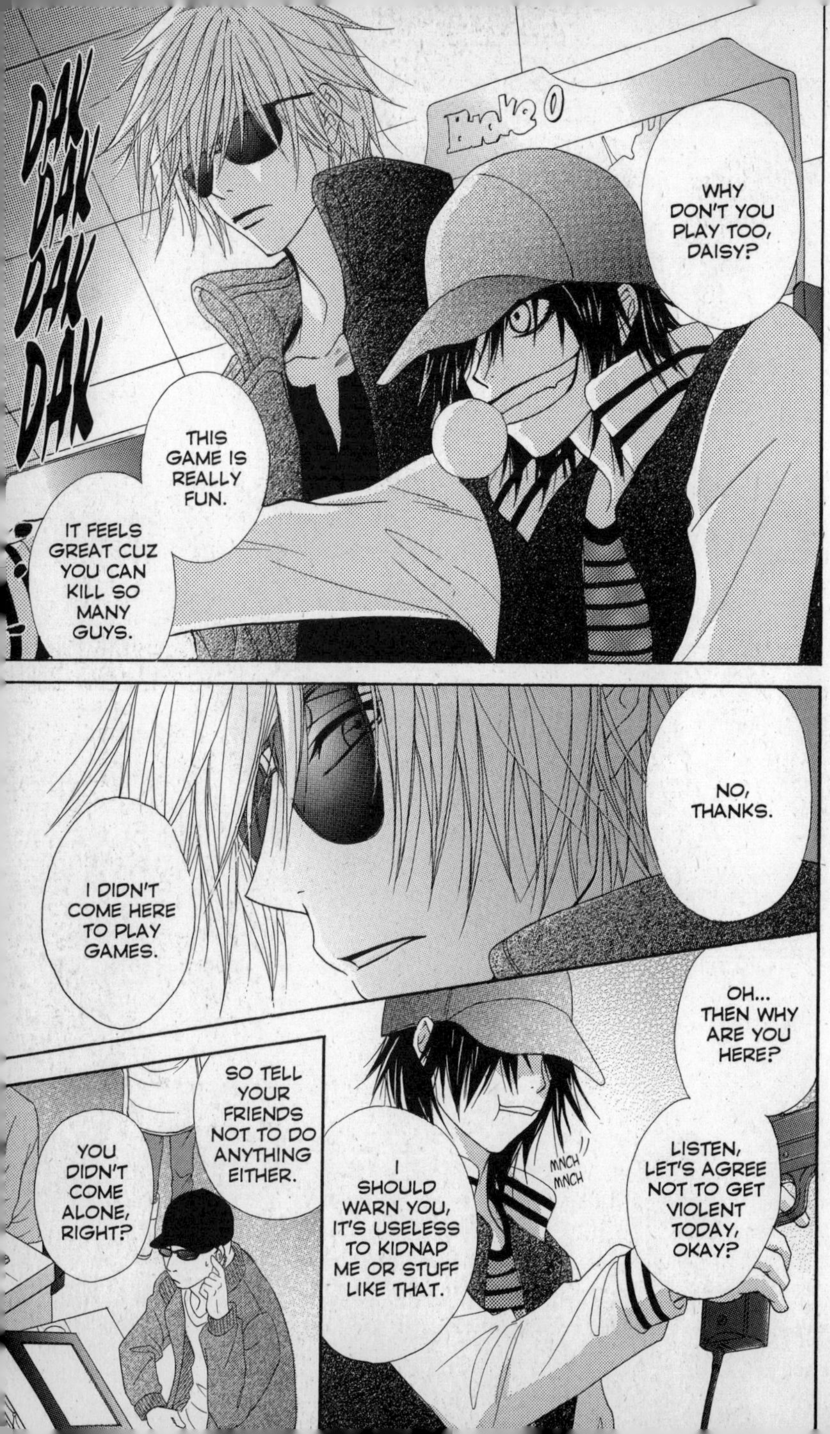
WHY DON'T YOU PLAY TOO, DAISY?
DAK DAK DAK DAK
THIS GAME IS REALLY FUN.
IT FEELS GREAT CUZ YOU CAN KILL SO MANY GUYS.
NO, THANKS.
I DIDN'T COME HERE TO PLAY GAMES.
OH... THEN WHY ARE YOU HERE?
LISTEN, LET'S AGREE NOT TO GET VIOLENT TODAY, OKAY?
MNCH MNCH
I SHOULD WARN YOU, IT'S USELESS TO KIDNAP ME OR STUFF LIKE THAT.
SO TELL YOUR FRIENDS NOT TO DO ANYTHING EITHER.
YOU DIDN'T COME ALONE, RIGHT?

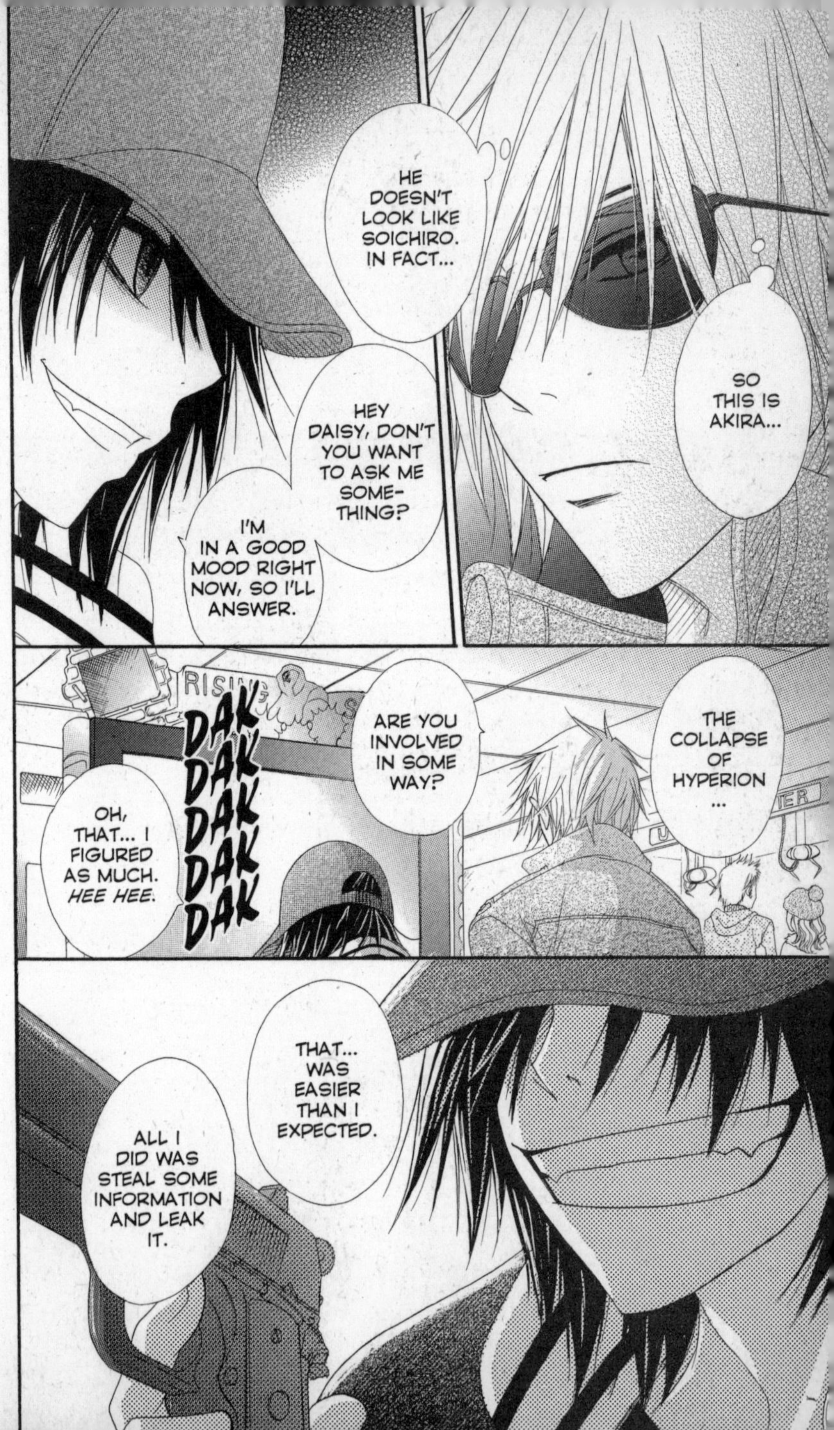
SO THIS IS AKIRA...
HE DOESN'T LOOK LIKE SOICHIRO. IN FACT...
HEY DAISY, DON'T YOU WANT TO ASK ME SOME-THING?
I'M IN A GOOD MOOD RIGHT NOW, SO I'LL ANSWER.
THE COLLAPSE OF HYPERION ...
ARE YOU INVOLVED IN SOME WAY?
RISING
DAK DAK DAK DAK DAK DAK
OH, THAT... I FIGURED AS MUCH. *HEE HEE.*
THAT... WAS EASIER THAN I EXPECTED.
ALL I DID WAS STEAL SOME INFORMATION AND LEAK IT.

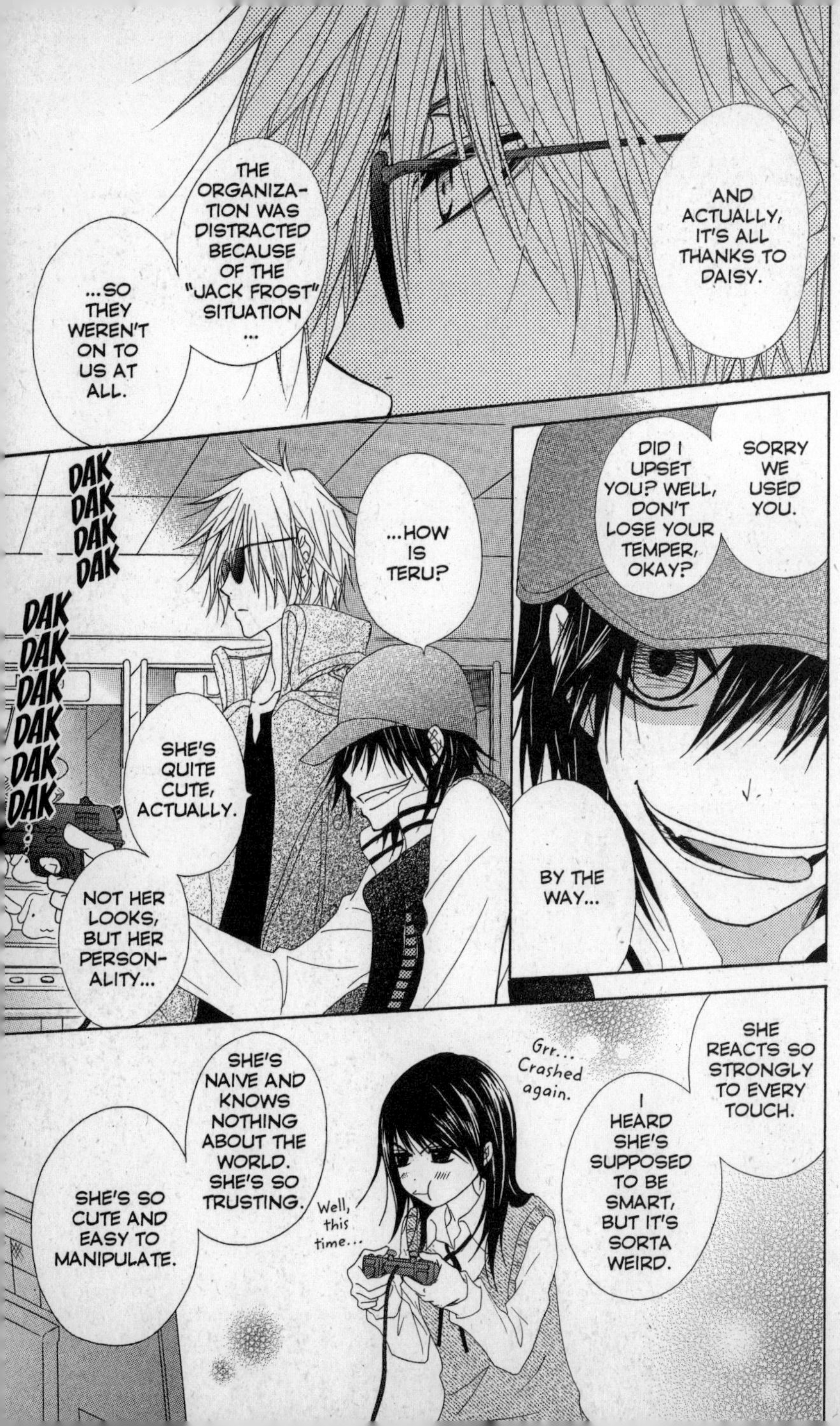
AND ACTUALLY, IT'S ALL THANKS TO DAISY.
THE ORGANIZATION WAS DISTRACTED BECAUSE OF THE "JACK FROST" SITUATION ...
...SO THEY WEREN'T ON TO US AT ALL.
SORRY WE USED YOU.
DID I UPSET YOU? WELL, DON'T LOSE YOUR TEMPER, OKAY?
BY THE WAY...
...HOW IS TERU?
DAK DAK DAK DAK
DAK DAK DAK DAK DAK DAK
SHE'S QUITE CUTE, ACTUALLY.
NOT HER LOOKS, BUT HER PERSONALITY...
SHE REACTS SO STRONGLY TO EVERY TOUCH.
I HEARD SHE'S SUPPOSED TO BE SMART, BUT IT'S SORTA WEIRD.
Grr... Crashed again.
SHE'S NAIVE AND KNOWS NOTHING ABOUT THE WORLD. SHE'S SO TRUSTING.
Well, this time...
SHE'S SO CUTE AND EASY TO MANIPULATE.

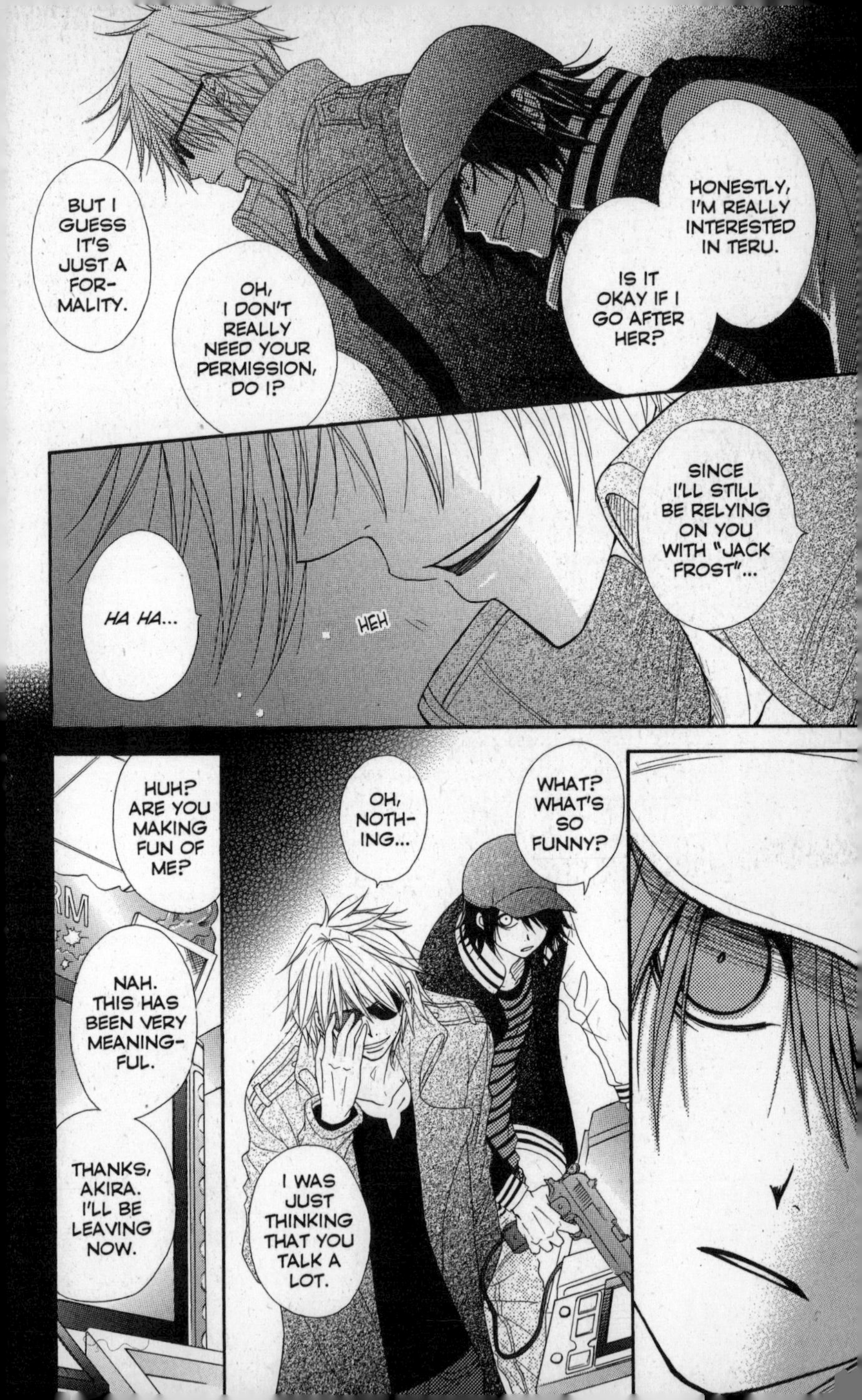
HONESTLY, I'M REALLY INTERESTED IN TERU.
IS IT OKAY IF I GO AFTER HER?
OH, I DON'T REALLY NEED YOUR PERMISSION, DO I?
BUT I GUESS IT'S JUST A FOR-MALITY.
SINCE I'LL STILL BE RELYING ON YOU WITH "JACK FROST"...
HEH
HA HA...
WHAT? WHAT'S SO FUNNY?
OH, NOTH-ING...
I WAS JUST THINKING THAT YOU TALK A LOT.
HUH? ARE YOU MAKING FUN OF ME?
NAH. THIS HAS BEEN VERY MEANING-FUL.
THANKS, AKIRA. I'LL BE LEAVING NOW.

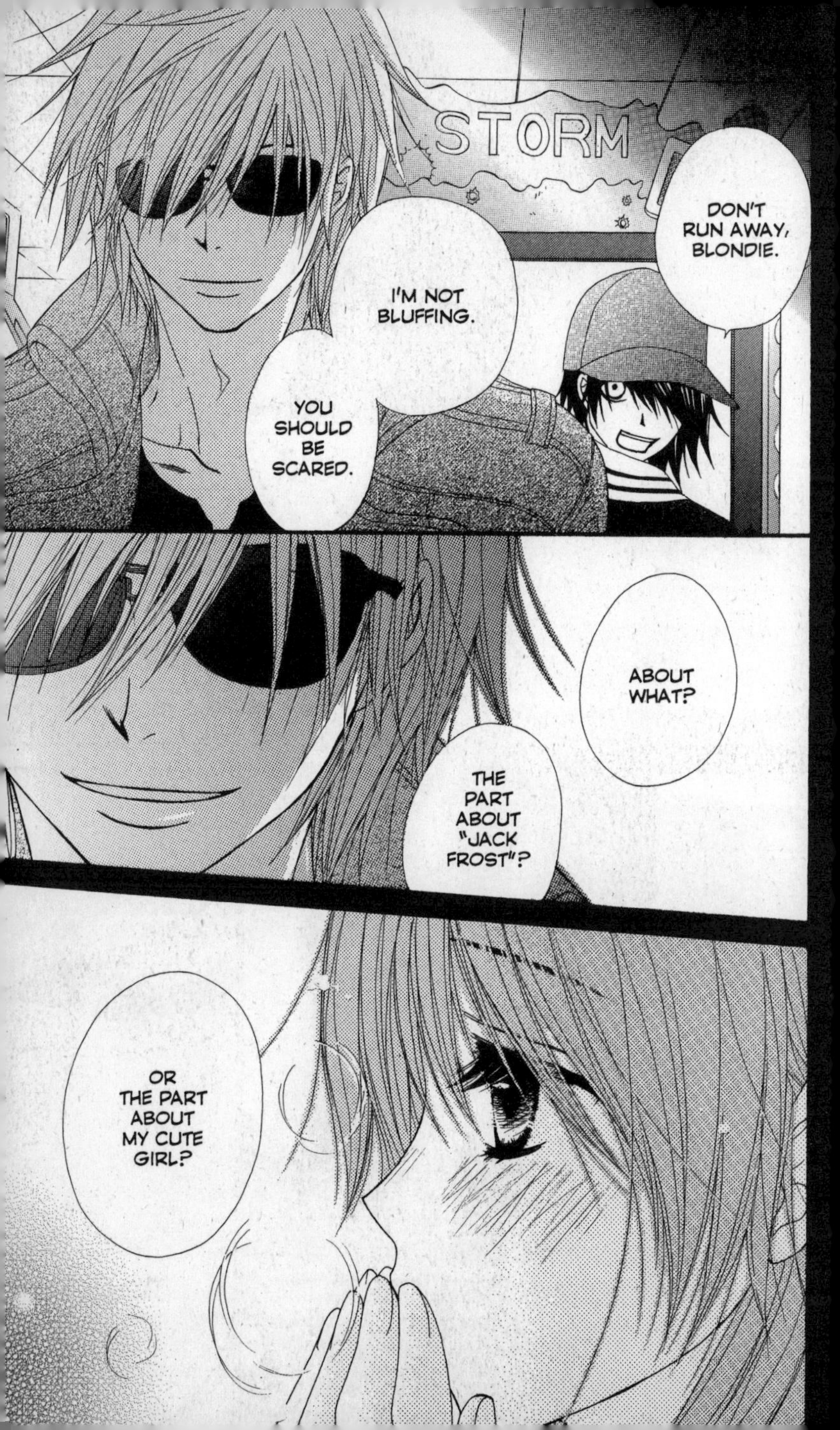
STORM
DON'T RUN AWAY, BLONDIE.
I'M NOT BLUFFING.
YOU SHOULD BE SCARED.
ABOUT WHAT?
THE PART ABOUT "JACK FROST"?
OR THE PART ABOUT MY CUTE GIRL?

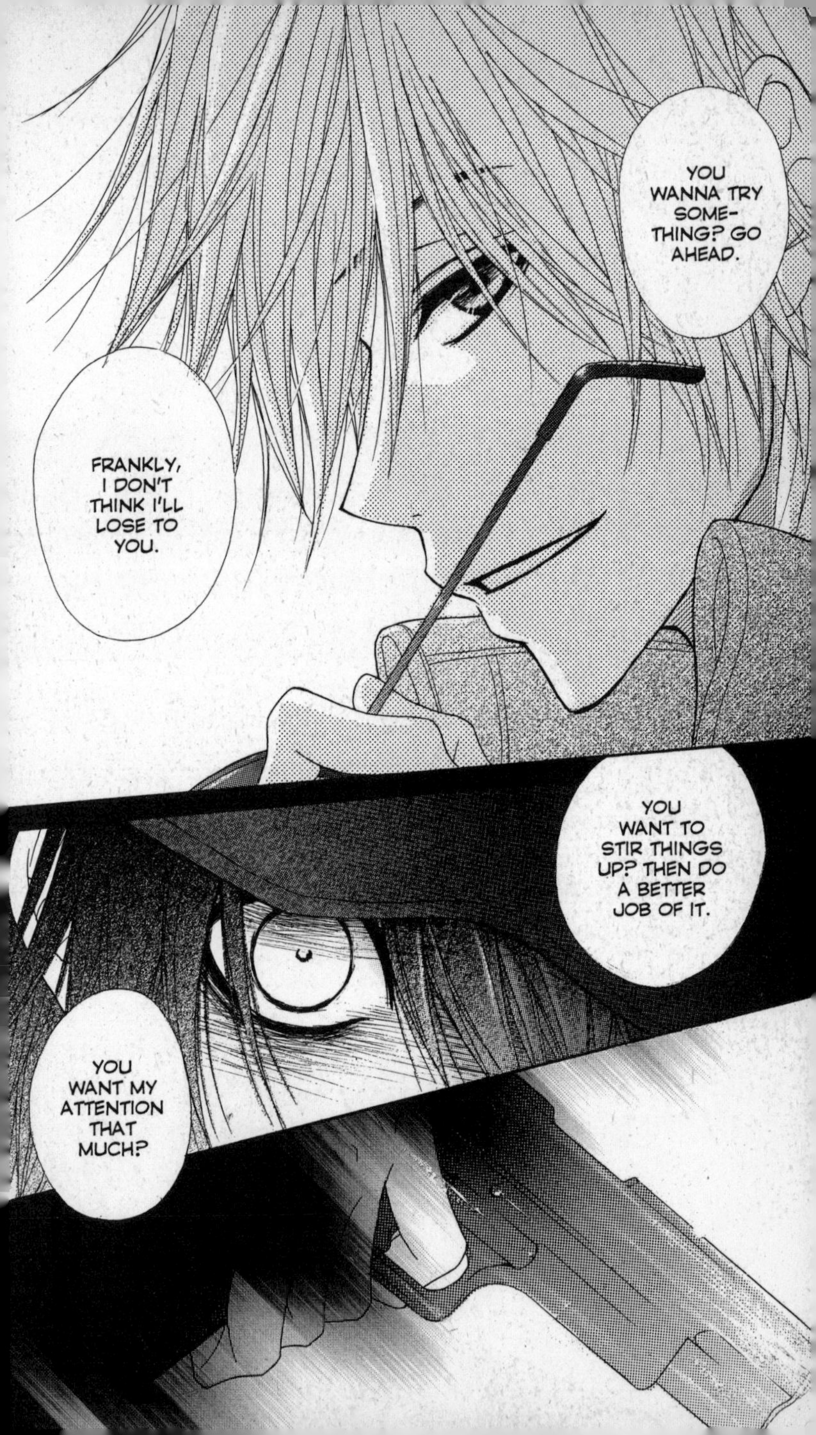
YOU WANNA TRY SOME-THING? GO AHEAD.
FRANKLY, I DON'T THINK I'LL LOSE TO YOU.
YOU WANT TO STIR THINGS UP? THEN DO A BETTER JOB OF IT.
YOU WANT MY ATTENTION THAT MUCH?

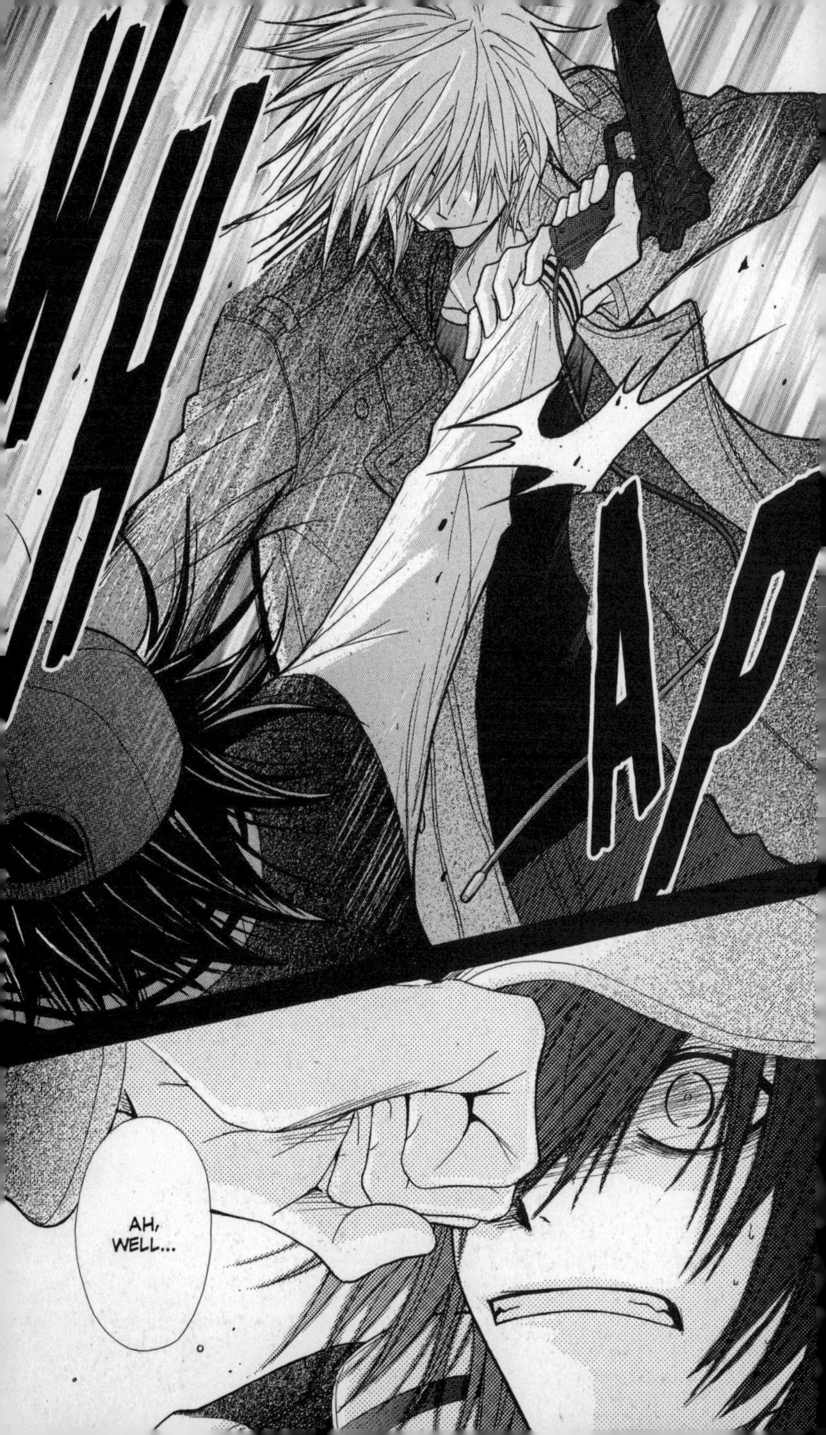
AH, WELL...

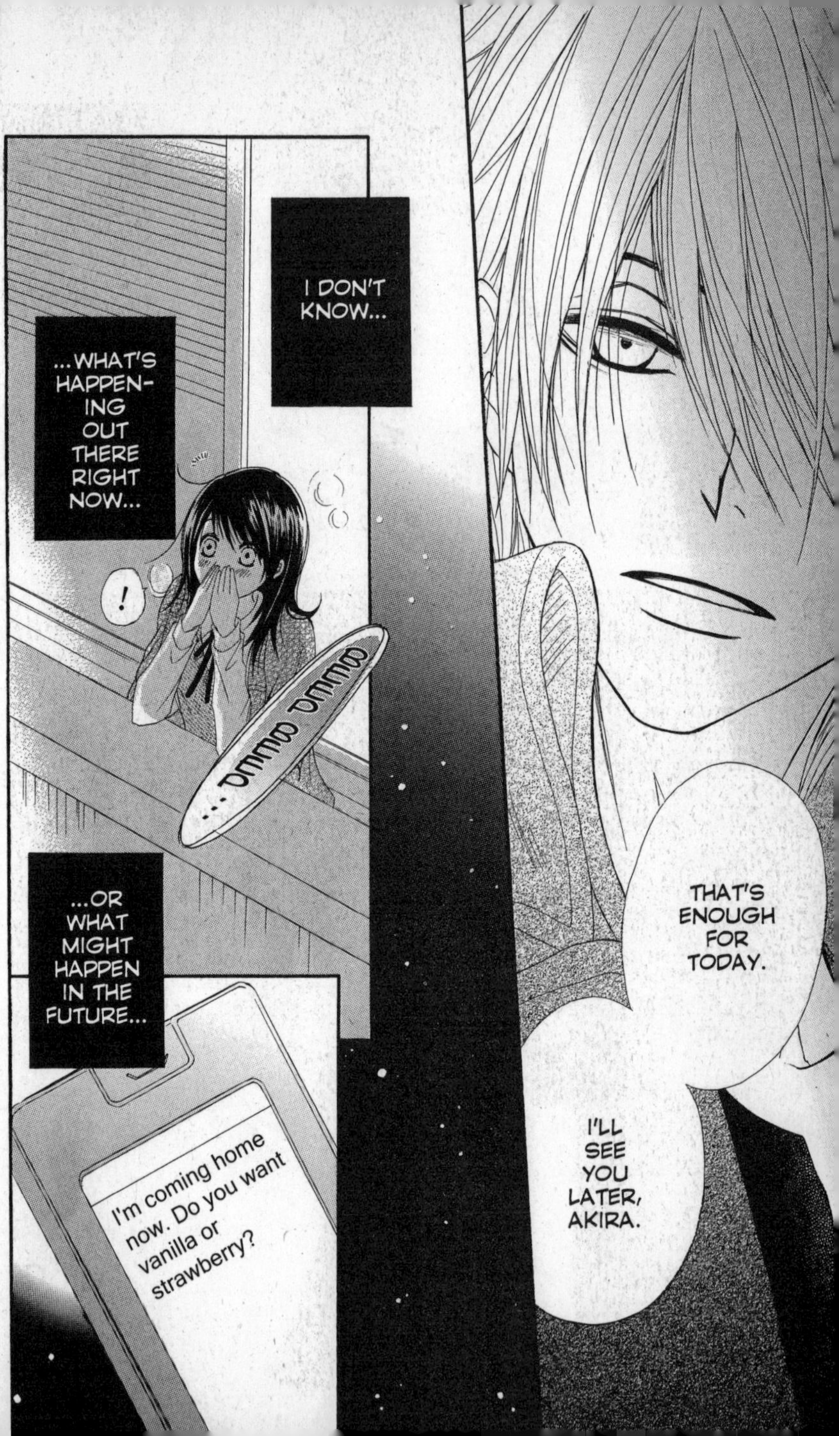
THAT'S ENOUGH FOR TODAY.
I'LL SEE YOU LATER, AKIRA.
I DON'T KNOW...
...WHAT'S HAPPENING OUT THERE RIGHT NOW...
!
...OR WHAT MIGHT HAPPEN IN THE FUTURE...
I'm coming home now. Do you want vanilla or strawberry?

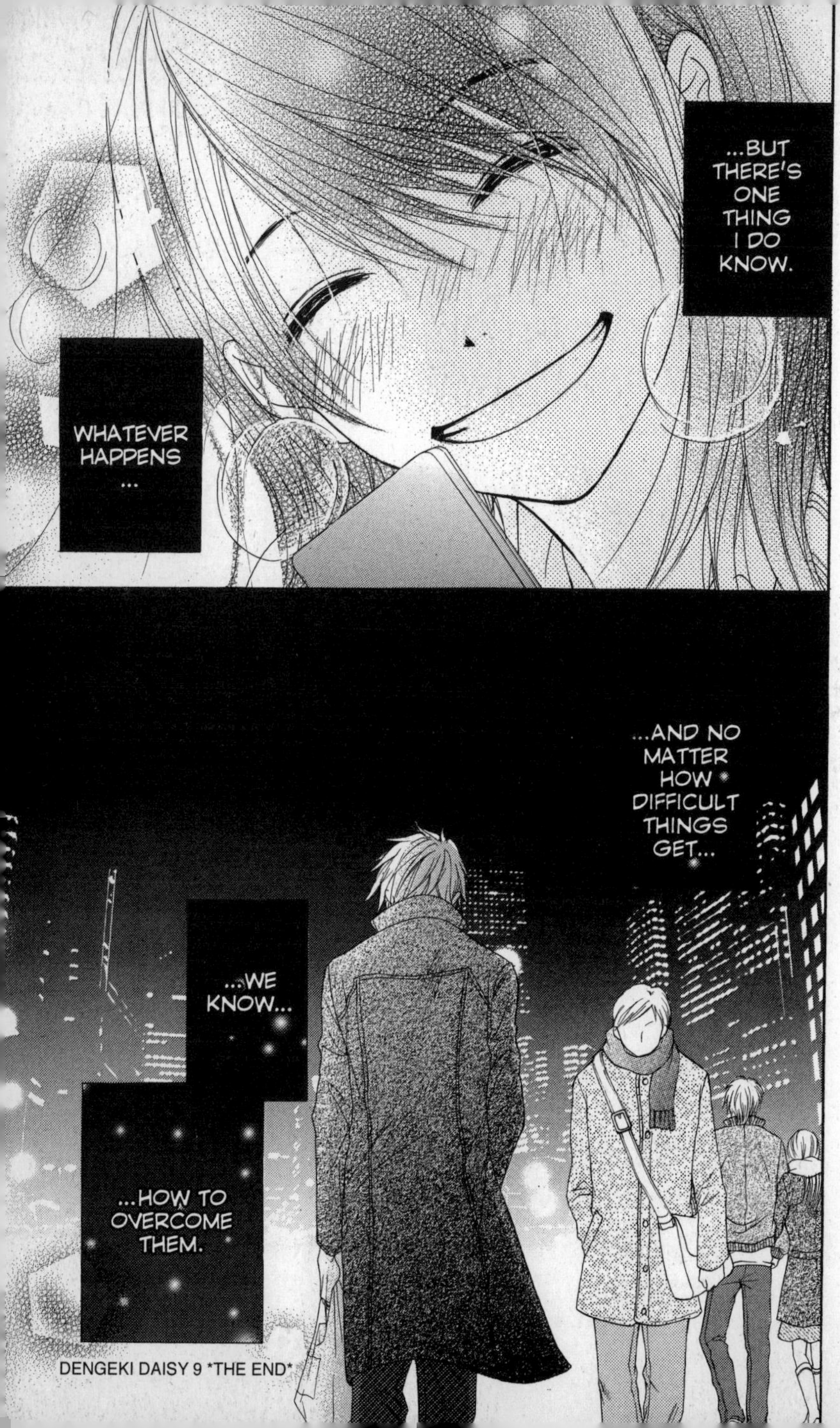
...BUT THERE'S ONE THING I DO KNOW.
WHATEVER HAPPENS ...
...AND NO MATTER HOW DIFFICULT THINGS GET...
...WE KNOW...
...HOW TO OVERCOME THEM.
DENGEKI DAISY 9 *THE END*

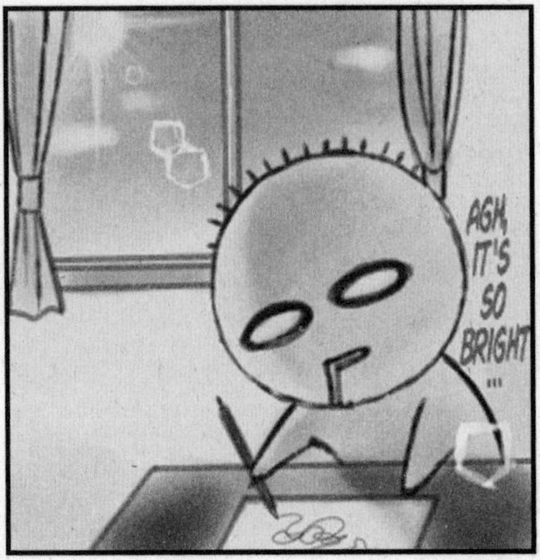
AGH, IT'S SO BRIGHT...

I've been writing as usual, but this is not a healthy lifestyle. I tried to change and work during the day, but found that the morning sun saps my energy. So what am I going to do...?

-Kyousuke Motomi

Born on August 1, Kyousuke Motomi debuted in *Deluxe Betsucomi* with *Hetakuso Kyupiddo* (No-Good Cupid) in 2002. She is the creator of *Otokomae! Biizu Kurabu* (Handsome! Beads Club), and her latest work, *Dengeki Daisy*, is currently being serialized in *Betsucomi*. Motomi enjoys sleeping, tea ceremonies and reading Haruki Murakami.

DENGEKI DAISY

VOL. 9

Shojo Beat Edition

STORY AND ART BY
KYOUSUKE MOTOMI

Translation & Adaptation/JN Productions
Touch-up Art & Lettering/Rina Mapa
Design/Nozomi Akashi
Editor/Amy Yu

Printed in the U.S.A.

Published by VIZ Media, LLC
P.O. Box 77010
San Francisco, CA 94107

10 9 8 7 6 5 4 3 2 1
First printing, March 2012

www.viz.com www.shojobeat.com

PARENTAL ADVISORY
DENGEKI DAISY is rated T+ for Older Teen and is recommended for ages 16 and up. This volume contains suggestive themes.

RATED T+ FOR OLDER TEEN

ratings.viz.com

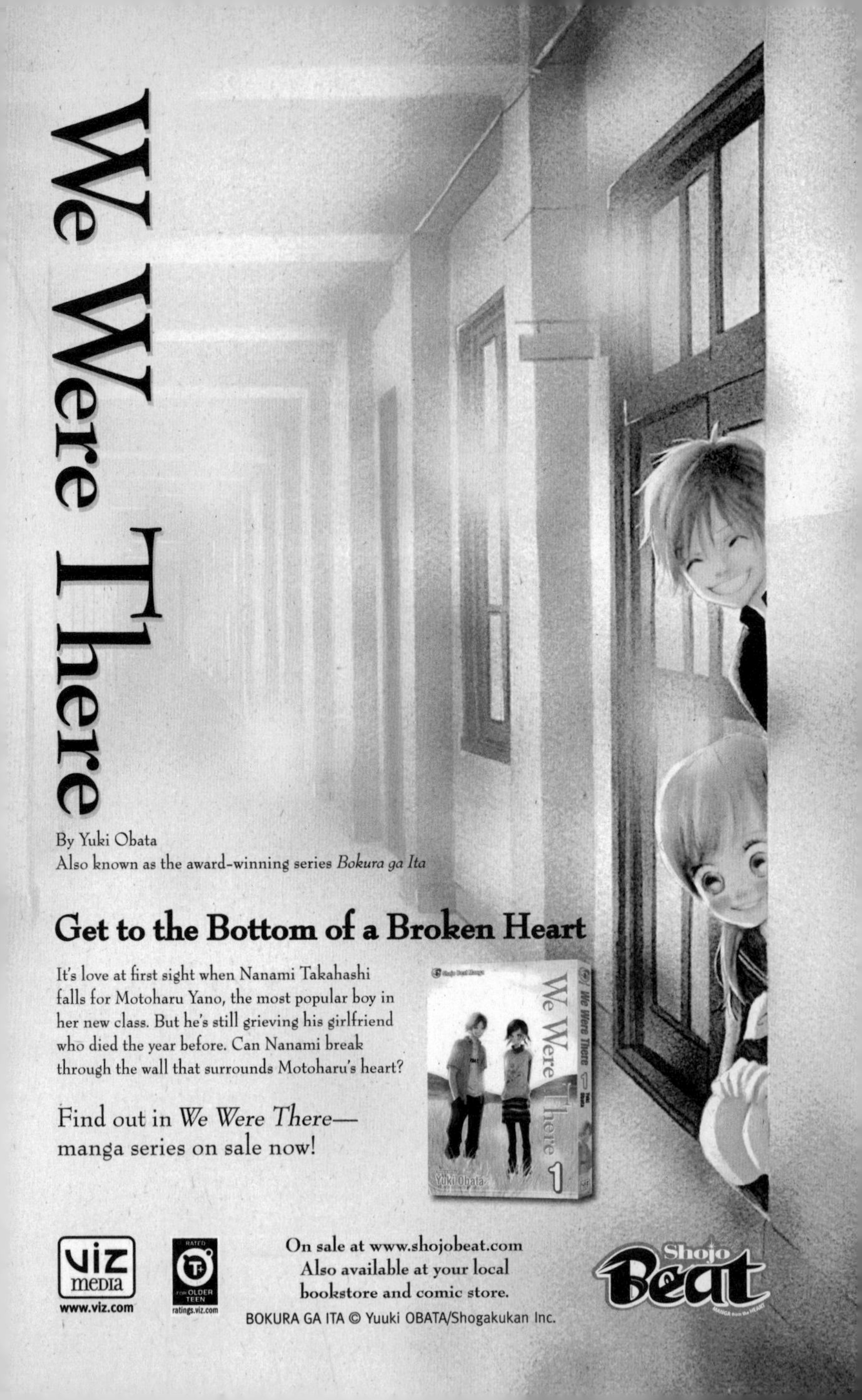
We Were There
By Yuki Obata
Also known as the award-winning series *Bokura ga Ita*
Get to the Bottom of a Broken Heart
It's love at first sight when Nanami Takahashi falls for Motoharu Yano, the most popular boy in her new class. But he's still grieving his girlfriend who died the year before. Can Nanami break through the wall that surrounds Motoharu's heart?
Find out in *We Were There*—
manga series on sale now!
We Were There 1
Yuki Obata
viz media
www.viz.com
RATED T+ FOR OLDER TEEN
ratings.viz.com
On sale at www.shojobeat.com
Also available at your local
bookstore and comic store.
BOKURA GA ITA © Yuuki OBATA/Shogakukan Inc.
Shojo Beat

TOKYO BOYS & GIRLS

By Miki Aihara, the creator of *Hot Gimmick*

Mimori's dream comes true when she's accepted to Meidai Attached High School, especially since she'll get to wear their super-fashionable uniform! Freshman year's bound to be exciting, but as Mimori soon discovers, looking great and feeling great don't always go hand-in-hand...

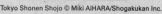

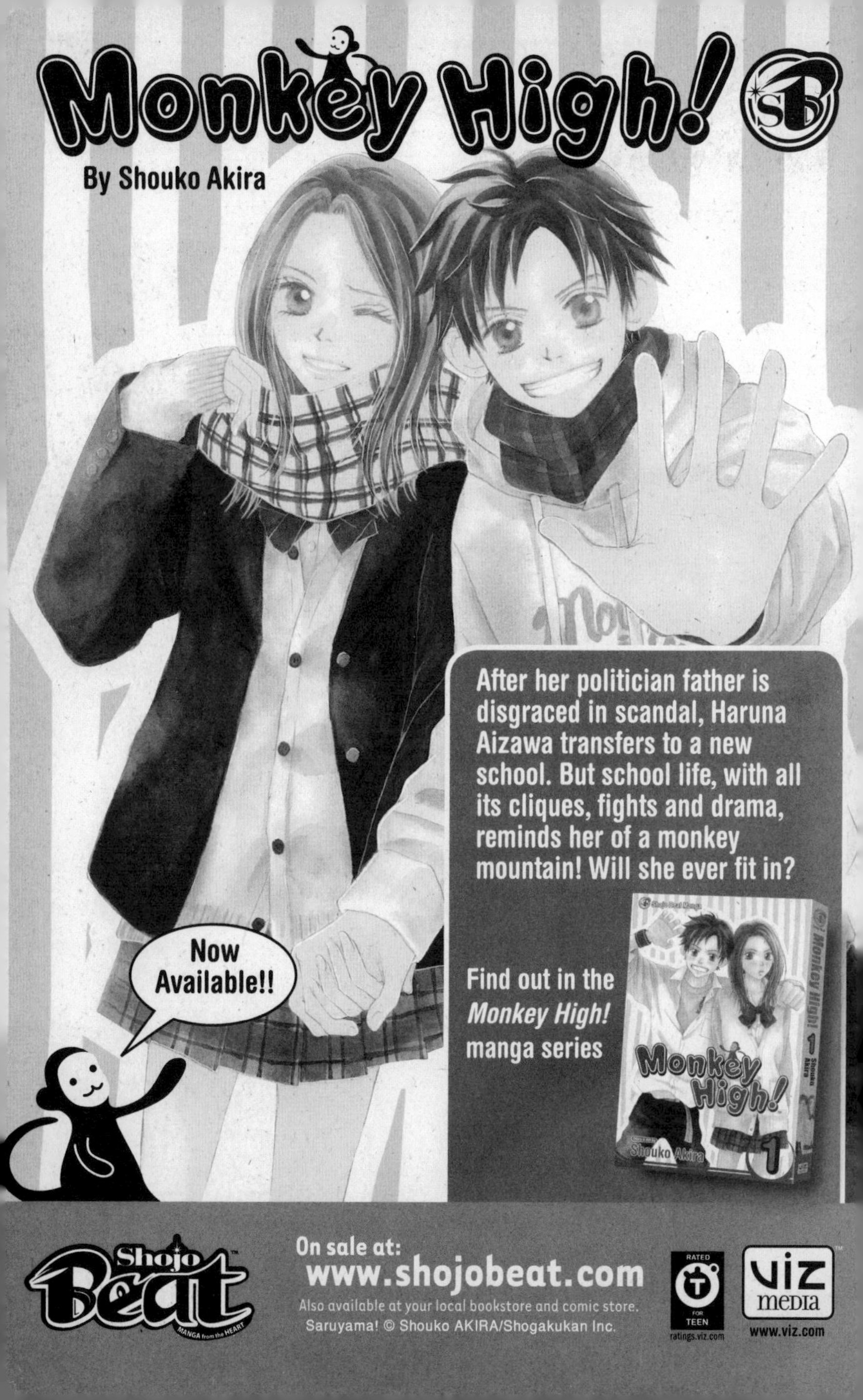
Monkey High!
By Shouko Akira
After her politician father is disgraced in scandal, Haruna Aizawa transfers to a new school. But school life, with all its cliques, fights and drama, reminds her of a monkey mountain! Will she ever fit in?
Now Available!!
Find out in the *Monkey High!* manga series
Monkey High!
Shouko Akira
1
Shojo Beat
MANGA from the HEART
On sale at:
www.shojobeat.com
Also available at your local bookstore and comic store.
Saruyama! © Shouko AKIRA/Shogakukan Inc.
RATED
T
FOR
TEEN
ratings.viz.com
VIZ MEDIA
www.viz.com

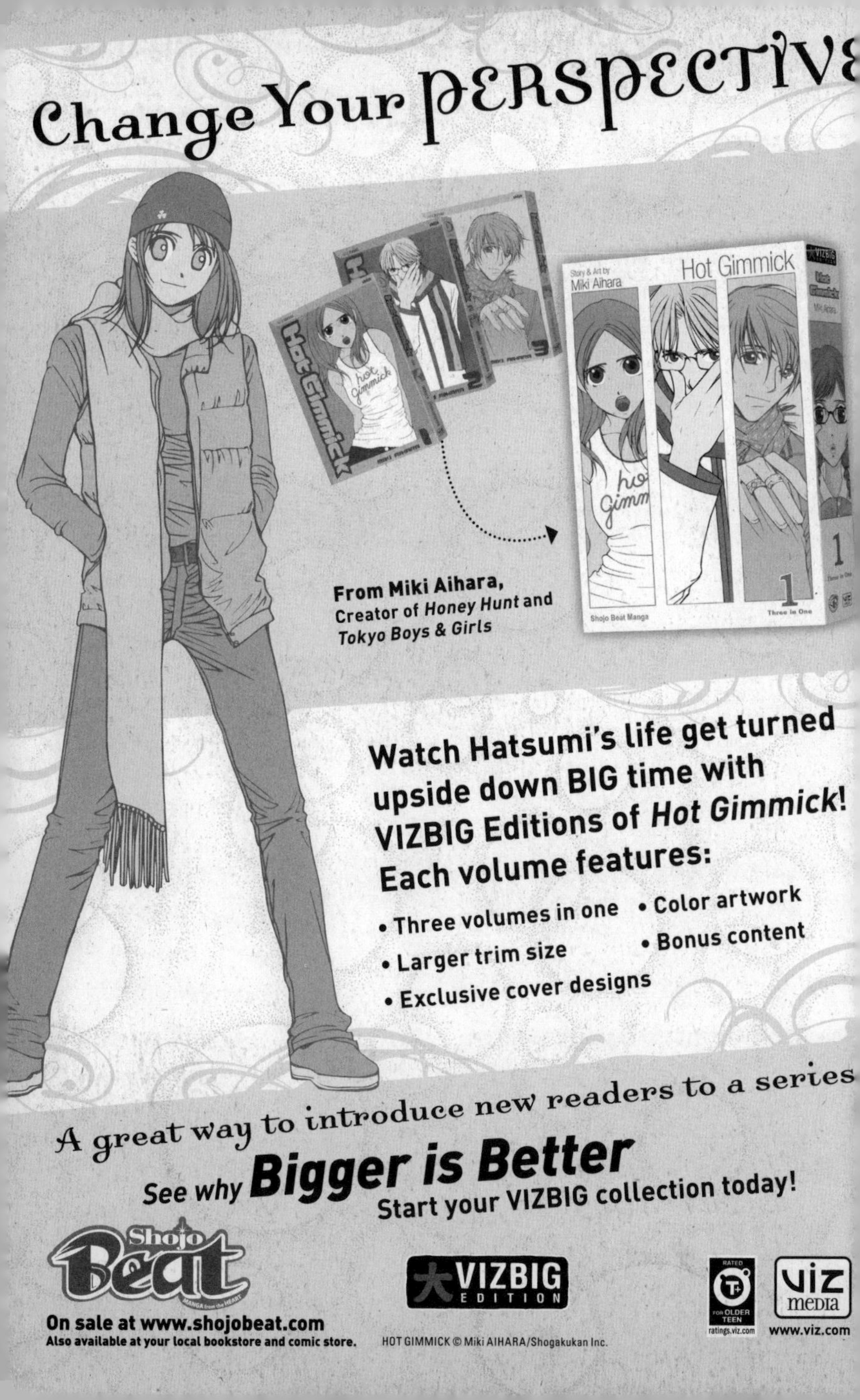
Change Your PERSPECTIVE
Story & Art by Miki Aihara
Hot Gimmick
1
Shojo Beat Manga
Three in One
From Miki Aihara,
Creator of *Honey Hunt* and *Tokyo Boys & Girls*
Watch Hatsumi's life get turned upside down BIG time with VIZBIG Editions of *Hot Gimmick*!
Each volume features:
• Three volumes in one
• Color artwork
• Larger trim size
• Bonus content
• Exclusive cover designs
A great way to introduce new readers to a series
See why Bigger is Better
Start your VIZBIG collection today!
Shojo Beat
MANGA from the HEART
On sale at www.shojobeat.com
Also available at your local bookstore and comic store.
VIZBIG EDITION
HOT GIMMICK © Miki AIHARA/Shogakukan Inc.
RATED T+ FOR OLDER TEEN
ratings.viz.com
viz media
www.viz.com